Buddhism in South Asia

Buddhism in South Asia

Dr Arvind Kumar Singh

MD Publications Pvt Ltd
New Delhi
www.mdppl.com

Published by :

MD Publications Pvt Ltd
'MD House', 11, Darya Ganj
New Delhi - 110 002
Phone : +91-11-41563325 (Customer Service)
+91-11-41562846 (Editorial)
E-mail (orders): contact@mdppl.com
Website: www.mdppl.com

ISBN : 978-81-7533-167-9

Published and Printed by Mrs. Rajni Gupta on behalf of **MD Publications Pvt Ltd** at Times Press, New Delhi.

CONTENTS

CONTENTS

PREFACE

Buddhism is one of the oldest religions in the world. It is a path of practice and spiritual development leading to insight into the true nature of life. Buddhist practices such as meditation are means of changing oneself in order to develop the qualities of awareness, kindness, and wisdom. The experience developed within the Buddhist tradition over thousands of years has created an incomparable resource for all those who wish to follow a path — a path which ultimately culminates in Enlightenment.

The basic tenets of Buddhist teaching are straightforward and practical: nothing is fixed or permanent; actions have consequences; change is possible. Thus Buddhism addresses itself to all people irrespective of race, nationality, or gender. It teaches practical methods (such as meditation) which enable people to realize and utilize its teachings in order to transform their experience, to be fully responsible for their lives and to develop the qualities of Wisdom and Compassion. There are millions of Buddhists in the world today and their numbers are growing with every passing day. Different people follow different paths, but all traditions are characterized by non-violence, lack of dogma, tolerance of differences, and, usually, by the practice of meditation.

Buddhism is one of the prominent religions in South Asia. In countries like Sri Lanka and Bhutan, it is the main state religion. There are a sizable number of Buddhists in South Asian region. This book traces the various aspects of Buddhism in South Asia including its history, development, prominent thinkers and much more which we believe will be very interesting for the readers.

I am very grateful to Mr. Pranav Gupta, Director, MD Publications Pvt Ltd, New Delhi who readily expressed acceptance and supported me fully for completing this book.

Dr Arvind Kumar Singh

Chapter - 1

Buddhism

An Introduction

Buddhism is both a world religion and a philosophy with between 230 and 500 million adherents worldwide. It is based on the teachings of Buddha Shakyamuni, sometimes known simply as "the Buddha", (Siddhârtha Gautama) who lived c. 5th century BCE in ancient India, in parts of what is now Nepal and the Indian states of Uttar Pradesh and Bihar.

Buddhism has spread through two main traditions; Theravada which extended south and east and now has widespread following in Southeast Asia, and Mahayana, which diffused first west, then north and later east throughout East Asia. Both traditions have since spread throughout the world. There are considerable differences between the various existing traditions regarding their canon of authentic scriptures, their emphasis on specific parts of what they respectively consider the Buddha's teachings and their subsequent interpretations as well as in the practices they consider most beneficial.

All traditions recognize the Buddha as an enlightened teacher who shared his insights in order to help sentient beings end their suffering in accordance with the laws of Karma by realizing the true nature of phenomena and thereby escaping the cycle of involuntary rebirths known to Buddhists as Samsara. Among the methods Buddhist sects apply towards that goal are ethical conduct, altruistic behaviour, renunciation of wordly matters, the training of one's mind through learning and meditation, devotional practices and the invocation of holy beings to seek their help in achieving Enlightenment. Followers of the Buddhist path take refuge in The Three Jewels: **Buddha** (*The Enlightened* or *Awakened One*), **Dharma** (*The Teaching*), and **Sangha** (*The Community*).

GAUTAM BUDDHA

Siddhârtha Gautama (Sanskrit; Pali: **Siddhattha Gotama**) was a spiritual teacher from ancient India and the founder of Buddhism. He is generally recognized by Buddhists as the Supreme Buddha (Sammâsambuddha) of our age. The time of his birth and death are uncertain: most early 20th-century historians date his lifetime from *circa* 563 BCE to 483 BCE; more recently, however, at a specialist symposium on this question, the majority of those scholars who presented definite opinions gave dates within 20 years either side of 400 BCE for the Buddha's death, with others supporting earlier or later dates.

Gautama, also known as **Sâkyamuni** or **Shakyamuni** ("sage of the Shakyas"), is the key figure in Buddhism, and accounts of his life, discourses, and monastic rules were said to have been summarized after his death and memorized by the sangha. Passed down by oral tradition, the *Tripitaka*, the collection of teachings attributed to Gautama by the Theravada, was committed to writing about 400 years later. "Scholars are increasingly reluctant to make unqualified claims about the historical facts of the Buddha's life and teachings."

The prime sources of information regarding Siddhârtha Gautama's life are the Buddhist texts. The Buddha and his monks spent four months each year discussing and rehearsing his teachings, and after his death his monks set about preserving them. A council was held shortly after his death, and another was held a century later. At these councils the monks attempted to establish and authenticate the extant accounts of the life and teachings of the Buddha following systematic rules. They divided the teachings into distinct but overlapping bodies of material, and assigned specific monks to preserve each one. This was done orally until three generations after the Buddha's death, when they were recorded. By this point, the monks had added or altered some material themselves, in particular magnifying the figure of the Buddha.

The ancient Indians were not concerned with chronologies, being far more focused on philosophy. The Buddhist texts reflect this tendency, and we have a much clearer picture of what the Buddha thought than of the dates of the events in his life. These texts contain descriptions of the culture and daily life of ancient India which can be corroborated from the Jain scriptures, and make the Buddha's time the earliest period in Indian history for which substantial accounts exist. The following is a summary of what is found in these texts.

CONCEPTION AND BIRTH

According to tradition, Siddhârtha was born more than 200 years before the reign of the Maurya king Asoka (273–232 BCE). Siddhartha was born in Lumbini and raised in the small kingdom or principality of Kapilvastu, both of which are in modern day Nepal. Culturally, these can be considered part of the broader region of Ancient India. His father was King Suddhodana, the chief of the Shakya nation, one of several ancient tribes in the growing state of Kosala; Gautama was the family name. His mother, Queen Maha Maya (Mâyâdevî) and Suddhodana's wife, was a Koliyan princess. On the night Siddhartha was conceived, Queen Maya dreamt that a white elephant with six white tusks entered her right side, and ten lunar months later Siddhartha was born from her right side. As was the Shakya tradition, when his mother Queen Maya fell pregnant, she returned to her father's kingdom to give birth, but after leaving Kapilvastu, she gave birth along the way at Lumbini in a garden beneath a sal tree.

The day of the Buddha's birth is widely celebrated in Theravada countries as Vesak. Various sources hold that the Buddha's mother died at his birth, a few days or seven days later. The infant was given the name Siddhartha (Pâli: Siddhatta), meaning "he who achieves his aim". During the birth celebrations, the hermit seer Asita journeyed from his mountain abode and announced that the child would either become a great king (chakravartin) or a great holy man. This occurred after Siddhartha placed his feet in Asita's hair and Asita examined the birthmarks. Suddhodarna held a naming ceremony on the fifth day, and invited eight brahmin scholars to read the future. All gave a dual prediction that the baby would either become a great king or a great holy man. Kaundinya (Pali: Kondanna), the youngest, and later to be the first arahant, was the only one who unequivocally predicted that Siddhartha would become a Buddha.

While later tradition and legend characterized suddhodana as a hereditary monarch, the descendant of the Solar Dynasty of Ikshvâku (Pâli: Okkâka), many scholars believe that Suddhodana was the elected chief of a tribal confederacy.

EARLY LIFE AND MARRIAGE

Siddhartha, destined to a luxurious life as a prince, had three palaces (for seasonal occupation) especially built for him. His father, King Suddhodana, wishing for Siddhartha to be a great king, shielded his son from religious teachings or knowledge of human suffering. Siddhartha was brought up by his mother's younger sister, Maha Pajapati.

As the boy reached the age of 16, his father arranged his marriage to Yaúodharâ (Pâli: Yasodharâ), a cousin of the same age. In time, she gave birth to a son, Rahula. Siddhartha spent 29 years as a Prince in Kapilavastu. Although his father ensured that Siddhartha was provided with everything he could want or need, Siddhartha felt that material wealth was not the ultimate goal of life.

THE GREAT DEPARTURE

At the age of 29, Siddhartha left his palace in order to meet his subjects. Despite his father's effort to remove the sick, aged and suffering from the public view, Siddhartha was said to have seen an old man. Disturbed by this, when told that all people would eventually grow old by his charioteer Channa, the prince went on further trips where he encountered, variously, a diseased man, a decaying corpse, and an ascetic. Deeply depressed by these sights, he sought to overcome old age, illness, and death by living the life of an ascetic.

Siddhartha escaped his palace, accompanied by Channa aboard his horse Kanthaka, leaving behind this royal life to become a mendicant. It is said that, "the horse's hooves were muffled by the gods" to prevent guards from knowing the Bodhisatta's departure. This event is known as "The Great Departure".

Siddhartha initially went to Rajagaha and began his ascetic life by begging for alms in the street. Having been recognised by the men of King Bimbisara, Bimbisara offered him the throne after hearing of Siddhartha's quest. Siddhartha rejected the offer, but promised to visit his kingdom of Magadha first, upon attaining enlightenment.

Siddhartha left Rajagaha and practiced under two hermit teachers. After mastering the teachings of Alara Kalama, Siddhartha was asked by Kalama to succeed him, but moved on after being unsatisfied with his practices. He then became a student of Udaka Ramaputta, but although he achieved high levels of meditative consciousness and was asked to succeed Ramaputta, he was still not satisfied with his path, and moved on.

Siddhartha and a group of five companions led by Kondanna then set out to take their austerities even further. They tried to find enlightenment through near total deprivation of worldly goods, including food, practicing self-mortification. After nearly starving himself to death by restricting his food intake to around a leaf or nut per day, he collapsed in a river while bathing and almost drowned. Siddhartha began to reconsider his path. Then, he remembered a moment in childhood in which he had been watching his father start the season's plowing, and he had fallen into a naturally concentrated and focused state that was blissful and refreshing, the jhana.

THE GREAT ENLIGHTENMENT

After asceticism and concentrating on meditation and Anapana-sati (awareness of breathing in and out), Siddhartha is said to have discovered what Buddhists call the Middle Way—a path of moderation away from the extremes of self-indulgence and self-mortification. He accepted a little milk and rice pudding from a village girl named Sujata, who wrongly believed him to be the spirit that had granted her a wish, such was his emaciated appearance. Then, sitting under a pipal tree, now known as the Bodhi tree in Bodh Gaya, he vowed never to arise until he had found the Truth. Kaundinya and the other four companions, believing that he had abandoned his search and become undisciplined, left. After 49 days meditating, at the age of 35, he attained Enlightenment; according to some traditions, this occurred approximately in the fifth lunar month, and according to others in the twelfth. Gautama, from then on, was known as the *Buddha* or "Awakened One." Buddha is also sometimes translated as "The Enlightened One." Often, he is referred to in Buddhism as Shakyamuni Buddha or "The Awakened One of the Shakya Clan."

At this point, he realized complete awakening and insight into the nature and cause of human suffering which was ignorance, along with steps necessary to eliminate it. These truths were then categorized into the Four Noble Truths; the state of supreme liberation—possible for any being—was called Nirvana. He then came to possess the Nine Characteristics, which are said to belong to every Buddha.

According to one of the stories in the *Âyâcana Sutta* (Samyutra Nikaya VI.1), a scripture found in the Pâli and other canons, immediately after his Enlightenment, the Buddha was wondering whether or not he should teach the *Dharma* to human beings. He was concerned that, as human beings were overpowered by greed, hatred and delusion, they would not be able to see the true *dharma*, which was subtle, deep and hard to understand. However, a divine spirit, Brahmâ Sahampati, interceded and asked that he teach the *dharma* to the world, as "there will be those who will understand the *Dharma*". With his great compassion to all beings in the universe, the Buddha agreed to become a teacher.

FORMATION OF THE SANGHA

After becoming enlightened, two merchants whom the Buddha met, named Tapussa and Bhallika became the first lay disciples. They are given some hairs from the Buddha's head, which are believed to now be enshrined in the Shwe Dagon Temple in Rangoon, Burma. The Buddha intended to visit Asita, and his former teachers, Alara Kalama and Uddaka Ramaputta to explain his findings, but they had already died.

The Buddha thus journeyed to Deer Park near Vârânasî (Benares) in northern India, he set in motion the Wheel of Dharma by delivering his first sermon to the group of five companions with whom he had previously sought enlightenment. They, together with the Buddha, formed the first sangha, the company of Buddhist monks, and hence, the first formation of Triple Gem (Buddha, Dharma and Sangha) was completed, with Kaundinya becoming the first stream-enterer. All five soon become arahants, and with the conversion of Yasa and fifty four of his friends, the number of arahants swelled to 60 within the first two months. The conversion of the three Kassapa brothers and their 200, 300 and 500 disciples swelled the sangha over 1000, and they were dispatched to explain the dharma to the populace.

MINISTRY

For the remaining 45 years of his life, the Buddha is said to have traveled in the Gangetic Plain, in what is now Uttar Pradesh, Bihar and southern Nepal, teaching his doctrine and discipline to an extremely diverse range of people— from nobles to outcaste street sweepers, mass murderers such as Angulimala and cannibals such as Alavaka. This extended to many adherents of rival philosophies and religions. The Buddha founded the community of Buddhist monks and nuns (the *Sangha*) to continue the dispensation after his Parinirvâna (Pâli: Parinibbâna) or "complete Nirvâna", and made thousands of converts. His religion was open to all races and classes and had no caste structure. He was also subject to attack from opposition religious groups, including attempted murders and framings.

The sangha travelled from place to place in India, expounding the dharma. This occurred throughout the year, except during the four months of the vassana rainy season. Due to the heavy amount of flooding, travelling was difficult, and ascetics of all religions in that time did not travel, since it was more difficult to do so without stepping on submerged animal life, unwittingly killing them. During this period, the sangha would retreat to a monastery, public park or a forest and people would come to them.

The first vassana was spent at Varanasi when the sangha was first formed. After this, he travelled to Rajagaha, the capital of Magadha to visit King Bimbisara, in accordance with his promise after enlightenment. It was during this visit that Sariputta and Mahamoggallana were converted by Assaji, one of the first five disciples; they were to become the Buddha's two foremost disciples. The Buddha then spent the next three seasons at Veluvana Bamboo Grove monastery in Rajagaha, the capital of Magadha. The monastery, which was of a moderate distance from the city centre was donated by Bimbisara.

Upon hearing of the enlightenment, Suddhodana dispatched royal delegations to ask the Buddha to return to Kapilavastu. Nine delegations were sent in all, but the delegates joined the sangha and became arahants. Neglecting worldly matters, they did not convey their message. The tenth delegation, lead by Kaludayi, a childhood friend, resulted in the message being successfully conveyed as well as becoming an arahant. Since it was not the vassana, the Buddha agreed, and two years after his enlightenment, took a two month journey to Kapilavastu by foot, preaching the dharma along the way. Upon his return, the royal palace had prepared the midday meal, but since no specific invitation had come, the sangha went for an alms round in Kapilavastu. Hearing this, Suddhodana hastened to approach the Buddha, stating "Ours is the warrior lineage of Mahamassata, and not a single warrior has gone seeking alms", to which the Buddha replied

"That is not the custom of your royal lineage. But it is the custom of my Buddha lineage. Several thousands of Buddhas have gone by seeking alms"

Suddhodana invited the sangha back to the royal palace for the meal, followed by a dharma talk, after which he became a sotapanna. During the visit, many members of the royal family joined the sangha. His cousins Ananda and Anuruddha were to become two of his five chief disciples. His son Rahula also joined the sangha at the age of seven, and was one of the ten chief disciples. His half-brother Nanda also joined the sangha and became an arahant. Another cousin Devadatta also became a monk although he later became an enemy and tried to kill the Buddha on multiple occasions.

Of his disciples, Sariputta, Mahamoggallana, Mahakasyapa, Ananda and Anuruddha comprised the five chief disciples. His ten foremost disciples were completed by the quintet of Upali, Subhoti, Rahula, Mahakaccana and Punna.

In the fifth vassana, the Buddha was staying at Mahavana near Vesali. Hearing of the impending death of Suddhodana, the Buddha went to his father and preached the dharma, and Suddhodana became an arahant prior to death. The death and cremation led to the creation of the order of nuns. Buddhist texts record that he was reluctant to ordain women as nuns. His foster mother Maha Pajapati approached him asking to join the sangha, but the Buddha refused, and began the journey from Kapilavastu back to Rajagaha. Maha Pajapati was so intent on renouncing the world that she lead a group of royal Sakyan and Koliyan ladies, following the sangha to Rajagaha. The Buddha eventually accepted them five years after the formation of the Sangha on the grounds that their capacity for enlightenment was equal to that of men, but he gave them certain additional rules (Vinaya) to follow. This occurred after Ananda interceded on their behalf. Yasodhara also became a nun, with both becoming arahants.

During his ministry, Devadatta (who was not an arahant) frequently tried to undermine the Buddha. At one point Devadatta asked the Buddha to stand aside to let him lead the sangha. The Buddha declined, and stated that Devadatta's actions did not reflect on the Triple Gem, but on him alone. Devadatta conspired with Prince Ajatasattu, son of Bimbisara, so that they would kill and usurp the Buddha and Bimbisara respectively. Devadatta attempted three times to kill the Buddha. The first attempt involved the hiring of a group of archers, whom upon meeting the Buddha became disciples. A second attempt followed when Devadatta attempted to roll a large boulder down a hill. It hit another rock and splintered, only grazing the Buddha in the foot. A final attempt by plying an elephant with alcohol and setting it loose again failed. Failing this, Devadatta attempted to cause a schism in the sangha, by proposing extra restrictions on the vinaya. When the Buddha declined, Devadatta started a breakaway order, criticising the Buddha's laxity. At first, he managed to convert some of the bhikkhus, but Sariputta and Mahamoggallana expounded the dharma to them and succeeded in winning them back. When the Buddha reached the age of 55, he made Ananda his chief attendant.

THE GREAT PASSING

According to the Mahaparinibbana Sutta of the Pali canon, at the age of 80, the Buddha announced that he would soon enter Parinirvana or the final deathless state abandoning the earthly body. After this, the Buddha ate his last meal, which, according to different translations, especially the religious texts knowledge of Heenyan texts was pork, which he had received as an offering from a blacksmith named Cunda. Falling violently ill, Buddha instructed his attendant Ânanda to convince Cunda that the meal eaten at his place had nothing to do with his passing and that his meal would be a source of the greatest merit as it provided the last meal for a Buddha. The demolition of the Bahmiyan Buddha statues by the Al-Queda builder terror mafia or Taliban was due to the last meal being of Pork as Muslims are forbidden to have anything to do with liquor and pork or pig's meat.

The Buddhas of Bamiyan were two monumental statues of standing Buddhas carved into the side of a cliff in the Bamyan valley of central Afghanistan, situated 230 km (143 miles) northwest of Kabul at an altitude of 2500 meters (8,202 feet).It was a Buddhist religious site from the second century up to the time of the Islamic invasion in the ninth century. Built during the sixth century, the statues represented the classic blended style of Indo-Greek art. Bamyan lies on the Silk Road, a caravan route linking the markets of China & India with those of Central Asia, the Middle East, and Europe. This Silk Route is used by drug peddlars and illegal hawala dealers;to send dirty money of terrorists and big companies of India. The statues were destroyed by dynamite over several weeks, starting in early March, carried out in different stages. Initially, the statues were fired at for several days using anti-aircraft guns and artillery. This damaged them but did not obliterate them Then the Taliban placed anti-tank mines at the bottom of the niches, so that when chunks of rock broke off from artillery fire, the statues would fall and be blown up again. In the end, the Taliban tied ropes around some local Hazara men, lowered them down the cliff face, and forced them to place explosives into holes in the Buddhas.

DYNAMITING AND DESTRUCTION, MARCH 2001

On March 6, 2001 The Times quoted Mullah Mohammed Omar as stating, "Muslims should be proud of smashing idols. It has given praise to God that we have destroyed them." He had clearly changed his position from being in favor of the statues to being against them. During a March 13 interview for Japan's Mainichi Shimbun, Afghan Foreign Minister Wakil Ahmad Mutawakel stated that the destruction was anything but a retaliation against the international community for economic sanctions: "We are destroying the Buddha statues in accordance with Islamic law and it is purely a religious issue".

The Mahayana Vimalakirti Sutra explains, that the Buddha doesn't really become ill or old but purposely presents such an appearance only to teach those born during the five defilements the impermanence and pain of defiled worlds and to strive for Nirvana.

"'Reverend Ánanda, the Tathágatas have the body of the Dharma - not a body that is sustained by material food. The Tathágatas have a transcendental body that has transcended all mundane qualities. There is no injury to the body of a Tathágata, as it is rid of all defilements. The body of a Tathágata is uncompounded and free of all formative activity. Reverend Ánanda, to believe there can be illness in such a body is irrational and unseemly!' Nevertheless, since the Buddha has appeared during the time of the five corruptions, he disciplines living beings by acting lowly and humble."

Ananda protested Buddha's decision to enter Parinirvana in the abandoned jungles of Kuúinâra (Pâli: Kusinâra) of the Mallas. Buddha, however, reminded Ananda how Kusinara was a land once ruled by a righteous wheel-turning king that resounded with joy:

"44. Kusavati, Ananda, resounded unceasingly day and night with ten sounds — the trumpeting of elephants, the neighing of horses, the rattling of chariots, the beating of drums and tabours, music and song, cheers, the clapping of hands, and cries of "Eat, drink, and be merry!"

Buddha then asked all the attendant Bhikshus to clarify any doubts or questions they had. They had none. He then finally entered Parinirvana. The Buddha's final words were, "All composite things pass away. Strive for your own liberation with diligence." The Buddha's body was cremated and the relics were placed in monuments or stupas, some of which are believed to have survived until the present. For example, The Temple of the Tooth or "Dalada Maligawa" in Sri Lanka is the place where the relic of the right tooth of Buddha is kept at present.

According to the Pâli historical chronicles of Sri Lanka, the Dîpavamsa and Mahâvamsa, the coronation of Asoka (Pâli: Asoka) is 218 years after the death of Buddha. According to one Mahayana record in Chinese, the coronation of Asoka is 116 years after the death of Buddha. Therefore, the time of Buddha's passing is either 486 BCE according to Theravâda record or 383 BCE according to Mahayana record. However, the actual date traditionally accepted as the date of the Buddha's death in Theravâda countries is 544 or 543 BCE, because the reign of Asoka was traditionally reckoned to be about 60 years earlier than current estimates.

At his death, the Buddha told his disciples to follow no leader, but to follow his teachings (dharma). However, at the First Buddhist Council, Mahakasyapa was held by the sangha as their leader, with the two chief disciples Mahamoggallana and Sariputta having died before the Buddha.

PHYSICAL CHARACTERISTICS

Buddha is perhaps one of the few sages for whom we have mention of his rather impressive physical characteristics. A kshatriya by birth, he had military training in his upbringing, and by Shakyan tradition was required to pass tests to demonstrate his worthiness as a warrior in order to marry. He had a strong enough body to be noticed by one of the kings and was asked to join his army as a general. He is also believed by Buddhists to have "the 32 Signs of the Great Man".

The Brahmin Sonadanda described him as "handsome, good-looking, and pleasing to the eye, with a most beautiful complexion. He has a godlike form and countenance, he is by no means unattractive."(D,I:115).

"It is wonderful, truly marvellous, how serene is the good Gotama's appearance, how clear and radiant his complexion, just as the golden jujube in autumn is clear and radiant, just as a palm-tree fruit just loosened from the stalk is clear and radiant, just as an adornment of red gold wrought in a crucible by a skilled goldsmith, deftly beaten and laid on a yellow-cloth shines, blazes and glitters, even so, the good Gotama's senses are calmed, his complexion is clear and radiant." (A,I:181)

A disciple named Vakkali, who later became an Arahant, was so obsessed by Buddha's physical presence that Buddha has to tell him to stop and reminded Vakkali to know Buddha through the Dhamma and not physical appearances.

Although the Buddha was not represented in human form until around the 1st century CE, the physical characteristics of fully-enlightened Buddhas are described by the Buddha in the Digha Nikaya's *Lakkhana Sutta* (D,I:142). In addition, the Buddha's physical appearance is described by Yasodhara to their son Rahula upon the Buddha's first post-Enlightenment return to his former princely palace in the non-canonical Pali devotional hymn, *Narasîha Gâthâ* ("The Lion of Men").

TEACHINGS

Some scholars believe that some portions of the Pali Canon and the Agamas could contain the actual substance of the historical teachings (and possibly even the words) of the Buddha. This is not the case for the later Mahayana sutras. The scriptural works of Early Buddhism precede the Mahayana works chronologically, and are treated by many Western scholars as the main credible source for information regarding the actual historical teachings of Gautama Buddha.

The following points are the a few of the fundamentals of the teachings of Gautama Buddha:

- The Four Noble Truths: that suffering is an inherent part of existence; that the origin of suffering is ignorance and the main symptoms of that ignorance are attachment and craving; that attachment and craving can be ceased; and that following the Noble Eightfold Path will lead to the cessation of attachment and craving and therefore suffering.
- The Noble Eightfold Path: right understanding, right thought, right speech, right action, right livelihood, right effort, right mindfulness, and right concentration.
- Dependent origination: that any phenomenon 'exists' only because of the 'existence' of other phenomena in a complex web of cause and effect covering time past, present and future. Because all things are thus conditioned and transient (anicca), they have no real independent identity (anatta).
- Rejection of the infallibility of accepted scripture: Teachings should not be accepted unless they are borne out by our experience and are praised by the wise.
- Anicca (Sanskrit: anitya): That all things are impermanent.
- Anatta (Sanskrit: anâtman): That the perception of a constant "self" is an illusion.
- Dukkha (Sanskrit: dukkha): That all beings suffer from all situations due to unclear mind.

However, in some Mahayana schools, these points have come to be regarded as more or less subsidiary. There is some disagreement amongst various schools of Buddhism over more esoteric aspects of Buddha's teachings, and also over some of the disciplinary rules for monks.

According to tradition, the Buddha emphasized ethics and correct understanding. He questioned the average person's notions of divinity and salvation. He stated that there is no intermediary between mankind and the divine; distant gods are subjected to karma themselves in decaying heavens; and the Buddha is solely a guide and teacher for the sentient beings who must tread the path of NirvâGa (Pâli: Nibbâna) themselves to attain the spiritual awakening called *bodhi* and see truth and reality as it is. The Buddhist system of insight and meditation practice is not believed to have been revealed divinely, but by the understanding of the true nature of the mind, which must be discovered by personally treading a spiritual path guided by the Buddha's teachings.

LANGUAGE

It is unknown what language the Buddha spoke, and no conclusive documentation has been made at this point. However, some modern scholars, primarily philologists, believe it is most likely that the Buddha spoke a vulgate then current in eastern India, Mâgadhî Prakrit.

IMPORTANT CONCEPTS OF BUDDHISM

Not all traditions of Buddhism share the same philosophical outlook, or treat the same concepts as central. Each tradition, however, does have its own core concepts, and some comparisons can be drawn between them.

Mahayana Buddhism shows a great deal of doctrinal variation and development over time, and even more variation in terms of practice. While there is much agreement on general principles, there is disagreement over which texts are more authoritative.

KARMA AND REBIRTH

Rebirth has no discernible beginning, and takes place in a variety of types of life, later formally classified as the Five or Six Realms.

The karma of kusala (skillful) and akusala (unskillful) actions produces "seeds" in the mind which come to fruition either in this life or in a subsequent one. These may be either rebirths themselves or events therein. The content of unwholesome actions and the lower types of wholesome actions belongs to the subject of Sila or conduct. Higher rebirths can be attained by the practice of forms of meditation later classified as samatha or samadhi.

Many Buddhists believe that there is no otherworldly salvation from one's karma. The suffering caused by the karmic effects of previous thoughts, words and deeds can be alleviated by following the Noble Eightfold Path, although the Buddha of some Mahayana sutras, such as the Lotus Sutra, the Angulimaliya Sutra and the Nirvana Sutra, also teaches that powerful sutras such as the above-named can, through the very act of their being heard or recited, wholly expunge great swathes of negative karma.

THE FOUR NOBLE TRUTHS

The Four Noble Truths (or The Four Truths of the Noble Ones) (Sanskrit: catvri ryasatyni; Tibetan: 'phags pa'i bden pa bzhi; Pali: cattâri ariyasaccâni) are one of the most fundamental Buddhist teachings. In broad terms, these truths relate to suffering's nature, origin, cessation and the path leading to the cessation. They are among the truths Gautama Buddha is said to have realized during his experience of enlightenment.

The Four Noble Truths appear many times throughout the most ancient Buddhist texts, the Pali Canon. Mahayana Buddhism regards these as a preliminary teaching for people not ready for its own teachings.

Some may see "truths" as a mistranslation (one author sites that "realities" may be better: these are "things", not statements, in the original grammar.) However, the original Tibetan Lotsawas (Sanskrit: locchâwa; Tibetan: lo ts'a ba), who studied Sanskrit grammar thoroughly, did translate the term from Sanskrit into Tibetan as "bden pa" which has the full meaning of "truth".

Why the Buddha is said to have taught in this way is illuminated by the social context of the time in which he lived. The Buddha was a Sramana, a wandering ascetic whose "aim was to discover the truth and attain happiness." He is said to have achieved this aim while under a bodhi tree near the River Neranjana; the Four Noble Truths are a formulation of his understanding of the nature of "suffering", the fundamental cause of all suffering, the escape from suffering, and what effort a person can make so that they themselves can *"attain happiness."*

These truths are not expressed as a hypothesis or tentative idea, rather the Buddha says:

"These Four Noble Truths, monks, are actual, unerring, not otherwise. Therefore, they are called noble truths. "

The Buddha says that he taught them...

"...because it is beneficial, it belongs to the fundamentals of the holy life, it leads to disenchantment, to dispassion, to cessation of suffering, to peace, to direct knowledge, to enlightenment, to Nirvana. That is why I have declared it."

This teaching was the basis of the Buddha's first discourse after his enlightenment. In early Buddhism this is the most advanced teaching in the Buddha's Gradual Training.

PALI CANON TEXT

1. The Nature of Suffering (*Dukkha*):

"Now this ... is the noble truth of suffering: birth is suffering, aging is suffering, illness is suffering, death is suffering; sorrow, lamentation, pain, grief and despair are suffering; union with what is displeasing is suffering; separation from what is pleasing is suffering; not to get what one wants is suffering; in brief, the five aggregates subject to clinging are suffering."

2. Suffering's Origin (*Samudaya*):

"Now this ... is the noble truth of the origin of suffering: it is this craving which leads to renewed existence, accompanied by delight and lust, seeking delight here and there, that is, craving for sensual pleasures, craving for existence, craving for extermination."

3. **Suffering's Cessation (*Nirodha*):**

"Now this ... is the noble truth of the cessation of suffering: it is the remainderless fading away and cessation of that same craving, the giving up and relinquishing of it, freedom from it, nonreliance on it."

4. **The Way (*Mârga*) Leading to the Cessation of Suffering:**

"Now this ... is the noble truth of the way leading to the cessation of suffering: it is the Noble Eightfold Path; that is, right view, right intention, right speech, right action, right livelihood, right effort, right mindfulness, right concentration."

MAHAYANA UNDERSTANDING OF THE FOUR NOBLE TRUTHS

Certain major Mahayana sutras, including the Mahaparinirvana Sutra and the Angulimaliya Sutra, present variant versions of the Four Noble Truths of the Buddha:

- the Truth of Suffering relates to the failure to recognize the eternity of the Buddha;
- the Truth of the Cause of Suffering concerns the perversion and distortion of the True Dharma (i.e. wrongly insisting that the Buddha and Dharma are impermanent);
- the Truth of the Cessation of Suffering relates to the correct meditative cultivation of the tathagatagarbha (in dwelling Buddha Nature in all beings) and not erroneously viewing it as non-Self and empty; cessation of suffering also arises with the elimination of inner defilements, when one can then enter into the Buddhic Essence within oneself: "When the afflictions have been eradicated, then one will perceive entry into the tathâgata-garbha";
- the Truth of the Path to the Cessation of Suffering entails envisioning the Buddha, Dharma and Sangha as eternal, unshakable and indestructible.

The Angulimaliya Sutra similarly emphasises the seeing and knowing of the Buddha's eternality, immutability and peace as the key factors in liberation from suffering; failure to see this eternal nature of ultimate reality is said to constitute the primary cause of beings' continued entrapment in the sufferings of samsara.

It should be noted that this view is specific to certain Mahayana schools, most notably the Tathagatagarbha and Jonangpa traditions. The ideas that the Buddha and his Dharma are eternal and that one's inner Buddhanature is not empty would be denied in other Buddhist traditions such as Madhyamaka and Zen.

NOBLE EIGHTFOLD PATH

The **noble eightfold path** is, in the teachings of the Buddha, declared to be the way that leads to the cessation of suffering (*dukkha*) and the achievement of self-awakening. The noble eightfold path is used as an instrument of discovery to gradually generate insights unveiling the ultimate truth of things. It is a technique used to eradicate greed, hatred and delusion. The last of the four noble truths is the noble eightfold path, while the first factor of the noble eightfold path is the understanding of the four noble truths. In all of the elements of the noble eightfold path, the word "Right" is a translation of the word *samyaka* (Sanskrit) or *sammâ* (Pâli), which denotes completion, togetherness, and coherence, and which can also carry the sense of "perfect" or "ideal". In Buddhist symbolism, the noble eightfold path is often represented by means of the dharma wheel, whose eight spokes represent the eight elements of the path.

According to the Pali canon discourses, the noble eightfold path was rediscovered by Gautama Buddha during his quest for enlightenment. It is believed to be an ancient path which has been followed and practiced by all the previous Buddhas. The noble eightfold path is a practice that will lead its practitioner toward self-awakening and liberation. It was revealed by the Buddha to his disciples, so that they could follow the very same path.

> "In the same way I saw an ancient path, an ancient road, traveled by the Rightly Self-awakened Ones of former times. And what is that ancient path, that ancient road, traveled by the Rightly Self-awakened Ones of former times? Just this noble eightfold path: right view, right aspiration, right speech, right action, right livelihood, right effort, right mindfulness, right concentration...I followed that path. Following it, I came to direct knowledge of aging & death, direct knowledge of the origination of aging & death, direct knowledge of the cessation of aging & death, direct knowledge of the path leading to the cessation of aging & death...Knowing that directly, I have revealed it to monks, nuns, male lay followers & female lay followers..."

The practice of the noble eightfold path varies between different Buddhist schools. Today the path either has been modified, is practiced only in part, or is practiced as a whole. Each Buddhist practice lineage claimed they are able to implement the Noble Eightfold Path in the manner most condusive to the development of their students. In some cases that has led to aspects of the Noble Eightfold Path to be abandoned.

THE PRACTICE

According to the Buddhist monk and scholar Walpola Rahula, the divisions of the noble eightfold path "are to be developed more or less simultaneously, as far as possible according to the capacity of each individual. They are all linked together and each helps the cultivation of the others." Bhikkhu Bodhi explained "with a certain degree of progress all eight factors can be present simultaneously, each supporting the others. However, until that point is reached, some sequence in the unfolding of the path is inevitable".

According to the Pali Canon discourses, right view, right resolve, right speech, right action, right livelihood, right effort, and right mindfulness are used as the support and requisite conditions for the practice of right concentration. Understanding of the right view is the preliminary role, and is also the forerunner of the entire Noble Eightfold

Path. The practitioner should first try to understand the concepts of right view. Once right view has been understood, it will inspire and encourage the arising of right intention within the practitioner. Right intention will lead to the arising of right speech. Right speech will lead to the arising of right action. Right action will lead to the arising of right livelihood. Right livelihood will lead to the arising of right effort. Right effort will lead to the arising of right mindfulness. The practitioner must make the right effort to abandon the wrong view and to enter into the right view. Right mindfulness is used in order to constantly remain in the right view. This will help the practitioner restrain their greed, hatred and delusion.

Once these support and requisite conditions have been established, the practitioner can then practice right concentration with ease. During the practice of right concentration, the practitioner will need to use right effort and right mindfulness to aid their concentration practice. In the state of concentration, the practitioner will need to investigate and verify their understanding of right view. This will then result in the arising of right knowledge, which will eliminate greed, hatred and delusion. The last and final factor to arise is right liberation.

*WISDOM (*PRAJÑÂ • PAÑÑÂ*)*

"Wisdom", sometimes translated as "discernment" at its preparatory role, provides the sense of direction with its conceptual understanding of reality. It is designed to awaken the faculty of penetrative understanding to see things as they really are. At a later stage, when the mind has been refined by training in moral discipline and concentration, and with the gradual arising of right knowledge, it will arrive at a superior right view and right intention.

Right view

Right view can also be translated as "right perspective", "right vision" or "right understanding". It is the right way of looking at life, nature and the world as they really are. It is to understand how reality works. It acts as the reasoning for the practictioner to start practicing the path. It explains the reasons for human existence, suffering, sickness, aging, death, the existence of greed, hatred and delusion. It gives direction and efficacy to the other seven path factors. Right view begins with concepts and propositional knowledge but through the practice of right concentration it gradually becomes transmuted into wisdom which can eradicate the fetters of the mind. Understanding of right view will inspire the person to lead a virtuous life in line with right view. In the Pali Canon, it is explained as:

> "And what is right view? Knowledge with reference to stress (dukkha can also be translated as suffering), knowledge with reference to the origination of stress (or suffering), knowledge with reference to the cessation of stress (or suffering), knowledge with reference to the way of practice leading to the cessation of stress (or suffering): This is called right view."

There are two types of right view:

1. **View with taints** – this view is mundane. Having this type of view will bring merit and will support the favourable existence of the sentient being in the realm of samsara.
2. **View without taints** – this view is supramundane. It is a factor of the path and will lead the holder of this view toward self-awakening and liberation from the realm of samsara.

Right view has many facets, its elementary form is suitable for lay followers, while the other which requires deeper understanding is suitable for monastic. Usually it involves understanding the following reality:

1. **Moral law of karma** - Every action (by way of body, speech and mind) will have karmic results. Wholesome and unwholesome actions will produce results and effects that correspond with the nature of that action. It is the right view about the moral process of the world.
2. **The three characteristics** – everything that arises will cease (impermanence). Mental and body phenomena are impermanent, source of suffering and not-self.
3. **Suffering** - Birth, aging, sickness, death, sorrow, lamentation, pain, grief, distress and despair are suffering. Not being able to obtain what one wants is also suffering. The arising of craving is the root cause of the arising of suffering and the cessation of craving is the root cause of the cessation of the suffering. The way leading to the cessation of suffering is the noble eightfold path. This type of right view is explained in term of Four Noble Truths.

Right view for monastics is explained in detail in the *Sammâditthi Sutta* ("Right View Discourse"), in which Ven. Sariputta instructs that right view can alternately be attained by the thorough understanding of the unwholesome and the wholesome, the four nutriments, the twelve *nidanas* or the three taints. "Wrong view" arising from ignorance (*avijja*), is the precondition for wrong intention, wrong speech, wrong action, wrong livelihood, wrong effort, wrong mindfulness and wrong concentration. The practitioner should use right effort to abandon the wrong view and to enter into right view. Right mindfulness is used in order to constantly remain in right view.

The purpose of right view is to clear one's path of the majority of confusion, misunderstanding and deluded thinking. It is a means to gain right understanding of reality. According to the Pali Canon commentary, right view should be held with a flexible, open mind, without clinging to that view as a dogmatic position. In this way, right view becomes a route to liberation rather than an obstacle. Direct realization of the Four Noble Truths may come at the peak level of self-development during the practice of right concentration.

RIGHT INTENTION

Right intention can also be translated as "right thought", "right resolve", or "right aspiration" or "the exertion of our own will to change". In this factor, the practitioner should constantly aspire to rid themselves of whatever qualities that they know are wrong and immoral. Correct understanding of right view will help the practitioner to discern the differences between right intention and wrong intention. In the Pali Canon, it is explained as:

"And what is right resolve? Being resolved on renunciation, on freedom from ill will, on harmlessness: This is called right resolve."

It means the renunciation of the worldly things and an accordant greater commitment to the spiritual path; good will; and a commitment to non-violence, or harmlessness, towards other living beings.

RIGHT CONDUCT

In order for the mind to be unified in concentration, it is necessary to restrain from unwholesome deeds of body and speech to prevent the faculties of bodily action and speech from becoming tools of the defilements. Ethical conduct is used primarily as aids for mental purification.

RIGHT SPEECH

Right speech, deals with the way in which a Buddhist practitioner would best make use of their words. In the Pali Canon, it is explained as:

"And what is right speech? Abstaining from lying, from divisive speech, from abusive speech, & from idle chatter: This is called right speech."

The *Samaññaphala Sutta, Kevatta Sutta* and *Cunda Kammaraputta Sutta* elaborate:

"Abandoning false speech...He speaks the truth, holds to the truth, is firm, reliable, no deceiver of the world..."

"Abandoning divisive speech...What he has heard here he does not tell there to break those people apart from these people here...Thus reconciling those who have broken apart or cementing those who are united, he loves concord, delights in concord, enjoys concord, speaks things that create concord..."

"Abandoning abusive speech...He speaks words that are soothing to the ear, that are affectionate, that go to the heart, that are polite, appealing and pleasing to people at large..."

"Abandoning idle chatter...He speaks in season, speaks what is factual, what is in accordance with the goal, the Dhamma, and the Vinaya. He speaks words worth treasuring, seasonable, reasonable, circumscribed, connected with the goal..."

The *Abhaya Sutta* elaborate:

"In the case of words that the Tathagata knows to be unfactual, untrue, unbeneficial (or: not connected with the goal), unendearing & disagreeable to others, he does not say them."

"In the case of words that the Tathagata knows to be factual, true, unbeneficial, unendearing & disagreeable to others, he does not say them."

"In the case of words that the Tathagata knows to be factual, true, beneficial, but unendearing & disagreeable to others, he has a sense of the proper time for saying them."

"In the case of words that the Tathagata knows to be unfactual, untrue, unbeneficial, but endearing & agreeable to others, he does not say them."

"In the case of words that the Tathagata knows to be factual, true, unbeneficial, but endearing & agreeable to others, he does not say them."

"In the case of words that the Tathagata knows to be factual, true, beneficial, and endearing & agreeable to others, he has a sense of the proper time for saying them. Why is that? Because the Tathagata has sympathy for living beings."

RIGHT ACTION

Right action (*samyak-karmânta* • *sammâ-kammanta*) can also be translated as "right conduct" . In this factor, the practitioner should train themselves to be morally upright in their activities, not acting in ways that would be corrupt or bring harm to themselves or others. In the Pali Canon, it is explained as:

"And what is right action? Abstaining from taking life, from stealing, & from illicit sex (or sexual misconduct). This is called right action."

"And what, monks, is right action? Abstaining from taking life, abstaining from stealing, abstaining from unchastity: This, monks, is called right action."

For the lay follower, the *Cunda Kammaraputta Sutta* elaborates:

"And how is one made pure in three ways by bodily action? There is the case where a certain person, abandoning the taking of life, abstains from the taking of life. He dwells with his...knife laid down, scrupulous, merciful, compassionate for the welfare of all living beings. Abandoning the taking of what is not given, he abstains from taking what is not given. He does not take, in the manner of a thief, things in a village or a wilderness that belong to others and have not been given by them. Abandoning sensual misconduct, he abstains from sensual misconduct. He does not get sexually involved with those who are protected by their mothers, their fathers, their brothers, their sisters, their relatives, or their Dhamma; those with husbands, those who entail punishments, or even those crowned with flowers by another man. This is how one is made pure in three ways by bodily action."

For the monastic, the *Samaññaphala Sutta* adds:

"Abandoning uncelibacy, he lives a celibate life, aloof, refraining from the sexual act that is the villager's way."

RIGHT LIVELIHOOD

In this factor, the practitioners ought not to engage in trades or occupations which, either directly or indirectly, result in harm for other living beings. In the Pali Canon, it is explained as:

> "And what is right livelihood? There is the case where a disciple of the noble ones, having abandoned dishonest livelihood, keeps his life going with right livelihood: This is called right livelihood."

The five types of businesses that are harmful to anyone are:

1. **Business in weapons** – trading in all kinds of weapons and instruments for killing.
2. **Business in human beings** – slave trading, or prostitution, or the buying and selling of children or adults
3. **Business in meat** - "meat" refers to the bodies of beings after they are killed. Breeding animals for slaughter
4. **Business in intoxicants** – manufacturing or selling intoxicating drinks, or addictive drugs.
5. **Business in poison** - all kinds of toxic products designed to kill.

RIGHT CONCENTRATION

Samadhi is literally translated as "concentration", it is achieved through training in the higher consciousness, which brings the calm and collectedness needed to develop true wisdom by direct experience.

RIGHT EFFORT

Right effort can also be translated as "right endeavor". In this factor, the practitioners should make a persisting effort to abandon all the wrong and harmful thoughts, words, and deeds. The practitioner should instead be persisting in giving rise to what would be good and useful to themselves and others in their thoughts, words, and deeds, without a thought for the difficulty or weariness involved. In the Pali Canon, it is explained as:

And what, monks, is right effort?

(i) There is the case where a monk generates desire, endeavors, activates persistence, upholds & exerts his intent for the sake of the non-arising of evil, unskillful qualities that have not yet arisen.

(ii) He generates desire, endeavors, activates persistence, upholds & exerts his intent for the sake of the abandonment of evil, unskillful qualities that have arisen.

(iii) He generates desire, endeavors, activates persistence, upholds & exerts his intent for the sake of the arising of skillful qualities that have not yet arisen.

(iv) He generates desire, endeavors, activates persistence, upholds & exerts his intent for the maintenance, non-confusion, increase, plenitude, development, & culmination of skillful qualities that have arisen:

This, monks, is called right effort.

Although the above instruction is given to the male monastic order, it is also meant for the female monastic order and can be practiced by lay followers from both genders.

The above four phases of right effort mean:

1. make effort to prevent the unwholesome that has not yet arisen in oneself.
2. make effort to destroy the unwholesome that has arisen in oneself.
3. make effort to arouse the wholesome that has not yet arisen in oneself.
4. make effort to maintain the wholesome that has arisen in oneself.

RIGHT MINDFULNESS

Right mindfulness, also translated as "right memory", "right awareness" or "right attention". In this factor, the practitioner should constantly keep their mind alert to phenomena as they are affecting the body and mind. They should be mindful and deliberate, making sure not to act or speak through the power of inattention or forgetfulness. In the Pali Canon, it is explained as:

And what, monks, is right mindfulness?

(i) There is the case where a monk remains focused on the body in & of itself — ardent, aware, & mindful — putting away greed & distress with reference to the world.

(ii) He remains focused on feelings in & of themselves — ardent, aware, & mindful — putting away greed & distress with reference to the world.

(iii) He remains focused on the mind in & of itself — ardent, aware, & mindful — putting away greed & distress with reference to the world.

(iv) He remains focused on mental qualities in & of themselves — ardent, aware, & mindful — putting away greed & distress with reference to the world.

This, monks, is called right mindfulness.

Although the above instruction is given to the male monastic order, it is also meant for the female monastic order and can be practiced by lay followers from both genders.

Bhikkhu Bodhi, a monk of the Theravadin tradition, further explain the concept of mindfulness as follows:

The mind is deliberately kept at the level of *bare attention*, a detached observation of what is happening within us and around us in the present moment. In the practice of right mindfulness the mind is trained to remain in the present, open, quiet, and alert, contemplating the present event. All judgments and interpretations have to be suspended, or if they occur, just registered and dropped.

RIGHT CONCENTRATION

Right concentration, as its Pali and Sanskrit name indicates, is the practice of concentration (*samadhi*). The practitioner will have to concentrate on an object of attention until it reaches full concentration and then into the state of meditative absorption (*jhana*). Traditionally, the practice of samadhi can be developed from mindfulness of breathing, from visual objects (*kasina*), and repetition of phrases. Samadhi is used to suppress the five hindrances in order to enter into jhana. Jhana is an instrument used for developing wisdom by cultivating insight and use it to penetrate the true nature of phenomena through direct cognition, which will then lead to cutting off the defilements, realize the dhamma and self-awakening. During the practice of right concentration, the practitioner will need to investigate and verify their right view, in the process right knowledge will arise and then followed by right liberation. In the Pali Canon, it is explained as:

And what is right concentration?

(i) Herein a monk aloof from sense desires, aloof from unwholesome thoughts, attains to and abides in the first meditative absorbtion (jhana) which is detachment-born and accompanied by applied thought, sustained thought, joy, and bliss.

(ii) By allaying applied and sustained thought he attains to, and abides in the second jhana which is inner tranquillity, which is unification (of the mind), devoid of applied and sustained thought, and which has joy and bliss.

(iii) By detachment from joy he dwells in equanimity, mindful, and with clear comprehension and enjoys bliss in body, and attains to and abides in the third jhana which the noble ones (ariyas) call: 'Dwelling in equanimity, mindfulness, and bliss.

(iv) By giving up of bliss and suffering, by the disappearance already of joy and sorrow, he attains to, and abides in the fourth jhana, which is neither suffering nor bliss, and which is the purity of equanimity-mindfulness.

This is called right concentration.

Although the above instruction is given to the male monastic order, it is also meant for the female monastic order and can be practiced by lay followers from both genders.

According to the Pali canon, right concentration is dependent on the development of preceding path factors:

"The Blessed One said: "Now what, monks, is noble right concentration with its supports & requisite conditions? Any singleness of mind equipped with these seven factors — right view, right resolve, right speech, right action, right livelihood, right effort, & right mindfulness — is called noble right concentration with its supports & requisite conditions."

THE ACQUIRED FACTORS

In the *Mahâcattârîsaka Sutta* , which appears in the Pali canon, the Buddha explains that cultivation of the noble eightfold path leads to the development of two further factors, which are right knowledge/insight (*sammâ-ñâna*) and right liberation/release (*sammâ-vimutti*). These two factors fall under the category of wisdom (*paññâ*).

RIGHT KNOWLEDGE AND RIGHT LIBERATION

Right knowledge is seeing things as they really are by direct experience, not as they appear to be, nor as the practitioner wants them to be, but as they truly are. A result of Right Knowledge is the tenth factor - Right liberation.

These two factors are the end result of correctly practicing the noble eightfold path, which arise during the practice of right concentration. The first to arise is right knowledge: this is where deep insight into the ultimate reality arises. The last to arise is right liberation: this is where self-awakening occurs and the practitioner has reached the pinnacle of their practice.

THE NOBLE EIGHTFOLD PATH AND COGNITIVE PSYCHOLOGY

Buddhism has always been concerned with feelings, emotions, sensations, and cognition. The Buddha points both to cognitive and emotional causes of suffering. The emotional cause is desire and its negative opposite, aversion. The cognitive cause is ignorance of the way things truly occur, or of three marks of existence: that all things are unsatisfactory, impermanent, and without essential self.

The noble eightfold path is, from this psychological viewpoint, an attempt to change patterns of thought and behavior. It is for this reason that the first element of the path is right understanding (*sammâ-ditthi*), which is how one's mind views the world. Under the wisdom subdivision of the noble eightfold path, this worldview is intimately connected with the second element, right thought, which concerns the patterns of thought and intention that controls one's actions. These elements can be seen at work, for example, in the opening verses of the *Dhammapada*:

Preceded by perception are mental states,

For them is perception supreme,

From perception have they sprung.

If, with perception polluted, one speaks or acts,

Thence suffering follows
As a wheel the draught ox's foot.
Preceded by perception are mental states,
For them is perception supreme,
From perception have they sprung.
If, with tranquil perception, one speaks or acts,
Thence ease follows
As a shadow that never departs.

Thus, by altering one's distorted worldview, bringing out "tranquil perception" in the place of "perception polluted", one is able to ease suffering. Watson points this out from a psychological standpoint:

Research has shown that repeated action, learning, and memory can actually change the nervous system physically, altering both synaptic strength and connections. Such changes may be brought about by cultivated change in emotion and action; they will, in turn, change subsequent experience.

MIDDLE WAY

An important guiding principle of Buddhist practice is the Middle Way which was said to have been discovered by the Buddha prior to his enlightenment (**bodhi**). The *Middle Way* or *Middle Path* has several definitions:

1. It is often described as the practice of non-extremism; a path of moderation away from the extremes of self-indulgence and opposing self-mortification.
2. It also refers to taking a middle ground between certain metaphysical views, e.g. that things ultimately either exist or do not exist.
3. An explanation of the state of nirvana and perfect enlightenment where all dualities fuse and cease to exist as separate entities.
4. Another term for emptiness, the ultimate nature of all phenomena, lack of inherent existence, which avoids the extremes of permanence and nihilism or inherent existence and nothingness.

Theravâda promotes the concept of Vibhajjavada (Pali), literally "Teaching of Analysis". This doctrine says that insight must come from the aspirant's experience, critical investigation, and reasoning instead of by blind faith.

In Theravâda Buddhism, the cause of human existence and suffering is identified as the craving, which carried with it the various defilements. These various defilements are traditionally summed up as greed, hatred and delusion. These defilements are believed to be parasites that have infested the mind and create suffering and stress. It is believed that in order to be free from suffering and stress these defilements need to be permanently uprooted through internal investigation, analyzing, experiencing, and understanding the true nature of those defilements by using jhana, a technique which is part of the Noble Eightfold Path. It will then lead the meditator to realize the Four Noble Truths, Enlightenment and Nibbana. Nibbana is the ultimate goal of Theravadins.

REALITY IN BUDDHISM

Buddhism evolved a variety of doctrinal/philosophical traditions, each with its own **ideas of reality**. The following are still regularly studied in some branches of the Buddhist tradition: Theravada, Vaibhashika, Sautrantika, Jojitsu, Madhyamika, Yogacara, tiantai, Huayan. Some of these are divided into subschools, and all are subject to interpretation, both by Buddhist teachers and by academic scholars. In addition to these, some less doctrinal traditions and individual teachers have their own ideas on the subject.

Some views of reality in Buddhism are relevant to the issue of dependent origination and some to teachings beyond cause and effect. Examples are discussed below.

- Some consider that the concept of the unreality of "reality" is confusing. They posit that, in Buddhism, the perceived reality is considered illusory not in the sense that reality is a fantasy or unreal, but that our perceptions and preconditions mislead us to believe that we are separate from the elements that we are made of. Reality, in Buddhist thought, would be described as the manifestation of karma, part of the process of impermanence, similar to the Hindu concept of Maya.
- Other schools of thought in Buddhism (e.g., Dzogchen), consider *perceived reality* literally unreal. As a prominent contemporary teacher puts it: "In a real sense, all the visions that we see in our lifetime are like a big dream [...]". In this context, the term 'visions' denotes not only visual perceptions, but appearances perceived through all senses, including sounds, smells, tastes and tactile sensations.

Different schools and traditions in Tibetan Buddhism give different explanations of the mechanism producing the illusion usually called "reality".

Reality in Buddhist sutras

Buddhist sutras devote considerable space to the concept of reality, with each of two major doctrines — the Doctrine of Dependent Origination (*pratitya-samutpada*) and the Doctrine of Cause and Effect (*karma* and *vipaka*) — attempting to incorporate both the natural and the spiritual into its overall world view. While there is no prime force setting the universe in motion, no "First Cause", Buddhist teachings continue to explore the nature of the world and our place in it.

The Theravada school teaches that there is no universal personal god. The world as we know it does not have its origin in a primordial being such as Brahman or God. What we see is only a product of transitory factors of existence, which depend functionally upon each other. The Buddha is said to have said: "The world exists because of causal actions, all things are produced by causal actions and all beings are governed and bound by causal actions. They are fixed like the rolling wheel of a cart, fixed by the pin of its axle shaft." (Sutta-Nipata 654)

The word 'illusion' is frequently associated with Buddhism and the nature of reality. Some interpretations of Buddhism teach that reality is a coin with two sides: impermanence or *anicca* and the "not-self characteristic" or *anatta,* referred to as "emptiness" in some Mahayana schools. Dzogchen, as the non-dual culmination of the Ancient School (a school with a few million followers out of a few hundred million Buddhists) of Mantrayana, resolves atman and anatman into the Mindstream Doctrine of Tapihritsa. The Buddha Shakyamuni is said to have taught the variously understood and interpreted concept of "not-self" in the Anatta-lakkhana Sutta. In this sutta, he lists the characteristics that we often associate with who we are, and found that these characteristics, ultimately, are not who we are because they are subject to change. He further illustrates the changing nature of our feelings, perceptions, and consciousness.

We can look at the concepts of impermanence and not-self in objective terms, for example by deconstructing the concept of an aggregated object such as a lotus and seeing that the flower is made up entirely of non-flower elements like soil, nutrients, photosynthetic energy, rain water and the effort of the entities that nourished and grew the flower. All of these factors, according to the Diamond Sutra, co-exist with each other to manifest what we call a 'flower'. In other words, there is no essence arisen from nothingness that is unique and personal to any being. In particular, there is neither a human soul that lives on beyond the death of the physical body nor one that is extinguished at death since, strictly speaking, there is nothing to extinguish.

The relative reality (i.e., the illusory perceived reality) comes from our belief that we are separate from the rest of the things in the universe and, at times, at odds with the processes of nature and other beings. The ultimate or absolute reality, in some schools of Buddhist thought, shows that we are inter-connected with all things. The concept of non-discrimination expands on this by saying that, while a chair is different from a flower, they 'inter-are' because they are each made of non-flower and non-chair elements. Ultimately those elements are the same, so the distinction between chair and flower is one of quantity not of quality.

The Diamond Sutra, a Mahayana scripture, has many passages that use the formula: A is not A, therefore A is called A.

From a metaphysical standpoint, some subschools of the Mahayana school have posited the idea of this ultimate reality of inter-connectedness as a unity with all things, a buddha-nature which illuminates or personifies the 'ultimate dimension' of reality.

The Mahayana Uttaratantra Shastra, one of the 'Five Treatises', presents what are alleged by some Mahayanists to be the Buddha's definitive teachings on how we should understand this ground [definition needed] of enlightenment and clarifies the nature and qualities of buddhahood (Dharmakaya). The Buddha Nature is declared to be the True Self of Buddha, both within and beyond samsara; and that True Self is stated by the Buddha in what is traditionally said to be his final Mahayana sutra, the Mahaparinirvana Sutra, to be "sovereign/ autonomous" (*aishvarya*), "real", "true", and "eternal" (*nitya / sasvata*). It is dependent on nothing — but is utterly free.

Reality and dreams in Dzogchen

In Dzogchen, perceived reality is considered to be unreal. According to contemporary teacher Chögyal Namkhai Norbu Rinpoche, all appearances perceived during the whole life of an individual, through all senses, including sounds, smells, tastes and tactile sensations in their totality, are like a big dream. It is claimed that, on careful examination, the dream of life and regular nightly dreams are not very different, and that in their essential nature there is no difference between them. The non-essential difference between the dreaming state and ordinary waking experience is that the latter is more concrete and linked to attachment; the dreaming experience while sleeping is slightly detached.

Also according to this teaching, there is a correspondence between the states of sleep and dream and our experiences when we die. After experiencing the intermediate state of bardo, an individual comes out of it, a new karmic illusion is created and another existence begins. This is how transmigration happens.

According to Dzogchen teachings, the energy of an individual is essentially without form and free from duality. However, karmic traces contained in the individual's mindstream give rise to two kinds of forms:

- forms that the individual experiences as his or her body, voice and mind
- forms that the individual experiences as an external environment.

What appears as a world of apparently external phenomena, is the energy of the individual him or herself. There is nothing external or separate from the individual. Everything that manifests in the individual's field of experience is a continuum. This is the 'Great Perfection' that is discovered in Dzogchen practice.

It is possible to do yogic practice such as Dream Yoga and Yoga Nidra whilst dreaming, sleeping and in other bardo states of trance. In this way the yogi can have a very strong experience and with this comes understanding of the dream-like nature of daily life. This is also very relevant to diminishing attachments, because they are based on strong beliefs that life's perceptions such as objects are real and as a consequence: important. If one really understands what Buddha Shakyamuni meant when he said that everything is unreal, then one can diminish attachments and tensions.

The teacher advises that the realization that life is only a big dream can help us finally liberate ourselves from the chains of various emotions, different kinds of attachment and the chains of ego. Then we have the possibility of ultimately becoming enlightened.

Reality in the Tathagatagarbha Sutras

Contrasting with some forms of Buddhism, the Buddha's teaching on 'reality' in the Tathagatagarbha Mahayana scriptures - which the Buddha states constitute the ultimate manifestation of the Mahayana Dharma (other Mahayana sutras make similar claims about their own teachings) - insists that there truly *is* a sphere or realm of ultimate truth - not just a repetitious cycle of interconnected elements, each dependent on the others. That suffering-filled cycle of x-generating-y-and-y-generating-z-and-z-generating-a, etc., is *Samsara,* the prison-house of the reincarnating non-self; whereas liberation from dependency, enforced rebirth and bondage is nirvana or reality / spiritual essence (*tattva / dharmata*). This sphere also bears the name *Tathagatagarbha* (Buddha matrix). It is the deathless realm where dependent origination holds no sway, where non-self is supplanted by the everlasting, sovereign (*aishvarya*) self (atman) (as a trans-historical, unconditioned, ultimate, liberating, supra-worldly yet boundless and immanent awakened mind). Of this real truth, called nirvana - which, while salvationally infused into samsara, is not bound or imprisoned in it - the Buddha states in the Mahayana Mahaparinirvana Sutra:

"What is the Real (*tattva*)? Knowledge of the true attributes of Nirvana; the Tathagata, the Dharma, the Sangha, and the attributes of space ... is the Real. What is knowledge of the attributes of Nirvana? The attributes of Nirvana are eightfold. What are these eight? Cessation [of ignorance and suffering]; loveliness/ wholesomeness; Truth; Reality; Eternity, Bliss, the Self [*atman*], and complete Purity: that is Nirvana."

He further comments: " ... that which is endowed with the Eternal, Bliss, the Self, and Purity is stated to be the meaning of 'Real Truth' ... Moreover, the Real is the Tathagata [i.e., the Buddha]; the Tathagata is the Real ... The Tathagata is not conditioned and not tainted, but utterly blissful: this is the Real ...".

Thus, in such doctrines, a very positive goal is envisioned, which is said to lie beyond the grasp of the five senses and the ordinary, restless mind, and only attainable through direct meditative perception and when all inner pollutants (twisted modes of view, and all moral contaminants) are purged, and the inherently deathless, spotless, radiantly shining mind of Buddha stands revealed. This is the realm of the *Buddha-dhatu* (popularly known as buddha nature) - inconceivable, beginning-less, endless, omniscient truth, the Dharmakaya (quintessential body-and-mind) of the Buddha. This reality is empty of all falsehood, impermanence, ignorance, afflictions, and pain, but filled with enduring happiness, purity, knowingness (*jnana*), and omni-radiant loving-kindness (*maitri*).

ENLIGHTENMENT AND ENLIGHTENED BEINGS

All traditional Buddhists agree that Shakyamuni or Gotama Buddha was not the only Buddha: it is generally taught that there have been many past Buddhas and that there will be future Buddhas too.

Mahayana Buddhism generally regards as its most important teaching the path of the bodhisattva. This already existed as a possibility in earlier Buddhism, as it still does in Theravada today, but the Mahayana gave it an increasing emphasis, eventually saying everyone should follow it.

In the Mahayana, the Buddha tends not to be viewed as merely human, but as the earthly projection of a beginningless and endless, omnipresent being beyond the range and reach of thought. Moreover, in certain Mahayana sutras, the Buddha, Dharma and Sangha are viewed essentially as One: all three are seen as the eternal Buddha himself.

Bodhi (Pâli and Sanskrit, lit. *awakening*) is a term applied to the experience of Awakening of Arahants. Bodhi literally means "awakening", but is more commonly referred to as "enlightenment".

EARLY BUDDHISM

Bodhi carries a meaning synonymous to Nirvana, using only some different similies to describe the experience, which implied the extinction of raga (greed), dosa (hate) and moha (delusion).

Theravada

A person may awaken from the "sleep of ignorance" by directly realizing the true nature of reality; such people are called arahants. After numerous lifetimes of spiritual striving they have also reached the end of the compulsive cycle of rebirths, no longer reincarnating as human, animal, ghost, or other being.

These people, also occasionally referred to as buddhas, are classified into three types.

- Sammasambuddha, usually just called Buddha, who discovers the truth by himself and teaches the path to awakening to others
- Paccekabuddha, who discovers the truth by himself but lacks the skill to teach others
- Sâvakabuddha, who has followed the teaching of a Buddha, and may use it to guide others

Bodhi and Nirvana carry the same meaning, that of being freed from craving, hate and delusion. The Arahant, according to Theravada doctrine, has thus overcome greed, hatred, *and* delusion, attaining Bodhi. In Theravada Buddhism, the extinction of only greed (in relation to the sense sphere) and hatred, while a residue of delusion remains, is called Anagami.

Mahayana

Celestial Buddhas are individuals who no longer exist on the material plane of existence, but who still aid in the enlightenment of all beings.

Nirvana came to refer only to the extinction of greed and hate, implying that delusion was still present in one who attained Nirvana. Bodhi became a higher attainment that eradicate delusion entirely. Thus, the Arahant attains Nirvana but not Bodhi, thus still being subject to delusion, while the Buddha attains Bodhi.

The method of self-exertion or "self-power" - without reliance on an external force or being - stands in contrast to another major form of Buddhism, "Pure Land", which is characterised by utmost trust in the salvific "other-power" of Amida Buddha. Pure Land Buddhism is a very widespread and perhaps the most faith-orientated manifestation of Buddhism and centres upon the conviction that faith in Amitabha Buddha and/or the chanting of homage to his name will provide the spiritual energy that will liberate one at death into the "happy land" (*sukhavati*) or "pure land" of Amitabha (called Amida in Japanese) Buddha. This Buddhic realm is variously construed as a foretaste of Nirvana, or as essentially Nirvana itself. The great vow of Amitabha Buddha to rescue all beings from samsaric suffering is viewed within Pure Land Buddhism as universally efficacious, if only people will have faith in the power of that limitless great Vow, or will utter the liberational chant of Amida's name.

Nearly all Chinese Buddhists accept that the chances of attaining sufficient enlightenment by one's own efforts are very slim, so that Pure Land practice is essential as an "insurance policy" even if one practises something else.

PRACTICE

Devotion

Buddhist devotion is an important part of the practice of most Buddhists. According to a spokesman of the Sasana Council of Burma, it is essential for the realization of truth. In particular, most Buddhists use ritual in pursuit of their spiritual aspirations.

Examples of devotional practices:

- bowing:
  - to images of the Buddha, and in Mahayana also of other Buddhas and bodhisattvas; such images originated some centuries after the Buddha's time
  - to religious superiors:
    - a monk to a monk ordained earlier
    - a nun to a nun ordained earlier
    - a nun to a monk, regardless of date of ordination
    - a lay person to a monk or nun
- offering flowers, incense etc. to images
- chanting:
  - the Three Refuges
  - protective chanting: in texts recognized by most scholars as early, the Buddha is portrayed recommending certain texts for protection from snakebite and evil spirits

  - o mantras and dharanis in Mahayana: includes the Heart Sutra and om mani padme hum
  - o homage to Amitabha in Pure Land Buddhism
  - o homage to the Lotus Sutra in Nichiren Buddhism
- pilgrimage:
  - o according to sources recognized by most scholars as early, the Buddha, shortly before his death, recommended pilgrimage to four places:
    - ♣ his birthplace (Lumbini, now Rummindei in Nepal)
    - ♣ the site of his enlightenment (Bodh Gaya)
    - ♣ the site of the preaching of his first sermon (near Benares)
    - ♣ the place of his death (Kusinara)

Other places were later added, particularly in other countries, where pilgrimage to the original sites would be daunting.

A very important form of Buddhist devotion is Pure Land Buddhism, which is practised by most Chinese monks, some combining it with Chan (Zen). It exists as a group of independent denominations in Japan, the most radical, and largest, of which, Jodo Shinshu, holds to a subtle idea of effortless salvation.

REFUGE IN THE THREE JEWELS

Traditionally, the first step in most forms of Buddhism requires taking refuge, as the foundation of one's religious practice, in Buddhism's Three Jewels. The practice of taking refuge on behalf of young or even unborn children is mentioned in the Majjhima Nikaya, recognized by most scholars as an early text. Tibetan Buddhism sometimes adds a fourth refuge, in the lama. The person who chooses the bodhisattva path makes a vow/pledge. This is considered the ultimate expression of compassion in Buddhism.

The **Three Jewels** are:

- The **Buddha**. This is a title for those who attained Awakening similar to the Buddha and helped others to attain it. The Buddha could also be represented as the wisdom that understands Dharma, and in this regard the Buddha represents the perfect wisdom that sees reality in its true form.
- The **Dharma**: The teachings or law as expounded by the Buddha. Dharma also means the law of nature based on behavior of a person and its consequences to be experienced (action and reaction). It can also (especially in Mahayana Buddhism) connote the ultimate and sustaining Reality which is inseverable from the Buddha.
- The **Sangha**: This term literally means "group" or "congregation," but when it is used in Buddhist teaching the word refers to one of two very specific kinds of groups: either the community of Buddhist monastics (bhikkhus and bhikkhunis), or the community of people who have attained at least the first

stage of Awakening (Sotapanna (pali)—one who has entered the stream to enlightenment). According to some modern Buddhists, it also consists of laymen and laywomen, the caretakers of the monks, those who have accepted parts of the monastic code but who have not been ordained as monks or nuns.

According to the scriptures, The Buddha presented himself as a model, however, he did not ask his followers simply to have faith in his example of a human who escaped the pain and danger of existence. In addition, he encouraged them to put his teachings to the test and accept what they could verify on their own, provided that this was also "praised by the wise". The Dharma, i.e. the teaching of the Buddha, offers a refuge by providing guidelines for the alleviation of suffering and the attainment of enlightenment. The Sangha (Buddhist Order of monks) is considered to provide a refuge by preserving the authentic teachings of the Buddha and providing further examples that the truth of the Buddha's teachings is attainable.

MORALITY

Sîla (Sanskrit) or **sîla** (Pâli) is usually translated into English as "virtuous behavior", "morality", "ethics" or "precept". It is an action committed through the body, speech, or mind, and involves an intentional effort. It is one of the *three practices* (sila, samadhi, and panya) and the second pâramitâ. It refers to moral purity of thought, word, and deed. The four conditions of **sîla** are chastity, calmness, quiet, and extinguishment.

Sîla is the foundation of Samadhi/Bhâvana (Meditative cultivation) or mind cultivation. Keeping the precepts promotes not only the peace of mind of the cultivator, which is internally, but also peace in the community, which is externally. According to the Law of Kamma, keeping the precepts are meritorious and it acts as causes which would bring about peaceful and happy effects. Keeping these precepts keeps the cultivator from rebirth in the four woeful realms of existence.

Sîla refers to overall (principles of) ethical behavior. There are several levels of sila, which correspond to 'basic morality' (five precepts), 'basic morality with asceticism' (eight precepts), 'novice monkhood' (ten precepts) and 'monkhood' (Vinaya or Patimokkha). Lay people generally undertake to live by the five precepts which are common to all Buddhist schools. If they wish, they can choose to undertake the eight precepts, which have some additional precepts of basic asceticism.

The five precepts are not given in the form of commands such as "thou shalt not ...", but are training rules in order to live a better life in which one is happy, without worries, and can meditate well.

1. To refrain from taking life. (non-violence towards sentient life forms)
2. To refrain from taking that which is not given. (not committing theft)
3. To refrain from sensual (sexual) misconduct.
4. To refrain from lying. (speaking truth always)

5. To refrain from intoxicants which lead to loss of mindfulness. (refrain from using drugs or alcohol)

In the eight precepts, the third precept on sexual misconduct is made more strict, and becomes a precept of celibacy.

The three additional rules of the eight precepts are:

6. To refrain from eating at the wrong time. (only eat from sunrise to noon)
7. To refrain from dancing, using jewelry, going to shows, etc.
8. To refrain from using a high, luxurious bed.

MONASTIC LIFE

Vinaya is the specific moral code for monks and nuns. It includes the Patimokkha, a set of 227 rules for monks in the Theravadin recension. The precise content of the vinayapitaka (scriptures on Vinaya) differ slightly according to different schools, and different schools or subschools set different standards for the degree of adherence to Vinaya. Novice-monks use the ten precepts, which are the basic precepts for monastics.

In Eastern Buddhism, there is also a distinctive Vinaya and ethics contained within the Mahayana Brahmajala Sutra (not to be confused with the Pali text of that name) for Bodhisattvas, where, for example, the eating of meat is frowned upon and vegetarianism is actively encouraged. In Japan, this has almost completely displaced the monastic vinaya, and allows clergy to marry.

MEDITATION

Buddhist meditation is fundamentally concerned with two themes: transforming the mind and using it to explore itself and other phenomena.

SAMÂDHI/BHÂVANÂ (MEDITATIVE CULTIVATION)

In the language of the Noble Eightfold Path, **samyaksamâdhi** is "right concentration". The primary means of cultivating **samâdhi** is meditation. According to Theravada Buddhism the Buddha taught two types of meditation, viz. **samatha** meditation (Sanskrit: **samatha**) and **vipassanâ** meditation (Sanskrit: **vipasyanâ**). In Chinese Buddhism, these exist (translated chih kuan), but Chan (Zen) meditation is more popular. Throughout most of Buddhist history before modern times, serious meditation by lay people has been unusual. Upon development of **samâdhi**, one's mind becomes purified of defilement, calm, tranquil, and luminous.

Once the meditator achieves a strong and powerful concentration, his mind is ready to penetrate and gain insight (vipassanâ) into the ultimate nature of reality, eventually obtaining release from all suffering. The cultivation of mindfulness is essential to mental concentration, which is needed to achieve insight.

Samatha Meditation starts from being mindful of an object or idea, which is expanded to one's body, mind and entire surroundings, leading to a state of total concentration and tranquility (jhâna). There are many variations in the style of meditation, from sitting cross-legged or kneeling to chanting or walking. The most common method of meditation is to concentrate on one's breath, because this practice can lead to both samatha and vipassana.

In Buddhist practice, it is said that while samatha meditation can calm the mind, only vipassanâ meditation can reveal how the mind was disturbed to start with, which is what leads to **jñâna** (Pâli **ñâna** knowledge), **prajñâ** (Pâli **paññâ** pure understanding) and thus can lead to **nirvâna** (Pâli **nibbâna**). When one is in **jhana**, all defilements are suppressed temporarily. Only **prajñâ** or vipassana eradicates the defilements completely. Jhanas are also resting states which arahants abide in order to rest.

PRAJÑÂ (WISDOM)

Prajñâ (Sanskrit) or **paññâ** (Pâli) means wisdom that is based on a realization of dependent origination, The Four Noble Truths and the three marks of existence. Prajñâ is the wisdom that is able to extinguish afflictions and bring about bodhi. It is spoken of as the principal means, by its enlightenment, of attaining nirvâna, through its revelation of the true nature of all things as dukkha (unsatisfactory), anicca (impermanence) and anatta (devoid of self). Prajñâ is also listed as the sixth of the six pâramitâs of the Mahayana.

Initially, prajñâ is attained at a conceptual level by means of listening to sermons (dharma talks), reading, studying and sometimes reciting Buddhist texts and engaging in discourse.

Once the conceptual understanding is attained, it is applied to daily life so that each Buddhist can verify the truth of the Buddha's teaching at a practical level. It should be noted that one could theoretically attain nirvana at any point of practice, while listening to a sermon, while conducting business of daily life or while in meditation.

ZEN

Ch'an (Chinese) or Zen (Japanese) Buddhism (whose name is derived from the Sanskrit term, *dhyana* - "meditation") is a form of Buddhism that became popular in China and Japan and that lays special emphasis on meditation. According to Charles S. Prebish (in his *Historical Dictionary of Buddhism*, Sri Satguru Publications, Delhi, 1993, p. 287): "Although a variety of Zen 'schools' developed in Japan, they all emphasize Zen as a teaching that does not depend on sacred texts, that provides the potential for direct realization, that the realization attained is none other than the Buddha nature possessed by each sentient being ...". Zen places less emphasis on scriptures than some other forms of Buddhism and prefers to focus on direct spiritual breakthroughs to truth.

Zen Buddhism is divided into two main schools: Rinzai and Soto, the former greatly favouring the use in meditation of the koan (meditative riddle or puzzle) as a device for spiritual break-through, and the latter (while certainly employing koans) focussing more on *shikantaza* or "just sitting". Prebish comments (op. cit., p. 244): "It presumes that *sitting in meditation itself* (i.e. *zazen*) is an expression of Buddha nature." The method is to detach the mind from conceptual modes of thinking and perceive Reality directly. Speaking of Zen in general, Buddhist scholar Stephen Hodge writes (*Zen Masterclass*, Godsfield Press, 2002, pp. 12–13): "... practitioners of Zen believe that Enlightenment, the awakening of the Buddha-mind or Buddha-nature, is our natural state, but has been covered over by layers of negative emotions and distorted thoughts. According to this view, Enlightenment is not something that we must acquire a bit at a time, but a state that can occur instantly when we cut through the dense veil of mental and emotional obscurations."

Zen Buddhist teaching is often full of paradox, in order to loosen the grip of the ego and to facilitate the penetration into the realm of the True Self or Formless Self, which is equated with the Buddha himself. Commenting on Rinzai Zen and its Chinese founder, Linji, Hisamatsu states: "Linji indicates our true way of being in such direct expressions as 'True Person' and 'True Self'. It is independent of words or letters and transmitted apart from scriptural teaching. Buddhism doesn't really need scriptures. It is just our direct awakening to Self ...". Nevertheless, Zen does not neglect the scriptures.

TANTRA

Though thoroughly based upon Mahâyâna, Tibeto-Mongolian Buddhism is also one of the schools that practice **Vajrayâna** or "Diamond Vehicle" (also referred to as Mantrayâna, Tantrayâna, Tantric Buddhism, or esoteric Buddhism). It therefore accepts all the basic concepts of Mahâyâna, but also includes a vast array of spiritual and physical techniques designed to enhance Buddhist practice. One component of the Vajrayâna is harnessing psycho-physical energy as a means of developing profoundly powerful states of concentration and awareness. These profound states are in turn to be used as an efficient path to Buddhahood. Using these techniques, it is claimed that a practitioner can achieve Buddhahood in one lifetime, or even as little as three years.

MAIN TRADITIONS

Scholars usually categorize Buddhist schools by the ancient languages of surviving Buddhist religious scripture. These are the Pâli, Tibetan, Mongolian and Chinese collections, along with some texts that still exist in Sanskrit and Buddhist Hybrid Sanskrit. While practical, this method doesn't always correspond to doctrinal divisions. Despite these differences, there are several concepts common to both major Buddhist branches:

- Both accept the Buddha as their teacher.
- Both accept the middle way, dependent origination, the four noble truths and the noble eightfold path, in theory, though in practice these have little or no importance in some traditions.
- Both accept that members of the laity and of the sangha can pursue the path toward enlightenment (bodhi).
- Both consider buddhahood to be the highest attainment; however Theravadins

consider the nirvana (nibbana to the Theravadins) attained by arahants as identical to that attained by the Buddha himself, as there is only one type of nirvana. According to Theravadins, a Buddha is someone who has discovered the path all by himself and taught it to others.

Chapter - 2

Early Development and Rise of Buddhism

The history of Buddhism spans the 6th century BCE to the present, starting with the birth of the Buddha Siddhartha Gautama. This makes it one of the oldest religions practiced today. Starting in India, the religion evolved as it spread through Central Asia, East Asia, and Southeast Asia. At one time or another it affected most of the Asian continent. The history of Buddhism is also characterized by the development of numerous movements and schisms, foremost among them were the Theravada, Mahâyâna and Vajrayana traditions, with contrasting periods of expansion and retreat.

According to the Buddhist tradition, the historical Buddha Siddhartha Gautama was born to the Shakya clan, at the beginning of the Magadha period (546–324 BCE), in the plains of Lumbini in Ancient India. He is also known as the *Shakyamuni* (literally "The sage of the Shakya clan").

After an early life of luxury under the protection of his father, Suddhodana, the ruler of Kapilavastu (later to be incorporated into the state of Magadha), Siddhartha entered into contact with the realities of the world and concluded that life was inescapably bound up with suffering and sorrow. Siddhartha renounced his meaningless life of luxury to become an ascetic. He ultimately decided that asceticism couldn't end suffering, and instead chose a middle way, a path of moderation away from the extremes of self-indulgence and self-mortification.

Under a fig tree, now known as the Bodhi tree, he vowed never to leave the position until he found Truth. At the age of 35, he attained Enlightenment. He was then known as Gautama Buddha, or simply "The Buddha", which means "the enlightened one", or "the awakened one".

For the remaining 45 years of his life, he traveled the Gangetic Plain of central India (the region of the Ganges/Ganga river and its tributaries), teaching his doctrine and discipline to a diverse range of people.

The Buddha's reluctance to name a successor or to formalise his doctrine led to the emergence of many movements during the next 400 years: first the schools of Nikaya Buddhism, of which only Theravada remains today, and then the formation of Mahayana and Vajrayana, pan-Buddhist sects based on the acceptance of new scriptures and the revision of older techniques.

Soon after the Buddha's death, the monks gave up the practice of begging for alms and wandering from place and place. They settled down for a sedentary life in monasteries, built by kings and wealthy merchants who were inspired by the teachings and the events of the Buddha's life and became his ardent followers. With generous donations and material contributions from these patrons, the monasteries thrived as Buddhism took deep roots in the subcontinent, despite stiff competition from sectarian movements within the Vedic religion and other religious movements such as Jainism.

During his life time on earth, the Buddha attracted the attention of many people. His exemplary life, the fact that he descended from a princely family, the simplicity of his teachings and his opposition to ritualism and casteism, drew the attention of many from all ranks and contributed to the immense popularity of Buddhism. The Buddha was aware of the problems of monastic life that could surface within the monastic order over a period of time. He therefore established well defined code of conduct for the monks to ensure that they followed the right way of life during their practice of the Dhamma in general and the eightfold path in particular.

His parinirvana must have left a big vacuum in the Order. None of his followers had his great stature and his personal appeal, though they had an infinite capacity to remain loyal to his teachings and the discipline he established. They were incapable of filling the void he left behind and needed a leading and guiding source of inspiration that would keep them firmly abide by the Buddha, the Dhamma and the Sangha, the three cardinal principles of Buddhism.

The best that they could do in such circumstances was to preserve the teachings of the Buddha in a systematic manner and use them as points of reference in times of doubt and confusion. This would help them preserve his teachings for the future generations, strengthen the roots of Buddhism and create a universal code of conduct that could be implemented uniformly in all the monasteries that were know during that period.

And this was probably one of the objectives of the First Buddhist Council which was convened by the early followers of the Buddha after the Buddha's parinirvana. We understand that soon after the Buddha's parinirvana, his chief disciples, Ananda and Upali recited his teachings to the gathered assembly and thus laid the foundation stone for the Buddhist Canon, that was to emerge later in the form of three Pitakas - Vinaya, Sutta and Abhidhamma.

The Buddha admitted all types of people into the Order, irrespective of their social and religious backgrounds. This practice contributed greatly to the popularity of the religion. But in many respects it also proved to be its weakness, for it admitted into the Order many who were ill qualified for a strict monastic discipline. It helped the Order to grow into an organized body of huge proportions. But at the same time it sowed the seeds of internal dissension and divisions, that finally led to the break up of the Order into various sects and sub-sects.

It is difficult to say how far the immediate disciples and followers of the Buddha succeeded in their efforts to preserve his teachings. The early history of Buddhism does not offer many clues. It is possible that during the life time of the Buddha, his followers might have done some ground work to organize his teachings and preserve them for posterity. True to the ancient Indian tradition, some of the teachings might have been preserved through the oral tradition and in the form of descriptive fables and parables.

We do not know much about the relationship the followers of Buddhism and the Buddha himself maintained during the early days of Buddhism with other religions and faiths. We know that there were occasions in the life of the Buddha when he personally engaged himself in religious debates and discussions with other sects such as the Jainas and the Ajivakas to disprove their theories and beliefs. It is hard to attribute any reason for such debates and discussions on the part of the Buddha, other than unbound compassion the Buddha had towards others and his attempts to bring them to the Dhamma and Sangha in order to help them in their salvation.

The fledgling new faith needed immunity from the corruption of teachings, a strong leadership and a distinct identity of its own to distinguish itself from other religions, gain a strong foothold in the subcontinent, keep the Dhamma and Sangha intact and attract new followers and converts to the faith.

As a scion of a ruling family, and having been tutored in the early part of his life, the Buddha was familiar with the art of leadership, organization and administration. He was also aware of the implications of creating a large body of Buddhist monks who would have to stay together and practice Dhamma under the most challenging circumstances. We know that at times he was disappointed with the behavior and insincerity of some of his followers. He knew the evils of decay and disintegration inherent in all component things, which he reminded his followers to remember even from his death bed.

He therefore organized the Buddhist Monastic Order on the basis of an established code of conduct, a hierarchy with in the Order and a daily and seasonal routine for the community of the monks within the Order. He also maintained a rigid stance when it came to admitting women who he believed would disturb the Order with their very presence and created a procedure to admit them. He exhorted his followers to be wary of the temptations of *samsara* by remaining focused on the Four Noble Truths and the Eightfold path. He did not designate a successor as he truly believed his followers to be lamps unto themselves and follow the Dhamma as it was taught to them.

One of the new practices that began after his passing away was the veneration of the chaityas or the sacred spots. This practice was already prevalent in ancient India in some rudimentary form and the Buddhists adopted it as their own. Another new practice adopted by The Buddhists was the building of the stupas. Originally stupas were built to designate the places where the ashes of the Buddha were buried as a mark of honor and symbols of veneration. In course of time stupas were being built for other reasons as well such as to express devotion or to honor the relics of a Buddhist monk.The third development was the development of sacred places and objects like the Bodhi tree, the Deer Park etc., which were associated with the Buddha's life and activities. These places became sacred places of pilgrimage and veneration for the followers of Buddhism.

These new developments contributed to the popularity of Buddhism outside the monastic order. But rituals were still looked with disfavor and the worship of the Buddha or his images, perhaps, did not yet begin.

These changes gradually led to the emergence of a new schools of Buddhism that were radically different in several respects from the original teachings of the Buddha. The changes helped the new religion adapt itself to the growing demands of a wider population and helped it emerge as a major world religion.

By the time Asoka became the emperor, Buddhism was already a well established religion in several parts of the Indian subcontinent, competing vigorously with other religious movements, especially the dominant Brahminical religion with its roots deep in several parts of the subcontinent, and the nascent Jainism that was competing for supremacy in certain pockets of the country having secured the support of eminent personalities like Chandragupta Maurya and the royal patronage of the kings of Orissa in the east.

Asoka began his career in a controversial manner. We do not have detailed accounts of his early life, but it seems his accession to the throne was not smooth. According to traditional accounts, he had to wage a war of succession against his own brothers for nearly four years and kill them all before ascending the throne. During the early part of his reign he led several campaigns either to suppress rebellions or expand his empire. He established friendly relations with foreign powers but maintained a policy of conquest within the subcontinent.

The Kalinga war brought a radical change in his thinking and approach heralded an era of peace within the subcontinent. He became convinced about the evils of war and converted to the path of Buddhism and the philosophy of non-violence. His direct involvement with Buddhism, led to the expansion of Buddhism on unprecedented scale to the far corners of India and the outside world.

Available evidence suggest that although he was converted to Buddhism, he maintained a very tolerant attitude towards other faiths and treated his subjects fairly irrespective of their religious beliefs. He preached and propagated a form of Dhamma or the law of piety in his empire which was partly Buddhist, partly Brahmnical and partly administrative or empirical in its approach.

While personally following the teachings of the Buddha and spending time in the company of the Buddhist monks, Asoka maintained a very tolerant attitude towards other religions. Despite his interest in the Buddhist way of life, he did not abdicate his responsibilities as the emperor. His inscriptions suggest that he worked relentlessly for the welfare of the people whom he considered as his children. He gave them generous donations and allowed them to preach and practice their respective religions in his empire. He also gave donations for building cave dwellings for a religious sect named Ajivakas.

Although he propagated his law of piety with the flavor of Buddhism, he called himself *devanampriya* or the beloved of the gods. In many ways his law of piety was above sectarian approach. It represented his effort to resolve the social, moral and religious issues of his time in a secular manner without adding to the religious tension that was already brewing between the orthodox and the the heterodox sections of society. Asokas' Dhamma was more a code of conduct used to inculcate moral discipline and social responsibility among his people than a theological sermon intended to convert them to Buddhism.

However there is little doubt that his commitment to the cause of Buddhism was unquestionable. He gave up vihara yatras or tours of pleasure and instead went on dharma yatras or tours of piety to preach Buddhism. He replaced his policy of political conquest with that of *Dhamma Vijaya* or the conquest of the Dhamma. He instructed important members of his administration to go on tours and preach the Dhamma to the masses. He got the relics of the Buddha recovered from the earlier stupas and redistributed them at various other places by building several new stupas. He also played a prominent role in convening the third Buddhist Council to resolve several issues concerning Buddhism. Because of his direct patronage, Buddhism became very popular in various parts of India and led to the establishment of several Buddhist centers, especially the places like the present day Andhrapradesh, Maharashtra, Madhyapradesh, Orissa and Karnataka. He dispatched Buddhist missions to various parts of the world, such as present day Afghanistan, Syria, Egypt, Cyrene, Macedonia and Emirus. Within the subcontinent, he sent missionaries to several places. like Kashmir, the Himalayan country, Maharashtra, Varanasi, Mysore and so on.

While we do not know much about the impact his missions to other countries created, his mission to Ceylon was a great success. It contributed directly to the spread of Buddhism in the island country. Because of his efforts, Buddhism was an instant success in Ceylon. According to the Chronicles of Ceylon, Mahendra (Mahinda), who was either a brother or son of Asoka, went to Ceylon, where he converted the king and his 40000 subjects to Buddhism. It was followed by another mission, which was headed by Sanghamitra, who was said to be a daughter of Asoka himself. According to tradition she carried along with her a branch of the original Bodhi tree under which the Buddha got enlightenment and planted it there in the Ceylonese soil. The tree that grew out of the sapling is still there for visitors to see. Sanghamitra converted many female members of the Ceylonese royal family to Buddhism.

POST MAURYAN PERIOD

After the death of Asoka, the Mauryan empire declined. But Buddhism grew in strength. The Sungas succeeded the Mauryans in the north. They were staunch supporters of the orthodox Brahmincial religion and revived the vedic practices. Some of them were very hostile to Buddhism. Pushaymitra Sunga, one of the most prominent Sunga rules and hero of the literary work *"Malaviakagnimitram"*, said to have indulged in the religious persecution of Buddhist monks in his empire and rewarded those who persecuted the Buddhist monks.

The Bactrian Greeks who invaded India during this time, brought under their control the whole part of what is now known as Western Pakistan and parts of northern India comprising Malwa, parts of Rajasthan, modern U.P and Bihar. Little is known about their religious and social institutions. Some of them adopted Buddhism and supported it like king Menander who ruled Punjab, with Sakala as his capital and was acclaimed by the Buddhist texts as a great warrior king. The famous Pali Buddhist text, Milindapatha, records his conversations with monk Nagasena.

THE SUNGAS

The Mauryas were succeeded by the Sungas, who ruled large parts of northern India between 185 B.C. and 73 B.C., with Vidisa in eastern Malwa as their capital. The Sungas were avowed followers of Vedic religion and showed little respect for other religions. They promoted Hinduism actively and were intolerant towards Buddhism. According to Buddhist tradition, they made serious attempts to suppress the religion and even indulged in religious persecution. Pushyamitra Sunga, one of the most prominent ruler of the dynasty, was said to be a great persecutor of Buddhism. Apart from patronizing Brahminism at the expense of other faiths, he was referred as a religious bigot who indulged in the destruction of several Buddhist monuments, including a famous monastery at Pataliputra. He said to have even offered monetary reward for killing the Buddhist monks. Some historians do not agree with this theory and point out the construction of the Buddhist stupas and railings at Barhut and the uninterrupted existence of several other stupas and Buddhist monuments throughout the kingdom of the Sungas as evidence of their religious tolerance.

THE SATAVAHANAS

The Satavahanas ruled large parts of Andhrapradesh, Maharashtra and central India between 200 BC and 250 AD. Like the Sungas they were Brahmin rulers, but unlike the former, displayed exemplary tolerance towards other religions. Both Buddhism and Hinduism flourished and coexisted peacefully during their reign. They made generous grants for the construction and maintenance of several monasteries, cave dwellings and residential quarters for the Buddhist monks. Several Buddhist centers flourished and gained prominence like the ones at Amaravathi and Nagarjunakonda in Andhrapradesh during their period.

KANISHKA

Emperor Kanishka was a Saka-Kushana king. He is remembered in Indian history as a great patron of Buddhism, next to Asoka. He ruled parts of central Asia and north Western India some time during the early Christian era. The fourth Buddhist council was held in Kashmir under his patronage.

During this period, the Mahayana school of Buddhism became popular in the north while Hianayana remained popular in the south and in Ceylon. The Mahayana doctrines crossed the frontiers of the sub-continent and traveled eastwards to China and other far eastern countries.

GUPTA PERIOD

The Guptas ruled large tracts of the Indian subcontinent from the fourth century A.D. to the sixth century A.D. They were great patrons of Vedic religion. Fahien, a Chinese Buddhist monk visited India during the reign of Chandra Gupta II and stayed in India for six years.

His travel account throws considerable light on the socio-religious life in the country during this period. Fahien noted that Buddhism was still popular, though Hinduism was gaining ground under the patronage of the Guptas. He also commented that due to the influence of Buddhism and Jainism many people from higher sections of society had become vegetarians.

POST GUPTA PERIOD

At the close of the fifth century A.D., the Huna began their invasions into India. The Hunas were the most cruel foreign rulers to invade India in ancient times. They were also known for their religious intolerance. Both Hsuan Tsang and the famous Kashmiri poet, Kalhana, recorded the cruel persecution they meted out to Buddhists. Fortunately the Hunas had a short reign in the country and thereby the native religions escaped from a great destruction.

HARSHAVARDHANA

In the first decade of seventh century A.D., Harshavardhana ascended the throne at the age of sixteen. He ruled large parts of central and northern India. His reign lasted for about forty one years. He is also known in Indian history as a great patron of Buddhism, and a man of considerable virtues.

Hsuan Tsang, the famous Buddhist scholar from China, visited India during his reign and stayed in his court for seven years. Like Fa-hien, his predecessor, he also recorded his experiences in India in the form of a book. He gave a fairly accurate picture of the conditions prevailing in the country during his several years' stay. He described Nalanda as a great center of learning for Buddhist monks.

Harshavardhana was a follower of Buddhism. But like many other emperor in the recorded history of India, he was tolerant of other religions and also worshipped some Hindu gods. He saved Buddhism from the hands of Sasanka, who was bent upon destroying Buddhist monuments and harassing Buddhist followers. Despite of support from Harshavardhana, Buddhism was in decline in various parts of the country.

VAJRAYANA BUDDHISM

During the early eight century A.D. Vajrayana Buddhism appeared in eastern India. It gained wider acceptance in Bihar and Bengal. The Vikramasila monastery in Bihar was popular center for this new sect, which was partly based upon the ancient Vedic Tantric practices and worship of Mother Goddess. In subsequent times, Tibet and Nepal came under the influence of Vajrayana Buddhism. Sub-sects such as Sahajayana, Kalachakrayana, and Mantrayana soon arose out of this new sect.

DECLINE

Despite of the support and patronage by Harshavardhana and by Pala kings, who came later, by the end of twelfth century A.D, Buddhism declined as a major religious force in the sub-continent . The growing influence of Bhakti movement and the religious bigotry of the Muslim invaders sealed what ever opportunities it had for revival and renewal. However Buddhism continued to flourish in other parts of the world, especially in China, Korea, Japan, Cambodia, Thailand and other far eastern countries.

Today Buddhism is practised in various parts of the world. In India it has the dubious distinction of a separate religion as well as a movement with in Hinduism. The Hindus consider the Buddha as an incarnation of Lord Vishnu. But the Buddhists disagree. As a religion, except in certain parts like Sikkhim, Ladakh, Buddhism is a minority religion in India.

But in neighboring Nepal, Bhutan and Ceylon it is still very popular religion. Though it greatly disappeared in main land China, it still survives in many far eastern countries and Japan. The west was introduced to Buddhism mainly in the last century. It is presently attracting many new followers from the western world. As a religion and as a way of life, Buddhism has a great religions appeal to the educated and liberal minded people of the west. It has an inherent strength, a certain dignified charm. It will continue to attract many new followers.

GRECO-BUDDHIST INTERACTION (2ND C. BCE–1ST C. CE

In the areas west of the Indian subcontinent, neighboring Greek kingdoms had been in place in Bactria (today's northern Afghanistan) since the time of the conquests of Alexander the Great around 326 BCE: first the Seleucids from around 323 BCE, then the Greco-Bactrian kingdom from around 250 BCE.

The Greco-Bactrian king Demetrius I invaded India in 180 BCE as far as Pataliputra, establishing an Indo-Greek kingdom that was to last in various part of northern India until the end of the 1st century BCE. Buddhism flourished under the Indo-Greek kings, and it has been suggested that their invasion of India was intended to show their support for the Mauryan empire, and to protect the Buddhist faith from the alleged religious persecutions of the Sungas (185–73 BCE).

One of the most famous Indo-Greek kings is Menander (reigned c. 160–135 BCE). He apparently converted to Buddhism and is presented in the Mahayana tradition as one of the great benefactors of the faith, on a par with king Ashoka or the later Kushan king Kanishka. Menander's coins bear the mention "Saviour king" in Greek, and sometimes designs of the eight-spoked wheel. Direct cultural exchange is also suggested by the dialogue of the Milinda Panha between Menander and the monk Nagasena around 160 BCE. Upon his death, the honour of sharing his remains was claimed by the cities under his rule, and they were enshrined in stupas, in a parallel with the historic Buddha (Plutarch, Praec. reip. ger. 28, 6). Several of Menander's Indo-Greek successors inscribed the mention "Follower of the Dharma" in the Kharoshthi script on their coins, and depicted themselves or their divinities forming the *vitarka* mudra.

The interaction between Greek and Buddhist cultures may have had some influence on the evolution of Mahayana, as the faith developed its sophisticated philosophical approach and a man-god treatment of the Buddha somewhat reminiscent of Hellenic gods. It is also around that time that the first anthropomorphic representations of the Buddha are found, often in realistic Greco-Buddhist style: "One might regard the classical influence as including the general idea of representing a man-god in this purely human form, which was of course well familiar in the West, and it is very likely that the example of westerner's treatment of their gods was indeed an important factor in the innovation" (Boardman, "The Diffusion of Classical Art in Antiquity").

CENTRAL ASIAN EXPANSION

A Buddhist gold coin from India was found in northern Afghanistan at the archaeological site of Tillia Tepe, and dated to the 1st century CE. On the reverse, it depicts a lion with a nandipada, with the Kharoshthi legend "Sih[o] vigatabhay[o]" ("The lion who dispelled fear"). On the obverse, an almost naked man only wearing an Hellenistic chlamys and a petasus hat (an iconography similar to that of Hermes/ Mercury) rolls a Buddhist wheel. The legend in Kharoshthi reads "Dharmacakrapravata[ko]" ("The one who turned the Wheel of the Law"). It has been suggested that this may be an early representation of the Buddha.

RISE OF MAHAYANA (1ST C. BCE–2ND C. CE)

The rise of Mahayana Buddhism from the 1st century BCE was accompanied by complex political changes in northwestern India. The Indo-Greek kingdoms were gradually overwhelmed, and their culture assimilated by the Indo-Scythians, and then the Yuezhi, who founded the Kushan Empire from around 12 BCE.

The Kushans were supportive of Buddhism, and a fourth Buddhist council was convened by the Kushan emperor Kanishka, around 100 CE at Jalandhar or in Kashmir, and is usually associated with the formal rise of Mahayana Buddhism and its secession from Theravada Buddhism. Theravada Buddhism does not recognize the authenticity of this council, and it is sometimes called the "council of heretical monks".The new form of Buddhism was characterized by an almost God-like treatment of the Buddha, by the idea that all beings have a Buddha-nature and should aspire to Buddhahood, and by a syncretism due to the various cultural influences within northwestern India and the Kushan Empire.

THE TWO FOURTH COUNCILS

The Fourth Council is said to have been convened in the reign of the Kushan emperor Kanishka, around 100 CE at Jalandhar or in Kashmir. Theravada Buddhism had its own Fourth Council in Sri Lanka about 200 years earlier in which the Pali Canon was written down *in toto* for the first time. Therefore there are two Fourth Councils: one in Sri Lanka (Theravada), and one in Kashmir (Sarvastivadin).

It is said that for the Fourth Council of Kashmir, Kanishka gathered 500 monks headed by Vasumitra, partly, it seems, to compile extensive commentaries on the Abhidharma, although it is possible that some editorial work was carried out upon the existing canon itself. Allegedly, during the council there were all together three hundred thousand verses and over nine million statements compiled, and it took twelve years to complete. The main fruit of this Council was the compilation of the vast commentary known as the Mahâ-Vibhâshâ ("Great Exegesis"), an extensive compendium and reference work on a portion of the Sarvâstivâdin Abhidharma.

Scholars believe that it was also around this time that a significant change was made in the language of the Sarvâstivâdin canon, by converting an earlier Prakrit version into Sanskrit. Although this change was probably effected without significant loss of integrity to the canon, this event was of particular significance since Sanskrit was the sacred language of Brahmanism in India, and was also being used by other thinkers (regardless of their specific religious or philosophical allegiance), thus enabling a far wider audience to gain access to Buddhist ideas and practices. For this reason, there was a growing tendency among Buddhist scholars in India thereafter to write their commentaries and treatises in Sanskrit. Many of the early schools, however, such as Theravada, never switched to Sanskrit, partly because Buddha explicitly forbade translation of his discourses into Sanskrit because it was an elitist religious language (like Latin was in Europe in earlier times). He wanted his monks to use a local language instead; a language which could be understood by all. Over time however, the language of the Theravadin scriptures (Pali) became a scholarly or elitist language as well.

MAHAYANA EXPANSION (1ST C. CE–10TH C. CE)

From that point on, and in the space of a few centuries, Mahayana was to flourish and spread in the East from India to South-East Asia, and towards the north to Central Asia, China, Korea, and finally to Japan in 538 CE.

INDIA

After the end of the Kushans, Buddhism flourished in India during the dynasty of the Guptas (4th-6th century). Mahayana centers of learning were established, especially at Nalanda in north-eastern India, which was to become the largest and most influential Buddhist university for many centuries, with famous teachers such as Nagarjuna. The Gupta style of Buddhist art became very influential from South-East Asia to China as the faith was spreading there.

Indian Buddhism had weakened in the 6th century following the White Hun invasions and Mihirkulas persecution.

Xuanzang reports in his travels across India during the 7th century of Buddhism being popular in Andhra, Dhanyakataka, and Dravida which today roughly correspond to the modern day Indian states of Andhra Pradesh and Tamil Nadu. While reporting many deserted stupas in the area around modern day Nepal and the persecution of Buddhists by Ssanka in the Kingdom of Gouda. (In modern day West Bengal) Xuanzang compliments the patronage of Harshavardana during the same period.

After Harshavardanas kingdom, the rise of many small kingdoms that lead to the rise of the Rajputs across the gangetic plains and marked the end of Buddhist ruling clans along with a sharp decline in royal patronage until a revival under the Pala Empire in the Bengal region. Here Mahayana Buddhism flourished and spread to Bhutan and Sikkim between the 8th and the 12th century before the Palas collapsed under the assault of the Hindu Sena dynasty. The Palas created many temples and a distinctive school of Buddhist art. Xuanzang noted in his travels that in various regions Buddhism was giving way to Jainism and Hinduism. By the 10th century Buddhism had experienced a sharp decline beyond the Pala realms in Bengal under a resurgent Hinduism and the incorporation in Vaishnavite Hinduism of Buddha as the 9th incarnation of Vishnu.

A milestone in the decline of Indian Buddhism in the North occurred in 1193 when Turkic Islamic raiders under Muhammad Khilji burnt Nalanda. By the end of the 12th century, following the Islamic conquest of the Buddhist strongholds in Bihar, and the loss of political support coupled with social and caste pressures, the practice of Buddhism retreated to the Himalayan foothills in the North and Sri Lanka in the south. Additionally, the influence of Buddhism also waned due to Hinduism's revival movements such as Advaita, the rise of the bhakti movement and the missionary work of Sufis.

CENTRAL AND NORTHERN ASIA

Central Asia

Central Asia had been influenced by Buddhism probably almost since the time of the Buddha. According to a legend preserved in Pali, the language of the Theravada canon, two merchant brothers from Bactria, named Tapassu and Bhallika, visited the Buddha and became his disciples. They then returned to Bactria and built temples to the Buddha (Foltz).

Central Asia long played the role of a meeting place between China, India and Persia. During the 2nd century BCE, the expansion of the Former Han to the west brought them into contact with the Hellenistic civilizations of Asia, especially the Greco-Bactrian Kingdoms. Thereafter, the expansion of Buddhism to the north led to the formation of Buddhist communities and even Buddhist kingdoms in the oases of Central Asia. Some Silk Road cities consisted almost entirely of Buddhist stupas and monasteries, and it seems that one of their main objectives was to welcome and service travelers between east and west.

The Theravada traditions first spread among the Turkic tribes before combining with the Mahayana forms during the 2nd and 3rd centuries BCE to cover modern-day Pakistan, Kashmir, Afghanistan, eastern and coastal Iran, Uzbekistan, Turkmenistan and Tajikistan. These were the ancient states of Gandhara, Bactria, Parthia and Sogdia from where it spread to China. Among the first of these Turkic tribes to adopt Buddhism was the Turki-Shahi who adopted Buddhism as early as the 3rd century BCE. It was not, however, the exclusive faith of this region. There were also Zoroastrians, Hindus, Nestorian Christians, Jews, Manichaeans, and followers of shamanism, Tengrism, and other indigenous, nonorganized systems of belief.

Various Nikaya schools persisted in Central Asia and China until around the 7th century CE. Mahayana started to become dominant during the period, but since the faith had not developed a Nikaya approach, Sarvastivadin and Dharmaguptakas remained the Vinayas of choice in Central Asian monasteries.

Various Buddhism kingdoms rose and prospered in both the Central Asian region and downwards into the Indian sub-continent such as Kushan Empire prior to the White Hun invasion in the 5th century where under the King Mihirkula they were heavily persecuted.

Buddhism in Central Asia started to decline with the expansion of Islam and the destruction of many stupas in war from the 7th century. The Muslims accorded them the status of dhimmis as "people of the Book", such as Christianity or Judaism and Al-Biruni wrote of Buddha as prophet "burxan".

Buddhism saw a surge during the reign of Mongols following the invasion of Genghis Khan and the establishment of the Il Khanate and the Chagatai Khanate who brought their Buddhist influence with them during the 13th century, however within a 100 years the Mongols who remained in that region would convert to Islam and spread Islam across all the regions across central Asia. Only the eastern Mongols and the Mongols of the Yuan dynasty would keep Vajrayana Buddhism.

Parthia

Buddhism expanded westward into Arsacid Parthia, at least to the area of Merv, in ancient Margiana, today's territory of Turkmenistan. Soviet archeological teams have excavated in Giaur Kala, near Merv, a Buddhist chapel, a gigantic Buddha statue, as well as a monastery. Parthians were directly involved in the propagation of Buddhism: An Shigao (c. 148 CE), a Parthian prince, went to China, and is the first known translator of Buddhist scriptures into Chinese.

Tarim Basin

The eastern part of central Asia (Chinese Turkestan, Tarim Basin, Xinjiang) has revealed extremely rich Buddhist works of art (wall paintings and reliefs in numerous caves, portable paintings on canvas, sculpture, ritual objects), displaying multiple influences from Indian and Hellenistic cultures. Serindian art is highly reminiscent of the Gandharan style, and scriptures in the Gandhari script Kharosthi have been found.

Central Asians seem to have played a key role in the transmission of Buddhism to the East. The first translators of Buddhists scriptures into Chinese were either Parthian (Ch: Anxi) like An Shigao (c. 148 CE) or An Hsuan, Kushan of Yuezhi ethnicity like Lokaksema (c. 178 CE), Zhi Qian and Zhi Yao, or Sogdians (Ch: SuTe/Ÿ l yr) like Kang Sengkai. Thirty-seven early translators of Buddhist texts are known, and the majority of them have been identified as Central Asians.

Central Asian and East Asian Buddhist monks appear to have maintained strong exchanges until around the 10th century, as shown by frescoes from the Tarim Basin.

These influences were rapidly absorbed however by the vigorous Chinese culture, and a strongly Chinese particularism develops from that point.

China

Buddhism probably arrived in China around the 1st century CE from Central Asia (although there are some traditions about a monk visiting China during Ashoka's reign), and through to the 8th century it became an extremely active center of Buddhism.

The year 67 CE saw Buddhism's official introduction to China with the coming of the two monks Moton and Chufarlan. In 68 CE, under imperial patronage, they established the White Horse Temple, which still exists today, close to the imperial capital at Luoyang. By the end of the second century, a prosperous community had been settled at Pengcheng (modern Xuzhou, Jiangsu).

The first known Mahayana scriptural texts are translations made into Chinese by the Kushan monk Lokaksema in Luoyang, between 178 and 189 CE. Some of the earliest known Buddhist artifacts found in China are small statues on "money trees", dated circa 200 CE, in typical Gandharan style (drawing): "That the imported images accompanying the newly arrived doctrine came from Gandhara is strongly suggested by such early Gandhara characteristics on this "money tree" Buddha as the high ushnisha, vertical arrangement of the hair, moustache, symmetrically looped robe and parallel incisions for the folds of the arms."

Buddhism flourished during the beginning of the Tang Dynasty (618–907). The dynasty was initially characterized by a strong openness to foreign influences, and renewed exchanges with Indian culture due to the numerous travels of Chinese Buddhist monks to India from the 4th to the 11th century. The Tang capital of Chang'an (today's Xi'an) became an important center for Buddhist thought. From there Buddhism spread to Korea, and Japanese embassies of Kentoshi helped gain footholds in Japan.

However foreign influences came to be negatively perceived towards the end of the Tang Dynasty. In the year 845, the Tang emperor Wuzong outlawed all "foreign" religions (including Christian Nestorianism, Zoroastrianism, and Buddhism) in order to support the indigenous Taoism. Throughout his territory, he confiscated Buddhist possessions, destroyed monasteries and temples, and executed Buddhist monks, ending Buddhism's cultural and intellectual dominance.

However, about a hundred years after the Great Anti-Buddhist Persecution, Buddhism revived during the Song Dynasty (1127–1279).

Pure Land and Chan Buddhism, however, continued to prosper for some centuries, the latter giving rise to Japanese Zen. In China, Chan flourished particularly under the Song dynasty (1127–1279), when its monasteries were great centers of culture and learning.

Today, China boasts one of the richest collections of Buddhist arts and heritages in the world. UNESCO World Heritage Sites such as the Mogao Caves near Dunhuang in Gansu province, the Longmen Grottoes near Luoyang in Henan province, the Yungang Grottoes near Datong in Shanxi province, and the Dazu Rock Carvings near Chongqing are among the most important and renowned Buddhist sculptural sites. The Leshan Giant Buddha, carved out of a hillside in the 8th century during Tang Dynasty and looking down on the confluence of three rivers, is still the largest stone Buddha statue in the world.

Korea

Buddhism was introduced around 372 CE, when Chinese ambassadors visited the Korean kingdom of Goguryeo, bringing scriptures and images. Buddhism prospered in

Korea, and in particular Seon (Zen) Buddhism from the 7th century onward. However, with the beginning of the Confucean Yi Dynasty of the Joseon period in 1392, Buddhism was strongly discriminated against until it was almost completely eradicated, except for a remaining Seon movement.

Japan

The Buddhism of Japan was introduced from Three Kingdoms of Korea in the sixth century. The Chinese priest Ganjin offered the system of Vinaya to the Buddhism of Japan in 754. As a result, the Buddhism of Japan has developed rapidly. Saichô and Kûkai succeeded to a legitimate Buddhism from China in nine century.

Being geographically at the end of the Silk Road, Japan was able to preserve many aspects of Buddhism at the very time it was disappearing in India, and being suppressed in Central Asia and China.

From 710 CE numerous temples and monasteries were built in the capital city of Nara, such as the five-story pagoda and Golden Hall of the Hôryû-ji, or the Kôfuku-ji temple. Countless paintings and sculptures were made, often under governmental sponsorship. The creation of Japanese Buddhist art was especially rich between the 8th and 13th century during the periods of Nara, Heian, and Kamakura.

From the 12th and 13th, a further development was Zen art, following the introduction of the faith by Dogen and Eisai upon their return from China. Zen art is mainly characterized by original paintings (such as sumi-e and the Enso) and poetry (especially haikus), striving to express the true essence of the world through impressionistic and unadorned "non-dualistic" representations. The search for enlightenment "in the moment" also led to the development of other important derivative arts such as the Chanoyu tea ceremony or the Ikebana art of flower arrangement. This evolution went as far as considering almost any human activity as an art with a strong spiritual and aesthetic content, first and foremost in those activities related to combat techniques (martial arts).

Buddhism remains very active in Japan to this day. Around 80,000 Buddhist temples are preserved and regularly restored.

Southeast Asia

During the 1st century CE, the trade on the overland Silk Road tended to be restricted by the rise in the Middle-East of the Parthian empire, an unvanquished enemy of Rome, just as Romans were becoming extremely wealthy and their demand for Asian luxury was rising. This demand revived the sea connections between the Mediterranean and China, with India as the intermediary of choice. From that time, through trade connection, commercial settlements, and even political interventions, India started to strongly influence Southeast Asian countries. Trade routes linked India with southern Burma, central and southern Siam, lower Cambodia and southern Vietnam, and numerous urbanized coastal settlements were established there.

For more than a thousand years, Indian influence was therefore the major factor that brought a certain level of cultural unity to the various countries of the region. The Pali and Sanskrit languages and the Indian script, together with Theravada and Mahayana Buddhism, Brahmanism, and Hinduism, were transmitted from direct contact and through sacred texts and Indian literature such as the Ramayana and the Mahabharata.

From the 5th to the 13th century, South-East Asia had very powerful empires and became extremely aciive in Buddhist architectural and artistic creation. The main Buddhist influence now came directly by sea from the Indian subcontinent, so that these empires essentially followed the Mahayana faith. The Sri Vijaya Empire to the south and the Khmer Empire to the north competed for influence, and their art expressed the rich Mahayana pantheon of the Bodhisattvas.

Srivijayan Empire (7th–13th century)

Srivijaya, a maritime empire centered at Palembang on the island of Sumatra in Indonesia, adopted Mahayana and Vajrayana Buddhism under a line of rulers named the Sailendras. Yijing described Palembang as a great centre of Buddhist learning where the emperor supported over a thousand monks at his court. Atisha studied there before travelling to Tibet as a missionary. Srivijaya spread Buddhist art during its expansion in Southeast Asia. Numerous statues of Bodhisattvas from this period are characterized by a very strong refinement and technical sophistication, and are found throughout the region. Extremely rich architectural remains are visible at the temple of Borobudur (the largest Buddhist structure in the world, built from around 780 CE), in Java, which has 505 images of the seated Buddha. Srivijaya declined due to conflicts with the Chola rulers of India, before being destabilized by the Islamic expansion from the 13th century.

Khmer Empire (9th–13th century)

Later, from the 9th to the 13th century, the Mahayana Buddhist and Hindu Khmer Empire dominated much of the South-East Asian peninsula. Under the Khmer, more than 900 temples were built in Cambodia and in neighboring Thailand. Angkor was at the center of this development, with a temple complex and urban organization able to support around one million urban dwellers. One of the greatest Khmer kings, Jayavarman VII (1181–1219), built large Mahayana Buddhist structures at Bayon and Angkor Thom.

Vietnam

Following the destruction of Buddhism in mainland India during the 11th century, Mahayana Buddhism declined in Southeast Asia, to be replaced by the introduction of Theravada Buddhism from Sri Lanka.

EMERGENCE OF THE VAJRAYANA (5TH CENTURY)

Vajrayâna Buddhism, also called Tantric Buddhism, first emerged in eastern India between the 5th and 7th centuries CE. It is sometimes considered a sub-school of Mahayana and sometimes a third major "vehicle" (*Yana*) of Buddhism in its own right. The Vajrayana is an extension of Mahayana Buddhism in that it does not offer new philosophical perspectives, but rather introduces additional techniques (upaya, or 'skilful means'), including the use of visualizations and other yogic practices. Many of the practices of Tantric Buddhism are common with Hindu tantricism (the usage of mantras, yoga, or the burning of sacrificial offerings). This school of thought was founded by Padmasambhava.

Early Vajrayana practitioners were forest-dwelling mahasiddhas who lived on the margins of society, but by the 9th century Vajrayana had won acceptance at major Mahayana monastic universities such as Nalanda and Vikramashila. Along with much of the rest of Indian Buddhism, the Vajrayana was eclipsed in the wake of the late 12th century Muslim invasions. It has persisted in Tibet, where it was wholly transplanted from the 7th to 12th centuries and became the dominant form of Buddhism to the present day, and on a limited basis in Japan as well where it evolved into Shingon Buddhism.

THERAVADA RENAISSANCE

From the 11th century, the destruction of Buddhism in the Indian mainland by Islamic invasions led to the decline of the Mahayana faith in South-East Asia. Continental routes through the Indian subcontinent being compromised, direct sea routes between the Middle-East through Sri Lanka and to China developed, leading to the adoption of the Theravada Buddhism of the Pali canon, introduced to the region around the 11th century CE from Sri Lanka.

King Anawrahta (1044–1077); the historical founder of the Burmese empire, unified the country and adopted the Theravada Buddhist faith. This initiated the creation of thousands of Buddhist temples at Pagan, the capital, between the 11th and 13th century. Around 2,000 of them are still standing. The power of the Burmese waned with the rise of the Thai, and with the seizure of the capital Pagan by the Mongols in 1287, but Theravada Buddhism remained the main Burmese faith to this day.

The Theravada faith was also adopted by the newly founded ethnic Thai kingdom of Sukhothai around 1260. Theravada Buddhism was further reinforced during the Ayutthaya period (14th–18th century), becoming an integral part of the Thai society.

In the continental areas, Theravada Buddhism continued to expand into Laos and Cambodia in the 13th century. However, from the 14th century, on the coastal fringes and in the islands of South-East Asia, the influence of Islam proved stronger, expanding into Malaysia, Indonesia, and most of the islands as far as the southern Philippines.

However, since 1966 with Soeharto's rise of power in the aftermath of the bloody events after the so called "September 30th, 1965 murders", allegedly executed by the Communists Party, there has been a remarkable renaissance of Buddhism in Indonesia. This is partly due to the Soeharto's New Order's requirements for the people of Indonesia to adopt one of the five official religions: Islam, Protestantism, Catholicism, Hinduism or Buddhism. Today it is estimated there are some 10 millions Buddhists in Indonesia. A large part of them are people of Chinese ancestry.

EXPANSION OF BUDDHISM TO THE WEST

After the Classical encounters between Buddhism and the West recorded in Greco-Buddhist art, information and legends about Buddhism seem to have reached the West sporadically. An account of Buddha's life was translated into Greek by John of Damascus, and widely circulated to Christians as the story of Barlaam and Josaphat. By the 1300s this story of Josaphat had become so popular that he was made a Catholic saint.

The next direct encounter between Europeans and Buddhism happened in Medieval times when the Franciscan friar William of Rubruck was sent on an embassy to the Mongol court of Mongke by the French king Saint Louis in 1253. The contact happened in Cailac (today's Qayaliq in Kazakhstan), and William originally thought they were wayward Christians (Foltz, "Religions of the Silk Road").

Major interest for Buddhism emerged during colonial times, when Western powers were in a position to witness the faith and its artistic manifestations in detail. European philosophy was strongly influenced by the study of oriental religions during that period.

The opening of Japan in 1853 also created a considerable interest for the arts and culture of Japan, and provided access to one of the most thriving Buddhist cultures in the world.

Buddhism started to enjoy a strong interest from the general population in the West following the turbulence of the 20th century.

Buddhism has been displaying a strong power of attraction, due to its tolerance, its lack of deist authority and determinism, and its focus on understanding reality through self inquiry.

Chapter - 3

Buddhism and Its Branches

Mahayana Buddhism (Sanskrit for "Greater Vehicle"), along with Theravada Buddhism, are the two principal branches of Buddhist belief. Mahayana originated in India and subsequently spread throughout China, Korea, Japan, Tibet, Central Asia, Vietnam, and Taiwan. Followers of Mahayana have traditionally regarded their doctrine as the full revelation of the nature and teachings of the Buddha, in opposition to the earlier Theravada tradition, which they characterize as the Lesser Vehicle (Hinayana).

In contrast to the relative conservatism of earlier Buddhist schools, which adhered closely to the recognized teachings of the historical Buddha, Mahayana embraces a wider variety of practices, has a more mythological view of what a Buddha is, and addresses broader philosophical issues.

MAHAYANA BUDDHISM

Mahayana Buddhism emerged in the first century CE as a more liberal, accessible interpretation of Buddhism. As the "Greater Vehicle" (literally, the "Greater Ox-Cart"), Mahayana is a path available to people from all walks of life - not just monks and ascetics.

Mahayana Buddhism is the primary form of Buddhism in North Asia and the Far East, including China, Japan, Korea, Tibet and Mongolia, and is thus sometimes known as Northern Buddhism. Mahayana Buddhists accept the Pali Canon as sacred scripture with the Theravadans, but also many other works, the Sutras, which were written later and in Sanskrit. Theravada and Mahayana Buddhists differ in their perspective on the ultimate purpose of life and the way in which it can be attained. Theravada Buddhists strive to become *arhats*, or perfected saints who have attained enlightenment and nirvana. This is considered to only be possible for monks and nuns, who devote their entire lives to the task. The best outcome the laity can hope for is to be reborn in the monastic life.

Mahayana Buddhists, on the other hand, hope to become not *arhats* but *boddhisatvas*, saints who have become enlightened but who unselfishly delay nirvana to help others attain it as well, as the Buddha did. Perhaps more significantly for one who would choose between the paths, Mahayana Buddhists teach that enlightenment can be attained in a single lifetime, and this can be accomplished even by a layperson. The various subdivisions within the Mahayana tradition, such as Zen, Nichiren, and Pure Land, promote different ways of attaining this goal, but all are agreed that it can be attained in a single lifetime by anyone who puts his or her mind (and sometimes body) to it.

The Mahayana form of Buddhism tends to be more religious in nature than its Theravadan counterpart. It often includes veneration of celestial beings, Buddhas and boddhisatvas, ceremonies, religious rituals, magical rites, and the use of icons, images, and other sacred objects. The role of such religious elements varies, however: it is central to Tibetan/Tantric Buddhism, but is highly discouraged by Zen practitioners, who have been known to burn statues of the Buddha to demonstrate their unimportance.

Two major Mahayana schools arose in India: Madhyamika (Middle Path) and Vijñanavada (Consciousness Only; also known as Yogachara). With the spread of Mahayana Buddhism beyond India, other indigenous schools appeared, such as Pure Land Buddhism and Zen.

ORIGINS AND DEVELOPMENT

The most probable forerunners of Mahayana were the Mahasanghikas (Followers of the Great Assembly), a liberal branch of the Buddhist community that broke away from the more conservative mainstream some time before the reign of Indian king Ashoka in the 3rd century BC. Mahayana thinkers of later periods categorized the Mahasanghikas as one of the 18 schools of Hinayana Buddhism, but when Mahayana first emerged, it resembled Mahasanghika in several areas of doctrinal interpretation. The most significant Mahayana innovation was the view of the Buddha as a supernatural being who assumed a transformation body (nirmana-kaya) to be born as the historical Buddha.

Precisely when and where Mahayana arose in India is unclear, but its origin can be traced to between the 2nd century BC and the 1st century AD. The early growth of Mahayana was promoted by Indian philosopher Nagarjuna, who founded the Madhyamika school. His influential writings provide some of the most persuasive early formulations of Mahayana. The Madhyamika school proliferated into a number of sects, and was carried to China in the early 5th century by Buddhist missionary Kumarajiva, who translated Nagarjuna's work into Chinese. By 625 Madhyamika had reached Japan by way of Korea, though everywhere it remained more influential among the scholarly elite than the common people.

The **Pure Land** school of Mahayana, based on the 1st-century Sukhavativyuha Sutra (Pure Land Sutra; a sutra is a writing that purports to record a discourse of the Buddha), was established in China in the 4th century by Chinese scholar Huiyuan, who formed a devotional society for meditating on the name of Amitabha Buddha (Buddha of Infinite Light). This sect grew and spread through the 6th and 7th centuries, especially among the common people.

The **Vijñanavada** (Consciousness Only) school maintained that consciousness alone is real. Vijñanavada first arose in India about the 4th century and was taken to China two centuries later by Chinese monk and pilgrim Xuanzang (Hsuan-tsang). A Japanese disciple, Dosho, who arrived to study with him in 653, conveyed it to Japan. A native Chinese Mahayana school, Avatamsaka (Huayan in Chinese), was established in the 7th century by Chinese monk Dushun around a Chinese translation of its basic text, the Avatamsaka Sutra (Garland Sutra). The school reached Korea in the late 7th century, and between 725 and 740 was carried to Japan, where it was known as Kegon. Another important Chinese school, the Tiantai (Tendai in Japanese), was founded by Chinese monk Zhiyi, who organized the entire Buddhist canon around the cardinal Mahayana scripture, the Saddharmapundarika Sutra (Lotus Sutra). This school became very influential in China and Korea, and also in Japan, where it served as a means for introducing Pure Land doctrines.

The Mahayana school called **Dhyana** (Sanskrit for "meditation"; known in Chinese as **Chan** and in Japanese as **Zen**) was supposedly introduced into China in 520 by Indian monk Bodhidharma, but **actually arose from cross-fertilization between Mahayana and Chinese Daoism (Taoism).** Chan split into a number of schools and was introduced into Korea and into Japan in the 7th century, though its full development occurred later. Zen and Pure Land both spread into Vietnam (under Chinese rule at the time) in the 6th century. Beginning in the 7th century the Indian form of Mahayana Buddhism was gradually introduced into Tibet.

Mahayana thus was established as the dominant Buddhist school of East Asia by about the 7th century. Some Mahayana influences penetrated into Sri Lanka, Indonesia, and other Southeast Asian countries - for example, the great Cambodian monuments of Angkor Thum reflect a 12th-century Mahayana tradition. These influences were later superseded by Theravada, Hinduism, and Islam.

Buddhism in China suffered persecution under the emperor Wuzong in 845, and subsequently was overshadowed by the state cult of Confucianism, but remained an integral part of Chinese life. In Korea, where the Zen school (known as Son in Korean) had become dominant, Mahayana flourished in the Koryo period (935-1392), but was restricted under the Yi dynasty (1392-1910). Japan supported a vibrant Mahayana culture, which after the 12th century gave rise to new Zen and Pure Land sects under such reformers as Japanese monks Dogen and Honen, as well as to Japan's only entirely indigenous Buddhist sect, Nichiren Buddhism. Japanese Mahayana lost much of its vitality in the Edo period (1600-1868), during which the Tokugawa shogunate used it for social control through registration of parishioners. The anti-Buddhist policy of Japan's new rulers in the first decade following the Meiji Restoration of 1868 foreshadowed much of Mahayana's experience in the 20th century, in which Communist regimes in China, Vietnam, and North Korea prohibited worship, and in which the Chinese annexation of Tibet led to considerable persecution of Mahayana practitioners. The easing of doctrinaire

Communism led to a revival of Mahayana in some of these areas. Mahayana has also spread into new territory with the growing popularity in the West of Zen and other Mahayana schools.

ORGANIZATION

Within the Mahayana tradition, the notion of the sangha, or Buddhist monastic community, is much broader and less restrictive than in early Buddhism. Mahayana takes as its ideal the path of the bodhisattva - one who aspires to bodhi, or enlightenment. Since this ideal can be pursued by both monks and lay believers, the Mahayana sangha includes both laity and monks. Monks follow the rules of one of the Vinayas (prescriptions for monastic life) in the Tipitaka, the sacred canon of Theravada, but do so through the Mahayana interpretation. Monks also take a vow to strive to become a bodhisattva, and those who pursue the esoteric practices of Tantric Buddhism receive Tantric vows and initiations.

Although Mahayana monks generally follow the Buddhist rules of poverty and celibacy, some sects - notably the Japanese Shin sect of Pure Land Buddhism - permit clerical marriage. In pre-modern China, an aspiring monk was traditionally admitted on probation for one year before becoming a novice, often the limit of progress for those without government connections. The unordained laity includes those who take the bodhisattva vow but who do not become monks: some may live as ordinary householders; others join religious communities with their own specific vows or Tantric initiations.

Relations between Mahayana sangha and governments have varied among countries with strong Mahayana traditions. In the early Tang (T'ang) dynasty in China (7th and 8th centuries), Buddhism was organized under the state, with a government commissioner for religion. However, beginning in 845, Chinese Buddhists were persecuted by the government. In Vietnam, after independence from Chinese rule was achieved in the 10th century, a Confucian bureaucracy continued to supervise monasteries. In Japan, Buddhist temples were often powerful autonomous institutions with their own lands and armies of soldier-monks. After 1603 the Tokugawa regime took control of the temples and integrated them into the Japanese government.

Mahayana generally offers more hope of enlightenment for the lay believer than Theravada: the compassionate bodhisattvas can supposedly transfer their merit to worshippers; Zen is notoriously disdainful of the formalities of creed and hierarchy; the Pure Land is an interim paradise on the road to salvation attainable by the pious. Consequently, Mahayana lay movements have abounded through the centuries. Pure Land sects in particular tend to actively evangelize. In China, Pure Land groups were sometimes associated with secret societies and peasant revolts. In Japan, Pure Land Buddhism became the people's version of Buddhism and periodically spawned millenarian movements (movements that looked for the establishment of an earthly paradise). The Japanese Nichiren sect also focused on the common people and produced many lay societies of worshippers. The extreme of Mahayana lay participation is perhaps Japan's Sôka Gakkai movement, an entirely lay group with definite secular aims and a policy of aggressive evangelization.

DOCTRINE

Mahayana goes beyond the core doctrine contained in the Theravada Tipitaka in several important respects. It accepts as canonical other sutras not in the Tipitaka; this literature is known as the Buddhavacana (Revelation of the Buddha). The most notable Buddhavacana texts are the Saddharmapundarika Sutra (Lotus of the Good Law Sutra, or Lotus Sutra), the Vimalakirti Sutra, the Avatamsaka Sutra (Garland Sutra), and the Lankavatara Sutra (The Buddha's Descent to Sri Lanka Sutra), as well as a collection known as the Prajñaparamita (Perfection of Wisdom). The Lotus Sutra helps to explain the Mahayana view of Buddhist revelation through its rendition of one of the Buddha's sermons. In a parable, the Buddha shows how he grants provisional revelations appropriate to the limited faculties of particular beings, until finally they are ready to receive his full revelation. The sutra recounts how 5000 listeners depart in arrogance before the parable is preached, thus projecting the cause of schisms in thecommunity of the faithful back to the days of the Buddha.

Mahayana attitudes toward Buddhist teachings are in part a consequence of the Mahayana view of the Buddha. Whereas Theravadins regarded the Buddha as a supremely enlightened man, most Mahayana thought treats him as a manifestation of a divine being. This view was formalized as the doctrine of the threefold nature, or triple body (trikaya), of the Buddha. The Buddha's three bodies are known as the body of essence (dharmakaya), the sum of the spiritual qualities that make him Buddha; the body of communal bliss, or enjoyment body (sambhoga-kaya), a godlike form revealed to the Mahayana initiate during contemplation; and the body of transformation (nirmana-kaya), a mortal body that appears in the transient world of death and rebirth to lead sentient beings (beings that possess senses) to enlightenment. The body of communal bliss appears in various manifestations, notably that of the five cosmic Buddhas, the eternal Buddhas that comprise and sustain the cosmos: Vairocana, Aksobhya, Ratnasambhava, Amitabha (or Amida), and Amoghasiddhi. The body of essence is seen as the universal ground of being, revealed for many Mahayana believers in the Lotus Sutra; other sects regard it as present within oneself and accessible through meditation. The historical Buddha is believed to be one transformation body emanated by the body of essence. Consequently, his teachings can be supplemented or superseded by further revelations.

Mahayana posits an infinite number of Buddhas, or transformation bodies and enjoyment bodies of the essential Buddha, appearing in innumerable worlds to help sentient beings reach enlightenment. These Buddhas are paralleled by bodhisattvas, enlightened beings who, through compassion, delay their final passage to the transcendent state of nirvana in order to labor on behalf of universal salvation. A bodhisattva can transfer his supreme merit to others, and is thus regarded in Mahayana as superior to the arhat, the ideal Theravadin who has achieved enlightenment but can do little else for other beings.

A Mahayana worshipper can aspire to become a bodhisattva, rising through ten stages of perfection, and approaching ever closer to Buddha's body of essence, until finally bodhisattva and essential Buddha are one. Certain bodhisattvas are themselves worshipped as virtual deities. These include Avalokiteshvara (Guanyin in China, where he came to be regarded as the female protector of women, children, and sailors), the personification of compassion, and Maitreya (the only bodhisattva also recognized by Theravadins), the future Buddha who waits in the Tsuhita Heaven to be reborn and lead all beings to enlightenment. Even the Buddha Amitabha, creator of the Pure Land who leads mortals to his paradise, began as a monk who became a bodhisattva.

Another important Mahayana doctrine is the emptiness (sunyata) of all things. In the formulation of Indian philosopher Nagarjuna, the familiar world of experience is the product of thought forms imposed on the Absolute, which is entirely unconditioned (not subject to limitations of any kind). These thought forms are the categories that reason creates in its attempt to apprehend the nature of reality. Since all phenomena in the world of experience depend upon these constructs of reason, they are purely relative and therefore ultimately unreal. The Absolute, on the other hand, is empty in the sense that it is totally devoid of artificial conceptual distinctions.

This teaching was variously interpreted, with the Vijñanavada school maintaining that nothing exists outside the mind. The teaching's most influential version holds that there is an eternal, mutually sustaining dialectic between the Absolute and relative reality: although phenomena are false and void in absolute terms, they are true and real in relative terms. The Mahayana goal was to transcend these opposites in ultimate enlightenment. This doctrine made Zen and other schools turn from the practice of renunciation and withdrawal to embrace the world in the belief that nirvana could be found within the transience (samsara) of ordinary life.

Within the Buddhist tradition, Mahayana has produced important innovations in three principal areas. The first area concerns the spiritual goal of Buddhism. The ideal of the arhat (taught by the historical Buddha to his immediate disciples) was replaced in Mahayana by the bodhisattva ideal, regarded as superior and open to all followers. Every person who professes Mahayana Buddhism can take the bodhisattva vow, which expresses the aspiration to attain enlightenment just as the Buddha did and to help all beings on their way to nirvana. The bodhisattva path can be undertaken in either a monastic or a secular context, depending on individual circumstances.

The second area of Mahayana innovation concerns the interpretation of the Buddha's nature. In addition to producing a systematic doctrine of the various Buddha bodies, Mahayana practitioners have accepted the existence of countless Buddhas who preside over countless universes. These divine beings are far different from the single supremely gifted yet mortal human sage whom Theravada Buddhists revere as the sole originator of their faith.

The third area of Mahayana innovation covers doctrine and philosophy. Early Buddhists rejected the existence of any permanent self or soul (atman) and taught the no-soul (anatman) theory. However, they also accepted the reality of the elements (dharmas) of existence. A famous example of this duality is the early Buddhist parable of the cart: the components of a cart exist, but the cart itself, being a mere concept, does not exist. Similarly, the components or aggregates of living beings exist, but the single permanent entity (atman) postulated as uniting them does not. The Mahayana sutras and their interpreters rejected this realistic and limited interpretation. They reaffirmed the nonexistence of the soul, but also denied the existence of the components.

They argued that since there is no permanent foundation beneath or within all things, the things themselves do not and indeed cannot exist. This doctrinal position is encapsulated in Madhyamika school's doctrine of sunyata, discussed earlier. The concept of emptiness in its basic scope means that all things and their characteristics are deprived (empty) of reality and individual existence. In its mystic dimensions, emptiness is seen as a meditational process through which one purges one's mind. The Vijñanavada school of Mahayana also accepted this notion, but for the purposes of spiritual practices taught that the mind alone exists and that the whole external world is an illusion projected by the mind. The dispelling of that illusion through meditation was presented as the path to enlightenment. In order to retain the basic assumption of Buddhism, the Vijñanavada school taught that after a full realization of the nature of all things, the mind dissolves in emptiness.

A final important Mahayana teaching, never embodied in a formal school but nonetheless permeating all layers of the Mahayana approach, concerns the Buddha nature (tathagata-garbha) of all living beings and their capacity to become Buddhas. Although certain isolated texts taught that some living beings are barred from deliverance, Mahayana Buddhism maintains that any sentient thing can gain Buddhahood-that gods, humans, and animals alike have the seeds of Buddha nature within them.

THERAVADA BUDDHISM

Theravada Buddhism, along with Mahayana Buddhism, are the two principal branches of Buddhist belief. It is most widespread in Sri Lanka, Myanmar (formerly known as Burma), Laos, Cambodia, and Thailand. Like Mahayana Buddhism, Theravada (Pali for "School of the Elders") claims to perpetuate the true teachings and practices of the Buddha.

The Theravada school traces its descent from the original sangha, or monastic community, that first followed the Buddha. Its canon of scripture consists of the Tipitaka

(Three Baskets), the first great compendium of Buddhist writings, composed in the Pali language. Theravada tends toward doctrinal conservatism, exemplified in a cautious interpretation of its canon. Because of this, it has been given the pejorative name Hinayana (Sanskrit for "Lesser Vehicle") by its rivals, who call their own tradition Mahayana ("Greater Vehicle"). The goal of the Theravadin, or devotee of Theravada, is to become an arhat, a sage who has achieved nirvana (enlightenment) and will never be reborn. Mahayana traditionally prefers the figure of the bodhisattva - who, out of compassion, helps others toward salvation - to the arhat, who is concerned chiefly with his own salvation.

ORIGINS AND DEVELOPMENT

Theravada was the only tradition among the so-called Eighteen Schools of early Buddhism to survive the first centuries after the Buddha's death in the 5th century BC. Some authorities trace its origins to the events following the second great council of Buddhism at Vaishali, India, in 383 BC, in which novel interpretations of doctrine were condemned by conservatives - the Theras (Elders) - who thereby became the originators of Theravada orthodoxy. The reformers, in turn, accused the conservatives of being too self-absorbed and dogmatic. The ideological split was confirmed at the third council, convened by King Ashoka at Pâtaliputra (now Patna, India) in about 250 BC. After that, according to tradition, the orthodox school is said to have been spread to Sri Lanka by Ashoka's son, the monk Mahinda. There it became a national creed, centered at the great monastery of Mahavihara and closely associated with the Sri Lankan monarchy. Ashoka's missionaries also spread Theravada Buddhism to Myanmar and Thailand. For much of the 1st millennium AD, Theravada existed alongside Mahayana and esoteric Buddhism in all these areas.

While other early sects died out or were absorbed into Mahayana Buddhism, Theravada retained its identity. Similarly, when Buddhism died out in India after the 12th century AD, Theravada kept its hold in Sri Lanka and Southeast Asia. In about the 10th century, a Theravada reform movement began in Sri Lanka that consolidated the kingdom as a Theravada monarchy. The reform movement spread to Burma and Thailand, where it revitalized the Theravada tradition and ensured its supremacy over other Buddhist sects. Reformers also carried the creed into Cambodia and Laos, where the geographical limits of Theravada predominance were reached. Despite some Theravada followers in Vietnam and elsewhere, Mahayana Buddhism became the dominant tradition in the rest of the Buddhist world.

Despite the European colonialism that began in the early 19th century, Theravada continued in Sri Lanka and Southeast Asia, in some areas becoming identified with nascent nationalist movements. In Sri Lanka, during the 18th and 19th centuries, Theravada split into factions, mostly over questions regarding the caste of worshippers. Thailand began reform of its Theravada tradition in the 19th century as part of the general national reform initiated in response to European colonialism, and the country has remained a fertile source of Theravada reform movements. In the 1980s and 1990s, Theravada became an important factor in civil strife between the Buddhist Sinhalese majority and the Tamil minority of Sri Lanka, with some militant Buddhists promoting a vigorous Sinhalese nationalism. In Myanmar, Theravada has become one element of the rigidly conservative political and social policies of the country's military rulers. Theravada in Laos and Cambodia suffered a setback during the Vietnam War (1959-1975) and the subsequent Communist domination but appeared to be reviving in the 1990s. **Theravada has been reestablished in India in the modern era by the mass conversion to Theravada Buddhism of Harijans** (the so-called Untouchables, who fall outside the traditional class divisions of Hindu society), who are attracted by Buddhism's indifference to Hindu concepts of caste.

ORGANIZATION

Theravada organization is in principle based on the original instructions of the Buddha as laid down in the Vinaya Pitaka, the compendium of 227 rules for monastic discipline that forms part of the Tipitaka. Since the sangha is the core institution of Buddhism, its structure is the basis of Theravada organization. Theravada monks were traditionally criticized by Mahayana believers for being too concerned with their own salvation and for indifference to the lay community. Theravada doctrine holds that only a monk can attain nirvana and that the laity can only aspire to be reborn as a monk after many reincarnations spent discharging the burden of karma (intentional action that determines one's future destiny). However, in some countries, especially Myanmar and Thailand, young men are placed in monasteries temporarily as part of their education, thus fostering lay involvement in the sangha.

Most countries with large numbers of Theravada adherents exhibit strong historical ties between the Buddhist hierarchy and the government. In such countries, Ashoka's beneficent propagation of Buddhism has been accepted as the exemplar of wise and legitimate government and as a precedent for state involvement in religious affairs. The state and the sangha are often seen as complementary and mutually supportive, ministering respectively to the secular and religious needs of the people. The temples themselves are loosely coordinated in most Southeast Asian countries, with little in the way of formal hierarchy between them. In early Sri Lankan Buddhism, a short-lived and limited practice of clerical marriage developed, and charge of particular temples was passed from father to son.

Theravada has a notable tradition of forest-dwelling hermits who exist outside the monastic organizations. In contrast to Mahayana Buddhism, since about AD 500, Theravada has had no orders of Buddhist nuns. There is limited participation in the sangha by women and lay people, who generally wear white robes and take up asceticism (self-denial) without entering a monastic order.

DOCTRINE

Theravada claims to abide by the original teachings of the historical Buddha, Siddhartha Gautama. Theravada doctrine reveres the Buddha as a single supremely gifted, yet mortal, teacher, in contrast to the succession of transcendent beings postulated by Mahayana. Some Theravada scriptures list other Buddhas, but in general the emphasis is on the one historical Buddha, on the grounds that no universe can bear more than one Buddha without shattering.

The dharma, or teachings, of the historical Buddha are usually regarded as being contained in the Tipitaka. Unlike Mahayana, which has generated a vast number of additional sutras (scriptural texts), Theravada confines itself to this core dharma. The Theravada canon is recorded in Pali, a dialect popular during the Buddha's lifetime. Other works highly esteemed in Theravada - particularly the dialogues in the Milindapanha (2nd century AD; translated as Questions of King Milinda, 1963), and the Visuddhimagga (5th century AD; Path of Purification, 1964) by the great Buddhist commentator Buddhaghosa - are regarded by most scholars as authoritative collections rather than as the fruit of further revelations of dharma (although the Milindapanha is considered canonical by the Myanmar).

The dharma of Theravada regards human existence as a complex of various transient aspects, also called dharmas. These dharmas are grouped in overlapping categories of 5 components (skandhas), 12 bases (ayatana), and 18 perceptual elements (dhatu). The 5 components are the physical body (rupa), feelings (vedana), cognitive perception (sanna), mental predispositions (sankhara), and consciousness (vijñana). The 12 bases are the 5 sensory organs with their 5 sensory fields, plus the mind and the object of mental perception. The 18 elements are the 5 sensory organs plus the mind, their 6 associated objects, and the 6 so-called consciousnesses of ear, eye, nose, mouth, body, and mind. These dharmas create a composite being not united by any enduring soul (atman) or identity: There is no self in the strict sense. The Theravadin endeavors to manipulate the dharmas so as to suspend the action of karma and thereby to achieve nirvana. Theravada is therefore less a philosophical doctrine than an almost scientific discipline, although it depends on a complex cosmology of cyclical, multiple worlds and an involved scheme of reincarnation.

OTHER FORMS OF BUDDHISM

LAMAISM

Lamaism is the Tibetan religion of about 3 million Tibetans and 7 million Mongols and others. The Dalai Lama is the equivalent of the Pope for them. A secondary leader is the Teshu Lama (or Panchen Lama). These two are regarded as 'Living Buddhas', being reincarnations of Buddha passing from one existence to another. When one dies, his successor is sought from among the baby boys born at the time the leader passed away because it is believed that the soul of the Buddha has only passed into another existence.

Lamaism is considered a corrupt form of Buddhism. It is sometimes called the Yellow Religion. In some areas it has degenerated into a form of spirit worship.

Tibetan Buddhism, also called Lamaism, is a distinctive form of Buddhism that arose (7th century) in Tibet and later spread throughout the Himalayan region, including the neighboring countries of Bhutan, Nepal, and Sikkim. The history of Tibetan Buddhism can be divided into three periods. During the 7th - 9th century AD Buddhism was first introduced from India and was slowly accepted under Buddhist kings in the face of opposition by adherents of the indigenous shamanistic religion of Tibet, Bon. Instrumental in this process were the Indian Mahayana Buddhist masters Padmasambhava and Shantarakshita. During the 9th century, however, King gLang Dar Ma persecuted the new faith and effectively eclipsed it for some time.

The second period began with the reintroduction of Buddhism from India and its successive reform in the 11th century. Powerful ecclesiastical organizations were established and soon began to rule the countryside in alliance with clans of nobles or the distant Mongol rulers. During this period the Tibetan Buddhist canon (notable for its accurate translations of now - lost Sanskrit texts and its helpful commentaries) was compiled, and some of the sects that have persisted to the present were formed. These include the Sa - skya - pa, the rNying - ma - pa (who traced their roots back to Padmasambhava), and the bKa'rgyud - pa (to which belonged the famous yogi Milarepa).

The third period began with the great reformer Tsong - kha - pa (1357 - 1419), who founded the dGe - lugs - pa sect - the so called Yellow Hats - to which the line of the Dalai Lamas belongs. Each of these lamas was thought to be the reincarnation of his predecessor (as well as that of the bodhisattva Avalokitesvara) and became, at least nominally, the religious and secular ruler of the country. In 1959 the present, or 14th, Dalai Lama fled the Chinese presence in Tibet along with thousands of ordinary Tibetans and many other high incarnate lamas. Since then they have all been living in exile, primarily in India but also in Nepal and elsewhere.

Among the characteristic features of Tibetan Buddhism are its ready acceptance of the Buddhist Tantras as an integral and culminating part of the Buddhist way; its emphasis on the importance of the master - disciple relationship for both religious scholarship and meditation; its recognition of a huge pantheon of Buddhas, bodhisattvas, saints, demons, and deities; its sectarianism, which resulted less from religious disputes than from the great secular powers of the rival monastic organizations; and, finally, the marked piety of both monastic and lay Tibetan Buddhists, which receives expression in their spinning of prayer wheels, their pilgrimages to and circumambulation of holy sites, prostrations and offerings, recitation of texts, and chanting of Mantras, especially the famous invocation to Avalokitesvara Om Mani Padme Hum.

ZEN BUDDHISM

This a recognized denomination of Buddhism. It is popular among non Buddhists in the U S; it seeks to transmit the spirit of Buddhism without demanding allegiance to all the teachings of Buddha. It uses mondo, a question - and - answer technique to reveal truths (some religious) from within the seeker which will bring bodhi (enlightenment). Wisdom and love are major emphases.

Many critics see Zen Buddhism as non religious, as a sham religion. True Buddhists see it as an attempt as a short cut to true enlightenment. Others see it as an atheistic approach to life.

Zen or Ch'an Buddhism represents a sectarian movement within the Buddhist religion that stresses the practice of meditation as the means to enlightenment. Zen and Ch'an are, respectively, Japanese and Chinese attempts to render the Sanskrit word for meditation, dhyana.

Zen's roots may be traced to India, but it was in East Asia that the movement became distinct and flourished. Like other Chinese Buddhist sects, Ch'an first established itself as a lineage of masters emphasizing the teachings of a particular text, in this case the Lankavatara Sutra. Bodhidharma, the first Ch'an patriarch in China, who is said to have arrived there from India c. 470 AD, was a master of this text. He also emphasized the practice of contemplative sitting, and legend has it that he himself spent 9 years in meditation facing a wall.

With the importance of lineages, Ch'an stressed the master - disciple relationship, and Bodhidharma was followed by a series of patriarchs each of whom received the Dharma (religious truth) directly from his predecessor and teacher. By the 7th century, however, splits in the line of transmission began to develop, the most important of which was between Shen - hsiu (606 - 706) and Hui - neng (638 - 713), disciples of the 5th patriarch, Hung - jen. According to a later and clearly biased legend, Hui - neng defeated Hung - jen in a stanza - composing contest, thereby demonstrating his superior enlightenment. He was then secretly named 6th patriarch but had to flee south for fear of his rival's jealousy.

The split between Shen - hsiu and Hui - neng accounts for the southern and northern branches of Ch'an, which competed vigorously for prestige and state support. Hui - neng's branch dominated in the long run, and by 796 an imperial decree settled the matter in his favor posthumously. By then, however, Hui - neng's branch was itself beginning to subdivide into several different schools.

The subsequent history of Ch'an in China was mixed. The sect suffered from the great persecution of Buddhism in 845. It recovered better than many Buddhist schools, however, partly because, in contrast to other monastic communities, Ch'an monks engaged in physical labor, which made them less dependent on state and lay support. During the Sung dynasty (960 - 1279), Ch'an again prospered and was a leading influence on the development of Chinese art and neo - Confucian culture.

It was during this period that Ch'an was first established in Japan. Within 30 years of each other, two Japanese monks, Eisai (1141 - 1215) and Dogen (1200 - 53), went to

China, where they trained respectively in the Lin - chi (Japanese, Rinzai) and Ts'ao - tung (Japanese, Soto) schools of Ch'an. These were then introduced into Japan. Rinzai emphasizes the use of Koans, mental stumbling blocks or riddles that the meditator must solve to the satisfaction of his master. Soto lays more stress on seated meditation without conscious striving for a goal (zazen). Both schools fostered good relations with the shoguns and became closely associated with the Japanese military class. Rinzai in particular was highly influential during the Ashikaga period (1338 - 1573), when Zen played an important role in propagating neo - Confucianism and infusing its own unique spirit into Japanese art and culture.

The heart of Zen monasticism is the practice of meditation; it is this feature that has been most popular in Zen's spread to the West. Zen meditation highlights the experience of enlightenment, or satori, and the possibility of attaining it in this life. The strict training of Zen monks, the daily physical chores, the constant wrestling with koans, the long hours of sitting in meditation, and the special intensive periods of practice are all directed toward this end.

At the same time, enlightenment is generally thought of as being sudden. The meditator needs to be jolted awake, and the only one who can do this is his Zen master. The master - disciple relationship often involves private interviews in which the Zen trait of unconventionality sometimes comes to the fore; the master will allow no refuge in the Buddha or the sutras but demands from his disciple a direct answer to his assigned koan. Conversely, the master may goad the disciple by remaining silent or compassionately help him out, but with the constant aim of trying to cause a breakthrough from conventional to absolute truth.

TANTRA

The term Tantra refers to a pan Indian religious movement (also called Tantrism) that arose in about the 6th century AD within both Buddhism and Hinduism and to the texts (either Buddhist or Hindu) setting forth its practices and beliefs. The main emphasis of Tantrism is on the development of the devotee's dormant psychophysical powers by means of special meditations and ritual techniques. These are essentially esoteric and must be passed on personally from master to initiate. Stressing the coordination of body, speech, and mind, they include the use of symbolic gestures (mudras); the uttering of potent formulas (Mantras); the entering (through meditation) of sacred diagrams (Mandalas) and yantras; the meditator's creative visualization of and identification with specific divine forms; and the physical, iconographic, or mental use of sexual forces and symbols.

Because of the last of these emphases, Tantra has sometimes been considered as a degenerate form of religion rather than as the final outgrowth of trends whose roots reach deep into Yoga and Indian cosmology. Although the particulars of practice vary between the Buddhist and Hindu Tantras and within each of these traditions from one text or lineage to another, they all stress the realization, within the body, of the union of polar opposites, whether these be conceived of as devotee and goddess, the masculine principle (Shiva) and the feminine (Shakti), reason and compassion, or samsara and nirvana. Tantrism is traditionally practiced in Tibet, Nepal, Bhutan, and other countries where Tibetan Buddhism is followed, as well as in India.

Chapter - 4

Early Buddhism and Its Various Schools

MAJOR SCHOOLS OF THE EARLY BUDDHISTS: MAHÂSÂMGHIKA

It has been noted earlier that at the time of the first of two Buddhist councils held at *Pâtaliputra* during the reign of *Mahâpadma Nanda* (approximately 346 B.C.), the Buddhist Samgha divided itself into two groups, the *Sthaviras* and the *Mahâsâmghikas.* Historically, our information on the second of these groups is scanty. The records of Chinese pilgrims who traveled to India (*Fa-hien* A.D. 399-414, *Hsüan-tsang* A.D. 629-645, *I-tsing* A.D. 671-695) seem to indicate that the Mahâsâmghikas flourished in *Magadha* in general and Pâtaliputra in particular. Views coincident with specific Mahâsâmghika doctrines are recorded in the Pâli Abhidharma text of the *Kathâvatthu,* said to have been composed around 250 B.C. as a result of the council convened under *Asoka,* and the phrase "some Mahâsâmghikas" also appears in the text. Epigraphical evidence, dating as early as 120 B.C., has been found in the ancient city of *Mathurâ.* As for the rest, it can only be inferred from a careful reading of the texts of the schools themselves and the secondary sources focusing on Buddhist sectarianism. Nevertheless, given certain limits, we can state with assurance that within several centuries the Mahâsâmòghikas divided internally, resulting in several subsects, the most important of which are the *Ekavyâvahârikas, Lokottaravâdins, Gokulikas,Bahusrutîyas, Prajñaptivâdins,* and *Caitîyas.*

LITERATURE

The canon of the Mahâsâmghikas includes:

A. *Vinaya Pitaka* — Basket of Discipline

B. *Sûtra Pitaka* — Basket of Discourses: 1. *Dîrgha Âgama* — Discourses; 2. *Madhyama Âgama* — Middle Length Discourses; 3. Samyukta Âgama — Linked Discourses; 4. Ekottara Âgama — Increased by One Discourses; 5. Khuddaka Âgama — Miscellaneous Discourses

C. *Abhidharma Pitaka* — Basket of Higher Philosophy

D. *Samyukta* or *Khuddaka Pitaka* — Basket of Miscellaneous Matters

Little of this canon is preserved today. We are told that Fa-hien discovered a manuscript of the Mahâsâmghika Vinaya at Pâtaliputra in A.D. 414 which he translated into Chinese. In 1934 several Sanskrit Vinaya fragments of this school were discovered in Tibet by Râhula Sâmkrtyâyana. Of the Sûtra Pitaka, only the Ekottara Âgama exists, in Chinese translation, and none of the other texts are extant, although Fa-hien is recorded to also have found the Abhidharma pitòaka at Pâtaliputra. We do have one complete text, the *Mahâvastu* (in Buddhist Hybrid Sanskrit), claiming to be the Vinaya of the Lokottaravâdin subsect, but actually representing a detailed account of the life of the Buddha, as well as a storehouse for many doctrinal matters. Most scholars agree that the actual linguistic medium of the Mahâsâmghikas was Prakrit, and on examination of the Sanskrit texts that have come down to us, this hypothesis seems likely.

DOCTRINES

We have already seen that the Mahâsâmghikas held a thoroughly progressive view with regard to the arhants. They also represent the first school of Buddhism to speculate about the nature of the Buddha. The orthodox Buddhism of the time held Buddha to be a human being, but one who had distinguished himself among men by attaining full enlightenment, and as a corollary of this complete perfect enlightenment (*samyaksambuddha*), omniscience. The docetic speculations of the Mahâsâmghikas were founded in statements made by the Buddha:

He who sees the Dharma, sees me; He who sees me, sees the Dharma. Or, Victorious over all things, I am omniscient, Unstained among all things, Abandoning everything, released through the destruction of craving, By knowing for myself, to whom should I point?

There is no teacher for me, One like me does not exist in the world with its gods, There is no one equal to me.

As a result of statements such as these, the Mahâsâmghikas held Buddha to be supramundane and possessed of all perfections (*pâramitâs*). As a result of his past stock of meritorious actions (*punòyakarma*) and current attainments, they speculated that, for example, Buddha's material body was unlimited, as was his length of life and divine power. He could comprehend all things in a moment and was always plunged in meditation, never sleeping or dreaming. This speculation set the stage for the later development of the *Mahâyâna,* expressed first in the *Prajñâpâramitâ-sûtras.*In view of the deprecation of the arhant ideal, the Mahâsâmghikas offered a new interpretation of the path to the goal.

In orthodox doctrine there was only one *Bodhisattva,* or "Buddha to be" Siddhârtha Gautama. The Mahâsâmghikas, however, note that others can follow this path and thus, in the Mahâvastu, establish a ten-step path for Bodhisattvas to follow. Although the stages outlined in the Mahâvastu do not all coincide with the ten Mahâyâna stages (*bhûmis*), they do represent a fundamental point of departure from which the Mahâyâna developed its mature Bodhisattva doctrine, emphasizing that all sentient creatures may strive for and attain complete perfect enlightenment. Apart from some rather sophisticated notions concerning the doctrine of the act and the nature of Buddha's teaching, it represents the main contributions of the Mahâsâmghikas to early Buddhist doctrinal development. We can unequivocally state that in setting forth these progressive doctrinal statements, in emphasizing an attempt to live by the spirit of the law rather than its letter, monastically, the Mahâsâmghikas played an extremely significant role in shaping the future of Buddhism.

MAJOR SCHOOLS OF THE EARLY BUDDHISTS: THERAVÂDA

The *Theravâda* school of Buddhism, flourishing today in Ceylon, Burma, Thailand, Laos, and Cambodia, represents both the only surviving school of so-called *Hînayâna* Buddhism and that school about which we have the most information. The name of the school, Theravâda in Pâli, corresponds exactly to the Sanskrit *Sthaviravâda,* the name of one of the two great schools separating at the time of the great schism around 346 B.C., and this small but significant detail has caused scholars more than a fair share of confusion. The logical tendency is to simply equate the two schools, but this is not the case. By the time of the council held by Asoka around 250 B.C., the Sthavira school had split itself into primarily three groups: the *Vâtsîputrîya-Sammatîyas,* the *Sarvâstivâdins,* and the *Vibhajyavâdins.* In the course of time (perhaps 100 years) the Vibhajyavâdin school splintered into two primary schools: the *Mahîsâkas* and the *Theravâdins.*

One must then ask how this school managed to implement itself so strongly throughout Asia. King Asoka, in his missionary zeal, sent his son Mahinda to the island of *Lankâ* or Ceylon, establishing Buddhism as the state religion. Apparently, the form of Buddhism exported was the Vibhajyavâda. Ceylon, however, was constantly threatened in its early history by Tamil invasions from South India. When King Dutòtòhagâminòî of Ceylon, during the first century B.C., finally drove the Tamils from the island, Theravâda emerged and consolidated itself into a distinct school, dominant on the island. It is most probably this isolation in Ceylon which allowed Theravâda to prosper, while its continental counterpart, the Mahîsâkas, eventually died out in India.

LITERATURE

The canon of the Theravâdins includes:

A. *Vinaya Pitaka* — Basket of Discipline: 1. *Suttavibhanga* — Analysis of a Sutta, including *Mahâvibhanga* — Great (or Monks') Analysis and *Bhikkhunîvibhanga* — Nuns' Analysis; 2. *Khandhaka* — Division, including *Mahâvagga* — Great Section and *Cullavagga* — Small Section; 3. *Parivâra* -The Accessory.

B. *Sutta Pitaka* — Basket of Discourses: 1. *Dîgha Nikâya* — Long Discourses; 2. *Majjhima Nikâya* — Middle Length Discourses; 3. *Samyutta Nikâya* — Linked Discourses; 4. *Anguttara Nikâya* — Increased by One Discourses; 5. *Khuddaka Nikâya* — Miscellaneous Discourses,

C. *Abhidhamma Pitaka* — Basket of Higher Philosophy: 1. *Dhammasangani* — Explication of Dhammas; 2. *Vibhanga* — Divisions; 3. *Dhâtukathâ* — Discourse on the Elements; 4. *Puggalapaññatti* — Descriptions of Persons; 5. *Kathâvatthu* — Subjects of Discussion; 6. *Yamaka* — Pairs; 7. *Patthâna* — Causal Relations.

We are fortunate to have the entire *Tripitaka* of the Theravâdins preserved in Pâli. The texts were committed to writing for the first time during the reign of *Vattagâmanî* in Ceylon (29-17 B.C.). Apart from the canonical literature of the Theravâdins, their school provides us with a rich and full commentatorial tradition. For each text of the Pâli Canon there is a major commentary, usually attributed to either *Buddhaghosa* or his successor *Dhammapâla,* and a host of subcommentaries. In addition, there are several texts which serve as compendiums of doctrine, such as Buddhaghosa's *Visuddhimagga* ("Path of Purity") or the *Milindapañha* ("The Questions of King Milinda"), recording conversations between the learned monk *Nâgasena* and the Bactrian king *Menander*.

DOCTRINES

While accepting all the early doctrines outlined in lecture six, the Theravâdins make a number of specific pronouncements with regard to items of contention between the various schools. With respect to Gautama the Buddha, the Theravâdins maintain and stress his humanity. Although representing an example of perfection, he is only a man possessed of a physical body (*Rûpakâya*). The *Dharmakâya,* later to be metaphysically interpreted by the Sarvâstivâdins as the "Body of Essence" or "Buddhahood" and by the *Mahâyânists* as "Ultimate Reality," represents for the Theravâda school only the sum total of Buddha's teachings; in other words, the "Body of Doctrine." For the Theravâdins there is but one *Bodhisattva,* Gautama. Aspiring to complete perfect enlightenment is an option simply not open to all sentient beings. In Theravâda there is just one unconditioned state (*asamòskrta dharma*), *nirvâna.* All other things in the world of *samsâra* are conditioned (*samskrta*).

MAJOR SCHOOLS OF THE EARLY BUDDHISTS: SARVÂSTIVÂDA

There is a great deal of mystery surrounding the rise and early development of the *Sarvâstivâdin* school. On the one hand, we have the tradition of Asoka's council, stating the schismatic group in the Samgha was expelled from Magadha, migrating to Northwestern India and evolving into the Sarvâstivâdin school. On the other hand, we have the attempts of several scholars to ascribe the rise of the school to one of Asoka's missions — that sending *Majjhantika* to *Gandhâra,* an early seat of the school. This episode corresponds well with one Sarvâstivâdin tradition stating that *Madhyântika* (the Sanskrit counterpart of the Pâli Majjhantika) converted the city of *Kashmîr,* which seems to have close ties with Gandhâra. Still another tradition establishes a community of Sarvâstivâdin monks at *Mathurâ,* founded by the patriarch *Upagupta.* Be that as it may, until the reign of King *Kaniska,* around the turn of the Christian era, the history of the school is at best sketchy.

Upon his accession to power, Kaniska extended his rule over a substantial empire and in his own distinctive way set out to be a second Asoka, i.e., a pious ruler, governing in accordance with the Dharma. During his reign yet another council was held, at Kaúmîr. This council marks the emergence of the Sarvâstivâdins as a pervasive school in Buddhism. Some 500 monks gathered, under the presiding eye of the monk *Vasumitra,* with the majority being Sarvâstivâdins. In addition to the canonical texts of the school being established, extensive commentaries on the Vinaya, SU_016Btras, and Abhidharma (the *Upadeúa-sâstra,Vinayavibhâcâ-sâstra,* and *Abhidharmavibhâsâ-sâstra,* respectively) were composed. These treatises, when completed, were written on copper plates and enclosed in a memorial mound or *stûpa.*

Strengthened by Kaniska's patronage, the Sarvâstivâdins were to prosper for 1,000 years in India. Being located on the trade route between China and the West, this school was invariably responsible for much of the Buddhist literature finding its way into China, and consequently occupied a doubly important role in the religious history of Buddhism.

LITERATURE

The canon of the Sarvâstivâdins includes:

A. ***Vinaya Pitaka*** — Basket of Discipline. The Vinaya of the Sarvâstivâdins is known as the "Vinaya in Ten Recitations" (*Dasâdhyâya Vinaya*). The recitations are: 1-3. *Prâtimoksa* — Monastic Code; 4. *Saptadharma* — 7 Sections; 5. *Actadharma* — 8 Sections; 6. *Kcudrakaparivarta* — Miscellaneous Points; 7. *Bhikkhunî Vinaya* — Nuns' Vinaya; 8. *Ekottaradharma* — Preceding Rules Arranged in Ascending Order, Adding One at a Time; 9. *Upâliparipròcchâ* — The Questions of Upâli (A Mahâyânist Vinaya Treatise); 10. *Kusalapativarta* — Good Points (Preface to the Vinaya).

B. ***Sûtra Pitaka*** — Basket of Discourses: 1. *Dîrgha Âgama* — Long Discourses; 2. *Madhyama Âgama* — Middle Length Discourses; 3. *Samyukta Âgama* — Linked Discourses; 4. *Ekottara Âgama* — Increased by One Discourses.

C. ***Abhidharma Pitaka*** — Basket of Higher Philosophy: 1. *Jñânaprasthâna* of Ârya *Kâtyâyanîputra;* 2. *Saingîtiparyâya* of *Mahâkaucthila* (Tibetan tradition) or *Sâriputra* (Chinese tradition); 3. *Prakaranapâda* of *Vasumitra;* 4. *Vijñânakâya* of *Devasarmâ;* 5. *Dhâtukâya* of *Pûrna* (Tibetan tradition) or *Vasumitra* (Chinese tradition); 6. *Dharmaskandha* of Ârya *Sâriputra* (Tibetan tradition) or *Mahâmaudgalyâyana* (Chinese tradition); 7. *Prajñapti-sâstra* of *Mahâmaudgalyâyana.*

One early Buddhist commentator, *Yasomitra,* states that, regarding the Abhidharma, the Jñânaprasthâna can be compared to the body of a being and the other six texts to its legs.

The Sarvâstivâdin canon was originally composed in Sanskrit. All that remains of these early Sanskrit texts are a few scattered fragments. Nevertheless, the whole of the canon has been faithfully preserved in Chinese, and several portions of it in Tibetan. Perhaps the most striking feature of the Sarvâstivâdin canon is its extremely developed Abhidharma tradition. The Sarvâstivâdin tradition is rich in its commentatorial literature, particularly on Abhidharma texts. Three texts, at least, are worthy of special mention. First, *Kâtyâyanîputra's* own commentary of the *Jñânaprasthâna.*

It is unfortunately incomplete, but another commentary on the Jñânaprasthâna, compiled by 500 arhants and called the *Abhidharmamahâvibhâsâsâstra,* is not. These two texts seem to result in their adherents developing into another sect, the *Vaibhâsikas,* having their home in Kashmîr and making much headway in the Buddhist community. Finally, *Vasubandhu,* probably one of the two greatest Buddhist commentators (with Buddhaghosa), wrote his magnificent Abhidharma treatise, the *Abhidharmakosa,* covering almost all the philosophical topics espoused in the Sarvâstivâdin Abhidharma books and offering many refutations of Vaibhâsika viewpoints. The Sarvâstivâdins represent the chief exponents of "Hînayâna Scholasticism," as attested to by their scriptures and commentaries.

DOCTRINES

Since the Sarvâstivâdin doctrines are complicated and complex, we shall outline here only the main features of the school. The school takes its name from the Sanskrit phrase *sarvam asti,* or "all is," thus we translate their name to mean "those who hold the doctrine that all is." In other words, although usually understood as exponents of the doctrine of impermanence (*anitya*), which excludes the existence of the past and future, they do hold that the past is made manifest in the present and the future is latent in the present through the transmission of dharmas. These dharmas fall into five categories basic to all existents: form (*rûpa*) — 11 items; mind (*citta*) -1 item; mental constituents (*caitasikas*) — 46 items; things not associated with formor mind (*rûacittaviprayukta-samòskâras*) — 14 items; and unconditioned states (*asamskrta*) — 3 items. These five major groups of dharmas, when applied to the present, seem to indicate that each presently existing object or being is the resultant of these persistent dharmas, while at the same time providing the potential for future events.

Although affirming with the other Sthaviras that Buddha was indeed but a mortal man possessed of a form-body (*Rûpakâya*), the Sarvâstivâdins recognize a problem inherent after Buddha's death. While Buddha lived, taking refuge in the Three Jewels (*triratna*) provided no difficulty. What happens, however, when Buddha dies and there is no living leader? What does taking refuge in Buddha then mean? In the

Abhidharmakosa, Vasubandhu responds to this problem in two ways. First, he states that *Dharmakâya,* previously referred to as simply the Body of Dharma or the totality of Buddha's teachings, actually represents the sum of all things constituting a Buddha, or more simply, the essence of Buddha. Second, Vasubandhu conceives of Dharmakâya as a foundation of pure dharmas, consonant with the doctrine that an individual is only a combination of physical and mental dharmas. Thus Vasubandhu has given the notion of Buddhahood a rather metaphysical interpretation, one which is carried to its radical conclusion by the *Mahâyânists.*

The Sarvâstivâdins also provide us with an emphasis on the practice of the six *pâramitâs* or perfections — charity or giving (*dâna*), morality (*sîla*), patience (*ksanti*), vigor (*vîrya*), trance (*samâdhi*), and wisdom (*prajñâ*). The doctrine of the practice of the pâramitâs was later to become one of the primary tenets of the Mahdâyânists, thus we see that the Sarvâstivâdins, like the Mahâsâmsghikas, provided much of the soil from which the Mahâyâana emerged. Just as the Mahâsâmsghikas expressed critical concern regarding the nature of the *arhant,* so did the Sarvâstivâdins, going as far as to say that the arhant could regress. For this school the arhants were not free from their past karmic influence or dependent origination. Fortunately, however, while the arhant could fall back, the streamwinner could not, insuring at least no bad rebirths or loss of the path. In summary, we can say that on doctrinal matters the Sarvâstivâdins added much to early Buddhism in both philosophical and practical matters.

MAJOR SCHOOLS OF THE MAHÂYÂANA: MÂDHYAMIKA

In the Indian schema of orthodox (âstika, explicitly acknowledging allegiance to the authority of the *Vedas*) and unorthodox philosophical schools (darsanas), Mâdhyamika belongs in the latter unorthodox category. Its early and middle developments occurred in the Indian context; however, it was also of tremendous influence in Tibet and in China. As with much of early Buddhist culture, it reflects an integration, assimilation, or reaction to the Indian cultural milieu. In the Buddhist schema it is one of the major schools of Buddhism, along with *Sarvâstivâda, Sautrântika, Theravâda, Tantra,* and *Yogacâra.* The title, "Middle Position," refers to a philosophical position midway between the extreme metaphysical positions of postulating ontological ("existence," eternalism) categories of either (any) X, or its contradictory; i.e., that X does not exist, annihilation. One should note that the denial of a "known" thing is also a "position". The Mâdhyamikas deny *both* that other views are free from legitimate contradiction and that they possess a position (drsti) to defend.

The Mâdhyamika school was (probably) founded by Nâgâjuna during the second half of the third century A.D., in the developing Indian Mahâyâna complex. It purports to be and is a true and faithful development of the basic tenets of Buddhism. Its goal is ultimately soteriological (salvation-oriented), i.e., nirvâa.

Since the beginning of the last half of the nineteenth century when Mâdhyamika first came to the notice of the modern scholarly tradition, it has remained one of the most fascinating, enigmatic religio-philosophic sets of concepts surfacing from Asia upon the international (and Western) consciousness.

A great variety of labels have been projected upon Nâgârjuna (A.D. 200-300), e.g., absolute monist, radical pluralist, nihilist, negativist, relativist, logician, and dialectician. It seems fair to say that the different labels, approaches, and descriptions of Nâgârjuna's writings found in the history of modern scholarship reflect almost as much about the viewpoints of the scholars involved as do they reflect the content of Nâgârjuna's concepts. Representative samples of such scholarship may be found in the Suggested Reading at the conclusion of this lecture.

One popular biography of Nâgârjuna states that he was born in a South Indian brahman family, participated in a typical brâhmanòical education in religious and nonreligious subjects, and acquired some fame for his wide learning while still a young man. He was also considered by later writers to have been a *Bodhisattva.* His Sanskrit style exemplifies his classical training and his interest in rather hard-nosed argumentation. He is a "rationalist" in the broad sense of the term; he argues systematically.

The two texts of Nâgârjuna in which his philosophical position is exemplified most clearly are the *Mûla-Mâhyamika Kârikâs* (hereafter *MK*) and the *Vigraha-Vâvartanî.* These are essentially polemic treatises which purport to refute the philosophical positions of both other Buddhist schools and other non-Buddhist darœanas. Those major schools to which the Mâdhyamika polemics are directed are orthodox (âstika), *Samòkhya, NyâyaVaiseúika, Mîmâmòsâ,* and the other unorthodox (nâstika) Buddhist Abhidharma schools of the Sarvâstivâda and Sautrântika. Mâdhyamika exemplifies the growing methodological and stylistic influences of the epistemological (*pramâa-vâda*) inquiries of the early darsana systems.

Nâgârjuna's assimilation and extensive use of rhetorical figures (e.g., *reductio ad absurdum, prasanga*) and the style and vigor of the early protologicians helped to tighten the rules of polemic debate among the later Indian schools. An example — a prasanga — may help to illustrate these qualities: "That existents (bhâva) are without own-being (*svabhâva*) is because their alter-being is seen; an existence without own-being does not exist; hence the emptiness (*snyatâ*) of existents. If own-being does not occur, to whom might alter-being belong? If own-being does occur, to whom might alter-being belong?". If one compares this style with a late *Upanisad,* one is struck by the obvious development of argumentation. By such formalistic emphasis, Nâgârjuna paved the way for a more systematic logical development of the later darsanas.

AN EPISTEMOLOGICAL AND METAPHYSICAL OVERVIEW

One crucial feature in contrasting the Buddhist philosophical assumptions with that of their Indian background is to note the fundamental and farreaching change in Buddhist philosophy during the period from the late Upanishads to the explicit formulation of the early darœana systems (roughly 300 B.C. to A.D. 200). The change was essentially a metaphysical one. By a metaphysical position, I refer to the most fundamental conceptual elements and categories of description which represent the most basic ideas common to a particular cultural, philosophical, or religious world view.

These ideas in this period in ancient India were in the process of gradual but significant change. Prior to the time of the Buddhists, the Indians of the late Upanisadic and very early classical period held that the question for metaphysical knowledge involved an examination of the most fundamental concepts, metaphysical elements, or reals which, because they were most fundamental, were seen as incompatible with the variety of *actual* change that we observe in our everyday lives. That is, the metaphysical axiom was that *basic* realities (e.g., *prakrti* or nature, satya or realities, svabhâva or own-being) do not change. To *be* a "real X" means that such an X is not subject to causal conditioning. This quest for unchanging reals was essentially a quest for *stable* conceptual categories which describe things most fundamental in what appears (perhaps superficially) to be a very changing, fluxing world. It was a quest for elements different in *kind*, not merely in *degree*.

A significant feature of the Buddhist metaphysical position is that it contrasts strongly with its Indian predecessors. The Buddhists introduced a fundamental and radical change in the idea of the basic constituents of the Indian world view. This radical view is expressed in one of the oldest and most fundamental ideas of Buddhism: everything (involves) change (*sarvamò anityam.*) Rather than looking for stable constituents of a description which reflected the way the world is, the Buddhist concluded that the described world was only superficially a set of stable projected relationships, however described in language; it is a world which, if examined minutely, could be seen to be a set of ever-changing, fluxing, moving, momentary "states of affairs."

This is not to say that the early and the later Buddhists denied our everyday ordinary experience; on the contrary, they realized that language, the most widely used medium of human communication, expresses the commonalities shared in our public discussion of our individual experience first-person knowing relationships in third-person (publicly shared) language. What the Buddhists did hold is that the world is held together by a set of publicly agreed upon conceptual tools which "glues" the world together and renders it understandable in accordance with, and because of, our conceptual frameworks. In other words, they did not deny public reality; rather they held that it was simply not an accurate picture of the way the world really is (*yathâbhûtam.*) This shift from a quest for stable enduring realities to a viewpoint that the world consists of ever-changing, ever-shifting relationships, "mutually glued" together by language and public acceptance of conceptual categories upon which people then acted, represents a fundamental metaphysical shift in the history of early Indian philosophy.

Again to somewhat oversimplify, the metaphysical position of the Buddhist represents a fundamental change from a subject-attribute metaphysics (i.e., Sanskrit grammars of the world) to process metaphysics. The Buddhists were concerned with the problem of dealing with the static components of language and experience in their philosophic descriptions. They were striving to bridge the gap between the perception of the ordinary individual and the supreme goal of perceiving the world process as it appears in itself. In the perception of things as they really are, one is freed from the projected conceptual and emotional distortions generated through our mutually conditioned worldly experience.

One is also freed from our habitual, mutual and culturally generated epistemic (knowing) grids. The *relationship* between the knower and the background is also a product of these reified grids. There is no nongrided grid. The Buddhists suggest that language and the coordinated relationships presupposed by language and its constant cultural reinforcement through years of preadult development constitutes a framework or grid of reified static epistemic components projected (and reprojected) on both an ever-changing personal inner (first person) environment and a simultaneous outer (third person) environment. Of this total environment, it can be said (at best) that *it* is in a *continual* state of flux. The latter "it," of course, begs the epistemic question. Thus they were led to conclude that if one assumes that the categories of language mirror reality as it really is, one commits the logical fallacy of circular reasoning. In a very restricted sense, their position is somewhat (but *only* somewhat) similar to Kant's. However, the Buddhists and Kant remain epistemological apples and oranges, not different types of apples.

To the question, "What are the most fundamental basic elements or categories of description in our collective perception of the world?," the Buddhist would answer that the question was a *logically complex* one and presupposes a metaphysical schema of ontological categories and epistemic elements (e.g., the object-attribute-dichotomy) which simply does not fit the case of experience as it really is.

The *general* Buddhist position seems to be that experience, either first person experience (one's own inner experience) and third person language customs of description *about* first person experience, consists of an infinite series of staccato-like unique moments (*ksana.*) Unfortunately, that these moments are either unique *or* nonunique involves (at least the suspicion of) circularity. Without examining the long history of these related arguments, consider that to be able to answer the question of either the uniqueness or nonuniqueness of momentary experience presupposes first that there be a position independent of both the "world as it is" and our knowing of it, from which we might compare. This obviously seems impossible without further and equally weak appeals to assumptions which lead one to a circular argument. The "individual," in his selective awareness of his own personal field of epistemic relations, knows the "contents" of that experience by means of generic concepts and habitual correlations between the five senses plus various mental components which involve relationships of knowing and describing.

These conceptual correlations are descriptive because they render the inner and outer worlds intelligible; also they are ostensibly descriptive rather than overtly prescriptive. Sometimes, however, these correlations are mixed together in such words as "love, hate"; i.e., they are both descriptive and carry an evaluative force. We strive to describe our, inner world by means of such public words. We communicate to others by using these words, the meanings of which are held in common by various individuals. These meanings are verified by subsequent behavior patterns called conversations, communication, rapping, etc. However, those Buddhists who developed the Abhidharma literature devised a new set of first person epistemic descriptive categories modeled largely on experiences in meditation. These Abhidharma dharma analysis concepts were held to more accurately describe the way the inner world "really is". These words and (thus) categories, and not *necessarily* the experiences, are held in common; therefore they constitute a third person public language *about* "private" experiences. One should note that there is nothing necessarily mysterious about the generation of such a technical, esoteric language. Musicians, race drivers, pimps, and others continually use such special languages. Ask yourself: What is the singular "it" in "He's got it all together"?

CAUSATION AND LANGUAGE

One of the most fundamental ideas which puzzled all the early Indian philosophers, including the Buddhists and the Jains, was that of the problem of causation. All of us are familiar with the concept of change in causation. But have we stopped to consider the basic problems involved in identifying change? One may devise questions which seem trivial (and perhaps all too true) by asking: If there is something changing, then there is something which is different in each succeeding moment, different than "it" was in the preceding moment. Therefore one may ask: Why do we know that the "thing" which is *now* observed to be a changed "thing" is the *same* "thing" which we identified in the previous moment?

This simple example exemplifies the relationship (and therefore the problem) between the identification of entities as the same (or as a different) entity in a state of continual change, the identity relationship between those changing entities, and the presupposed stable references common to such descriptors in a publicly operative language. Language consists of relatively stable units of description and prescription; the world, however, is changing from moment to moment, from day to day, and from lifetime to lifetime. How then may we justify the use of a stable system of conceptual referring units of language to describe something which is in a continual process of change?

The Buddhists also considered several answers to this problem. A great deal of philosophical discussion revolved around the two interrelated concepts of relational or dependent coorigination (*pratîtya-samutpâda*) and the ontological status of certain words — in Mâdhyamika, "own-being" (svabhâva) and language-constructs (*prajñapti.*) The origins of this "causal" concept of the twelvefold prior conditions (*nidânas*) may be found in various of the earliest texts, such as the *Pâli Nikâyas*. With such statements as "this thing being, that becomes; from the arising of this, that arises; this not becoming, that does not become," the concept of Buddhist causality seems to imply, in some scholars' eyes, a chain of physical and mental causality. However, if one combines the concept of sequential causality with the additional and equally fundamental tenet that everything is impermanent, that everything consists of a series of unique staccato-like moments, then the problem of "causation" does *not* become one of sufficient and necessary causal conditions through succeeding public moments.

The problem *does* become that of trying to distinguish the ontological criteria for distinguishing what constitutes an ontological category in one succeeding moment and its relationship, if any, with a specific "event" in a succeeding moment. Can this be done without blatant circular reasoning? Does the ordinary use of a general term (e.g., self, *âtman, pudgala*) presuppose that no legitimate (or possible) falsification can ever occur? In other words, do we beg the question in the language we use about what (basically) exists? Are we merely assuming the naive idea that if there is a descriptive word then there must be a distinct knowable entity to which the word supposedly refers? The Mâdhyamikas suggest an affirmative answer to the latter two (rhetorical) questions. Consider then the following: What is the "it" in "it is raining"? Hence the problem of identifying entities through time about which there are sequential, causal relationships is a logically prior and soteriologically important question. The Mâdhyamikas hold that although words and the world they map seem to be stable units in a changing world, identity and time are actually born fresh at every moment.

The general Mâdhyamika problematic has been succinctly described by Professor Matilal in *Epistemology, Logic and Grammar in Indian Philosophical Analysis*: "If we assume any object 'X' to be independently existent, then either we cannot give any consistent (rational) account of that object, by which we can avoid logical contradiction or our assumption of its independent existence will lead to some absurd consequence which will run counter to our experience " We shall consider a part of this problematic.

METALANGUAGES AND LEVELS OF ABSTRACTION

Language is deceptively transparent in that we are so bombarded by it and immersed in it that we seldom take time to become aware of how complex and subtle many of our linguistic actions really are. We understandably perform these linguistic actions with a fantastic degree of *unawareness;* certainly we perform them every day. To understand some Mâdhyamika problems, such as the use of different levels of language and their functions in the process of reification, we need to be more aware of the subtleties and bewitching aspects of language.

All of us have had occasions in which our grammar or word choice has been corrected (or at least criticized). At such times it is quite easy to distinguish what we said from what was said *about* what we said. In this context we may note that the former (i.e., what we said) is on a lower level of abstraction than the specific criticisms *of* what we said. The latter (i.e., talking *about* what we said) constitutes a metalanguage to the former object language. The writing you are now reading constitutes a meta-metalanguage to what was said in the preceding sentences; it is also a self-referring sentence much as is the Mâdhyamika statement that "emptiness is empty too." This rational concept is important, for the Mâdhyamikas (and most Indian and Western philosophers) were concerned with the problems of how we *must* talk about the world and, second, the characteristics of how the world *is* (or may be) apart from the ways in which we talk *about* it.

If we assume (falsely, of course) that the categories of language always reflect the categories and distinctions of the way the world is apart from our talking about it, we are led to make judgments about the world which have a reality solely in pieces of language and not in pieces of the world. The structure of our descriptive language does not necessarily reflect or mirror the structure of the world; they do not stand in an isomorphic relationship. If we take a word which expresses a set of abstract relationships between aspects of the world, and if we presuppose that the reference of that relationship-word (e.g., self) is a thing, then we project this thing into our felt expectations of the world because of our language, and not in accordance with the particular reality of the world yathâbhâtam (i.e., the way the world really is). The latter projective process is called reification.

An example of a category mistake may help. If I guided you around the campus and introduced you to the students, faculty, administrators, and passers-by, and showed you the buildings, the grounds, and maintenance vehicles, I would have showed you the university. However, after meeting all those people and seeing all those things, if you then asked me to point out the university, you would be making a category mistake. A category mistake is, in this context, a request for an ostensive, guided experience enabling one (falsely here) to couple a particular experience with a specific linguistic label; that is, to see the thing for which the word is merely a label.

The university is a word which does not refer solely to the earth or the people on the campus. Rather it refers to a complex set of relationships between these peoples and certain portions of the earth. Therefore, to ask that the university be pointed out is to reify the word university as if it were a thing in ways in which trucks, pedants, and sidewalks are things. The Mâdhyamikas attempted to show that the categories of description, the words used to describe the world in ordinary and philosophical language, of other schools was mistaken because it involved this fatal mistake of reification and the collapsing of levels of abstraction in the description of the way the world "really is"; thus they make a category mistake. The Mâdhyamikas also held that they had no alternate position to defend. Their position was purely metacritical and soteriologically therapeutic.

The central problem of Buddhist causation is one which concerns identity and difference, epistemic correlation and the relationship of language to the world; this in turn effects one's self-image, social role, actions, and values. Note that these are grounded in and *about* words and in words about other words; such words are the means of one's *understanding* of the world. We need now to distinguish levels of abstraction in the *Mûla-*

Mâdhyamika Kârikâs. Words are the primary (but not the only) medium through which the world is both known individually and through which intrapersonal communication about it is achieved. We must therefore distinguish levels of reference and levels of abstraction to avoid reification and category mistakes.

There are at least four orders of description and abstraction operative in the *Mûla-Mâdhyamika Kârikâs.* First, there is the ordinary language abstraction level of "things" in the world, e.g., trees, stones, and properties of relationships such as hate, anger, and love. Second, there are rival metaphysical and epistemological theories which utilize such generic terms as Abhidharmic *dharmas,* prakròti, etc., which the *Mûla-Mâdhyamika Kârikâs* holds are incorrect and inherently contradictory. The general word (in the text) for such generic terms is own-being (*svabhâva.*) These rival metaphysical and epistemological theories are the objects of the polemics in the *MûlaMâdhyamika Kârikâs.* Third, there is the third-order capstone *reflexive* concept of emptiness (sûnyatâ). Everything is empty, including "emptiness" itself. Fourth, there are certain implicit prescriptive relationships which involve a fourth order abstraction level, the concept of language-constructs.

ABHIDHARMA DHARMA ANALYSIS

There is a special class of words which we use to describe experiences within the particular boundaries of our own consciousness, the contents of which are not open to public observation. We may call these words first person epistemic descriptive words. They are first person terms, on the analogy of the first person pronoun (e.g., I, *aham.*) They refer not to publicly observable aspects of experience, but to the intimate known experiences within our *own* minds. They are epistemic because they are words which refer to categories of the different *functional* levels of mental (*citta, manas*) components of knowing. The most general Buddhist epistemological interpretation seems to be that the specific individual characteristics of any known entity is dependent upon the totality of causes and conditions (*hetu, pratyaya*) present in any given moment of its perception.

Therefore the relationship of subject-object and the epistemic discriminations present in the field of experience to one individual is a product of the effects of those forces in his experience over which he has ordinarily no conscious control. Second and simultaneously, the interrelated set of concepts by which he sorts out the known perception enables him thereby to *recognize* it as a meaningful set of relationships to him. All too simply put, everything is *what* it is because of what we habitually conclude it is not. From this position, the world consists (to the individual) of a series of interrelated projections and reactions. The reflexive nature of the problem of Mâdhyamika epistemology revolves around the twin problems of generic concepts (e.g., ownbeing, svabhâva) and their reifications. The affective and emotive concomitants of believing that the categorized world as approved by and reinforced by one's own culture *is* really constituted in the manner in which we normally view it, is to generate ties of care and suffering (*dukkha.*) The word is not the thing, but the thing is known through word-relations; to know a thing is to know a word and its web-like context. The relationships between references to word (language constructs, prajñapti) and things (e.g., self) constitute a core problem in Mâdhyamika.

Let us examine the concept of a dharma in Abhidharma dharma-analysis (*dharmavicaya*). Against this the Mâdhyamikas reacted. A dharma is an epistemic and descriptive component (not a static entity) in a reductive (and phenomenological) analysis of first person epistemic relations. It is an alternate map of consciousness. The Abhidharmists held that third person epistemological situations commonly misdescribed in ordinary language (first order language) are better described by reference to their alternate epistemic second order relationships than by their opponents' metaphysical postulates and ordinary language epistemic categories. This better second order description (dharma-analysis, an alternate metalanguage) of reality is composed of a finite set (75 for the Sarvâstivâdins) of mutually exclusive, totally exhaustive epistemic components of description, i.e., dharmas. By postulating these evaluative and epistemic categories these pre-Mâdhyamika Buddhists offered an alternate descriptive world view, from a first person epistemological point of view, which contrasts markedly with ordinary (first person and third person) descriptive language. Dharma analysis is simply an alternative conceptual map. It is a map within which one must shift the gears of one's language categories and assume a *new* vocabulary and conceptual syntax. Terminology operative in one map may not be operative in the other. While becoming nimble in this new language-land, one notices that old, warm, familiar conceptual friends such as "the self " and "the will," strictly speaking, are no longer operative in the new epistemic landscape.

These Buddhist Abhidharmists postulated two kinds of reality or truth (Pâli: *sacca,* Sanskrit: *satya*) which correspond to two language frameworks — two coherent, consistent ways of talking. First, is the ultimate or highest reality (Pâli: *paramattha-sacca,* Sanskrit: *paramârtha-satya*), the highest level of philosophical insight and religious aspiration. The emphasis is epistemological, not ontological. Operationally, this is equivalent to both nirvâa and seeing things as they really are (yathâbhûtam). Second, is conventional or mundane reality (Pâli: *sammuti-sacca,* Sanskrit: *samvctisatya*). This refers to the world of samòsâra (birth and death), or the world as we usually know it. It is the world endowed by us as having coordinated objects in time and space. It is a flashing flux consisting of an almost infinite variety of things and their melting attributes. We shall see that the problem of these two truths will reoccur, in some cases, almost word for word within the Mâdhyamika context. We shall also find that some of the same problems and terminology, found here in the earlier works of the Abhidharmists, will occur again in the Buddhist context of Nâgârjuna. Mâdhyamika, like Zen, illustrates that although the vocabulary and expository structures may change through time, the basic Buddhist problematics continue to be developed.

What *is* a dharma? First, it is not a thing. Dharma analysis is a completely different and alternative conceptual language framework. When we refer to things we usually feel that there is some object out there to which the particular features (attributes) we know about the object somehow adheres or belongs to the object. There is no such terminological or ontological analogy in dharma analysis language. That is, a dharma is not an object which possesses attributes; a dharma is only the attribute, without an object. What we *do* know about an individual dharma is all we *can* know. There is nothing behind it which possesses or controls it. The Buddhists maintain that within the scope of this alternative epistemic language framework, there are only a finite number of these categories called dharmas.

They are mutually exclusive, and in combination they are totally exhaustive. The various combinations of most (but not necessarily all) dharmas that constitute the concrete particulars of the first person experienced world at any given moment may more accurately and less misleadingly describe such first person experience by means of these dharmic categories than can ordinary language. Also we must note that there are *no* inferred causal relations between dharmas; dharmas simply arise, endure for a moment, and then go out of existence. They go to and come from nowhere. The rest is inference. As with the concept of karma, there is no agent, no overseer or administrator of dharmas (or karma) in their experienced combinations. Dharmas in combination at any given second constitute the world as described by this alternative conceptual framework; within the descriptive confines of this framework the Abhidharmists hold that we can truthfully say that we *know* the world as it is.

Just as dharmas in their various, ever-changing combinations constitute an alternate description of the variety of the conventional world with which we are all too familiar, just so is the concept of a self (âtman, jîva, pudgala) merely another component in our familiar but alternative descriptive framework, ordinary language. However, within the dharma analysis framework there is neither need nor evidence for postulating the descriptive category of self (âtman); an accurate description of first person experience is possible solely by means of the categories of the dharma list.

In our everyday lives, we generally act as if there is an enduring personal entity which somehow is *there* "in the back of" or "possessing" the feelings and concepts we call our own. We easily, but inaccurately, utilize this assumption in ordinary first person language *about* our own experience. However, the self for the Buddhists is merely one more inaccurate component among many ordinary language components which do not accurately describe experience as it occurs within the first person context. Thus the particular and ever-changing combination of these dharmas allow one to pose (emphatically) the problem of the self in a familiar word; however, the word self represents merely a nominal but not an ultimate (ontological) reference.

The number of dharmic category elements operative varies from moment to moment; thus within the context of the various combinations of these epistemic categories the Abhidharmists suggest that there are value tendencies and specific reoccurring experiences which are important for the development of certain moral qualities within the context of religious language. Notice the shift in vocabulary.

There are multiple levels of reference *within* both the dharma list and in the implicit explanatory rules of its use, e.g., the class of the general functions contributing to wholesomeness (kusalmahâbhûmika) and one of its members, for example, the dharma energy (vîrya). These terms and levels represent (implicitly) descriptive differences and normative rules of conceptual syntax. These particular dharmas represent what we, in ordinary language, would call states of emotion and/or value references which even in the context of dharma analysis are said to be attributes that *should* be encouraged. One such dharma is that of insight or wisdom (Pâli: *paññâ*, Sanskrit: *prajñâ*). If such value dharmas, in combination with others, tend to predominate through the choice of the individual, then we may shift the gears of our language from the conceptual categories from dharma analysis language to that of the ordinary language framework. This enables one to refer to a development of wholesome qualities which lead "one" toward the "attainment" of nirvâna. Strictly speaking, there is no attainment and none to attain. In other words, we shift the vocabulary of our language to dharma analysis from the language of ordinary first person talk.

However, if there is no self, then who does the attaining? The simplified answer is: No one does. The world doesn't shift; only our conceptual language does. When the language shifts, it carries us "we's" along too.

One must remember that according to the Abhidharmists, the world as it is experienced *should* be analyzed according to this alternative dharma map of consciousness. Within this dharma context, there is simply no appropriate way to *speak* of such concepts as the self, of strictly anthropomorphic moral values without making category mistakes; nor is there an appropriate vocabulary to talk about the ontology of things which are said to exist or possess the attributes and qualities we see in the world *as described in* ordinary language. When we *talk* about moral development, we must shift the gears of our language so that we may then utilize ordinary language and thus use such anthropomorphic and ego-centered concepts as one's development toward religious and/or moral goals.

It is most important to note that certain terms or concepts which have a clear and unambiguous function within the operative framework of anthropomorphic religious language are not appropriate within the alternative language framework of dharmas analysis. Two examples of these inappropriate terms in the dharma language frameworks are "self" and the idea of an uncaused, unconditioned existing entity which "possesses" certain attributes. These two concepts are simply excluded from being operative in dharma analysis language. If such a concept is said not to be contextually applicable but is still used, we must then call the user's attention to the set of fallacious relationships called category mistakes.

Let us explicitly ask such an inappropriate question to illustrate the confusion of categories within these two epistemic and language frameworks, i.e., ordinary language descriptions and dharma analysis descriptions. First, if we were to say that we understood the concept of dharma analysis as an alternative map of consciousness and then, second, we were to go on to ask "to whom do these dharmas belong?," we would then be making a category mistake. We would be requesting an answer to a question wrongly put. The presupposition of the question is that there *is* someone or something which owns or possesses dharmas. It is a logically complex question. If we were to answer the question in the way in which it is posed to us, we would be implicitly agreeing to the underlying assumptions about the self and about such inaccurately described epistemic components, the inaccuracies of which dharma analysis was designed to clarify.

"SELF" AND LINGUISTIC SURROGATES

We now turn to a linguistic surrogate of the "self" concept. To keep from making a category mistake such as the one concerning the self, the Buddhists devised this elaborate and technical dharma analysis vocabulary to prevent such category mistakes and to render a more accurate description of first person experience. In place of the concept of "self" they use the surrogate term "stream" or "current" (as in a stream), *santâna.* It is neither a dharma nor a replacement for "self." This word does *not* refer to a self or to any entity which either owns dharmas or appropriates the feelings of which we all are aware and do describe in ordinary language. The word santâna is a dharma analysis explicit *metaphor* which is a surrogate substitute for talk about "self." It refers to those specific and concrete concatenations of dharmas which are juxtaposed through the single dharma of memory (smrti, and of course other dharmas too) which we habitually and inaccurately *wish* to call a "self." The generation of the metaphor santâna is an accommodation to the felt needs within ordinary language, about Abhidharma questions which cannot be answered conventionally concerning a *specific* concatenation of dharmas — the analogy of one's own dharmas. Speaking conventionally, questions about the features of my dharmas *are* important to me, but to speak in such a manner is inaccurate. Thus there is the need for a special term in the dharma analysis vocabulary which allows one provisionally to refer to the concerns without totally violating the rules of (the conceptual syntax in the) dharma analysis language.

To summarize, in our first person ordinary language way of speaking these "self" feelings are connected or juxtaposed in our memory as belonging somehow to the stream about which we feel the need to make first person statements in ordinary language. Again, santâna is *not* a person; it *is* a descriptive metaphor which is an accommodation to nonenlightened, human ways of describing something which, until we come to know better through dharma analysis and samadhi, we shall continue to call first person experience and to which we then apply ordinary first person language words such as "self," "my," and "mine." To know the real difference of the two, "self" and "santâna," is to have insight or wisdom (*prajñâ, vipaúyanâ*).

THE ABHIDHARMIC BACKGROUND OF PRAJÑAPTI

We now turn to two Abhidharma schools concerned with ordinary first person experience as described in dharma analysis. They are the Sarvâstivâdins and the Sautrântikas. The Sarvâstivâdins (all dharmas exist[through time]) postulated as an explanatory concept (somewhat similar to the early and rather naturalistic explanatory concept of karma as found in the speculative *Brhadâranyaka Upanisad*) a particular (and odd) meta-dharma called *prâpti* (adhesion). It was held to be a real agent which exists (*dravya-dharma*). To the extent to which one knows an individual stream (santâna), to that extent the adhesion dharma is operative; since without it there would be an absence of the coherence and consistency *presupposed* by the metaphor *santâna*. It was said to hold these dharmas in their specific experienced combinations. It is the agent which maintains the consistency and coherence one finds within the stream of one's single santâna. The other Abhidharma school, the Sautrântikas, also reacted to the same problem of explaining the consistency and coherence we find in *both* ordinary language *and* dharma analysis descriptions. Both schools set out to answer the question of what gives consistency, nonrandomness, and coherence to first person experiences. The Sautrântikas answered by saying that all dharmas are fruitful fictions, or language constructs (prajñapti).

The Sautrântikas criticized the Sarvâstivâdin adhesion dharma by saying essentially that by appeal to dharmic experience, there would be no possible way to *explain* how this particular adhesion dharma could somehow glue together *experienced* dharma moments in the fairly consistent and coherent manner that they *are* experienced, that is, the dharmas which constitute one's individual momentary santâna. A metalanguage term is not necessarily operative at the object language level. By controlling other dharmas *prâpti* functions as a metaterm; but there is, by definition, nothing behind coordinated dharmas. So either prâpti, as an object language term, cannot adhere or grasp other dharmas and thereby bring about cohesion of dharmic experience, which violates both the reason for their postulation and definition; *or* prâpti, as a metalanguage term, can coordinate and group dharmas violating the implicit Abhidharmic definition which excludes the assumption that there is anything behind or in addition to the flashing staccato-like dharmas.

Another way to say the same thing is that no falsification of the dharma "adhesion" could ever occur in any possible (or theoretical) set of epistemic circumstances imagined by any individual whether he spoke *either* in the vocabulary of ordinary language or in the dharma analysis language framework. Therefore the Sautrântikas held that the Sarvâstivâdins were simply wrong. Furthermore, the Sautrântikas held that *all* dharmas then were subject to the same criticism, i.e., that all dharmas were merely designations, pragmatic language constructs, conceptual concepts whether conditioned through ordinary language or ordinary Buddhist language. As this point was expanded by Mâdhyamikas, the most important point is that the very *same word* fruitful fiction or language-construct (prajñapti) is used to describe emptiness (sûnyatâ) in the *MK*. The passage in which it is so described constitutes the highest metalanguage level within the Mâdhyamika system.

LINGUISTIC RAFTS: UPÂYA AND PRAJÑAPTI

One may also note that there is an analogy between this use of the word language construct (prajñapti) and a word which has a more religious connotation, skillful means (upâya). The latter term is developed in the religious literature called Prajñpâramitâ ("Perfection of Wisdom") Sûtras. This literature contains many important Mâdhyamika concepts such as emptiness (sûnyatâ). (It is helpful to read it along with the *MK* to grasp the religious implications of Mâdhyamika.) The Buddhist concept of karma implies (implicitly) that there must be some sort of accommodation by means of a variety of religious doctrines which are appropriate and suitable to the different karmic endowments of individuals; likewise there must be some metaconcept (upâya) which expresses the conclusion that all Buddhist religious doctrines are relative to and appropriate for the different levels of individual karmic capacities following the Buddhist path. In other words, religious doctrines are (ultimately) "pedagogical devices, fruitful fictions, gimmicks, teaching devices, or religious tricks."

In a similar way, the concept of language constructs (prajñapti) is an accommodation to the Abhidharma Sautrântika answer that all dharmas are *prajñaptis*, i.e., fruitful fictions, appropriate but unconfirmable outside the systemic context of dharma analysis language. As we shall see, there is also a Mâdhyamika acknowledgment of this problematic. So, just as *prajñaptis* are fruitful fictions within the religious language frameworks, we find in a similar manner that the word emptiness (sûnyatâ) is said also to be merely a prajñapti; it is a fruitful fiction which, if reified, leads to confusions which obviate the desirable religious ends for which both the concepts of emptiness and dharma analysis have been generated. Another way to say the same thing is that prajñapti(s), upâyas, and the "emptiness of emptiness" are reflexive metagrids which refer to relationships of epistemic evaluation but not to the ontological entities presupposed by the world's way of talking.

The Mâdhyamikas strove to refute not only ordinary language concepts; in addition they strove to refute both the second order Abhidharma dharma analysis concepts and the rival second order concepts of own-being (svabhâva) held by members of opposing non-Buddhist schools. Such concepts of the rival schools are Sâmkhya's nature (prakrti) and Nyâya's ontological and epistemological map categories. Own-being is a Mâdhyamika generic (cover term) for such general epistemic and metaphysical concepts. Therefore, to assume a similarity between the concepts and categories of description used in ordinary language and those of the words things, trees, stones, and love, and the second order concepts of dharmas, nature, and own-beings, is imply to collapse levels and to make category mistakes. The values and possible ontologies associated with each level are of different orders of abstraction and of different methods of verification and justification.

EMPTINESS

It is said about emptiness, the Mâdhyamika third order concept, that "emptiness too is empty" (*MK*, 13:7-8). This reflexive third order concept of emptiness is derivative and logically dependent on the two concepts of dependent (or relational) origination and own-being. The *Mûla-Mâdhyamika Kârikâs* holds that emptiness is a reflexive designation (prajñapti); it is a descriptive device which has no ontological import. In fact to reify emptiness is again to make a category mistake. Emptiness is a third order contextrestricted term; emptiness denotes or designates nothing. In a context it describes the relationship in which, combined with other correlated descriptions, it does indirectly refer to the epistemic "world" we know; it functions as a rule, a boundary or limitation of what we can know and what there is "out there."

To suggest an oversimplified analogy, with respect to orders of abstraction, emptiness is somewhat like the difference between a particular sound and the musical transformation rule that the sound of G flat is identical with F sharp in the European well-tempered diatonic scale. Ultimately they may refer to the same thing, but to describe one is not to describe the other. The former is a sound; the latter is a rule about the identification of a sound. So it is with own-being and emptiness; the former is a second order description. The latter belongs to the third order description of the ways in which first and second order concepts and terms are epistemically evaluated (i.e., a rule) and descriptively manipulated. That emptiness is empty means that the term emptiness has a restricted epistemic role but not an ontological descriptive role. It is not a "thing" word; rather it is a relation-word, the function of which is to evaluate and contrast the differences between what-is-happening and the methods and structures by which we recognize and communicate about what-is-happening. Emptiness is a nonreferring word *about* referring words; it has merely nine letters!

LANGUAGE CONSTRUCT: PRAJÑAPTI

The implications of the ontological status of language-descriptions and their correlations with publicly known objects in the furniture of the world lead one to the conclusion that all ontological descriptions are merely pragmatically useful but provisional fictions. They guarantee only that what is known is simply (and tautologically) consistent with what *is* known. That is, no conclusions about the transcendental or ultimate nature (yathâbhûtam) are *authorized* by statements verified by public or private observation; rather, what can be known (explicitly) *is* to be known. Language and its correct, consistent use guarantees nothing except itself; it is empty. Words, then, are useful, pragmatic constructs constantly reinforced by personal, emotional, conceptual habits and general sociolinguistic cultural patterns. Nothing more is possible; nothing more can be described. However, a language which possesses a reflexive component can describe its own ontological *limitations.* The language of Mâdhyamika does just this in the metaconcepts of emptiness (Sûnyatâ) and language constructs (prajñapti). Therefore the highest possible level of reflexive abstraction and description is that found in *Mûla-Mâdhyamika Kârikâ* 24:18. "It is dependent co-arising (pratîtya-samutpâda) that we term emptiness; this is a designation (prajñapti, the fourth order) overlaid (on emptiness, the third order); it alone is the middle path." (This passage, from the *Prasannapadâ*, is quoted from Robinson , *Early Mâdhyamika in India and China*, p. 40. The parentheses have been added by the author of this lecture.)

THE DOCTRINE OF TWO TRUTHS

The Buddha's dharma explanation relies on two truths: the worldly, conventional truth (*samvrtisatya*), and the highest truth (*paramârtha-satya*). Those who do not know the distinction between these two truths do not know the deep reality in the Buddha's teaching. Without relying on the expressional (truth), the highest is not taught; without arriving at the highest, Nirvânòa is not reached. The *Mûla Mâdhyamika Kârikâs*, firmly welded in conventional truth, possesses this important passage: "Everything is legitimately said for that of which emptiness is legitimately said; nothing is legitimately said for that of which emptiness is not legitimately said." Here is the familiar Indian idea first developed in the late Upanishads: there are different levels of "truth" (satya) for different levels of individuals who possess varied capacities and levels of understanding in accordance with their personal karmic endowments.

Conventional truth (samvrti-satya) is the repository of the category mistakes and the projected conceptual distortions leading to suffering and existential illusion. However, the highest truth cannot be known except by *using* conventional truth as a ladder, each rung of which represents an epistemological metalanguage. Emptiness (úûnyatâ, a term derived from early Indian mathematicians), like the zero, is a high-level descriptive word whose meaning is determined by its mutually defined/conditioned relations with the other conceptual components of the metalanguage grid, i.e., conventional truth. Emptiness is a reflexive term, a self-describer; thus it refers to *no* space-time empirical thing in our experience.

The doctrine of the two truths indicates there are progressively higher and higher levels of abstraction in which there is operative a sequence of metacritical points of view generated within each preceding metacritical position. It is within language that we talk about language. Since there can be statements about statements about language (ad infinitum), the postulation of an almost infinite series of metalanguages within which we refer to descriptions and capacities of language to describe the world is not an unfamiliar idea. For example, English grammar books about the German language are metalanguages to the German language. One could extend this chain infinitely. The language you are reading now is a meta-meta-metalanguage concerning the preceding statements about German.

Although the doctrine of the two truths seems to be strange and potentially contradictory, we wish to suggest that there is nothing intrinsically unfamiliar about the explicit rational structure of this doctrine. It seems to maintain that one must progress to different levels of understanding, realizing that the word "level" is a metaphor (since we are not talking about spatial relationships), until one reaches a point in the process of articulation and metacriticism where one is able to realize that there is a *reflexive* metacriticism directed at our medium through which we speak and learn -language. The word emptiness refers to the nonontological, nonempirical, referential status of certain pieces of the object languages. It does *not* seem paradoxical to me to suggest that it is through language that we postulate that, except in episternically restricted contexts, some language is ontologically empty.

There is nothing intrinsically or ultimately mysterious about the rational structure of the doctrine of two truths. I assume that there are parallels and isomorphic experiences common to us all within which we can understand the progressively sophisticated and ontologically restricting levels of metalanguage postulated in the Mûla-Mâdhyamika Kârikâs descriptions concering language and the world.

Thus the Mâdhyamikas are left with a set of distinctions and vocabulary about the relationship of language and the world in which it is soteriologically necessary to point out that there are subpockets of language within which the referents of such language are other pieces of language and not a postulated circular set of epistemic-linguistic behavior patterns. The doctrine of the two truths is the expression of a metaphorical ladder on which one progresses (up the ladder) by climbing different metalanguage levels until one realizes the reflexive turn at the top of the ladder. Hence one realizes that the ladder one has been climbing (metalinguistically) is itself as empty as the shadow it casts from the sun.

The doctrine of the two truths and emptiness are therapeutic in the sense that they diminish the magical attachments *to* and obscuration *of* our inner language. Also both diminish potential reificaions of language and its conceptual and value relationships. Abhidharma dharma-analysis theory is a way tounreify the world; it is a new epistemic map. Mâdhyamika emptiness and the doctrine of two truths are additional Buddhist ways to unreify the world and its concomitant furniture and values by unreifying the Abhidharmist and non-Buddhist's metalanguage maps. It is a logician's joke; however, to get the joke, one must ask: Who's laughing?

VALUE IMPLICATIONS

In a world in which it is said that even the monks of the first century B.C. Mahâyâna countries were not free from avarice, arrogance, lust, and dissipation, reflection upon the reflexive concept of emptiness frees one from the reification of abstract terms, names, and the conventional human epistemic relationships which are mistakenly taken as real and soteriologically efficacious. The realization (or the potential realization) of the emptiness of all things is a therapeutic ploy by which one may realize the differences between languages and things (including the thing called "self "), by reflexively including one's own perception in that realization. After many years of assuming that Nirvâna is the goal and that samsâra is the starting point, the Mâdhyamikas make the following startling claims:

The own-being of the *Tathâgata* (i.e., the Buddha) is the own-being of this world; the Tathagata is without own-being, and this world is without own-being. Samsâra has nothing that distinguishes it from nirvânòa; nirvâna has nothing that distinguishes it from samsâra. The limit of nirvâna is the limit of sansâra; there is not even the subtlest something separating the two.

MAJOR SCHOOLS OF THE MAHÂYÂNA YOGÂCÂRA

Yogâcâra (literally, "practice of yoga," meaning here the entire path of practice of the *Bodhisattva*) is a *Mahâyâna* method for the alleviation of sufferings through the loosening and shedding of the mentally constructed. Its treatises include descriptions of progressive meditational practices as well as accumulations of various tentative theories, all of which serve as a temporary alleviating purpose before their implications lead to their own dissolutions. The meditational practices take one further and further in the realm of "signless cognition," and involve a complete revulsion, turningover, revolution, of the entire basis of "one's" being (*âúrayaparâvrtti*). In the central *Yogâcâra* theory of the three kinds of reality, the mentally constructed (parikalpita) is what must be cleansed away from the interdependent (or relative, *paratantra:* the world of change) before there can be a fulfilled, or accomplished, state (*parinicpanna*). Since all theories are mentally constructed, the best they can be is therapesutic aids to the dissolving of mental constructions.

BRIEF HISTORY OF THE SCHOOL IN INDIA

Yogâcâra has found the attention of writers with the most diverse additional interests, and the specific expedients they have evolved have been markedly varied, which has also given the method an extraordinary all-inclusiveness.

THE SÛTRAS

The expedient of the three natures exists already in the *Pañcavimò Batisâhasrikâ-prajñâpâramitâ-sûtra.* Other sûtra influences on *Yogâcâra* have come from the *Avatamòsaka,* with its statement that everything is *citta* only, and the *Tathâgatotpattigunakâranda,* with its mirror consciousness and Tathâgata's consciousness free from stains. The entire method, with its delineation of calm and insight meditations, its theory of an appropriating consciousness which carries karmic continuity and from which all developed consciousnesses evolve, the three natures leading to the realization of emptiness, the different stages in the realization of emptiness (including the discarding of notions of egolessness), apperception-only, fulfilled, etc., by the emptiness of ultimate truth, and finally, the abandonment of the idea of emptiness itself, through the emptiness of emptiness, is found in the *Samdhinirmocana-sûtra.* This realization may take eons, or it may take place in a moment, says the Samdhinirmocana.

It is the Samòdhinirmocana which has been the most influential in shaping *Yogâcâra* methods. Other *Mahâyâna* sûtras containing parts of the method are the *Lankâvatâra-sûtra* and the *Suvarnaprabhâsa-sûtra,* but these may not antedate the great treatise writers of *Yogâcâra,* as the Samdhinirmocana apparently does.

MAITREYANÂTHA, ASANGA, AND VASUBANDHU

Some time in the fourth century, a Gandhâran monk named Asanga in dissatisfaction left the *Mahîsâsaka Hînayâsists* under whom he had been trained, and went off to the forest to meditate. According to the traditional account, after twelve years Asamòga received a vision of the future Buddha *Maitreya,* who dictated to him the *Yogâcâra* works which go under the name of *Maitreya* (*nâtha*): *Abhisamayâlankâra, Mahâyânasûtrâlankâra, Madhyântavibhâga, Dharmadharmatâvibhâga.* Asanga himself then began writing a series of books further developing the method — *Mahâyâna-Samgraha, Commentary on the Samdhinirmocana, Bodhisattvabhûmi* (?) — and succeeded in converting his brother, the great Abhidharmika *Vasubandhu,* to Mahâyâna. Vasubandhu subsequently produced prodigious amounts of treatises systematizing *Yogâcâra:* commentaries on the works of Maitreyanâtha and Asanga, *Karma-siddhiprakarana, Vyâkhyâyukti, Dasabhumika-sâstra, Vimòsatikâ, Trimòsikâ, Trisvabhâvanirdeka,* etc.

STHIRAMATI AND DHARMAPÂLA

In the sixth century the method finds two sharply differing interpretations at the hands of *Sthiramati* and *Dharmapâla.* The latter is the basis of *Hsüantsang's Vijñânavâda* and of its living descendant, the *Hossô* of Japan. All Tibetan schools have also been influenced by *Yogâcâra* methods, and *rNying-ma-pa* and *dGe-lugs-pa* masters have written differing interpretations of key *Yogâcâra* concepts.

PRACTICES

The meditational practices described in *Yogâcâra* works usually begin with some form of the applications of mindfulness (*sm\tyupasthâna,*), meditations on the flow of the body, feelings, consciousness-moments, and all moment-events. In *Yogâcâra* they are not just to be done introspectively, but *Mahâyânistically* into the bodies of others, resulting in an extraordinary empathetic understanding and the annihilation of the boundary between self and others. They may be accompanied by special meditations called the aids to penetration (*nirvedhâbhîya*), which shatter the holding fast to any mental cognition. This Path of Application is followed by insight meditations on the Four Noble Truths (this part of the practice is called the Path of Seeing), followed in turn by the calm meditation directed at the eradication of all afflictions, and which take one progressively through the ten Bodhisattva stages, each of which involves the complete carrying through of one of the *paramitâs* (perfections), which finally culminates in Buddhahood.

SOME YOGÂCÂRA THEORIES FROM MAITREYANÂTHA'S MADHYÂNTAVIBHÂGA

The capacity, or seeming necessity, for human beings to mentally construct is called the constructing-all-around of that which was not (*abhûta-parikalpa*). It exists (for otherwise there would be no problem), but it can be destroyed, and it is through its destruction that deliverance from sufferings is reached. For all constructions result in constrictions, and hence in sufferings. Mental constructions, however, have the reality of anything produced in a magical show: they exist as long as they exist, but only as apparitions, and they can be made to disappear entirely without a trace. The constructing-all-around of that which was not is the constructing apart (*vikalpa,* i.e., discrimination) of grasped and grasper, i.e., the split between object and subject. This is the basis of all further construction. An actual duality of any kind, however, is not found, finally, to exist (and there are meditations which can aid in shattering all these constructed walls making for dualities), and the absence of all dualities is emptiness. The nature of the universe had always been empty and unafflicted: all afflictions are adventitious and the result of constructions.

FROM ASANGA'S MAHÂYÂNASAMÒGRAHA AND VASUBANDHU'S TRIMÒSIKÂ, AND TRISVABHÂVANIRDEÚA

In addition to the six kinds of consciousness accepted by Abhidharma, there must be something additional to account for the sense of ego, psychic continuity, and the retribution of acts. The sense of ego comes from a special kind of consciousness called *manas* — like other Abhidharma concepts this is a cover term for an infinite number of broadly typified moment-events. Underlying the entire complex of consciousnesses is a series of subconscious or supraconscious psychic moments, called the store consciousness (*âlaya-vijñâna*), in which are deposited seeds (*bîjas,* potential transformations of the series) from all the other consciousnesses, through a process called perfuming or penetrating (*vâsanâ*). Each consciousnessmoment deposits a seed in the store-consciousness, and these seeds in turn influence all future cognitions. If this is so, it follows that all of our normal ways of perceiving involve constructions (e.g., the construction of definite external objects) and that all definable natures and specifications assigned to things are constructions, including everything that has been hitherto or hereafter said. This realization is termed *vijñaptimâtra,* apperception-only, is equivalent to emptiness, and, of course, negates the possibility of holding fast to apperception-only or any other theory.

LATER YOGÂCÂRINS

For Sthiramati, Dharmapala, and later theorists following them, attention shifts from the three-nature method to the theory of consciousness. Asanga had assumed a three-part relation of the basic cognition capacity with an object part and subject part of consciousness. This division had been practically rejected by Vasubandhu, but was taken up again by his pupil *Dignâga* and forms one of the basic disagreements between Sthiramati and Dharmapâla. To Sthiramati, all parts of consciousness are constructed;

to Dharmapâla, the three-part relation is of interdependent reality and dominated and fashioned by a consciousness which remains an absolute basis. It is Dharmapâla's view which can be called *Vijñânavâda,* and with some reservations, idealism, and it seems far away from the *Yogâcâra* of Maitreyanâtha or Vasubandhu, where all theories must be dissolved.

Chapter - 5

Evolution of Buddhist Schools and Literature

Conceived in Asia, Buddhism is an historic expression of a universal human ideal. It offers any individual or society a voluntary way of thought and conduct, based upon an analysis of conditioned existence, dependent upon supreme human effort, and directed toward the realization of freedom in perfect existence.

As a way of life, Buddhism has been variously understood, followed, and expounded by its adherents, and variously studied, interpreted, and described by nonBuddhists. Ethnic traits and social customs, subjective interests and partial knowledge, and many other factors have influenced the development of Buddhist beliefs and practices and thus condition an understanding of the nature of Buddhism by all concerned.

In its historical development and geographical expansion—in twenty-five centuries, over thirty Asian countries, and some twenty-two Asian languages—Buddhism has been designated in several ways. The Theravâda Buddhists in South and Southeast Asia traditionally speak of, and live in, the Buddha Sâsana. The Pâli term *sâsana* means "teaching, doctrine, discipline, religion" and "is perhaps the nearest equivalent of the modern expression, Buddhism. In its developed sense, it denotes a System. It has a socioreligious content and is used as a term of delimitation, with a touch perhaps of communal consciousness too,-of within the *sâsana*' meaning 'within the Buddhist system of faith and its rule of living.'" Hence, the *Theravâda* conception of Buddhism connotes an emphasis upon community spirit and order in life. The *Mahâyâna* Buddhists in East Asia and elsewhere customarily refer to the Buddha Dharma in Sanskrit, Fo-chiao in Chinese, Bukkyô in Japanese, Pulgyo in Korean, or Ph-tGiáo in Vietnamese, all meaning "the Teaching of the Buddha," while Chös in Tibetan signifies the Dharma or simply "the religion." Thus the Mahâyâna conception of Buddhism embodies an emphasis on doctrinal guidance in the conduct of life.

On the other hand, most Westerners or non-Buddhists tend to view and define Buddhism as a philosophy, noting its humanistic concern with right action being based upon right knowledge, or as a religion, perceiving the frequent incorporation of folk religious beliefs and practices in its institutional development. But "philosophy" and "religion" are primarily Western concepts which have had various meanings in the course of Western thought; although they have been transposed and translated into Asian terms (for example, *chê-hsüeh* and *tsung-chiao* in Chinese, *tetsugaku* and *shûkyô* in Japanese) they should not be used contradistinguishably to dichotomize the essential unity of Buddhist thought and practice. In other respects, however, Buddhism may be described as a philosophic interpretation and religious expression of a way of life, Asian in origin but intended to be universally human in outlook.

The simple definition of the Buddha as "the Enlightened One" in both epistemological and metaphysical or existential respects and the meaning of Bodhi as supreme "Enlightenment" remind us that Buddhism, however conceived, is primarily experiential in nature and purpose. It concerns the life, here and now, of each sentient being and thus interrelatedly of all existence.

Where, then, should our exposition of Buddhism begin? The Buddhist, living within the circle of the Buddha *Sâsana/sâsana* and following the Buddha Dhamma/ Dharma, would suggest that we start from where we stand in life: our perspective normally develops from our present, conditioned state of being; how could we begin from where we are not? Similarly, the non-Buddhist, living outside the circle and facing it from any direction, might well begin where he is, reaching out and touching the circle at his special point of interest. In any case, whether in study or in practice, Buddhism invites and accepts us as we are and is characteristically tolerant of those views and ethnocentric mores which typify us. To start in Buddhism we need no doctrinal assumptions but simply an awareness of the conditioned existence of ourselves and all others.

This concern with conditioned existence and one's immediate perception and subsequent study of it, this tolerance of all right-minded inquiry and stress on right action guided by right understanding, this philosophical-religious way of life for any individual or society, this reliance upon supreme human effort and the possibility of experiencing freedom in perfect existence—these principles characterize Buddhism and express its point of view in life. In short, freedom in thought is a prerequisite for freedom in existence.

The Buddhist spirit of reasoned inquiry is exemplified in numerous accounts of the Buddha's own conduct and advice to others. Two examples from early Pâli texts may be cited here:

And the Bhagavâ [the Buddha] said: "Monks, if others speak against me, or against the Dhamma [the Teachings] or the Sangha [the Order], you should not on that account either have a grudge against them or suffer heart-burning or feel illwill. If you, on that account could be angry and hurt, that would become a danger to your own selves. If, when others speak ill of me, or of the Dhamma or the Sangha, you feel angry at that, and displeased, would you then be able to judge how far that speech is good or bad?"

"That would not be so, Lord."

"But when others speak ill of me, or of the Dhamma or of the Sangha, you should rebut their statement by saying: 'For this or that reason, this is not the fact, that is not so, such a thing does not exist among us, is not in us.'

"But also monks, if others should speak in praise of me, in praise of the Dhamma, in praise of the Sangha, you should not on that account be filled with pleasure and gladness, or be lifted up in mind.

"Monks, if others should speak in praise of me, in praise of the Dhamma, in praise of the Sangha, and you, on that account, be filled with pleasure or gladness, or be lifted up in mind, that also would become a danger to your own selves.

"Monks, when others speak in praise of me, or of the Dhamma or the Sangha, you should admit the fact as right, saying: 'For this or that reason this is the fact, that is so, such a thing exists among us, is in US.'"

Now the *Kâlâmas* of Kesaputta heard it said that Gotama the recluse, the Sakyans' son who went forth as a wanderer from the Sakyan clan, had reached Kesaputta. . . . So the *Kâlâmas* of Kesaputta came to see the Exalted One [Bhagavâ]. On reaching him, some saluted the Exalted One and sat down at one side: some greeted the Exalted One courteously, and after the exchange of greetings and courtesies sat down at one side: some raising their joined palms to the Exalted One sat down at one side: some proclaimed their name and clan and did likewise; while others without saying anything just sat down at one side. Then as they thus sat the *Kâlâmas* of Kesaputta said this to the Exalted One:

"Sir, certain recluses and brâhmins come to Kesaputta. As to their own view, they proclaim and expound it in full: but as to the view of others, they abuse it, revile it, depreciate and cripple it [lit., deprive it of its wings]. Moreover, sir, other recluses and brâhmins, on coming to Kesaputta, do likewise. When we listen to them, Sir, we have doubt and wavering as to which of these worthies is speaking truth and which speaks falsehood."

"Yes, Kâlâmas, you may well doubt, you may well waver. In a doubtful matter wavering does arise. Now look you, *Kâlâmas*. Be ye not misled by report or tradition or hearsay. Be not misled by proficiency in the collections [citing the authority of religious texts], nor by mere logic or inference, nor after considering reasons, nor after reflection on and approval of some theory [taking delight in speculative opinions], nor because it fits becoming [has seeming possibilities], nor out of respect for a recluse (who holds it). But, *Kâlâmas*, when you know for yourselves: These things are unprofitable, these things are blameworthy, these things are censured by the intelligent; these things, when performed and undertaken, conduce to loss and sorrow,—then indeed do ye reject them, *Kâlâmas*. . . .

"But if at any time ye know of yourselves: These things are profitable, they are blameless, they are praised by the intelligent: these things, when performed and undertaken, conduce to profit and happiness,—then, *Kâlâmas*, do ye, having undertaken them, abide therein."

Similarly, the Buddhist spirit of tolerance is related in the *Upâla-sutta* of the *Pâli Majjhima-Nikâya* and has been summarized by the Venerable Dr. Walpola Rahula:

Once in *Nâlandâ* a prominent and wealthy householder named Upâli, a well-known lay disciple of Niganòtòha Nâtaputta (Jaina Mahâvîra), was expressly sent by Mahâvîra himself to meet the Buddha and defeat him in argument on certain points in the theory of Karma, because the Buddha's views on the subject were different from those of Mahavira. Quite contrary to expectations, Upâli, at the end of the discussion, was convinced that the views of the Buddha were right and those of his master were wrong. So he begged the Buddha to accept him as one of his lay disciples (*Upâsaka*). But the Buddha asked him to reconsider it, and not to be in a hurry, for "considering carefully is good for well-known men like you." When Upâli expressed his desire again, the Buddha requested him to continue to respect and support his old religious teachers as he used to.

In the third century B.C., the great Buddhist Emperor Asoka of India, following this noble example of tolerance and understanding, honoured and supported all other religions in his vast empire. In one of his Edicts carved on rock, the original of which one may read even today, the Emperor declared:

"One should not honour only one's own religion and condemn the religions of others, but one should honour others' religions for this or that reason. So doing, one helps one's own religion to grow and renders service to the religions of others too. In acting otherwise one digs the grave of one's own religion and also does harm to other religions. Whosoever honours his own religion and condemns other religions, does so indeed through devotion to his own religion, thinking 'I will glorify my own religion.' But on the contrary, in so doing he injures his own religion more gravely. So concord is good: Let all listen, and be willing to listen to the doctrines professed by others.'"

The Buddhist principle of tolerance for everyone is experientially based, and expressed, in the belief and practice that all beings can attain freedom in perfect existence: Nibbâna (Pâli term) in the Theravâda tradition and Nirvâna (Sanskrit term) in the Mahâyâna and Vajrayâna traditions. Such an ideal gives a profound meaning and direction to life for those who seek, find, and follow the Buddha-view as the Buddhist way. Here, the teaching of sGam.po.pa (1079-1153 A.D.), the Tibetan philosopher-saint, is particularly relevant:

He is convinced that every sentient being is capable of attaining enlightenment which is not so much a change from one extreme, Samsâra, to another, Nirvâna, but the ineffable experience in which both have ceased to dominate the thought of man so that he begins to live his life as transformed by pure transcendence.

Samsâra and Nirvâna are not entities, but interpretations of our experiences, and as such are both Úûnyatâ, which again is an operational term, not an ontological concept.

Although all sentient beings may attain enlightenment by their own efforts, because each is a potential Buddha, human existence is the most suitable occasion for such striving. It is not something self-evident, although we can only act as human beings. We must always be aware of human dignity and so respect others as equally worthy beings. By this awareness we gain confidence in being able to realize a thoroughly human and humane goal, and find the meaning of life. In this striving we are in need of spiritual friends.

They may be found at any level, because, if Samsâra and Nirvâna as interpretations have their common root in transcendence, which from the ordinary point of view is just nothing (Sunyatâ), whatever and whomsoever we meet serves as a symbol and guide to transcendence. Since all our experiences, from the most sordid aspects of life to the most lofty ideals, are of a transitory nature, it is important for us always to be aware of this fact and not to build on them as a solid foundation which will only obscure our mind and expose us to unending sorrow. In this awareness the transitory does not lead us into despair, but serves as a lamp to the everlasting which no words can express and which pervades everything temporal. . . .

Thus in whatever we do we are in duty bound to be aware of being human beings and of our task which must not be allowed to glide into a betrayal of human dignity but must be expressive of this dignity in benevolence and compassion.

BUDDHIST HISTORICAL DEVELOPMENTS

Since the sixth century B.C., Buddhist beliefs and practices, literature, and institutions have been spreading, developing, and adjusting to diverse societal environments in more than thirty countries in Asia and, in turn, influencing their cultures and religious ways of life. Since the nineteenth century, Buddhist ideas have also been of interest to Western philosophy, literature, music, drama, and other cultural arts.

In these and other respects, Buddhist historical developments are so complex and ramified that it is difficult to view them comprehensively. In fact, most present histories of Buddhism relate only a few of its regional or topical developments, since the subject cannot be surveyed in its entirety until more source materials have been collected, evaluated, and interpreted, further political-social-cultural histories of Buddhist areas have been written and consulted for reference purposes, and the principles of accretion and concurrent growth in the nature of Buddhist expansion have been better determined and studied. In short, Buddhist historical research and writing need to be much increased before the subject can be properly understood. Nevertheless, an attempt will be made here to indicate some of the significant Buddhist developments within periods of five centuries each.

During the sixth to first centuries B.C., the Buddha was regarded as a Teacher (*Satthâ/Sâstar*) and conceived as a Great Man (*Mahâpurisa/Mahâpurusa*) and Universal Ruler (*Cakkavattin/Cakravartin*); popular veneration of him developed into a Buddha-cult

(*Buddha-pûjâ*), which expressed and facilitated belief in him as the Exalted One (*Bhagavâ or Bhagavant*). The Buddha Dhamma/ Dharma was developed in doctrinal statement and scholastic interpretation and textually begun in Pâli, Sanskrit, and Buddhist Hybrid Sanskrit. Several Buddhist Councils or Conferences (*Sangîti*) are traditionally believed to have been held in India: the First Council at Râjagaha/Râjagriha (*Râjgir*) shortly after the Buddha's demise [its nature has been questioned by scholars]; the Second Council at Vesâli/Vaisâli (*Besarh*) some 100 or I 10 years later; and, according to Theravâda accounts, a Third Council at Pâtaliputta/Pâtaliputra (*Patna*) allegedly convened by Emperor Asoka of the Maurya Dynasty sometime in the third century B.C. [its historicity or nature has been questioned]; a *Vinaya* recital in the *Thûpârâma at Anurâadhapura* in Ceylon (then called *Sinhala[dvîpa] or Lankâ*) in the mid-second century B.C. and a Fourth Council in the Aluvihâra at Mâtale in Ceylon in the late first century B.C. [these Ceylonese councils are recognized only by the Theravâda tradition]. Accordingly, various Buddhist schools arose, coalesced, disappeared, or developed—totaling more than eighteen-among which the Theravâda, Mahâsanghika, Sarvâstivâda, and Sautrântika became the most influential.

The Theravâda tradition was widespread but established itself permanently in Ceylon; the Mahâsasghika fostered dissension from the Theravâda which, together with other factors, eventually resulted in the rise of the Mahâyâna tradition; the Sarvâstivâda tradition likewise spread, particularly in north-central and northwest India and probably also in Suvannabhûmi/Suvarnabhûmi; and the Prajñâpâramitâ doctrinal literature and related Mahâyâna tradition began to evolve. Buddhist followers as wanderers (*pabbajakas/ parivrâjakas or pabbajitas/pravrâjitas) and mendicants (bhikkhus/bhikus = monks, bhikkhunîs/ bhikunîs = nuns*) settled in residences (at first as âvâsas during the Vassa or rainy season retreat, later established as *vihâras* including *parivenòas*; in the next period as *sanghârâmas*), became communities (*sanghas*), and thus established Buddhist monasticism. Buddhist architecture, sculpture, and literary arts also developed, and the Buddha Sâsana/sâsana was identified with political and social welfare in various countries in India and Ceylon.

During the first to fifth centuries A.D., Buddhism spread rapidly from India eastward to Bengal during the Gupta Dynasty rule; southeastward to Suvannabhûmi/ Suvarnabhûmi including Fu-nan (Cambodia) and Champa (Viet-nam), and to Suvarnòadvîpa (Malay Peninsula in Indonesia); northwestward to Kâúmîra (Kâshmîr), Gandhâra, Bactria (capital Balkh), Parthia, and Sogdiana (capital Samarkand); thence eastward through Tokharistan to Central Asia (Tarim or Taklamakan Desert): Kâshgar, Yarkand, Karghalik, Khotan, Niya, Tukhara (Endere), Calmadana (Cherchen), and Kroraina (later Loulan, now Shan-shan in the Lobnor region) on the southern route and Kâshgar, Yarkand, Bharuka (Uch-Turfan), Kucî (Kucha), Agni (Karasahr), Turfan, and Hami on the northern route, and Tun-huang, An-hsi, and Yu-mên-kuan at the east end; to China principally from Central Asia but also from Southeast Asia by sea (also by land); and from China northeastward to Kogury, Paekche, and Silla (Samguk in Korea). During 399-414 A.D., the Chinese Buddhist pilgrim Fa-hsien visited Central Asia, India,

Ceylon, and Java (dvîpa). In northwest India, a Buddhist Council or Conference was convened, either in Kâúmîra or in Gandhâra at Purusapura by King Kaniska of the Kusânna Dynasty sometime during the first century A.D. which strengthened the Sarvâstivâda tradition; its authority is not recognized by the Theravâdins but is generally regarded by others as the Fourth Council (or the Third for the Sarvâstivâdins).

The Theravâda tradition developed principally in Ceylon but was also known in northern India; the Sarvâstivâda tradition (under several School names, and finally as the Vaibhâsika) appears to have prevailed in Suvarnabhûmi, Suvarnadvîpa, Kâúmîra, Gandhâra, and Central Asia and was known elsewhere in India, China, and Korea. The Prajñâpâramitâ literature and related Mahâyâna tradition developed mainly in the Buddhist areas of India, Central Asia, China, and Korea; this movement was in two general directions, the Mâdhyamika School and the Yogâcâra School, each with varying subschools. Conceptions of the Buddha further developed into the Bodhisattva doctrine and numerous idealized Buddhas in the Mahâyâna tradition, while the Buddha-cult was aided by Hindu Bhakti devotional practices and acquired variant ethnic forms as it was being adopted by different peoples. The Dhamma in Pâli accumulated scholarly commentaries and treatises, for example, those by Buddhaghosa in the fifth century, and the Dharma in Buddhist Hybrid Sanskrit expanded into the canonical literatures of various non-Theravâda and Mahâyâna Schools through translations, commentaries, and original compositions in many languages. Buddhist monasticism became institutionalized as Sanghas (Communities) or Nikâyas (Groups) in various countries, usually in close cooperation with kingship which was the prevailing form of political authority. Also in this period, Buddhist cultural pursuits made remarkable progress and established their traditional place in the heritage of Asian art.

During the sixth to tenth centuries A.D., Buddhism continued to spread, principally from Korea and China to Japan, and from India to Nepal and thence to Tibet. Foreign travel by Buddhist pilgrims and scholars increased: notably, Sung-yün and Hui-sang during 518ca. 521 to Central Asia, Tokharistan, (Sogdiana), Udyâna, and Gandhâra; Hsüan-tsang (or Yüan-chuang, 596-664) during 629-645 to Central Asia and India; I-ching (or I-tsing, 635-713) during 671-695 to Sumatra and India; Chien-chên (Japanese: Ganjin, 688-763); during 724-754 to Japan, Hainan, and China; and the Japanese Ennin (Jikaku Daishi, 793-864) three times during 838-847 to China. The Theravâda tradition grew in Ceylon whereas the Sarvâstivâda was still prominent in Central Asia and respected in Tibet but declined elsewhere; the Mahâyâna tradition generally prevailed, often concurrently with non-Buddhist beliefs and practices, in China, India, Japan, Korea, Nepal, Úrîvijaya, and Tibet and at times in Ceylon (Anurâdhapura), Champa (ViÇt-Nam), Chen-la (Cambodia), and Pagân or Pukâm (north-central Burma); the Vajrayâna tradition developed principally in northern India, Bengal, Nepal, and Tibet while some of its beliefs and practices were incorporated into the Chinese (Mi-chiao), Korean (Milgyo), and Japanese (Mikkyô) esoteric forms of the Mahâyâna tradition and apparently were also known in Pagân, Ceylon, and Southeast Asia (Srîvijaya especially).

Mahâyâna literature continued to be written, translated, and studied, while Vajrayâna texts developed in relation to it and the Tantras in India. The Buddha-concept and Buddha-cult culminated in the Buddhist pantheons and elaborate rituals in the Mahâyâna and Vajrayâna traditions. In every Buddhist country or area, the Sangha progressed or declined according to favorable or unfavorable royal and public support, societal conditions, and its own observance or negligence of monastic discipline. In architecture, painting, sculpture, literature, and the handicrafts, Buddhism everywhere made historic contributions to the cultural arts of Asia. In many ways this period was perhaps the most remarkable and significant in the history of Buddhism.

During the eleventh to fifteenth centuries A.D., Buddhist institutions declined, disappeared, or were supplanted by Hinduism or Islam in most of India and Central Asia; they were established in Lang Chang (Laos), Mongolia, various Siamese states, and presumably in Bhutan and Sikkim; they progressed in Cambodia, Ceylon, and Japan but not notably in China, Korea, or Nepal. By the end of the period, the Theravâda tradition had supplanted any remaining Mahâyâna elements in Burma, Cambodia, Laos, and Siam, whereas a reformed Vajrayâna predominated in Tibetan cultural areas. The Buddha concepts, cults, and pantheons expanded in doctrine, practice, and art forms; Buddhist literature continued to be written, studied, and edited as canonical collections; and in all areas, SaEgha institutions were subjected to occasional persecutions, societal strife, and monastic reforms. The Buddhist cultural arts presented remarkable achievements in Burma (Pagân), Cambodia (Angkor Thom), Ceylon (Polonnaruva), Japan (Kamakura), and elsewhere.

During the sixteenth to twentieth centuries A.D., the most significant changes in Buddhist traditional beliefs, practices, and institutions occurred in their varied responses to the challenges presented by European colonialism, Westernized ideas and values, modern technology, and educational reforms. Henceforth, conceptions and cults of the Buddha are questioned from non-Buddhist viewpoints, the Buddha Dhamma/Dharma is reinterpreted by nontraditional scholarship, and the Safigha is conditioned by relatively new forms of political and public interest. Adherents of the Theravâda, Mahâyâna, and Vajrayâna are beginning to study each other's traditions as components of their common heritage, and are attempting to determine, describe, and support the role of the Buddha Sâsana/Úâsana in the present-day world.

Asian Buddhists are making pilgrimages and visits to each other's country on an unprecedented scale; they are conferring with each other more frequently and internationally, as in the case of the Sixth Great Council (Chattha Sangâyanâ) in Rangoon during May, 1954 - May, 1956 [the Fifth Burmese Council was convened by King Min-don-min at Mandalay in 1871], the Buddha Jayanti celebrations in Asia during May, 1956November, 1957, and the World Fellowship of Buddhists Conferences of 1950 (Colombo), 1952 (Tôkyô), 1954 (Rangoon), 1956 (Kathmandu), 1958 (Bangkok), and planned for 1961 (Phnom-Penh). The reorganization of monastic education in the form of Westernized or modern Buddhist schools, colleges, and universities; the exchange of Buddhist publications among the laity and between scholars; the increasing social consciousness of the Sangha and public welfare activity by Buddhist lay organizations; and the ideological and material exploitation of Buddhist beliefs, personnel, and facilities by Communist governments—these new factors may become significant in the future development of Buddhism.

TRADITIONAL BUDDHIST WAYS, SCHOOLS, AND PATHS

In the historical development of Buddhism, various ways (*yâna*), schools (*vâda* and *vâdin*), and paths (*magga/ mârga*) have been devised and instituted as *means* for the realization of the Buddhist way of life and attainment of Enlightenment (Bodhi). These have naturally acquired varying ethnic-cultural expressions and characteristics and have often induced proponents of a particular approach to differentiate their own means from those of others, but usually there is considerable unity among them.

With regard to major Buddhist ways, the word *yâna* in Pâli, Sanskrit, and Buddhist Hybrid Sanskrit signifies "the way, method, or means by which one may attain Enlightenment." Chinese-oriented Mahâyânists, perhaps precedented by the views of the early Mahâsanghika/ Mahâsânghika School, customarily distinguish two kinds of *yânas*: Mahâyâna, meaning the Expansive Way, Means, Career or the Great Method; and Hînayâna, meaning the Exclusive Way, Means, Career or the Lesser Method. (These terms are often misleadingly translated literally as the Great Vehicle and the Small Vehicle.) In Buddhist Hybrid Sanskrit texts, three *yânas* are ordinarily distinguished: the Srâvaka-yâna for Srâvakas (Pâli: Sâvakas; disciples who become Arahants/Arhats through hearing the Teachings of the Buddha and are unconcerned about the possible Enlightenment of others); the Pratyekabuddha-yâna or Pratyeka-yâna for Pratyeka-buddhas (Pâli: Paccekabuddhas; those who attain Enlightenment by themselves and are unconcerned about the Enlightenment of others); and the Bodhisattva-yâna for Bodhisattvas (in this sense not quite comparable to Pâli: Bodhisatta, a being destined to become Enlightened; those who qualify as Buddhas but postpone their Enlightenment in order to help all sentient beings) or sometimes called the Buddhayâna. In these respects, they equate the Srâvaka-yâna and Pratyekabuddha-yâna with the so-called Hînayâna and the Bodhisattva-yâna with the Mahâyâna. To this threefold classification of Buddhist ways, Tantric Buddhists add their own way, the Vajrayâna.

In general, Mahâyâna and Vajrayâna proponents do not disavow the Hînayâna, or Srâvaka-yâna and Pratyekabuddha-yâna, as the basis of their way but regard it historically as having been incorporated into their own system. However, this view is not acceptable to adherents of the Theravâda, which is the earliest Buddhist tradition continuing today. Instead, they regard the Theravâda as the Teaching of the Theras (senior bhikkhus) which transmits the orthodox Dhamma of the Buddha and thus is to be distinguished from other Buddhist schools. In such cases, Bhiksu Sangharaksita has proposed that followers of the major Buddhist ways mutually understand each other's practices through a historical-sociological, comparative study of rituals in the Sarvâstivâda, Mahâyâna, and Vajrayâna traditions.

With regard to the principal Buddhist schools which implement the major Buddhist ways, the suffixes *-vâda* and *vâdin* are often used in their Pâli/Sanskrit names to connote "doctrine, theory put forth, creed, belief, school, sect" and its "proponents, adherents, followers." Numerous Buddhist schools evolved primarily from the Buddhist Councils, or from their resultant conditions for the wellbeing and spread of the Buddha Sâsana/Sâsana. They have been established in many countries according to societal and monastic requirements, have assumed certain ethnic-cultural expressions and characteristics, and have either survived as traditional Buddhist institutions or succumbed to external and internal disintegrating forces. Here only the most influential schools in Buddhist historical developments can be mentioned.The so-called Hînayâna movement once comprised many schools, totaling more than eighteen, of which there are various lists. Among these the most important were:

1. The Theravâda (Sanskrit: Sthaviravâda; the Teaching of the Elders, senior bhikkhus) which has continued as the orthodox Pâli form of Buddhism in Burma, Cambodia, Ceylon, Laos, Thailand, and certain Buddhist communities elsewhere in South and Southeast Asia.
2. The Mahâsanghika (Sanskrit: Mahâsânghika) which is believed to have dissented from the Theravâda at the Second Council at Vesâli/Vaisâli and fostered views which later culminated in the Mahâyâna.
3. The Sarvâstivâda (Pâli: Sabbathavâda; the Teaching or Doctrine that All *dharmas* [elements] Exist; also later called in some areas Mula-Sarvâstivâda or Abhidharma [variously defined, e.g. Special Dharma, Higher Religion, for the attainment of Enlightenment] and finally Vaibhâsika because of its dependence upon commentaries, *vibhâsâ*) which was once widespread in Suvarnabhûmi and Suvarnadvîpa, Gandhâra, Kâsmîra, and elsewhere in India, Central Asia, Nepal, Tibet, China (as the P'i-t'an-tsung and Chü-shê-tsung), Korea, and Japan (Kusha-shu, later Kusha-shû). The Buddhist Council convened by King Kaniska of the Kusâna Dynasty was essentially a Sarvâstivâda Conference. Among the notable Sarvâstivâda writers may be mentioned: Ârya Kâtyayanîputra, Mahâkausthila, Sthavira Vasumitra, Sthavira Devaúarmâ, Pûrna, Ârya sâriputra, Ârya Maudgalyâyana, Vasubandhu (*ca.* 320-400 A.D.; later a Yogâcâra writer), Sanghabhadra, Dharmottara, Dharmatrâta, Yasomitra, and others.
4. Several transitional schools between the Sarvâstivâda and the Mahâyâna, such as the Vâtsîputriya (Pâli: Vajjiputtaka, Vajjiputtiya), which held the doctrine of *pudgala* (*puggala;* the individual is neither the same nor different from the five *skandhas/khandhas*, compounding elements of being or agglomerations

comprising "personality": rûpa [material qualities], *vedanâ* [feeling], *samjñâ* [*saññâ, perception*], *samskâra [sankhâra,* coefficients of consciousness], and *vijñâna* [*viññâna,* consciousness] and challenged the adequacy of the *dharma* exposition by the Sarvâstivâdins; and the Sautrântika or Sûitravâda (Pâli: Suttavâda; the reliance upon original texts, *sûtrânta* or *sûtra*), also called Sankrântivâda (the view that the *skandhas* transmigrate from the former world to the later world), which developed the doctrines of conceptual construction (*vikalpa*) and representative perception (*bâhyânumeya-vâda* or *jñânâkâra* as *visaya-sârûpya*). Later, *Sautrântika* ideas coalesced with, or influenced, Mahâyâna doctrines to help form the Sautrântika-Yogâcara system and especially the Sautrântika-Mâdhyamika-Svâtantrika School.

Another important development was the Ch'êng-shih-tsung (Satyasiddhi or Tattvasiddhi School) in China, the SyÒng-sil-jong in Korea, and Jôjitsu-shu (in the mid-eighth century renamed Jôjitsushû) in Japan. The principal text of this movement was the Ch'êng-shihlun in Chinese translation by Kumârajîva (344-413 A.D.) from a now lost work (*Satyasiddhî-sâstra Tattvasiddhi-sâstra*), attributed to Harivarman (in India ca. third century A.D.), which may have been an attempt to synthesize the Vaibhâsika and early Mahâyâna doctrines. It should be noted that in Japan, Sautrântika studies were affiliated with Mâdhyamika studies.

Similarly, the so-called Mahâyâna movement has comprised various developments which are too numerous to be listed here by country. In general, however, the Mahâyâna may be viewed according to the following major schools or textual aspects.

1. The Prajñâpâramitâ literature was a doctrinal development rather than a school, although a Pan-jo-tsung (Prajñâ School) existed in China from the early fifth to about the seventh centuries A.D. "The composition of Prajñâpâramitâ texts extended over about 1,000 years. Roughly speaking, four phases can be distinguished:

A. The elaboration of a basic text (*ca.* 100 B.C. to 100 A.D.), which constitutes the original impulse;

B. The expansion of that text (*ca.* 100 A.D. to 300); then, as the third, we get the re-statement of the doctrine in

C 1. short Sûtras and in

2. versified Summaries (ca. 300 to 500); and

D. the period of Tantric influence and of absorption into magic (600 to 1200)." These texts were basically in Buddhist Hybrid Sanskrit with translations and commentaries in Central Asian languages or scripts, Chinese, Japanese, Tibetan, and Mongolian. Prajñâpâramitâ doctrines stimulated the development and spread of the Mahâyâna in India, Central Asia, China, Korea, Japan, Nepal, Tibet, and Mongolia and were partly known in Cambodia (Khmer period), the Siamese and Indochinese states, Indonesia (Srîvijaya period), and probably also in Burma (Pagân period) and Ceylon (Anurâdhapura period).

2. The Mâdhyamika, a formative school of Mahâyâna thought which expounds the main doctrines contained in the Prajñâpâramitâ literature, signifies a doctrinal position: those who adhere to the middle view (*madhya*) devoid of duality or implied contradictions (*úûnya*), and thereby avoid all possible extremes (*madhyamâ pratipad*) in attaining transcendent comprehension and understanding (*prajñâ*) for Enlightenment (Bodhi). The name Mâdhyamika is formed from the Sanskrit word madhyama (superlative of *madhya* meaning "middle, neutral, non-dual") and the *taddhita* suffix *ika*.

As an exposition of the Buddha Dharma from the Prajñâpâramitâ viewpoint, the Mâdhyamika is also sometimes called Madhyamaka Darúana (the Middle View) or Sûnyavâda (the Teaching or Doctrine of sûnyatâ). The Mâdhyamika in India was established by Nâgârjuna (*ca.* 150-250 A.D.) possibly at Nâgârjunikonda in Ândhradçúa in the south and at Nâlandâ in Magadha in the north, and was continued by his disciple Âryadeva (*ca.* 170-270 A.D.) in Ândhradçúa as well as at Nâlandâ, Pâtaliputra, and elsewhere, and by Nâgabodhi (third century A.D.) and Râhula(bhadra) (third century A.D.).

The School later became divided into two main lines: the Mâdhyamika-Prâsangika School (fifth to eighth centuries A.D.), founded by Buddhapâlita (*ca.* 470-540) at Dantapurî and continued especially by Candrakîrti (*ca.* 600-650) at Nâlandâ, by Úântideva (*ca.* 691-743) at Nâlandâ, and by Dîpamìkara Úrîjñâna (Âcârya Atîúa, 980-1053) at Vikramasîla; and the Mâdhyamika Svâtantrika School (sixth to eleventh or later centuries), founded by Bhâvaviveka or Bhavya (*ca.* 490-570) near Dhânyakataka which subdivided into the Sautrântika Mâdhyamika-Svâtantrika led by Bhâvaviveka and apparently continued by Divâkara (613-687) in China during 676/ 680-687, and the Yogâcâra-Mâdhyamika-Svâtantrika led by Sântarakcita (*ca.* 705-762) at Nâlandâ and continued by Srîgupta (early eighth century) and his disciple Jñânagarbha (early eighth century), Kamalaúîla (ca. 713-763), Vimuktasena, Haribhadra (9th century) and his disciple Buddhajñânapâda. Concurrently, the Mâdhyamika School developed in other areas under different names and, with the exception of Tibet and possibly Central Asia, according to a different group of texts now mostly extant only in their Chinese translations by Kumârajîva (344-413) and others.

These area developments of the Mâdhyamika outside India are:

(a) in Central Asia (mid-fourth to ninth centuries) called the Chung-tsung (Middle School) by the Chinese, and introduced from India;

(b) in China (early fifth to eighth centuries) called the San-lun-tsung (Three [Mâdhyamika] Treatises School) and other names, and introduced from Central Asia;

(c) in Korea (early sixth to seventh or later centuries) known as Sam-non studies [also a school], and introduced from China;

(d) in Japan (early seventh to fourteenth or later centuries) called the Sanron-shu Treatises Study Group) and after the mid-eighth century the Sanron-shû Treatises School), and introduced first from Korea and then from China; and

(e) in Tibet (mid-eighth to eleventh or later centuries) called Dbu-ma-pa (Mâdhyamika), introduced from India via Nepal and still studied there in its Mâdhyamika-Prâsangika and Mâdhyamika-Svâtantrika forms.

The Yogâcâra School (which emphasized ethical and meditative practices), with its epistemological-metaphysical development, the Vijñānavâda (the Teaching or Doctrine [*vâda*] that only "discriminating consciousness" [*vijñāna*] exists), was concurrent with the Mâdhyamika School as a formative movement in Mahâyâna thought and generally has predominated, particularly in its Chinese expression and extension in Japan, Korea, and Vietnam. It was established in India by Ârya Maitreya(nâtha) (ca. 270-350 A.D.), the reputed author of the Mahâyâna-sûtrâlamòkâra(-nâma-kârikâ), the Madhyânta-vibhanga(-kârikâ), the Dharma-dharmatâ-vibhanga, the Ratnagotra-vibhâga Mahâyânottaratantra-sâstra or simply Uttaratantra (attributed to him by the Tibetan tradition, but probably by Sâramati [ca. 350-450 A.D.]; later valued from the Mâdhyamika-Prâsangika standpoint), and the Abhisamayâlamòkâra(-kârikâ) or Abhisamayâlamòkâra-nâma Prajñâpâramıtâ-upadesa-sastra (later valued from the Yogâcâra-Mâdhyamika-Svâatantrika standpoint).

He was followed by Ârya Asanga (ca. 310390), author of the Mahâyâna-samgraha, the Mahâyânasamuccaya, and other works; the Yogâcâra-bhûmi-sâstra (containing the Bodhisattva-bhûmi) is attributed to him by the Tibetan tradition but to Maitreya(nâtha) by the Chinese tradition. In turn, Asanga converted his brother Vasubandhu (ca. 320-400) from Sarvâstivâda views; Vasubandhu wrote numerous commentaries and various works among which his Vijñaptimâtratâ-siddhi: vimòsika and trimòsika are particularly well known. Thereafter, the philosophical Vijñânavâada developed, especially by the logicians Dignâga (or Dignâga, ca. 400-480) and Dharmakîti (late seventh-early eighth centuries) and the commentators Dharmapâla (ca. 530-561) and Sthiramati (ca. 470-500). The Yogâcâra School and especially its Vijñânavâda development spread to East Asia and is still studied in China (Wei-shih = Vijñaptimâtratâ) and Japan (Yuishiki = Wei-shih, Vijñaptimâtratâ) as well as in Tibet. The Ch'an-tsung (Dhyâna School) in China and its developments and modifications in Korea (T'an-jong), Japan (Zen-shû), Viê + òt-Nam and elsewhere may have been considerably influenced in yoga practice and vijñâna doctrine by the Yogâcâra School.

A so-called Sukhâvatî ("Land of Bliss = Pure Land") movement, centering around a Buddha-pûjâ veneration of Amitâbha ("of Infinite Light") or Amityâyus ("of Infinite

Life"), apparently in the early centuries A.D. arose in India, developed in Central Asia, and became established as various schools in China, Korea, Japan, and Vietnam; for example, in China the Chingt'u-tsung (Pure Land School) in four transmissions among which Hui-yüan (333-416), T'an-luan (476-542), Tao-ch'o (562-645), and Shan-tao (613-681) are usually regarded as important exponents, and in Japan the Yûzû-nembutsu-shû of Ryônin Shônin (1071-1132), the Jôdo-shû of Hônen Shônin (1133-1212), the Jôdo-Shin-shû development of Shinran Shônin (1173-1262), and the Ji-shû of Ippen Shônin (1238-1289; precedented by Kûya, 903-972).

The basic texts are the *Sukhâvafî-vyûha* in large and abridged versions and the *Amitâyur-dhyâna-sûtra.* Numerous texts, besides those already mentioned, influenced the foregoing developments and, in certain cases, engendered particular Mahâyâna schools devoted to their study and veneration. For example, the Lankâvatâra or Saddharma-Lankâvatâra-sûtra (especially important for Ch'an-tsung/Zen-shû doctrine), the Saddharma-pundarîka-sûtra (basic for the Fa-hua-tsung or T'ien-t'ai-tsung/Tendai-shû and Nichiren-shû and influential elsewhere), the Mahâyâna-sraddhotpâda ("The Awakening of Faith in the Mahâyâna," attributed to an Aúvaghosa different from the author of the Buddhacarita), the Samadhinirmocana-sûtra (fundamental for Yogâcâra studies), the Avatamìsaka-sûtra or Buddhâvatamìsaka-sûtra, the Nirvâna-sûtra (the basis for the Nieh-p'an-tsung), the Ratnagotra-vibhâga Mahâyânottaratantra-sâstra or Uttaratantra probably by Sâramati (ca. 350-450 A.D.), the Suvarnòaprabhâsa or Suvarnabhâsottama-sûtra, the Samâdhirâja or Candrapradîpa-sûtra, the Kâranòda-vyîha, the Râstorapâlaparipròcchâ, the Dasabhumika-sûtra, and numerous other works in Sanskrit, especially Buddhist Hybrid Sanskrit, and other Asian language versions or original compositions.

The Vajrayâna (the Way of the Vajra), as a major Buddhist *means* for attaining Enlightenment, bases its monastic order on the Sarvâstivâda Vinaya and derives many of its metaphysical doctrines from Mahâyâna texts (perhaps more from the Yogâcâra than the Mâdhyamika) with certain Vedântic and Tantric influences. In addition, it characteristically employs advanced meditative practices and special, esoteric media for rituals: equipped with *abhiseka* (empowerment to perform, received from the teacher), instructed by *tantra* (special directions), and often through the *mandala* (diagramed sphere of power), one may integrate personality in Body with *mudrâ* (special hand-gesture), Speech with *mantra* (special spell) and *dhâranî* (special formula), and Mind with *dhyâna* (concentrated thought).

Hence, as a composite system, the Vajrayâna is sometimes called Buddhist Tantra to distinguish it from Hindu Tantra (although both were probably influenced by a common, general source) or Tantra-yâna or Mantra-yâna or Kâlacakra-yâna (the Means of Protection against the Wheel of Time [Destruction]), but all these are actually aspects or phases of its development. Four principal Indian/Tibetan kinds of Vajrayâna may be listed here:

(1) Kriyâ-tantra-yâna,

(2) Caryâ-tantra-yâna or Upâya-tantra-yâna,

(3) Yoga-tantra-yâna/,

(4) Anuttarayoga-tantra-yâna/Blamed-rGyud-kyi-theg-pa. Just as the major Buddhist ways (*yâna*) of thought and practice for the attainment of Enlightenment have been diversified in numerous schools (*vâda* and *vâdin*), so these schools may be grouped and classified according to the nature of their functional approach or method for attaining Enlightenment.

In this respect, five Buddhist paths (*magga/mâga*) may be briefly noted of which one or more may typify a particular Buddhist school and all, in varying degrees, implement the principal Buddhist ways. These paths are correlated with the Threefold Training, when fundamentally integrated, they comprise but one path or One Way.

Sîla-magga/sîla-mârga is the path of discipline and virtuous conduct: followed by the Theravâda in its Vinaya (especially the Dasa-sikkhâpadâni, Dasa-sîla, Pañca-sîla, and the *Pâtimokkha*), the Sarvâstivâda in its Vinaya (especially the *Prâtimokca*) now largely preserved in the Mahâyâna and Vajrayâna traditions, the Mahâyâna (especially the six, later ten, Prajñâpâramitâs and Bodhisattva-sîla practiced by the Mâdhyamika, Yogâcâra, and other schools), and the Vajrayâna (especially the six Pâramitâs and the *samaya* regarding every *abhiceka*). For school examplès in Eastern Asia, note the Lü-tsung (Vinaya School) in China and the related Ritsu-shu (later called Ritsu-shû) in Japan.

Jhâna-magga/Dhyâna-mârga is the path of meditative concentration consisting of mindfulness (*sati/smrti*), concentrative absorption (*samâdhi*), and attentive concentration in two aspects of tranquillity and fixedness of mind = concentration and introspection and intuition = transcendent analysis or insight leading to transcendent comprehension and understanding for Enlightenment (Bodhi): followed by the Theravâda (especially active today in Burma), the Mahâyâna (various schools, less so in the Sukhâvatî movement), and the Vajrayâna (as stressed in Tibetan cultural areas). For Mahâyâna school examples, note the Ch'an-tsung in China, the related Zen-shû in Japan, and remaining elements in Korea and Viêtnam.

Paññâ-magga/Prajñâ-mârga is the path of transcendent comprehension and understanding for Enlightenment (Bodhi) in which three kinds of *paññâ/prajñâ* may be distinguished: *sutamayâ-paññâ/úrutamayñâ-prajñâ* (that transcendent comprehension, understanding, knowledge gained from oral tradition), *cintâmayâ-paññâ/cintâmayîprajñâ* (that . . . gained from pure thought), and *bhâvanâmayâ-paññâ/bhâvanâmayî-prajñâ* (that . . . gained from cultured thought). This path is followed by the Theravâda (especially its analysis of the relational structure of existence, or study of the *Patthâna* in the Abhidhamma Pitaka), the Sarvâstivâda (previously in its Abhidhamma), the Mahâyâna (especially by the Mâdhyamika, Yogâcâra and other Schools), and the Vajrayâna (as practiced in Tibetan cultural areas). For Mahâyâna (doctrinal examples, note the vast Prajñâpâramitâ literature.

Bhatti-magga/Bhakti-mârga is the path of devotional practice, with some expectation of spiritual aid in return, centering around the veneration (*pûjâ*) of the Buddha in various forms or manifestations, eminent School founders, and the Buddha Dhamma/ Dharma —not found in the Ti-sikkhâ/Tri-siksâ and probably a result of the influence of Hindu Bhakti cults on the development of popular Buddhist beliefs and practices. This path is followed by the Theravâda (especially its thûpa-*pûjâ*), the Mahâyâna (especially in its veneration of School founders and certain texts: Buddha-*pûjâ* and sûtra-*pûjâ*), and the Vajrayâna (especially in its esoteric rituals).

Buddhânusmròti-mârga is the path of complete reliance upon the efficacy of Karunâ as manifested and offered by the Amitâbha Buddha (A-mi-t'o-fu in Chinese, Amida-butsu in Japanese) who is thus comparable to the Bodhisattva Avalokiteúvara. The idea is embryonic in the Theravâda tradition as Buddhânussati (Pâli term) or "mindfulness of the Buddha" but in the Mahâyâna as Buddhânusmrti (Buddhist Hybrid Sanskrit term) this means is the culmination of the Sukhâvatî trend in the Bhakti-mârga. It begins with a profound pietism and recollection of the Buddha-object (often orally) and is fulfilled through utter faith by the devotee. In short, the devotion (*pûjâ*) of the Amitâbha devotee becomes total piety which is realized as the complete, universal saving-compassion (*karunâ*) of Amitâbha expressed to/through/in that devotee (*parinòâmana*). In the T'ien-t'ai/Tendai Schools and the Chên-yen/Shingon Schools, this path is esoteric with Amitâbha identified with the Mahâvairocana (the Great Sun Buddha) in the manòdòala; in the Ching-t'u/Jôdo Schools, the path is based upon the vows or resolutions (*pranidhâna*) of the Bodhisattva Dharmakâra as expressed or stated in the Sukhâvatî texts; in the Jôdo-Shin School, the path is centered on the eighteenth vow of the Bodhisattva Dharmakâra declared in the larger *Sukhâvartî-vyûha*.

The foregoing classification of five Buddhist paths, or rather a fivefold Buddhist path providing the means for attaining Enlightenment, is admittedly arbitrary and has been compositely formed from a survey of Buddhist principles and practices. An earlier, traditional Mahâyâna conception of the Buddhist path in five degrees or phases is given in the *Abhisamayâlamkâra(-kârikâ)*, or *Abhisamayâlamkâra-nâma Prajñâpâramitâ-upadeúa-sâstra*, by Ârya Maitreya(nâtha), (ca. 270-350 A.D.) which "is considered by the learned Tibetan tradition to be the most important [of the five treatises by him] as

1) a summary of the *Prajñâ-pâramitâ-sûtras*, and
2) as the text containing the special theory of the *mârga* or the Path to the attainment of Nirvâna according to the Mahâyânistic standpoint."

Now, what is this "Path," and in what sense is it to be understood? First of all we have to mention the tradition which takes into consideration 3 kinds of individuals, viz. the lowest, the intermediate and the highest. The first is the ordinary worldly being who cares only for worldly matters, and the highest aim he can pursue can be only a blissful existence in a future life. For the individual of the intermediate and the highest kinds, i.e. the Hînayânist (Srâvaka and Pratyekabuddha) and the Mahâyânist Bodhisattva, respectively, the Phenomenal World represents nothing but an object of disgust and sorrow.

Such individuals accordingly search for a path to attaining a position in which one is no more disturbed by worldly turmoil. It is through constant meditation on the true aspect of existence and the full cognition of it that the deliverance from Phenomenal Existence can be secured. Accordingly, the general definition of the Path for the individuals of both the intermediate and the highest order is "the intuition (*abhisamaya*) of the Truth which is conducive to the attainment of Enlightenment, Nirvâna, and the liberation from the bonds of Phenomenal Existence." Its synonyms are "the way to Final Deliverance," "the process of the cognition of Truth," "the Vehicle" (*yâna* = *theg-pa*). It has five principal degrees which are:—

The Path of Accumulating Merit (*sambhâra-mârga* = *tshogs-lam*).

The Path of Training (*prayoga-mârga* = *sbyor-lam*).

The Path of Illumination (*darúana-mârga* = *mtho-lam*).

The Path of Concentrated Contemplation (*bhâvanâmârga* = *sgom-lam*).

The Final Path, where one is no more subjected to training (*aœaikca-mârga* = *mi-slob-lam*).

The last three represent "the Path of the Saint" (*âryamârga*), whereas the first two are regarded as subservient degrees.

Such are the degrees of the Path in general. But in regard to the various individuals, progressing on this fivefold Path, there is another threefold division, viz. the Path of the *Srâvaka*, the Path of the *Pratyekabuddha*, and the Path of the Bodhisattva (or the *Mahâyânistic* Path). These 3 different forms correspond to the 3 varieties of the faculty of cognition of the Truth [note: *srâvaka-yâna-abhisamaya-gotra*, *pratyekabuddha yâna-abhisamaya-gotra* and *tathâgata-yâna-abhisamaya-gotra*.] The *Srâivaka*'s cognition is that of the unreality of the Ego or individual as an independent whole [*pudgalanairâtmya*]. The *Pratyekabuddha* comes to the intuition of the objective unreality of the external world, without becoming free from the imputation concerning the reality of the subject that perceives. Finally, the Bodhisattva on his Path cognizes the unreality of all the separate elements of existence [*dharmanairâtmya*], which are intuited by him as merged in the unique undifferentiated Absolute.

The first 2 varieties are characterized as having only an egoistic aim, the liberation of the stream of elements [*samòtâna*] constituting one's own personality from the bonds of the Phenomenal World. In that sense the Path of "the intermediate individual" is defined as "the mental activity characterized by the aversion towards Phenomenal Existence and the desire of attaining salvation exclusively for one's own self." The path of the Bodhisattva is on the contrary regarded as essentially altruistic; it has for its aim the attainment of Buddhahood in order to bring deliverance for other living beings.

The principal constituent members of this process of meditation and intuition, the chief factors for the realization of the Path, are two in number, viz. the perfect quiescence of the mind (*samatha* = *Ÿi-gnas*) and transcendental analysis (*vipaúyanâ* = *lhag-mthon*). All the merits and achievements of the Hînayânist and Mahâyânist Saints on their Paths, the mundane [*laukika*] as well as the super-mundane [*lokottara*], are regarded as the result of these 2 cooperating factors, the latter being the most essential part, the foundation, of every kind of transic meditation. We have accordingly to speak of the Path as conditioned by the joint agency of the said 2 elements. Therefore all the Yogins, all the meditators, all the Saints on their Paths, must at all times take recourse to mental quiescence and transcendental analysis.

THE NATURE OF BUDDHIST LITERATURE

A satisfactory presentation of the nature of Buddhist literature would require a historical survey of Buddhist languages and literary forms, councils and school developments, monastic practices and scholarship.

The various spoken languages and dialects in which the Buddha Dhamma/Dharma has been expounded since the sixth century B.C. are too numerous to be listed, but it should be mentioned that the Teachings were first stated and transmitted orally (as still emphasized by the Chinese Ch'an and Japanese Zen Schools) and that recitation of texts, usually from memory, is still customary in monastic ceremonies (such as the Pâtimokkha on alternate Uposatha days in Thailand), in scholastic examinations (such as those held annually in Burma for the Tipitakadhara Grade), and in debates (as in Vajrayâna monasteries where argumentation may be enhanced by the ready citation of relevant texts).

Written Buddhist literature may be briefly described here according to language, script, and canon of the major Buddhist traditions.

The Tipitaka ("three baskets = containers = collections") of the Theravâda tradition was presented in Pâli from oral accounts, then recorded into early Sinhalese script (by stenciling *ôla* leaves with a stylus and treating them with *dummâlâ* oil) and is preserved in various editions in Burmese script (several editions and a Burmese translation in progress), Cambodian or Khmer script (an edition and Cambodian translation in progress), canonical Lao or *nang su tham* script (manuscripts, edition suspended), Môn script (manuscripts), Sinhalese script (several incomplete editions, one in progress, and a Sinhalese translation; largely the basis for the Pâli Text Society's edition in roman letters), and Thai script (several editions, and a Thai translation).

The several Tripitaka canons of the Sarvâstivâda, Mahâyâna, and Vajrayâna traditions were originally written in Middle Indic dialects, of which Buddhist Hybrid Sanskrit was developed particularly for this use, in various scripts notably Brâhmî, Kharosthî. Gupta (especially Central Asian Slanting Gupta and Cursive Gupta), Devanâgarî, and sometimes

Siddhamâtrikâ (commonly called Hsi-t'an in Chinese, Shittan in Japanese, Siddham in English) and Kavi (Old Javanese). Translations from certain Pâli, Sanskrit, and especially Buddhist Hybrid Sanskrit texts were made into various languages and from these versions further translations were made into other languages in addition to new texts being composed in all these languages; for example, from Buddhist Hybrid Sanskrit into Khotanese (or Khotanî Saka; in Khotanese script), Sogdian (in Sogdian script), and Turkic (in Uigur script) in Central Asia; from Central Asian languages or scripts as well as from Buddhist Hybrid Sanskrit, and some Pâli and Sanskrit, into Chinese (with terms transliterated and later translated); from Chinese into Korean (in Chinese characters, or *hanmun*, with Korean pronunciation and later in several scripts, principally *Ònmun* which has been revised as *hangml* and used together with *hanmun* as *kuhanmun*; now *hangml* is exclusively official), Japanese (in Chinese characters, or *kanji*, with Japanese pronunciation as *go-on* and occasionally *tô-on* and later in *hiragana* script added to *kanji* or used exclusively), and Vietnamese (Vietnamese adaptations of Chinese characters with Vietnamese pronunciation now officially romanized); from Buddhist Hybrid Sanskrit and some Central Asian and Chinese languages into Tibetan (in *dbu-chan* script) and therefrom into Mongolian (especially in *ka-lekka* and *'p'ags-pa* or Pa-sse-pa scripts) and therefrom into Manchu (in Manchu script).

The Buddha commanded his disciples to use only popular dialects in reciting his teachings. They followed his instructions for a time. Many dialects all over North India were thus used by local schools of Buddhists. One such dialect, perhaps originally spoken at Ujjain [in Central Province; formerly Ujjenî/Ujjayinî, the ancient capital of Avantî/ Avanti], was Pali, which was carried to Ceylon, Burma, etc., and became the canonical language of Southern Buddhism. Another such dialect, of unknown original location, began after a time to be modified by the local Buddhists to make it look more like Sanskrit, the socially respected language of their brahman neighbors. This Sanskritization was at first slight and partial. As time went on it increased, but it never became complete. Prakritic forms continued to be used, and many forms were mixed or hybrid, neither genuine Prakrit nor standard Sanskrit. The vocabulary, especially, remained largely Prakritic. Thousands of words were used which are unknown in Sanskrit, or not used there with the same meanings. To this curious language, which became widespread in North India, I have given the name Buddhist Hybrid Sanskrit. . . .

To such localities [where thriving Buddhist centers were established], and there were doubtless many others, came Buddhist monks, who may have been themselves of very different origins, bringing with them a sort of canon: a body of sermons, sayings in prose and verse, narratives of the Buddha's life and of his previous incarnations, and rules laid down for the conduct of monks and nuns. Many of these canonical works no doubt went back to the earliest times, and were carried everywhere in similar forms; but there is . . . no reason to assume linguistic unity even in the texts as they were thus spread by missionaries; there is no reason to assume *any* single "original language of

Buddhism." And whatever the dialects of the missionaries may have been, the sacred texts were soon adapted to the speech native to each locality. Thus various Buddhist "canons," at first loose and fluid, sprang up all over North India. . . .

In some Buddhist Hybrid Sanskrit works, especially the Mahâvastu, the Lalitavistara, the Mahâparinvâna Sîtra, and a few Prâtimokca and other Vinaya texts, we find passages, in both prose and verse, which correspond more or less closely to passages of the Pali canon. (Many others which no longer exist in Indic are found in Tibetan and Chinese translations.)

In such passages the vocabulary used in Pali and in Buddhist Hybrid Sanskrit is very largely identical, though the phonetic and grammatical forms are different. This is natural, for both were inherited from a common tradition older than either. Neither was translated from the other; each was adapated independently to the dialect of its locality, but used a word-stock that was to a considerable extent identical. And such words, common to both, continued to be used in both languages in new compositions dealing with the Buddhist religion, which were composed in the separate monkish communities where Pali and Buddhist Hybrid Sanskrit flourished.

This explains the fact that there is a very extensive agreement in vocabulary between Pali and Buddhist Hybrid Sanskrit. They have a great many words in common, and many of these words are not used, at least with the same meanings, in Sanskrit, or often even in other Middle Indic dialects. They are words inherited from the dialects in which the oldest Buddhist traditions were handed down. Nor are they by any means limited to technical terms of the Buddhist religion. Equally common are words which belonged to ordinary secular language.

The components and forms of Buddhist literature are naturally varied and may be suggested here by the following list of definitions. In Pâli usage, *gâthâ* is "a verse, stanza, line of poetry"; *nikâya* means "a collection, group, division, or section of a literary work," and *nipâta* similarly is "a group or section composed of chapters"; sutta is "a chapter or text, especially in the sense of a dialogue, discourse," and *vagga* is "a chapter or section in a book." In Sanskrit and Buddhist Hybrid Sanskrit usage, *gâthâ* is "a verse or stanza, the metrical part of a *sûtra*," *kârikâ* is "a concise statement in verse (especially of philosophical and grammatical) doctrines"; *sûtra* means "basic teaching, text," whereas sâstra signifies "commentary, teaching, treatise (often re a *sûtra* or *kârikâ*)," and *stotra* is "an ode or hymn of praise, verses to be sung (in contradistinction to *úâstra* which is recited)"; bhâcya is "an exposition or commentary (especially re a technical *sûtra*)," whereas *tòîkâ* is "a commentary (especially on another commentary)." The term *âgama* in Pâli, Sanskrit, and Buddhist Hybrid Sanskrit means "traditional or canonical text" and, in the *Mahâyâna usage, is applied particularly to the Four (out of Five) Nikâyas of the Sutta/Sûtra Pitaka: Dîgha-Nikâya/Dîrghâgama, Majjhima-Nikâyɿ/ Madhyamâgama, Samyutta-Nikâya/Samyuktâgama, Anguttara-Nikâya/Ekottarâgama or Ekottarika.*

With regard to the nature of Buddhist manuscripts, the following description of Chinese manuscripts recovered from Tunhuang must suffice. The manuscripts described in this Catalogue once formed part of a huge collection which was discovered about fifty years ago in a walled-up chamber adjoining one of the "Caves of the Thousand Buddhas" (*Ch'ien Fo Tung*) a few miles south-east of the Tunhuang oasis on the border of Kansu. Hollowed out in irregular tiers along the face of a steep cliff, these cave-temples were known in the rang dynasty as *Mo Kao K'u*, or "Grottos of Surpassing Height." They are said to have owed their origin to a saintly monk, one Lo-tsun, who began the work of excavation in A.D. 366. An account of him is given in an inscription of 698, and his name occurs again in a topographical fragment some 200 years later. . . . The manuscripts, mostly in the shape of long paper rolls, together with a large number of religious paintings, would appear to have been removed from different monasteries in the neighbourhood and hurriedly stowed away here for safety on the approach of an invading tribe, probably the Hsi Hsia, early in the eleventh century. And here they lay, apparently undisturbed and forgotten, for a space of nearly 900 years. . . .

A prominent feature in the Buddhist sections is the tailpiece or "colophon" (as it is here somewhat loosely termed) which is sometimes appended to the copy of a sûtra or some other holy text. Its main purpose is to make known the person who has acquired "merit" by having the copy made at his own expense, and the beneficiary (usually deceased) in whose direction he wishes the merit to flow. An exact date is generally included. Many of these colophons run to a few words only, while others are long and elaborate compositions with a pronounced literary flavour about them. . . . Another occasional appendage to Buddhist sûtras, occurring for some reason with special frequency in copies of the *Chin kuang ming tsui shêng wang ching*.

Paper was still quite unknown in Europe during the whole period covered by the Tunhuang MSS. . . . Broadly, it may be said that even the earliest fifth-century papers known to us are of remarkably good quality: they are generally a dull or brownish buff in hue, for the application of colouring matter does not appear to have been practised much before A.D. 500. . . . An agreeable lemon-yellow is characteristic of the earlier part of the sixth century. . . . Then, a little later on, a beautiful golden-yellow paper, thin and crisp, makes its first appearance. More uncommon shades of colour are orange-yellow, slate-blue, greenish-buff, pink or pinkish, sulphur-yellow, etc. . . . And one roll is actually composed of twelve variously coloured sheets. The staining fluid was evidently of an oily nature; sometimes it has been applied on both sides of the paper, but usually on one only. During the seventh century and part of the eighth, the texture of the paper used in the monasteries continues to be fine and smooth, and its colour a bright or brownish-yellow; but after the An Lu-shan rebellion a marked deterioration sets in, and most of it now becomes coarse and drab-coloured.

The handwriting of the copyists also passes through a series of changes which are similarly useful in furnishing a rough clue to the date. Throughout the fifth century and perhaps even later, a stubby kind of brush seems to have been in common use which was incapable of producing the fine, delicate strokes that are characteristic of Chinese calligraphy at its best. It was during the Sui dynasty that the art of handwriting appears to have reached its zenith—at any rate, as far as the present Collection is concerned. . . . Only the most carefully trained scribes were entrusted with the task of copying sûtras (supposed to be the pronouncements of the Buddha himself), as opposed to Vinaya and Abhidharma texts, commentaries, and the like; and that is probably the main reason why we find the production of sûtras suddenly diminished almost to vanishing point after the disastrous upheaval, which must have affected every monastery in the country.

A new departure of another kind also begins to be noticeable during the tenth century at Tunhuang. Ever since the invention of paper by Ts'ai Lun eight hundred years before, books had been written and circulated in the form of long paper rolls; hence the use, down to the present day, of *chüan*, the word for "roll," to designate a section or chapter. By far the greater part of the Stein Collection consists of such rolls; they are made up of a number of sheets, each about 1 ½ feet in length, very neatly and efficiently fastened together with glue. The earliest dated roll, a Vinaya text of A.D. 406 (no. 4523), is 23 feet long, which is slightly less than the average length of ordinary sûtra rolls. The longest of all the rolls are to be found among the commentaries, of which nos. 5587 (99 feet), 5597 (90 feet), 5287 (86 feet), and 5523 (80 ¾ feet) head the list in this respect. The handling of such rolls, or even those of more moderate length, cannot but be awkward for the reader, who has to be constantly unrolling and rolling up again as he goes along, and any reference to a required passage may involve serious loss of time. It is surprising, therefore, that the invention of some more convenient device for the construction of books should have been so long delayed.

The first step in advance was taken when, instead of being rolled up, the paper was folded into leaves of a reasonable size thus forming a volume that could be quickly opened at any point and shut up after consultation. A fairly good specimen, containing as many as 211 leaves, is no. 5591 in the Catalogue. The next innovation was the stitching of all the leaves together at one side, so that they should no longer fly apart in a long chain. This is the style in which Chinese books are still produced. It has the disadvantage, however, of leaving one side of the paper unused; and as scarcity of paper was becoming a problem in the Tunhuang region, booklets were generally made up of small separate sheets, intended for writing on both sides, as with us in the West. Of these there are several hundred specimens, varying greatly in size, in the Stein Collection; but it is fairly clear that even by the end of the tenth century they were far from having superseded the roll, for of the last fifty dated manuscripts only two are in booklet form.

About 70 of our MSS. may be confidently assigned to the fifth century, and for the next 200 years or so the output continues steadily to increase. The great majority of these early MSS. are copies of Buddhist sûtras that happened to be in particular favour at the time. During the following period, when the Tunhuang district passed temporarily under Tibetan rule, the flow of Buddhist literature rapidly dried up, and never returned to anything like its earlier level.

A small but very precious part of the Collection consists of 20 early specimens of block-printing, one of which, a complete and remarkably well-preserved copy of the

Diamond Sutra, bears a date corresponding to the 11th May, A.D. 868. Among the other printed documents are two calendars of A.D. 877 and 882, several prayer-sheets from the middle of the tenth century, and a very well printed set of Buddhist verses on the 24 examples of filial piety.

THE THREE VALUED COMPONENTS OF BUDDHISM

Buddhist beliefs and practices are fundamentally centered in, and traditionally guided by, three valued components called Ti-ratana in Pâli by the Theravâda tradition and Tri-ratna in Sanskrit and Buddhist Hybrid Sanskrit by the Mahâyâna and Vajrayâna traditions, or as a triad *Ratana-ttaya/Ratna-traya*, literally meaning "The Three Treasures, Jewels, Gems, etc." They are the Buddha (the Enlightened One), the *Dhamma/Dharma* (the Teachings of the Buddha, Doctrine, Truth, Law, Norm), and the Sangha [or Samgha, often Sangha] (the Buddhist Order, Community, Ecclesia).

These three components of Buddhism are interrelated: the Buddha taught and exemplified the *Dhamma/ Dharma* which was subsequently taught as doctrine and expounded by his followers who together came to comprise the Sangha as a monastic organization. Consequently, in their veneration of the Buddha, his followers, both ecclesia and laity, have tended to idealize him more than remember him historically.

Formal recognition of the Ti-ratana/Tri-ratna has become the primary, requisite act of veneration in all Buddhist schools and sects. As the most elementary initiation-ritual, it is called *Ti-sarana-gamana/Tri-saranagamana*, often rather awkwardly translated as "Taking the Three Refuges." *Sarana* may have a literal sense of "protection, shelter, abode, refuge, willed or chosen resort, etc.," but in the Buddhist context it means "that whereby I will transcend conditioned life and experience freedom in perfect existence and thus attain Nibbâna/ Nirvâna," for which no single translation-word seems appropriate. *Gamana* has the sense here of "striving for . . . finding shelter in".

When expressed as a formula (*Saranòattaya/Trînisaranâni*), the *Ti-sarana-gamana/ Tri-sarana-gamana* becomes at once an act of veneration, resolution, and elementary training. It is stated in Pâli as follows:

Namo tassa Bhagavato Arahato Sammâsambuddhassa: Veneration to the Blessed One, the Enlightened One, the Perfectly Enlightened One: *Buddham saranamì gacchâmi* To the Buddha, the (chosen) resort, I go. *Dhammam saranamì gacchâmi* To [the] Dhamma, the (chosen) resort, I go. *Sangham sarana gacchâmi* To the Sangha, the (chosen) resort, I go. *Dutiyam pi buddham saranamì gacchâmi* For the second time to the Buddha, the (chosen) resort, I go. *Dutiyam pi dhammam saranamì gacchâmi* For the second time to [the] Dhamma, the (chosen) resort, I go. *Dutiyam pi sangham saranamì gacchâmi* For the second time to the Sangha, the (chosen) resort, I go.

Tatiyam pi buddham sarananamì gacchâmi For the third time to the Buddha, the (chosen) resort, I go. *Tatiyam pi dhammam saranamì gacchâmi* For the third time to [the] Dhamma, the (chosen) resort, I go. *Tatiyam pi sangham saranamì gacchâmi* For the third time to the Sangha, the (chosen) resort, I go. *Saranattayamò.*

And now I betake myself, Lord, to the Blessed One as my refuge, to the Truth, and to the Order. May the Blessed One accept me as a disciple, as one who, from this day forth, as long as life endures, has taken his refuge in them.

Statements about the Ti-ratana and Saranattaya are made in various places in the Sutta Pitaka of the Pâli Canon, for example,

Whatever spirits have come together here, either belonging to the earth or living in the air, let us worship the perfect (*tathâgata*) Buddha, revered by gods and men; may there be salvation.

Whatever spirits have come together here, either belonging to the earth or living in the air, let us worship the perfect (*tathâgata*) Dhamma, revered by gods and men; may there be salvation.

Whatever spirits have come together here, either belonging to the earth or living in the air, let us worship the perfect (*tathâgata*) Sangha, revered by gods and men; may there be salvation.

The complex, ever-developing nature of Buddhism may be comprehended more easily by viewing the *Tiratana/Tri-ratna* as the quintessence of its thought and the *Ti-sarana-gamana/Tri-saranòa-gamana* as the fundamental of its practice. In time the Buddha was given various interpretations and cultish veneration by the Sangha and lay devotees, the *Dhamma/Dharma* was much elaborated by various schools, and the Safigha was diversified in different areas by historical circumstances. The conception of the *Ti-ratana/ Tri-ratna* as a formula (*Saranattaya/ Trîni-saranòâni*) and ritual (*Ti-sarana-gamana/Tri-œaranòa-gamana*) was developed especially by the Mahâyâna. For example, the *Uttaratantra or Ratnagotra-vibhâga Mahâyânottaratantra-sâstra,* attributed to Ârya Maitreya (nâtha) (*ca.* 270-350 A.D.) by the Tibetan tradition but probably by Sâramati (*ca.* 350-450 A.D.), states:

Now, what aim did the Lord pursue when he established the 3 Refuges [*trîni sarannâni*]? In order to make known the virtues Of the Teacher, the Teaching, and the Disciples, For the sake of (the adherents of) the 3 Vehicles And those devoted to the 3 forms of religious observance,-The 3 Refuges have been proclaimed (by the Lord).

The commentator, Ârya Asanga (*ca.* 310-390 A.D.), gives the following reasons for the establishment of the *Tri Sarana-gamana*:

In order to show the virtues of the Teacher, with a view to those individuals who adhere to the Vehicle of the Bodhisattvas and wish to attain the character of a Buddha, as well as those who, (though they have not entered the Path), are devoted to the performance of religious observances which have the Buddha for their object, it has been spoken and ascertained: —the Buddha is the refuge, since he is the Highest of Men [*buddhamì saranamì gacchâmi dvipadânam agryam*].

In order to make known the virtues of the Doctrine, for the sake of those who belong to the Pratyekabuddha Vehicle and start an activity for an independent apprehension of the profound Doctrine of Causality, as well as those whose religious fervour is directed toward the Doctrine (exclusively), it has been declared:—The Doctrine is the Refuge, since it is the highest for those who become dispassionate [*dharmam saranam gacchâmi virâgânâm agryam*].

In order to show the virtues of the Disciples [the Arhats and Bodhisattvas], who have embraced the Doctrine of the Teacher, with regard to the individuals who adhere to the Vehicle of the Srâvakas and proceed on the Path in order to attain (the fruit of Arhatship) on the basis of the instructions heard of others, as well as those who are devoted to the worship of the Congregation, it has been proclaimed:—The Congregation is a refuge, since it is the highest of communities [*samgham saranamì gacchâmi gannâm agryam*].—Thus, in short, for 3 motives, and having in view 6 kinds of individuals, the Lord has proclaimed the 3 Refuges and shown them in their variety. This has been done in order to promote the living beings to the 3 Vehicles respectively, the matter being viewed from the Empirical standpoint [*samìvrti*].

The conception and practice of the *Tri-saranòa-gamana* were further developed by sGam.po.pa (1079-1153 A.D.), the Tibetan Vajrayâna Master, who states in his great work, *"Jewel Ornament of Liberation"*:

The mind is purified as the substance of enlightenment in the following manner. Thrice by day and by night, in the desire to attain Buddhahood for the sake of all sentient beings, and once an hour to form an enlightened attitude, we should repeat the following words:

Until I have attained enlightenment I take refuge In the Buddha, the Dharma, and the noble Sangha. By performing acts of liberality and other virtues May I realize Buddhahood for the benefit of the world.

To attain enlightenment or to realize Buddhahood . . . a special training is needed. It begins with taking refuge in the Three Jewels, the Buddha, the Dharma, and the Sangha, which is of three orders: an outer order in which the Buddha is represented by an image, the Dharma by the Mahâyâna texts, and the Sangha by the Bodhisattvas, those who strive continuously for enlightenment; an inner order, where the Buddha is the patterning of our life, the Dharma the experience of Nirvâna and tranquillization, and the Sangha the Bodhisattvas who have reached the highest level of spirituality; and a mystic order, where Buddhahood alone is the refuge, as the foundation, path and goal of our life. Taking refuge in this Mahâyânic sense is always accompanied by the resolution to adopt an attitude which is directed towards enlightenment and the earnest endeavour to develop and cultivate such an attitude.

Chapter - 6

Mainstream Buddhism Thoughts and Its Different Schools

SARVÂSTIVÂDA/VAIBHASIKA

As with Theravâda, there is a complete Sarvâstivâda Canon with a Sarvâstivâda Vinaya and a Sarvâstivâda ordination lineage to go with it. But the name 'Sarvâstivâda' means 'the doctrine *(vâda)* that all *(sarva)* exist *(asti)*', and holding this 'doctrine that all exist', whatever that involves, is not the same as being ordained into the Sarvâstivâda lineage. To hold and defend this doctrine, and other associated doctrines, is to follow Sarvâstivâda as a doctrinal school. Clearly it is logically possible to be a Sarvâstivâdin (one who follows Sarvâstivâda) monk by ordination without being a Sarvâstivâdin by doctrine, and vice-versa. The association between a Sarvâstivâda ordination lineage and Sarvâstivâda doctrines is a contingent one, although in practice it may well have turned out to be the case that they were often associated in those monks (no doubt the minority) who were particularly interested in the refinements of doctrinal study. But not all the great doctrinal schools of Buddhism (traditionally there is said to have been eighteen doctrinal schools related to non-Mahâyâna Buddhism) had Vinayas associated with them.

As far as we know, for example, 'Sautrântika' is only a doctrinal school. Thus there could easily have been a Sarvâstivâdin monk, i.e. one ordained according to the Sarvâstivâda Vinaya, holding Sautrântika views. And, as we have seen, Mahâyâna as such is neither a Vinaya tradition nor a doctrinal school. It is rather a vision or aspiration, and an understanding of what the final concern should be for all Buddhists. That final concern should be to obtain perfect Buddhahood for the benefit of all sentient beings, and perfect Buddhahood for all is very much superior simply to becoming an arhat, liberated from one's own suffering. Thus there would be no contradiction in being a Sarvâstivâdin monk holding Sautrântika doctrinal views and also being a Mahâyânist. The universal association of certain doctrinal schools, notably Madhyamaka and Yogâcâra, with Mahâyâna is again a contingent matter not one of necessary connection, notwithstanding the fact that the founders and all the great teachers associated with these doctrinal positions do indeed appear to have held the Mahâyâna vision as well.

Here I want to outline briefly some of the more significant positions associated with doctrinal schools *not* historically connected directly with Mahâyâna. The 'doctrine that all exist' was indeed so important to Sarvâstivâda as a doctrinal school that it became a name for the school. But from the time of the composition of the 'Great Commentary' *(Mahâvibhasâ)* in the second century CE perhaps the expression Vaibhasika ('Following the Commentary') was the more formal name for the school. Among the geographical areas associated with Sarvâstivâda, Northwest India (such as Kashmir) was particular important both in doctrinal terms and also for its influence on Afghanistan, Central Asia, and thence China.

The Sarvâstivâda appears to have had a particular interest in ontological issues. This interest should be seen as an understandable response to the basic Buddhist concern with the ontology of the Self, and with seeing things the way they really are. These are essentially ontological issues, and in its concern with ontology Sarvâstivâda is quintessentially Buddhist. We have seen already that Sarvâstivâda drew a systematic distinction between the way dharmas exist, and the way composite entities that are constructions out of dharmas exist. The former are 'primary existents' *(dravyasat),* and those composite entities constructed out of primary existents are 'secondary' or 'conceptual existents' *(prajñaptisat).* Both truly exist, although in different ways. The 'doctrine that all exist' concerns serious and perennial philosophical issues arising out of apparent paradoxes when referring to non-existence, specifically here past and future dharmas.

If a dharma is impermanent, and ceases soon after its arising, how can something which has ceased and is thus apparently non-existent *do* anything? How can it serve as the object of cognition (as in the case of memory), and how can it bring about an effect (as in the case of *karman*)? Moreover the same could be said about future dharmas. How can they serve as the objects of cognition or action, as occurs in anticipation and motivated activity? In consideration of all this, the Sarvâstivâdin response was that past and future dharmas, while clearly not existing in the same way as the momentary present dharmas, must nevertheless still *exist.* Something simply non-existent could not serve as a cognitive (an 'intentional') referent, nor could it bring about an effect, as in the case of pain now occurring due to wicked deeds done in the past. Thus the 'doctrine that all exist' is specifically the doctrine that if a dharma is a future, a present, or a past dharma it nevertheless still exists.

The idea that dharmas exist when future, present, and past was felt by rival schools (notably Sautrântika) to sail very close to an entailment that dharmas must actually be permanent. This need not follow, however, providing one distinguishes sufficiently adequately existing as past and future from existing as present. We find a number of attempts to do this even prior to the *Mahâvibhâsâ,* and detailed in that text with priority given to an explanation by a certain Vasumitra. For the Sarvâstivâdin it was felt to be clear, as SaCghabhadra (late fourth or early fifth century CE) pointed out, that past and future dharmas cannot possibly be absolutely non-existent. They are not non-existent in the way that, for example, the horn of a hare is simply non-existent (i.e. there is no such thing). Anything that can be a cognitive referent exists. But in order to distinguish between existing simply in the way past and future dharmas do, and existing as present (and of course in that respect impermanent) dharmas do, the Sarvâstivâdin brought into play the notion of the 'own-existence' *(svabhâva)* of a dharma.

The own-existence, as we have seen, is possessed by each dharma inasmuch as it is a dharma and not a conceptual construct. Its own-existence is what makes each dharma an individual unique thing. It was easy to slide from this to the own-existence as the 'what-it-is-ness' of the dharma, and thereby what is referred to every time one speaks of that dharma. Thus the Sarvâstivâdin wants to say past and future dharmas exist simply in the mode of their own-existence *(sasvabhâvamâtra)*. That is, each past and future dharma exists as its 'what-it-is-ness', and it is this that enables one to cognise and to speak about it. This sort of existence is always possessed by a dharma of that type. It is atemporal and is what makes the dharma the dharma it is. In the case of dharmas it enables us to talk in abstract, divorced from particular instances, about dharmas. Thus we can speak of dharmas as 'not further analysable', for example, and we can classify them into a list of dharmas.

It is what we might call 'intentional existence'. It is the sort of existence anything has solely inasmuch as it is an object of language and cognition. The Sarvâstivâdin wants to suggest that because a past dharma has this sort of existence there is also no longer any paradox in a result occurring of something that is past and otherwise non-existent. But in addition to existing this way, present dharmas also have their characteristic activity *(sakâritra)*. That is, a present dharma does what that dharma does, as this is understood in the Abhidharma. The dharma's not yet doing what it does is what makes it a future dharma. Its doing what it does when the appropriate causes and conditions come together makes it a present dharma, and its ceasing to do what it does when the causes and conditions cease is what renders it a past dharma. This 'doing-what-it-does' is instantaneous, momentary. Thus any dharma's being present is momentary. This is fully temporal, and since we live in time and the occurrence (i.e. being present) of a dharma in time is momentary, momentariness is preserved. A further interesting dimension of Sarvâstivâda thought worth noting in passing is its analysis of causation itself. This is because, in a way that shows remarkable philosophical flexibility and adventurousness, the Sarvâstivâdin has no objection to the simultaneity of cause and effect, and is even willing to entertain the possibility that the effect may occur *after* the cause.

Sarvâstivâda speaks of six types of causes *(hetu)* and four types of conditions. The first type of cause is the *kâranahetu*, the 'efficient cause'. This consists of every other dharma apart from the dharma that is the effect itself, inasmuch as every dharma either contributes directly towards bringing about a further dharma (the cause as an 'empowered' *kâranahetu*) or does not hinder its production (the cause as a 'powerless' *kâraanahetu*). Thus all things are one way or another linked into the mesh of cause and effect. Here the class of *kâranahetu* is specifically said to incorporate causes that can be either prior to or simultaneous with the effect. Simultaneity is even more obvious in the case of the 'simultaneous cause' *(sahabhûhetu)*, which occurs where dharmas arise in a simultaneous relationship of mutual cause and effect. Thus, for example, since in a particular composite mental event (like perceiving a strawberry) consciousness and its mental associates arise together, if the consciousness occurs the mental associates must occur, and if the mental associates occur the consciousness must occur.

If either consciousness or any of the mental associates is missing here, the others as parts of this composite mental event could not occur. Therefore they are here all mutually and simultaneously cause and effect. The 'homogeneous cause' *(sabhâgahetu)*, on the other hand, referring to cases of sequential concordance between causes and effects, must obviously be prior to its effect. Thus, for example, prior good causes give rise to subsequent good effects, prior bad causes to subsequent bad effects. The *Abhidharmakosabhâcya* considers also the possibility that the cause could occur chronologically after the effect, with support cited both for and against from the central Sarvâstivâdin canonical Abhidharma text, the *Jñânaprasthâna*. The *Kosabhâsya* itself rejects this possibility, but throughout this text its author Vasubandhu frequently rejects even established Sarvâstivâdin positions in a way which shows his considerable sympathy with Sautrântika. From a Sautrântika perspective it is axiomatic that the cause must precede its effect.

A unique Sarvâstivâdin doctrine, and once more a topic of intense debate with others, is that of 'possession' or 'ownership' *(prâpti)*. Supposing I have an intense wicked intention. That wicked intention is an unwholesome *karman*, which will eventually produce suffering for me. But the intention itself is impermanent. When it has ceased (in Sarvâstivâdin terms, passed from present into past) what entails that its karmic result will occur in the future to a future stage of the same psychophysical continuum in which the original intention occurred? In other words, in imprecise everyday terms, given the Buddhist stress on complete impermanence, what ensures that the karmic result of my wicked intention will occur to *me* (albeit perhaps my reincarnation)? In the future all the factors that make up 'me' will be completely different, even though causally linked, to the factors that make up 'me' now. The answer the Sarvâstivâdin wants to say is that when the original intention occurred it was *mine*. That is, in addition to the intention itself there was a further dharma occurring in the series called 'possession', *prâpti*. The intention 'ceased' (i.e. for the Sarvâstivâdin, passed into 'past-mode'). As an impermanent dharma, so did the *prâpti*. But the *prâpti* generated another *prâpti*, this time the possession of 'having had that wicked intention'.

This *prâpti* too is an impermanent dharma. On its cessation it too generates another similar possession. Thus as a result of the original wicked intention part of my psychophysical continuum consists of an ongoing stream of *prâptis:* 'having had that wicked intention.' Eventually, when the conditions are right, a suffering as the karmic result of that original intention will occur. The original intention still exists in past-mode. And the suffering will occur in the psychophysical continuum which has the *prâpti*-series 'having had that wicked intention', not in another one. The karmic result will occur to me because I am the one who has the *prâpti*-series—*I* am the one who possessed the original intention, not someone else. Similarly, an unenlightened being has a possession of the negative taints (passions/defilements). Thus even when these taints are not actually operative in an unenlightened person, he or she is still not equivalent to an enlightened person, since the unenlightened person still has a possession of the negative taints. But in the case of an enlightened person not only has the possession of negative taints been completely disconnected, there is also a different dharma present, called 'non-possession' *(aprâpti),* which keeps the negative taints from ever occurring again. Both *prâpti* and *aprâpti* were simply rejected as unnecessary—indeed a rather absurd reification of abstract qualities into fundamentally existent dharmas—by rival schools like Sautrântika.

SAUTRÂNTIKA

The name 'Sautrântika' refers to 'those who take the sûtras as valid authority *(pramâna),* rather than later treatises *(sâstras)'*—where 'later treatises' means the Abhidharma. It is not clear how early this term came to be used for the group, or how it relates to another expression 'Dârsmântika', 'those who utilise the method of examples'. According to the Japanese scholar Junsho Kato (in Cox 1995:38-9), Dârcmântika may have been an expression originally used for the followers of Sautrântika by their opponents, while 'Sautrântika' was their own name for themselves. As we have seen already, there is no Sautrântika ordination lineage. Monks who described themselves as 'Sautrântika' were no doubt frequently ordained according to the Sarvâstivâda rite. Their Sautrântika affiliation indicated a particular stance in rarefied doctrinal discussion and debate. They were suspicious of the claim of the *Abhidharma Pitaka* to be the word of the Buddha, and while in fact sharing much in common with their approach they were even more suspicious of the philosophising of certain later Abhidharma scholars. As Collett Cox puts it (drawing on the work of Kato):

> [It] is best not to construe the appellation 'Sautrântika' as entailing either a distinct ordination lineage or a defined set of doctrinal positions. Instead, it indicates a reliance only upon the Buddha's verified teaching in the *sûtras* that ensures consistency with correct principle in contrast to the faulty reasoning that it is assumed undermines Abhidharma treatises. Doctrinally, the Sautrântika perspective can be characterised only by a rejection of the definitive Sarvâstivâdin position that factors exist in the three time periods. Therefore the appellation 'Sautrântika' could have been used to encompass a broad range of individual opinions that conform to these general guidelines, rather than to a defined and delimited set of doctrinal opinions.

The presence of scholars favouring Sautrântika shows the vitality and vigour of philosophical debate within the Buddhist tradition. Doctrinal positions were not identical with ordination lineages, and within one monastic group no doubt in the same monastery there could be radical disagreement and discussion concerning doctrinal issues within the context of a common rule of conduct. Followers of Sautrântika rejected the existence of dharmas in the three times, which they saw as necessarily implying the permanence of dharmas. Actually only the present dharma exists. The past dharma did exist, and the future dharma (assuming the appropriate conditions come together) will exist. But only the present dharma actually exists. The Sautrântika took from the Sarvâstivâda, however, the idea that the present stage of a dharma lies in the dharma's exerting its characteristic activity.

Thus exerting activity now becomes the mark not of the present stage of the dharma as such, but its very existence. To be in fact *is* to exert activity. But it follows from this that a dharma cannot be something that remains for some time *and then* exerts its activity. If hypothetically it existed for some time before acting then in the moments during which the dharma is not acting it actually could not exist, since to be *is* to act. Likewise if the dharma hypothetically existed for some time *after* exerting its activity then during those moments too it could not actually exist. Thus the dharma must exist only in the moment in which it exerts its activity. And that moment cannot itself have any time span, since if the moment had a time span then there would be the first moment of a moment, the second moment of a moment, and so on.

If that were the case, then there would be the question of whether the dharma exerted its activity in the first moment of the moment, or in a subsequent moment of the moment. Whatever the answer, it would follow that the dharma actually existed in only one moment of the moment. And this process could be traced to infinity, unless one adopted the position that the temporal moment is not itself divisible into further moments. Thus the moment in which a dharma acts, in which existence occurs, has no time span beyond itself. It is absolutely instantaneous, so short that it can only be said to mark the infinitely short time-difference between the non-existence before its existence, and the non-existence after its existence. To be is to cease. Cessation is the very nature of being, and is said to occur to a dharma through its very nature as existing. We are here stretching the bounds of language. The existence of a dharma is so short in time that we can no longer speak of it in terms of 'being' at all. Life can best be viewed as an ever-flowing process, and all talk of things, of beings, is merely practical convenience that can easily mislead and engender attachment and consequential suffering.

The epistemology of all of this was particularly considered by the philosophers Dinnâga (fifth or sixth century CE) and Dharmakîrti (seventh century), although it is not clear what the relationship was between their views and the Sautrântika of, say, Vasubandhu in the *Abhidharmakosabhâsya*. If what actually exists endures for an infinitely small period of time before ceasing, then it follows that we never really see what we think we see. By the time we have seen something, in any normal sense of 'seeing', that thing has ceased to exist. According to DiEnâga only the very first moment of a veridical perceptual act apprehends what is actually there, the dharma.

This first moment is thus referred to as 'without construction' *(nirvikalpa)*. The subsequent moments of what we normally call a 'perception' bring about the construction of a 'thing seen', which as we understand it is of course not a momentary entity at all. These stages are called 'with construction' *(savikalpa)*. Since, however, non-momentary entities do not exist these subsequent stages embody a process of falsification through linguistic and conceptual reification, associating the actual momentary real (known as the *svalaksana,* that which is self-characterising) with a non-momentary recurrently instantiated universal *(sâmânya)* which as something non-momentary cannot really exist at all. Thus what we think we see is actually a constructed image, as such a fiction, and by the time the image *(âkâra)* has been fully constructed the original dharma has long ceased.

Followers of Sautrântika utterly rejected the Sarvâstivâdin theory of *prâpti,* possession, along with the idea that a past dharma is able to cause its effect because the past dharma still exists as past. According to the Sautrântika theory, what happens in the case of *karman* and its effect is that when e.g. a wicked intention occurs the subsequent psychological continuum or series *(samtâna)* of the person who has that intention is no longer what it was. It is directly modified, and each moment of that series now bears the modification (perhaps analogous to a genetic imprint). The last moment of the series *qua* modified series has a special capacity to produce the effect. Thus the effect is the direct result of the preceding moment of the modified series, which is a result of the previous moment, and so on back to the original unwholesome intention. The images used to explain this process are of a 'seed' and 'perfuming'. Thus the unwholesome intention is said to have deposited a seed in the mental continuum, the nature of which is to transform until it issues in a shoot and then a flower, the result.

The existence of a flower is the result of a process of transformation from the seed. Lest we are misled by this image to think of the modification of the continuum as itself an additional dharma, it is said that that the influence of the unwholesome intention is like perfuming—there is no additional thing, but the series is now imbued with a different fragrance. It is not obvious however that the 'seeds' and the 'perfuming' could actually be there in the normal everyday level of consciousness (they are not constantly *experienced* as such). Some Sautrântikas put forward the suggestion that there is a subtle level of consciousness in which this occurs. That subtle consciousness continues through the lifetimes up until its destruction at nirvana. It is held to contain not just the seeds laid down by our intentions but also seeds for the emergence of the whole phenomenal world, implicated as it is in mental construction. Possibly too there are even innate seeds for wholesome activity. These theories contributed to the Yogâcâra doctrine of the 'substratum consciousness'.

Finally, as we have seen, the Sarvâstivâda speaks of three unconditioned dharmas. The most important of these is nirvana itself. As dharmas these bear primary or fundamental existence (they are *dravyas*). Followers of Sautrântika refused to accept with Sarvâstivâda that any of these unconditioned dharmas are entities, or existents *(bhâva*). They are just ways of talking about negations. Nirvanais not a positive thing, but a simple negation, a non-existent *(abhâva)*, the simple cessation and therefore non-existence of greed, hatred and delusion, suffering, and all the factors of samsâra.

THERAVÂDA

It is normal in introductory works on Buddhism to equate Theravâda with the Buddhism of its canon, the Pâli Canon. Since for convenience and historical reasons the Pâli Canon is usually the source employed for outlining 'basic' and therefore presumably earliest Buddhism, it is often not properly appreciated that the Theravâda is actually both a Vinaya tradition and a doctrinal school in just the same way as Sarvâstivâda is. Both Theravâda and Sarvâstivâda considered themselves to be simply explicating and defending the original Buddhism of the Buddha. Both could claim great antiquity, and both were nevertheless schools that developed over many centuries. Both schools had a very great deal in common, but also doctrinal differences between themselves and with other schools. As does Sarvâstivâda, the Theravâda as a doctrinal school relies extensively on exegetical works, such as the *Milindapañha* ('Questions of [King] Milinda'), the commentaries to e.g. the *Abhidhamma Pitaka,* and particularly the great *Visuddhimagga* ('Path of Purity') of Buddhaghosa. The Theravâda also contains among the texts in its *Abhidhamma Pitaka* one work, the *Kathâvatthu* ('Points of Controversy') which set out to combat other views and thus position Theravâda as a doctrinal school in opposition to its rivals.

According to questionable tradition, doctrinal divisions occurred between Sarvâstivâda and a group known in Sanskrit as 'Sthaviravâda' ('the Doctrine of the Elders') over the issue of the existence of dharmas in the three times. The Sthaviravâdins declared themselves to be 'Distinctionists' (Sanskrit: *Vibhajyavâdins;* Pâli: *Vibhajjavâdins*). They accepted that dharmas exist in the present but denied that they exist in the future. As regards the past, the Distinctionists wished to make a distinction between a wholesome or unwholesome intention that has already issued its karmic fruit, which could no longer be said to exist, and that which has not issued its fruit, which must be held still to exist. The name 'Sthaviravâda' is in Pâli 'Theravâda', and Theravâdins are indeed happy also to be called 'Vibhajjavâdins'. However the Theravâdins clearly cannot actually be identical with the Sthaviravâdins of this ancient dispute since the traditional Theravâdin position on dharmas in the three times is that only the present dharma exists.

A unique Theravâdin doctrine is that of the *bhavanga*. The *bhavanga* is an inactive level of mind that is still present when no mental activity is occurring, as in the case of so-called 'unconsciousness', or deep sleep. When e.g. a visual perception occurs, the mind emerges from the state of *bhavanga* and 'adverts' to the visual object, taking its part in a complex process of experiencing, receiving the data, and possibly investigating the object, determining it, grasping, it, and identifying it. But the Theravâda view is that at the end of each process of consciousness the mind returns to the state of *bhavaEga,* no matter how short that return may be. The *bhavanga* is also the level of mind that makes the link between a dying person and the rebirth.

When the causal link occurs, and consciousness first arises in the embryo in the womb, that consciousness is the *bhavaEga,* determined by the karmic forces of previous lives. The link between the consciousness of the dying person and that of the rebirth is direct. The Theravâda denies that there is any intermediate state *(antarâbhava)* between death and rebirth, a theory accepted by Sarvâstivâda and more familiar in the West from its espousal by Tibetans in works like the *Bar do thos grol* (Bardo thödrol; the 'Tibetan Book of the Dead'). The particular *bhavanga* is thus the basic level of mind of an individual, linking together all the experiences of a lifetime and making the connection between death and rebirth.

The Theravâda appears to have been much less interested than schools like the Sarvâstivâda in issues concerning the ontology of the *dhamma.* Nevertheless the very nature of the Abhidhamma project necessitated drawing some distinction between entities like cabbages and kings which are constructed out of dhammas, and dhammas themselves which even if the results of causes and conditions are not constructs and thus have their own unshared, unique, existence. This point is reflected in the definition of the *dhamma* which occurs in post-canonical Pâli texts: 'Dhammas are so-called because they hold *(dhârentî)* their own-existence' (Pâli: *sabhâva;* Sanskrit: *svabhâva*). This is of course the same idea that is so central to Sarvâstivâda ontology, even if the Theravâda seems to have had little interest in its implications and development.

PUDGALAVÂDA

The Pudgalavâda, or 'Doctrine of the Person' *(pudgala)* is a notorious doctrine particularly associated with two schools and their offshoots, the Vâtsîputrîya and the Sâmmatîya. Unfortunately very little of their texts survives, and most of our knowledge of their unique doctrines comes from attacks by other schools. The Theravâdin *Kathâvatthu* begins with this doctrine, there is an important discussion in the Sarvâstivâdin Abhidharma work the *Vijñânakâya,* and a lengthy section of the *Abhidharmakosa* is also devoted to its criticism. The best known surviving Pudgalavâda text is only in Chinese translation, but has been given the Sanskrit title of *Sammitîyanikâya Sâstra.* There is also extant in Chinese another Pudgalavâdin work given the title of *Tridharmaka Sâstra.*

Scholars often refer to the calculation by the seventh-century Chinese pilgrim to India Hsüan-tsang, that about a quarter of the Buddhist monks in India at that time were followers of the Sâmmatîya (or Sâmmitîya) school. The doctrine of the *pudgala* (Pâli: *puggala*) appears on the surface to be in tension with the Buddhist espousal of Not-Self *(anâtman).* It was strongly opposed by other Buddhist schools. Followers of

Pudgalavâda were accused of having all but ceased to be Buddhist. I agree very much with Rupert Gethin, however, when he points out that even if Hsüan-tsang is right in his calculation this may well entail only that the Sâmmatîya was the most widespread and popular Vinaya (ordination) lineage. It need not entail that all the monks so ordained held to the actual doctrine of the *pudgala*. Nevertheless, it seems likely that, in spite of the dearth of Pudgalavâda texts, the espousal of its characteristic doctrine was by no means rare among Buddhists in ancient India.

Lance Cousins has suggested that the earliest source for the Pudgalavâda controversy is the *Kathâvatthu* (third century BCE). This text is quite clear that the Pudgalavâdins hold that there exists something called a *pudgala* ('person(hood)') *from an ultimate point of view, as a real thing*. That is, the *pudgala* has the status of an additional dharma, an irreducible datum, a primary existent. This contrasts with the position acceptable to other schools, like the Theravâda or Sarvâstivâda, that any personhood, any *pudgala*, is just a conceptual construct (*prajñapti;* secondary existent), a name we give for practical purposes to the patterned flow of dharmas explained in terms of the five aggregates.

That the Pudgalavâdins wished the *pudgala* to be seen as existing from an ultimate point of view is also confirmed by the later *Vijñânakâya*. The issue is complicated, however, by the fact that the *Sâmmitîyanikâya Úâstra* (pre-fourth or fifth centuries CE) asserts that the *pudgala,* while existing and a datum that has to be taken into consideration, is actually a conventional conceptual construct. At perhaps the same time Vasubandhu, in the *Abhidharmakosa,* portrayed the Pudgalavâdins as holding that the existence of the *pudgala* is neither by way of a primary existent (a *dravya*) nor by way of a secondary existent. It is possible that under criticism the Pudgalavâdins gradually clarified their position.

Adherents of the *pudgala* claim that it is neither the same as nor different from the aggregates. If it were the same as the aggregates then the *pudgala* would be conditioned, and when the aggregates were destroyed the person would be destroyed. This would be annihilationist, and it would also entail that after death the Tathâgata certainly could not be said to exist. In that case why did the Buddha refuse to answer the question concerning whether or not the Tathâgata exists after death? On the other hand if the *pudgala* were different from the aggregates it would be unconditioned, in fact a Self like the *âtman,* and subject to all the Buddhist criticisms of the concept of a Self. This would be to fall into the great mistake of eternalism. Thus the *pudgala* is neither identical to nor different from the aggregates, and neither conditioned nor unconditioned. In fact, it is said to be 'indefinable' *(avaktavya)*. The *pudgala* is the subject of experiences, the doer of wholesome and unwholesome deeds, the one that undergoes karmic results, and the *pudgala* is also said to be what transmigrates. It is the *pudgala* that attains nirvana. Unsurprisingly opponents felt that this is in fact the *âtman* in another guise. The so-called *pudgala* necessarily must be reducible to the dharmas which make up the aggregates—in which case the Pudgalavâdins would hold the same view as other Buddhists—or must be a separate reality, in which case the Pudgalavâdins would hold the *âtman* position of Brahmanic Hindus.

And yet it seems to me that the Pudgalavâdins were wrestling with genuine philosophical problems here, and their position is perhaps subtler than it is often portrayed. The Vâtsîputrîya-Sâmmitîya tradition may have had a particular interest in Vinaya matters, in which case their concern with personhood could have been significant in terms of an interest in moral responsibility. It is indeed persons who engage in moral acts, and attain enlightenment. For moral responsibility there has to be some sense in which the *same person* receives reward or punishment as the one who did the original deed. It is persons who have experiences of love and hate. All this, as Pudgalavâda sources make clear, has to be taken as given. The question is, what is the status of personhood? It is arguable that personhood is an irreducible datum, and cannot be explained away in terms of constructions out of arms, legs, feelings, intentions, and so on, or a series of ever-changing mental and physical moments.

Constructions *presuppose* the existence of persons. And it is also arguable that if we cannot say the same person is reborn, or the same person attains nirvana, there would be no point in considering rebirth or the spiritual path. If all this is correct then personhood would not be reducible to the aggregates. And yet it is also clear that it makes no sense to think of personhood as a separate real thing, as if it could float free from the living being of arms, legs, feelings, and so on. Personhood is a different logical category from arms and legs. If we were to take a living human being, or a tree, apart we would not find personhood, or treeness, as an additional component. Thus it seems to me it might make sense to speak of an irreducible datum which is neither the same as nor different from the constituents.

Possibly it was something like this that the Pudgalavâdins were thinking of (through a glass darkly) when they started by speaking of the *pudgala* as a reality, existing from the ultimate (i.e. irreducible) point of view, before switching to speaking of the *pudgala* as conceptualised in dependence upon the aggregates. The Pudgalavâdins were constrained almost to the point of absurdity by the language of Buddhist scholasticism. The *pudgala* in itself, personhood in itself, cannot be spoken of. One can only speak of personhood in dependence upon living beings, beings with e.g. arms, legs, feelings, and so on, even if personhood is not reducible to arms, legs, feelings, and so on. Thus personhood in itself is indeed indefinable, it is *sui generis,* and personhood can be spoken of, conceptualised in dependence upon the aggregates, without this making personhood a conceptual construction *(prajñapti)* in the way in which this is understood by other Buddhist schools, reducible to the aggregates. Yet personhood is also not a separate reality *(dravya)* capable of being encountered apart from the aggregates. Personhood is not itself a conditioned thing in the way that e.g. the human body is, and for the Pudgalavâdin personhood continues from life to life and into enlightenment. Nevertheless personhood also could not be an unconditioned dharma or an *âtman*. For personhood is (possessed by) this person, Archibald or Freda, and it is the person Archibald who marries the person Freda, not some separate eternal reality marrying some separate eternal reality.

The Pudgalavâdins found puzzlement and problems where their fellow Buddhists found clarity and simplicity. The problem with unclarity and puzzlement is that they can often seem absurd. But some absurdity, it seems to me, may be profounder than it seems.

MAHÂSAMGHIKAS

The best known Mahâsâmghika doctrine is that of the 'supramundane nature of the Buddha', and the Mahâsâmghika 'supramundane doctrine' *(lokottaravâda)* appears to be characteristic of the school. Indeed the Mahâsâmghikas split into a number of sub-schools, one of which is known specifically as the *Lokottaravâdins*. A single text of this school survives in Sanskrit, the *Mahâvastu* (the 'Great Affair'), which describes itself as the Vinaya of the Lokottaravâdin sub-school of the Mahâsamghikas. The supramundane doctrine itself is found expressed in only a small section of this text, however. Stated briefly, the doctrine asserts that all the actions of the Buddha which appear worldly *(laukika)*, to be the same actions as ordinary people engage in, are in reality extraordinary, 'supramundane' *(lokottara)*.

All Buddhist traditions agree that once a person has become a Buddha he is radically transformed and no longer the same as an ordinary person. Thus the Buddha has various miraculous powers not possessed by ordinary people, he has the 112 marks of a superior person, his skin is capable of glowing with a golden hue, and he is even said to be able to live for an aeon if he so wishes. A Buddha, as such, is said to be just that—neither a man nor a god, but a Buddha. There is a saying attributed to the Buddha preserved in the Pâli Canon to the effect that though the Buddha was born in the world, he was not tainted by it. Perhaps it was sayings such as this which suggested to the Mahâsâmghikas that although he appeared to need to eat, sleep, bathe, undergo the effects of *karman*, take medicine, get old, and so on, in reality the Buddha was not subject to any of these needs.

The Buddha had actually gone beyond all these needs, and did all these things simply in order to conform to the way of things in the world. He appeared to be like the rest of us, but inside he was really quite different. Actually Buddhas do not experience hunger, tiredness, dirt on their bodies, illness, or any of the other taints of ordinary life. Actually, although Buddhas appear to be sleeping or teaching, walking or talking, really they are in constant meditation. That is, a Buddha is not *laukika* (worldly, from Sanskrit *loka*, world). He is *lokottara*. The word *lokottara*, literally 'beyond the world', supramundane, is an expression used throughout Buddhism in the context of enlightenment, the higher reaches of the path to enlightenment, and enlightened beings. To say a Buddha is *lokottara* is to say that he is not *laukika*, that is, he is not unliberated, he really is enlightened. This would be acceptable to all Buddhists. And what a wonderful, almost inconceivable, thing it is to be enlightened. What the Mahâsâmghikas are doing is giving a specific gloss on what the implications of this supramundane status are. That gloss stretches language and our expectations in admiration and wonder.

Sometimes modern books suggest that the Mahâsamghika doctrine is that the Buddha was actually an illusory being, a mere appearance, or a fictitious being, a 'magical emanation' perhaps from some transcendent Buddha who is really on another plane. This is, I think, a misreading of the meaning of *lokottara* here, and is not the doctrine of the Mahâsâmghikas in the *Mahâvastu*. There is no suggestion in the *Mahâvastu* that the being who was to become the Buddha was not actually born in this world, and did not actually become enlightened here. His birth is indeed accompanied by many marvels, but that is only to be expected in the case of one who had just completed many aeons of progressively more extraordinary spiritual cultivation. What *is* illusory or fictitious about a Buddha, according to the Mahâsâmghikas, is not his body as such, but his being subject to the normal human needs of food, sleep, washing, and so on. In other words, the illusion of the Buddha is the illusion of an extraordinary being appearing to be ordinary. And, crucially, there is no suggestion in non-Mahâyâna sources like the *Mahâvastu* that the Buddha did not die when he appeared to die. Much about his life may have been mere appearance out of conformity to the world. But his death was not.

There is one other doctrine found among some Mahâsâmghikas that I also want to mention in passing. There is a text known as the *Lokânuvartana Sûtra* ('The Sûtra of Conformity with the World') which survives in Chinese and Tibetan translation and which also contains strongly expressed the Mahâsamghika supramundane teachings. It has been claimed that this sûtra may be one of the sources for the *Mahâvastu*. The *Lokânuvartana Sûtra* is quoted and described in a later Indian source as a scripture of the Pûrvaúailas, which is known to be one of the sub-schools of the Mahâsamghikas. In that sûtra it is stated that all things, including all dharmas, are lacking in fundamental primary existence, intrinsic existence. This doctrine, of the universal emptiness of all things, even dharmas, is often thought of as characteristic of Mahâyâna sources like the *Perfection of Wisdom* literature and the Madhyamaka. Yet perhaps that is wrong.

Chapter - 7

The Philosophy of Buddhism

The story of Buddhism might be said to have begun with a loss of innocence. Siddhartha Gautama, a young prince of the Shakhya clan in India, had been raised in a life of royal ease, shielded from the misery and cruelties of the world outside the palace gates, distracted by sensual pleasures and luxurious living. But one day the fateful encounter with the real world occurred, and Siddhartha was shaken to the core. There in his own kingdom, not far from his gardens and delights, he encountered people suffering from sickness, old age and death; he brooded over these things, deeply disturbed that such was the fate of all beings. Then he encountered an ascetic holy man, a renunciate dedicated to liberation. The prince then undertook the great renunciation, forsaking his family, fortune and kingdom in pursuit of the path of liberation. The central, profound question that burned in Gautama was this: "How may suffering be ended?"

He became a wandering ascetic, practiced yogic disciplines and meditation, studied with various teachers, and attained high states of consciousness; but still he did not find the answer to his question. He practiced severe forms of asceticism, almost to the point of death by starvation, all without gain. Finally he sat under a bodhi tree, determined not to rise from meditation until he had gained the insight he sought. Not long after, he attained enlightenment; he became the Buddha — the Awakened One. He had ascended through various stages of meditative awareness, he had seen all of his past lives, and he had seen directly into reality, into the nature of existence and the causes of suffering and rebirth. He pondered whether to try to teach these insights, so subtle and difficult to grasp to others; perhaps it would be futile. But finally he decided that at least some of the people would be able to understand; perhaps more importantly, they could be shown the path to arrive at these insights themselves. He gave his first sermon to a few disciples in the Deer park at Benares, and then continued to wander and teach for the next forty-five years, until his death at the age of eighty.

He was born in the 6th century BCE, a time of great turmoil and political change in India; many were unsatisfied with the Vedic religion, and new teachings had emerged, among them the Upanishads. The Buddha stood largely outside the Vedic tradition, criticizing many of its central teachings. Nevertheless, he had been influenced by that tradition and his teachings in turn would have a profound effect on later teachers in the Hindu tradition, such as Shankara; even in such Hindu classics as the Bhagavad Gita, some reaction can be seen to Buddhist teachings. But later centuries would see the Buddha's influence wane in India and instead spread to other Asian countries. Today Buddhism has spread throughout the world. Various sects have arisen as later teachers have reinterpreted and expounded upon the Buddha's basic teachings. Buddhism may be considered a religion, a philosophy, a way of life, or all three; here we will deal mainly with Buddhism as a philosophical system.

BUDDHIST METAPHYSICS

The Buddha's main concern was to eliminate suffering, to find a cure for the pain of human existence. In this respect he has been compared to a physician, and his teaching has been compared to a medical or psychological prescription. Like a physician, he observed the symptoms — the disease that human kind was suffering from; next he gave a diagnosis - the cause of the disease; then he gave the prognosis — it could be cured; finally he gave the prescription — the method by which the condition could be cured.

His first teaching, the Four Noble Truths, follows this pattern. First, the insight that "life is dukkha." Dukkha is variously translated as suffering, pain, impermanence; it is the unsatisfactory quality of life which is targeted here — life is often beset with sorrow and trouble, and even at its best, is never completely fulfilling. We always want more happiness, less pain. But this 'wanting more' is itself the problem: the second noble truth teaches that the pain of life is caused by 'tanha' — our cravings, our attachments, our selfish grasping after pleasure and avoiding pain. Is there something else possible? The third noble truth says yes; a complete release from attachment and dukkha is possible, a liberation from pain and rebirth. The fourth noble truth tells how to attain this liberation; it describes the Noble Eightfold Path leading to Nirvana, the utter extinction of the pain of existence.

Another main teaching of Buddhist metaphysics is known as the Three Marks of Existence. The first is Anicca, impermanence: all things are transitory, nothing lasts. The second is Anatta, No-Self or No-Soul: human beings, and all of existence, is without a soul or self. There is no eternal, unchanging part of us, like the Hindu idea of Atman; there is no eternal, unchanging aspect of the universe, like the Hindu idea of Brahman. The entire idea of self is seen as an illusion, one which causes immeasurable suffering; this false idea gives rise to the consequent tendency to try to protect the self or ego and to preserve its interests, which is futile since nothing is permanent anyway. The third mark of existence is that of Dukkha, suffering: all of existence, not just human existence but even the highest states of meditation, are forms of suffering, ultimately inadequate and unsatisfactory.

The three marks of existence can be seen as the basis for the four noble truths above; in turn the three marks of existence may be seen to come out of an even more fundamental Buddhist theory, that of Pratityasamutpada: Dependent Origination, or Interdependent Co-arising. This theory says that all things are cause and are caused by other things; all of existence is conditioned, nothing exists independently, and there is no First Cause. There was no beginning to the chain of causality; it is useless to speculate how phenomenal existence started. However, it can be ended, and that is the ultimate goal of Buddhism - the ultimate liberation of all creatures from the pain of existence.

Sometimes this causality is spoken of as a circular linking of twelve different factors; if the chain of causality can be broken, existence is ended and liberation attained. One of these factors is attachment or craving, tanha, and another is ignorance; these two are emphasized as being the weak links in the chain, the place to make a break. To overcome selfish craving, one cultivates the heart through compassion; to eliminate ignorance one cultivates the mind through wisdom. Compassion and wisdom are twin virtues in Buddhism, and are cultured by ethical behavior and meditation, respectively. It is a process of self-discipline and self-development which emphasizes the heart and mind equally, and insists that both working together are necessary for enlightenment.

If Buddhism can be seen as a process of personal development, one may well ask: what is a person, if not a soul or self? In keeping with the ideas of dependent origination, Buddhism views a person as a changing configuration of five factors, or 'skandhas.' First there is the world of physical form; the body and all material objects, including the sense organs. Second there is the factor of sensation or feeling; here are found the five senses as well as mind, which in Buddhism is considered a sense organ. The mind senses thoughts and ideas much the same as the eye senses light or the ear senses air pressure. Thirdly, there is the factor of perception; here is the faculty which recognizes physical and mental objects. Fourth there is the factor variously called impulses or mental formulations; here is volition and attention, the faculty of will, the force of habits. Lastly, there is the faculty of consciousness or awareness. In Buddhism consciousness is not something apart from the other factors, but rather interacting with them and dependent on them for its existence; there is no arising of consciousness without conditions. Here we see no idea of personhood as constancy, but rather a fleeting, changing assortment or process of various interacting factors. A major aim of Buddhism is first to become aware of this process, and then to eliminate it by eradicating its causes.

This process does not terminate with the dissolution of the physical body upon death; Buddhism assumes reincarnation. Even though there is no soul to continue after death, the five skandhas are seen as continuing on, powered by past karma, and resulting in rebirth. Karma in Buddhism, as in Hinduism, stems from volitional action and results in good or bad effects in this or a future life. Buddhism explains the karmic mechanism a bit differently; it is not the results of the action per se that result in karma, but rather the state of mind of the person performing the action. Here again, Buddhism tends to focus on psychological insights; the problem with bad or selfish action is that it molds our personality, creates ruts or habitual patterns of thinking and feeling. These patterns in turn result in the effects of karma in our lives.

Many other metaphysical questions were put to the Buddha during his life; he did not answer them all. He eschewed the more abstract and speculative metaphysical pondering, and discouraged such questions as hindrances on the path. Such questions as what is Nirvana like, what preceded existence, etc., were often met by silence or what may have seemed like mysterious obscurity. Asked what happens to an Arhant, an enlightened one, upon his death, the Buddha was said to have replied: "What happens to the footprints of the birds in the air." Nirvana means 'extinction' and he likened the death of an arhant to the extinction of a flame when the fuel (karma) runs out. He evidently felt that many such questions were arising out of a false attachment to self, and that they distracted one from the main business of eliminating suffering.

THE PATH TO LIBERATION: THE BUDDHIST WAY OF LIFE

The Buddha intended his philosophy to be a practical one, aimed at the happiness of all creatures. While he outlined his metaphysics, he did not expect anyone to accept this on faith but rather to verify the insights for themselves; his emphasis was always on seeing clearly and understanding. To achieve this, however, requires a disciplined life and a clear commitment to liberation; the Buddha laid out a clear path to the goal and also observations on how to live life wisely. The core of this teaching is contained in the Noble Eightfold Path, which covers the three essential areas of Buddhist practice: ethical conduct, mental discipline ('concentration; or 'meditation'), and wisdom. The goals are to cultivate both wisdom and compassion; then these qualities together will enable one ultimately to attain enlightenment.

The path is laid out in eight steps, but one may practice all of the steps simultaneously, since they work together.

The first two steps or factors constitute Wisdom. Right understanding (or right views) is the grasping of true reality, as seen in the Buddhist teachings; it is not merely an intellectual understanding, although this helps. Rather it is a direct insight and penetration into the nature of things. Right thought (or right intentions) is that frame of mind which is selfless, detached and free of malice; that generosity of spirit which extends loving benevolence to all beings.

The next three steps on the eightfold path constitute ethical conduct. Right speech involves abstaining from lies, from rude or malicious language, from foolish gossip, and from slander or backbiting that may cause disharmony. One should speak a gentle, kind, and useful truth, or not speak at all. Right action requires abstaining from killing and all violence, stealing, dishonest practices, intoxicating drinks and improper sexual behavior. Right livelihood means that one should abstain from any profession that brings harm to others, such as weaponry, butchering animals or selling liquor. Also one's career should develop one's talents, overcome the ego by joining in a common cause, and provide what is needed for a worthwhile existence — basic comforts and necessities, but not ostentatious luxuries.

The last three steps on the path are those which promote mental discipline. Right effort is the will to cultivate wholesome states of mind and eliminate evil or unwanted ones. Right mindfulness (or attentiveness) involves being keenly aware of the processes involved in one's daily existence, those of the body, the sensations, the mind and the experiencing of thoughts and ideas. Mindfulness is practiced in Buddhist forms of meditation such as vipassana, through techniques like observation of the breath and bodily sensations. Right concentration refers to the progressive stages of dhyana (this is closer to what is called meditation in most Hindu traditions). In this discipline, the mind is gradually cleared of passionate desires, then thoughts, then finally even feelings of joy, until only pure awareness remains, in a state of perfect calm and equanimity.

Other teachings speak of the Four Friends and the Five Hindrances that one encounters along the path; these are qualities in the heart which may aid or distract one from the process. The four friends are: loving kindness, compassion, sympathetic joy and equanimity. Loving kindness is universal love for all beings, without distinction. Compassion is the ability to empathize with others — to feel what they are feeling. Sympathetic joy is the quality that takes delight in the happiness of others. Equanimity is a calm acceptance of all that happens, based on the insight of the impermanence of all things; in the end, the only thing that really matters is liberation, so the vicissitudes of life don't really have much significance.

The five hindrances are: sensual desire; ill will; sloth and torpor; restlessness and worry, or distraction; and skeptical doubt. Everyone has these hindrances in common, so it is important to find ways of eliminating them; they are like toxins or weeds which prevent the cultivation of those qualities essential for self-discipline and stand in the way of our liberation.

The Buddha's teachings on ethics and living a good life also extended to the realm of the social and political. He was ahead of his time in many ways; considering all people as equal, he rejected the caste system and openly encouraged women to become students and teachers. He taught that governments had a responsibility to lead by example, to teach people ethics and to eliminate poverty by providing opportunities for the people to become prosperous. He was clearly opposed to all forms of war, and taught that violence can never create security. In keeping with these teachings, Buddhism is rare among world religions in that its followers never attempted to spread their beliefs through the use of force. Unique among victorious leaders, the Buddhist emperor Asoka in the third century BCE renounced violence and war, and put Buddhist ethical virtues at the center of his government.

Regarding the Buddhist path as a philosophy, one may consider its epistemology: certain claims of knowledge have been made, but how can they be known to be true? As stated above, the Buddha himself never asked anyone to accept unproven claims on faith, and in fact discouraged them from doing so. He maintained that his teachings could be verified by direct insight and reasoning, by anyone willing to consider them and to follow the necessary path of self-discipline. Starting from a few basic assumptions, such as impermanence and dependent origination, he derived a complex and consistent system of philosophy which has stood for centuries. Later teachers have validated his claim that others could reach the same insights, and they have expanded upon his basic teachings with impressive intuitive depth and intellectual rigor.

In this way the Buddhist teaching has itself become a kind of interactive and self-evolving process, much like its idea of pratityasamutpada. However, the end goal is still Nirvana, which is an experience ultimately beyond all concepts and language, even beyond the Buddhist teachings. In the end even the attachment to the Dharma, the Buddhist teaching, must be dropped like all other attachments. The tradition compares the teaching to a raft upon which one crosses a swift river to get to the other side; once one is on the far shore, there is no longer any need to carry the raft. The far shore is Nirvana, and it is also said that when one arrives, one can see quite clearly that there was never any river at all.

BUDDHIST PHILOSOPHY

It will be more difficult to give a definition or even a description of the term 'Philosophy'. It is however very clear that 'philosophy' in its Western (viz. Greco-Christian) context shows a different 'content' than that in the East (predominantly Indian and/or Chinese). From almost every definition of philosophy it goes to show that Western philosophy centers around the question of 'being', the 'first (or last) cause' and the 'absolute'. It tries to find an explanation, analyzes the experiential data and attempts to develop a dialectic around it.

Western philosophy then will be mainly concerned with metaphysics, and especially with ontological questions.

Another facet of Western philosophy (and mysticism) is that it places itself outside the realm of religion, even in those cases where its use lies in giving a coherent structure to religion (viz. Scholasticism).

In the East, philosophy endeavors towards a coherent scheme around which multiple soteriological practices can be weighed, evaluated and structured. The search here is not the search for an explanation (the why-question) but for an efficiency (the how-question). It is not so much the 'absolute truth' that counts, but the effectiveness of a given system or practice.

It is therefore not the question of 'being' but the question of 'knowledge and knowing' (epistemology versus ontology) (viz. Wisdom) that will be the center of philosophical thought in the East. There is the search for understanding the connections and inter-relationships between phenomena and the ability to express them. It is an attempt to translate the non-conceptual (meditative or mystical) into concepts and words, with the clear purpose of describing the salvific process or way to liberation (Enlightenment or Nirvana,...), without however confusing the 'description' with the 'described'.

Emphasis therefore is put on psychology and epistemology as the basis for the development of a soteriology.

Thus, there is no search for the 'absolute' as there is in the West, but an uninterrupted input of relativism and self-critique. It is therefore the religious aspect that is dominant, integrating both philosophy and mysticism. A non-religious philosophy, while characteristic for the West, is conceived as an impossibility in the Eastern context. Even Confucianism, with its initial rejection of all things supernatural takes into account the concept of Heaven (T'ien) and its Virtue (working or effectiveness).

A Buddhist 'philosophy' will make no exception to this rule.

FUNDAMENTS OF BUDDHISM

The basic principles of the Teaching of the Buddha are found within the Four Noble Truths :

1. The Universality of Suffering
2. The Cause of Suffering
3. The Cessation of Suffering
4. The Way that leads to the Cessation of Suffering

(1) and (2) are situated mainly on the psychological level of the world of experience. Both the 'inner' and 'outer' world are seen as nothing more than a representation of the mind. Our knowledge originates in the subject. Not the world is illusory, but the glasses through which I see the world makes that the world as it appears to me is an ego-illusion.

If one looks at the meaning of these Four Noble Truths, one comes to the conclusion that the first three Noble Truths point to a theoretical model in which (1) can be taken as consensual, generally acceptable and not necessarily Buddhist; while (2) and (3) are causal: (2) as the cause of suffering, and (3) as the cause of the cessation of suffering. Truth (4) on the contrary is typically Buddhist in its referral to a praxis.

The concept 'suffering' is usually misinterpreted, due to a Christian or materialistic point of view. The term 'dukkha', although mostly translated as 'suffering' reaches much further than our ordinary conception of the term suffering: it implies not just our bodily or social torments or vexations, but also - and primarily so - our mental torments. Therefore dukkha would be better described as 'universal unsatisfactoriness' or 'dissatisfaction with the existing situation'.

In a certain sense we can also consult philosophers from the West for possible 'better' translations of dukkha. John Locke 1 (1632-1704) speaks of 'uneasiness', thereby remarking that this is the basic feeling, the drive behind every thought or action of humanity. Also found are terms such as 'Unerfülltheit' etc. It is through the use of these, that the term 'suffering' can be taken out of its physical-material context.

In a certain sense we could look upon the Buddhist concept of 'suffering' as being the interval, the distance between the existentially experienced and our expectations, on the one hand 'desire' and 'attachment', on the other hand fear.

Suffering here, does not belong to the sphere of salvation or enlightenment - as is often the case in other religions -, but is a characteristic of the existential world in which existence unfolds. This 'suffering' stands loose from the sphere of nirvana : this becomes clear although paradoxically expressed in the 'Heart-Sutra' ("Here, there is no suffering, no cause of suffering, no cessation of suffering, no path that leads to the cessation of suffering.").

Dukkha indeed is one of the universal characteristics of that which exists, viz. the 'experienced'. As the locus typicus goes:

- All forms of existence are characterized by suffering;
- All forms of existence are characterized by impermanence;
- All elements of existence are characterized by non-self.

The distinction between 'forms of existence' and 'elements of existence' is of the utmost importance.

All 'things' or 'beings' are compound: these are the 'forms' that existence takes on. (samskara = compound).

This 'compound' is characterized by its composing elements or components (dharma = principle, basic principle, characteristic,...).

If one would use the example of computer science as a metaphor, one could picture a dharma as corresponding to a unit of communication (bit) or a unit of transmission (baud). Samskara than would correspond with a 'message' or 'data'.

Both samskara and dharma have in fact a multitude of meanings that are not always clearly distinguishable. The Monier-Monier Williams Sanskrit-English Dictionary for example gives the following lemma for 'samskara': "...the faculty of memory, mental impression or recollection, impression on the mind of acts done in a former state of existence. Buddh.: mental conformation or creation of the mind (such as that of the external world, regarded by it as real though actually non-existent...". In the Pali Text Society Dictionary on the other hand we read for the same lemma: "1. Aggregate of the conditions or essential properties of a given process or result e.g. the essentials or 'elements' of anything; - essential conditions, antecedents or synergy (co-ordinated activity), mental coefficients, requisite for act, speech, thought. 2. One of the five khandhas, or constitutional elements of physical life...".

'Suffering' is unavoidable since all 'things' are impermanent (not-remaining = Skt. anitya). This impermanence has given rise to a lot of esthetical expressions such as the inevitable withering of a flower, or morning dew, etc. Often this theme of impermanence is emotionally interpreted as the 'transitory nature of all things' through which a sense of doom is evoked, e.g. in poetry. Yet anitya should be understood as objectively neutral: if things where 'doomed' to perish or to disappear, than enlightenment would not be a possibility. Even impermanence can become a factor of enlightenment !

Besides this it is clear that every change in a 'subject' at the same time means a change in the experienced 'object'. In this way anitya in fact becomes a universal experience.

Things are impermanent because there can be no 'permanent' substance ('soul', 'atman', 'self', 'ego'). The 'elements of existence' (dharma) - and therefore also the 'forms of existence' which are composed by these elements - are 'self-less' (P. anatta). All that exists (the world of experience) is self-less, without self, without permanence, without absoluteness. This is the main criterion of the Teaching of the Buddha.

But : *if there is no 'self', than who is it that suffers?*

That which we call an 'individual', a 'personality', 'ego' or 'psyche', is in fact no more than a convergence of events, impulses, thought constructions, volitional actions, etc. In short, all that is conventionally understood under the term "mental activity". This collection (khandha, skandha) has no permanent substance or essence (atman). Just as no permanent 'house-entity' is found in a constructed house, in the same way no permanent 'entity' can be found within the different forms of existence including sentient beings. This compound nature of the forms of existence explains not only their impermanence but also their 'artificiality', their com-positeness (together + to put) (sam-skri), their polymer character.

The term 'samskara' has, as was mentioned before, a lot of meanings that can not be confused with one another. Each of these possible meanings however point to a compound nature, an aggregate; yet, the context in which the term is used can differ. Therefore it is necessary to make a clear distinction between its different uses: e.g. samskara is used to denote the fourth of the five skandha's (aggregates) in which case the connotations of 'karma' and 'will or volition' will be determining. When it is used as the second link of the pratitya samutpada (dependent co-origination), the emphasis will be put on the dynamic that runs from a (past) volitional action towards its (future) result, the fruit which conditions a future mental situation.

Every momentous 'being' is a compound of a series of ever-changing and impermanent aggregates called the 'five aggregates' (*pañca-skandha*).

- *rupa*: form, corporeality
- *vedana*: feeling, perception

- *samjña*: cognition, conception
- *samskara*: volition, karma-formations
- *vijñana*: consciousness, discrimination

These five skandha's are stages of perception, cognition and volition. They are NOT ontological elements. They give an approach of the mental process that is active in the 'psyche'. We thus can look upon them as psychological/epistemological elements.

It would therefore be wrong to consider each of these skandha's as an 'entity', a 'being'. Not only are they compound (ad infinitum), they also cannot exist by themselves but only in relation to and in function of the other skandha's. They are therefore without substance and without autonomy, the two prerequisites for the so-called 'atman'. Thus there is no 'atman'. Or to state it more clearly: concentrating on or around the idea of an atman is (according to Buddhist thought) an inefficient thought-error. Buddhism in all its forms and aspects is an-atman (anatta): non-self.

This strict norm is the main criterion to separate things Buddhist from things non-Buddhist.

Further: the fivefold classification of the personality into skandha's and the twelve-fold classification of karmic existence are not a "scientific neurological or neuro-psychological" analysis and make no statements concerning an objective, anatomical reality. We are to look upon these classifications as empirical 'expedient means' (upaya) used to gain an insight into the process which leads from an 'existence characterized by suffering' (samsara) to a state of 'non-suffering' (nirvana). We are therefore clearly dealing with a soteriological methodology and not with mere psychological data or metaphysical statements.

The illusion to have or to be an atman - or even to take it into consideration - is the deep origin of suffering. Suffering comes to an end through the destruction of the atman-delusion (avidya = ignorance, mis-conception). This delusion leads to desire (trisna, P. tanha = thirst) and hatred (dosa = aversion), out of which the whole world of dissatisfaction or unsatisfactoriness, in short 'duhkha' comes into existence.

The term 'desire, thirst' should not be interpreted to narrow, in the sense of merely emotional or psychological. Desire encompasses 'all beings'. So for instance we could say that 'the heart desires to beat' seeing that this is the hearts necessary function. We can even speak of a certain 'cosmic' desire, e.g. as is seen in the mutual attraction of two masses (Newton's Law). Seen as such, desire is not only the motive or drive of the individual, it can also be transposed to a collectivity, yes even cosmically as the drive or the motive of the universe.

This all leads us to conclude that 'suffering' has its origin in 'desire', which in its turn has its source in 'ignorance'. To often however this is interpreted as "my suffering has its origin in my desire which in its turn finds its source in my ignorance". Such an expression leads to irrelevant questions concerning e.g. the suffering of innocent children. This mistaken shifting of emphasis is based on the input of the concept of 'mine' there where 'it' is meant. The reduction to individuality is in contradiction with the presupposition of anatman or 'no-self' and leads to a methodological incoherence. In our discussion of causality we should continuously take this into account with every step in our train of thought.

This makes that the Third and Fourth Noble Truths should consequently be interpreted in a purely soteriological and pragmatic (i.e. effective) way. A further consequence of the anatman-idea is than that all concepts, all ideas, all forms of thought are anatman, and therefore have no absolute or adequate sense, i.e. they can only be understood as being relative (i.e. in relation to). Further: anatman is also applied to anatman, meaning even anatman is relative: it is only a form of expression in which the content is relative, interchangeable, impermanent. From this the concept of 'emptiness' (sunyata) originated. However, also the concept of sunyata is a mere concept.....therefore.....

Buddhist philosophy than will primarily be an epistemology, a philosophy of knowing and Buddhist soteriology will be a wisdom of knowing: seeing things as they are in se, in their emptiness, and not as they appear to our existential consciousness.

DIVERSIFICATION

The diversification of the Buddhist streams - reaching several climaxes between the 2nd Century BCE and the 5th Century CE - did not so much result from schisms concerning the fundamental doctrines - such as the Four Noble Truths or the doctrine of Dependent Co-Origination - as from the additions of elements not mentioned by the Buddha, or even elements which the Buddha refused to discuss.

At first, these additions remained peripheral, later however they became more far-reaching and radical (e.g. in the Pudgalavada-tradition where the concept of anatta was 'bypassed'). The diversification on the philosophical level concerns mainly two themes :

- **dharma**: principle, supporting characteristic, basic element of cognition;
- **buddha**: as historical figure, as transcendental being, as cosmic principle.

It is and remains agreed upon however that both are in fact identical, and thus interchangeable: "He who sees the Buddha, sees the Teaching; and he who sees the Teaching sees the Buddha", the Buddha more than once proclaimed. (e.g. in SN, IV-120)

Broadly speaking however, it could be said that the 'dharma-theme' was more emphasized within circles of monks and philosophers, whereas the 'buddha-theme' (certainly at the outset) was more appealing to lay-people, preachers and artists - as is apparent from the oldest archeological Buddhist findings in India. Also a lot of the early 'biographical' literature, e.g. Lalitavistara, Jataka's and Buddhacarita, refers mainly to the exemplary function of the 'buddha-theme'.

The diversification can (but therefore doesn't have to) happen by way of diverse, interactive points of view, coming from diverse angles, which will require us to look upon it in the light of a multidimensional complexity.

Apart then from disciplinary and/or soteriological problems, we can determine the following important points of view concerning the Teaching of the Buddha, without however being able to pinpoint in how far they are simultaneous or consecutive. Their chronology remains very uncertain.

A. Diversification according to the "addressee"

In the scriptures of the different schools we see that the Buddha addresses a great diversity of social and spiritual categories of listeners, thereby each time adapting his use of language and terminology in function of the social and/or educational level of his audience.

Grosso modo we can reduce this to three main groups of listeners:

- the monks: with a strong emphasis on meditative states and levels;
- lay-people: mainly concerning ethical questions;
- the "specialists" (e.g. brahmins, sramana's, muni's, etc.): questions regarding worldview and metaphysics.

A strong and definitive demarcation between these three groups is however impossible, since the Teaching of the Buddha starts out with the anatta-criterion, a criterion that covers all further consequences.

Tensions between (1) and (2) have led to the first known 'schism' (during the so-called Second Council at Vaisali, be this historically correct or not...) whereby - for purely disciplinary reasons - the Elders (Sthaviravada) who strongly held to the letter of the Vinaya, parted with the Greater Community (Mahasanghika) which consisted for a great part, if not the majority, of lay-people.

Tensions between (1) and (3) could have been the cause for the origination of the "pre-Mahayana".

B. Diversification according to Abhidharma

The Abhidharma (Pali: Abhidhamma) in its broadest meaning is the "Extended Teaching", viz. the systematically and philosophically structured envelopment of the actual soteriology. This later 'extension' differs strongly from school to school as becomes apparent from the transmitted Abhidharma-pitaka's. Certain schools even went as far as rejecting every form of Abhidharma. (e.g. Sautrantika)

The two extremes of this diversification according to importance given to, or rejection of the Abhidharma are:

- Buddhist 'Scholasticism', is most strongly represented by the Sarvastivada (e.g. their discussion concerning the dharma's, their classification, their existence and their time-value). Mostly practiced by monks and based on scriptural texts and commentaries. Leads towards abstraction and reduction to conceptual forms (e.g. buddha (buddhata)

- 'Devotion' and especially 'popular devotion', most strongly emphasized by the lay. Traces of this can be found back in the oldest Buddhist archeological monuments (e.g. Bharhut and Sanchi) and in the Edicts of Emperor Ashoka. Institutionally they are mostly represented in the Mahasanghika-stream (e.g. Lokottaravada, with its emphasis on the transcendence and the "deification" of the historical Buddha)

The synchronicity of diversifications A and B leads to new perspectives apart from the distinction between the Smaller Vehicle (Hinayana) and the Greater Vehicle (Mahayana). (Philosophically very artificial at first). The distinction between the two streams is in fact much more complex than conventionally presented. Many correlations and interactions have played an important role in this process.

Further we see an evolution in the thinking and living of the Teaching, in which the distinction between Smaller and Greater Vehicle has given way to the emphasis of either Buddha or Teaching (Dharma).

C. Diversification according to Dharma and Buddha

In connection to A and B we see the inclination towards an emphasis on either the expression of the Teaching or the 'person' of the Buddha:

1. Dharma: The historical Buddha is 'only' the bringer of the Teaching, which makes him 'subordinate' to the Teaching. This emphasis will be expressed the strongest in those currents that give importance to discussion and polemics, to scholasticism, ethics and psychology, such as there are
   - Sarvastivada and Theravada (i.e. Smaller Vehicle)
   - The Prajñaparamita schools in India and China (i.e. Greater Vehicle) E. Conze uses the term "Wisdom-schools".
2. Buddha: The Teaching is the manifestation of Buddhahood, with its inherent, open to human experience, characteristics of Wisdom and Compassion. Here we notice however again a distinction between:
   - Gautama Buddha as exclusive Buddha, be it as a historical figure or as manifestation of an "Eternal Buddha": e.g. Theravada (Smaller Vehicle); Lotus-sutra, Zen (Greater Vehicle).
   - Non-historical (so-called 'meditative') Buddha-figures who assume a cosmic scale (up to present only Mahayana): e.g. Vairocana in Avatamsaka and Tantra; Amitabha in Sukhavativyuha.

We need to underline however that within this complexity the actual soteriology remains centered around the Four Noble Truths, of which the coherence should be looked upon as exclusively soteriological, certainly not ontological.

Most 'additions' or 'extensions' are of a cognitive and explanatory nature. Within Mahayana philosophy they are regarded as 'expedient means' (upaya-kausalya), as are all forms of appearance of the Teaching.

NIRVANA

If there is one term in Buddhism that has given rise to a lot of confusion and misunderstanding, it must be nirvana. Nirvana, "the Great Nothing or Void as Supreme Bliss", is such an image that has more become - from Schopenhauer until present - a western pseudo-myth than the central concept of Buddhist soteriology.

The negative appreciation of nirvana as destruction of existence is in fact the result of a dichotomous approach. Although it is true that nirvana is in a sense a negative expression, it must be said that which is negated does not belong to the domain of ontology, not even the domain of general metaphysics. It is most certainly not a negation of "being", nor of "non-being". In Buddhism, 'being' and 'non-being' can neither be affirmed nor denied: they are concepts that do not belong into the soteriology. Sakyamuni Buddha himself classified questions of this nature in the category of theoretical irrelevancies.

The sense of nirvana therefore must be searched for within another domain. Time and again, the Buddha - and many masters after him - has emphasized that nirvana should be approached and interpreted in an (in a certain sense) epistemological, and primarily in a pragmatic-soteriological sense.

If we look at the etymology of the term we find that nirvana is a compound of the prefix ni[r]- (ni, nis, nih) which means "out, away from, without", and the root vâ[na] (P. vâti) which can be translated as "blowing" as in "blowing of the wind", but also as "smelling, etc"

The compound 'nirvâna' therefore undeniably has the meaning of "blowing out, putting out, extinguishing (of a lamp or of fire), setting (of the sun)". Used as an adjective it can mean "quiet, stilled, tamed, departed". MMW adds to this lemma that for Buddhists and Jains the term means "the absolute extinction or annihilation of individual existence or of all desires and passions". Nirvana thus means the "settling of the wind, the extinguishing of the fire". As a medical term it is also used as "stopping of the fever or stress".

Although all Buddhist schools in a way agree on this basic meaning of the term, diverse interpretations and connotations appear. Grosso modo we can make a distinction in interpretations between those of the Hinayana (especially the Sautrantika and Sarvastivada schools) and those of the Mahayana schools.

The Smaller Vehicle sees nirvana primarily - and almost exclusively - as an ethical event, attainable in this life (at least in theory) through the practice of morality, contemplation and insight. It is only within the Abhidharma-literature that the meaning of nirvana will somehow extend to a certain realm of existence of passionlessness, peace, etc.

Such an approach must necessarily lead to a strictly negative formulation, e.g. that of Udana viii. There, nirvana is described as the realization of the fourth proposition of the logical tetralemma: "neither [this]....nor [not this]....", with by the way a truly Nagarjunian sense for expression.

This negative formulation will be less the case in Mahayana-texts. Often, nirvana is here equated with sunyata (emptiness), which - one should keep in mind - for a Buddhist is a positive term, equivalent to 'availability' and even - especially in later Mahayana - 'totality'. Nirvana in this sense can be approached in a positive way as 'Enlightenment' (bodhi), Buddhahood (buddhata), etc.

The situation becomes more clear when nirvana is in the first place seen as the opposite of samsara: the world of suffering as the cycle of birth-and-death. Since samsara is in a sense "propelled" by karma-formations (volitional activity conditioned by desire, aversion and delusion), nirvana means - as the opposite of samsara - the halting of these (causative) karmic formations and therefore also the exhaustion of their karmic 'fruit' (results of volitional actions). The realization of nirvana is therefore the cessation of the karma-causality.

Mostly the commentators agree when it comes to the 'attributes' that can be ascribed to nirvana, this despite the fact that they - paradoxically enough - keep stressing that nirvana is "inconceivable, unthinkable, indescribable'. So, it is said that nirvana is the 'unconditioned' (asamkrita), peaceful (santa), unarisen (anutpada), etc.

Moreover distinctions were made between a 'temporal, created nirvana' (nirvana seen from the human condition, and therefore as a relative truth), and the 'perfect, definitive, uncreated nirvana' which belongs to the experience of ultimate (absolute) truth.

Or, a distinction is created between a 'place bound' nirvana (pratisthita-nirvana), which is realized in this existence and with this present body, and the 'nirvana of no-abode' (apratisthita-nirvana). Only this nirvana is complete as the realization of Buddhahood.

RELATIONSHIP HINAYANA/MAHAYANA

Taking into account the different diversification criteria, we can conclude that the Smaller Vehicle (Hinayana) and the Larger Vehicle (Mahayana) have (1) a lot of themes in common and (2) that they overlap each other on a number of topics. It should be noticed here however that to look upon these two streams as 'whole units', viz. completed and closed-off systems, is a fiction.

1. A lot of the so-called 'typical' Mahayana doctrinal points appear in the Pali-Canon, which is seen without a doubt as the Hinayana document par excellence. A great number of these doctrinal points are found in the oldest layers of the Pali-Canon and cannot be taken to be later interpolations.

2. Another remarkable fact is that within Indian Buddhism there rarely is any mention (not until very late) of separate Mahayana communities. Apparently the

monks of the divers streams lived among one another, following more or less the same Vinaya rules. Witness to this are the writings of the pilgrim monk Hsüan-chuang (600-664) who gives a detailed description of the situation of Buddhism in India. There is therefore no reason to speak of a 'schism' in the Christian sense of the word. It is impossible, given the present archeological research, where India is concerned to draw a sharp demarcation line between the two streams. It is only in China that the institutional separation of Hinayana/Mahayana becomes truly noticeable.

Also remarkable is that, on the doctrinal level, we notice an evolution (or better yet, an extension) of the original anatta-teaching. With the transmission of the term from Hinayana to Mahayana, we notice that the emphasis on its non-ontological character is preserved, whereas the dualism between self/non-self is transcended in the sense of the logical tetralemma (viz. the fourth lemma 'neither-nor').

At first, the term 'Mahayana' did not have the implication of being sectarian or schismatic, but it referred to a 'different approach' of the salvific problem.

The adjective maha(n)t, in compounds 'maha', does not just mean 'great', but also 'broad' or 'large'. It is exactly this meaning that lies at the basis for the term 'Mahayana': the 'broad or large vehicle'.

In this sense 'Mahayana' points primarily to a soteriology that is 'broader' [than for monks alone]; namely, that there is also a possibility for salvation outside of the strict observance of the Vinaya rules or the monastic discipline. The 'Way' (or path, Skt. Marga, Ch. Tao) is 'Broad' ! It is in this sense that the term appears, probably for the first time, in Asvaghosha's "Mahayana-sraddhotpada-sastra" (The Awakening of Faith in the Mahayana).

In a somewhat later evolution, the Mahayana evolves towards a stronger contrast in regards to the 'Smaller Vehicle', which emphasizes the effort towards individual salvation "Diligently strive towards your own salvation". In contradistinction to this the Mahayana posits "the salvation of all beings, regardless their numbers". This will go as far as the Mahayana accusing the 'Smaller Vehicle' of mere self-concern and a lack of compassion.

This polemic will appear most clearly in the controversy Arhant/Bodhisattva as the proposed ideal set to be followed by the 'adept'.

ARAHANT (P.) - ARHANT (SKR.)

It is stated that the adept meditator has to transgress four stages on his way to enlightenment:

- sotapanna: the 'stream-enterer'
- sakadagami: the 'once-returner'
- anagami: the 'none-returner'
- arahant: the 'praiseworthy' or the 'holy one'

The arahant, the final stage of this evolution, is the one who is no longer subject to the cycle of birth-and-death. By overcoming the fundamental ignorance he has become desireless and has been freed of every ego-illusion. Because he gives no more rise to desire, no more karma-formations (volitions, acts of will) arise and he is no longer reborn.

He has reached this state through his own efforts by practicing the Dharma, the Vinaya and the "Four Levels of Meditation" (P. jhana; Skt. dhyana). When he experiences suffering as a result of past karma, there is no more mental reaction against this suffering in him. He lives in a state of 'emotional non-reaction', equanimity an invulnerability, a state to which every being should strive.

This ideal state is difficult to describe, and even more difficult to realize. The subject in any case brought along a lot of discussion within the different Hinayana-schools (e.g. concerning the question whether the Arahant can 'regress' to a lower state or not).

In the Mahayana-schools the Arahant-ideal was mostly the subject of sharp attacks. He was blamed for working exclusively towards his own salvation. It is true that he functions as an example and that in this way he arouses the desire in others to walk the same way, but besides this he is inactive. He sits alone in a 'small vehicle' and lacks the element of Compassion.

DIFFERENCE BETWEEN ARAHANT/BUDDHA

- The arahant needs the Teachings (Dharma) set forth by the Buddha, whereas the Buddha discovered the Dharma.
- The arahant puts the Teachings into practice, whereas the Buddha established the practice.
- The arahant has put an end to the causes of suffering, but is not necessarily capable of transmitting this experience to others; whereas the Buddha necessarily shares his experience with others.
- The arahant has a passive knowledge (jñana) of the Teaching, but lacks Wisdom (prajña); whereas the Buddha has (is) active Wisdom.
- The arahant misses compassion (karuna); whereas the Buddha has (is) Great Compassion (maha-karuna).

PRATYEKABUDDHA (P. PACCEKABUDDHA)

At a certain moment, another distinction between a Buddha or 'Sammasambuddha' versus a 'pratyekabuddha' is introduced. A pratyekabuddha or a 'solitary Buddha' discovers the Teaching by himself, and fathoms its Wisdom, but he dies without having proclaimed it (viz. the Compassion-element) to others. A lot of interpretations concerning the pratyekabuddha are possible ! (e.g. the possibility of enlightened beings outside the realm of Buddhism).

BODHISATTVA (P. BODHISATTA)

Enlightenment-being - Being towards Enlightenment - Being focused on Enlightenment.

This term is difficult to translate, even more difficult to describe.

1. *Evolution of the term*

The term bodhisatta is already found in the Pali-Canon, be it with a limited meaning: Bodhisatta is Siddharta Gautama before he realized Enlightenment. Therefore we see two phases in his biography: bodhisatta before, and Buddha after his Enlightenment.

Therefore: Bodhisattva is the stage that precedes Enlightenment; however, the way of the arahant excludes Perfect Enlightenment (sammasambodhi). The arahant realizes Complete and Final Nirvana at the moment of his death, not being reborn again he does not pass through the stages of the bodhisattva. The way of the bodhisattva leads towards Enlightenment; not just his own enlightenment, but the Enlightenment of all beings indiscriminately.

In the Mahasanghika-school a more liberal interpretation of the bodhisattva-idea will come to light and gradually the ideal of the bodhisattva will become the Mahayana counterpart of the arahant ideal in the Hinayana. The bodhisattva is a 'being' that refuses to remain (some would say 'enter') in Nirvana because of its vow to help others; the bodhisattva chooses to remain in the world of suffering and rejects Complete and Final Nirvana (in the sense as stated before).

This will become the 'leitmotiv' for Mahayana Thought: the bodhisattva chooses Enlightenment for himself and all other beings over his own, individual Enlightenment (cfr. the anatta-doctrine). Besides this, every being (and therefore every human being) has within itself a conscious or unconscious drive towards Enlightenment: the Mind of Enlightenment (bodhicitta), through which it has the potential to realize the bodhisattva within itself.

2. *Different 'kinds' of bodhisattva's*

It doesn't hold to classify bodhisattva's into different 'kinds' or 'categories'. If we do so, than it is exclusively with the intention to smoothen the approach of the problem. Because, every distinction lies exactly within the approach. So it goes that the Buddha-characteristics of Wisdom and Compassion in se are not different, and yet we experience them as two separate characteristics. It is important to keep in mind that the bodhisattva does not have a separate existence; he is mainly an ideal-projection of - and in - our mind.

Bodhisattva-Mahasattva

The "Great Being Bodhisattva's" traditionally number about 10. They are in fact manifestations of a Buddha 'quality'. The two most important 'qualities' we ascribe to a Buddha are 'Wisdom' (prajña) and 'Compassion' (karuna). Thus we see two kinds of manifestations:

'Wisdom Bodhisattva's' such as Mañjusri (cognitive wisdom) or Mahasthamaprapta (intuitive or emotional wisdom). The Wisdom Bodhisattva's have multiplied almost infinite in number, especially in Tibetan Buddhism.

'Compassion Bodhisattva's' such as Avalokitesvara (the most popular, spread over the divers Buddhist cultures, very important in popular devotion); Samantabhadra (active compassion); Maitreya (the Peaceful, Buddha of the future).

'Human' Bodhisattvas

Since all beings have bodhicitta within them, human beings are also potential bodhisattva's. Here we distance ourselves from the metaphysical structure of the term and emphasize more the emotional element: every human being can be bodhisattva in the perception of every other human being. In this way a human relationship can through the capacity of wisdom and compassion rise above ordinary human standards.

The 'Cosmos' as bodhisattva

When all beings can become bodhisattva, the term bodhisattva will gain an strong expansion. So the feeling of interaction will arise through which all beings out of their true nature are inclined to bring all beings to Enlightenment. Through contact with all beings, any being can experience the Teaching of the Buddha.

From the limited understanding of 'bodhisattva as manifestation of Buddhahood' we will arrive to the embracing of the totality of human occurrences and from there to the embracing of the totality of existence in all its manifest forms. All beings and things participate in each others bodhisattvahood. Certainly in Chinese Buddhism this thought has found a vivid expression, maybe through interaction with Taoism.

3. *Difference Buddhahood/bodhisattva*

Buddhahood surpasses the existential and is related to 'true nature': availability, totality, sunyata.

The bodhisattva stands in relative existence and is subject to anatta. He has no objective 'being'. He is the existential reflection of Enlightenment; he outlines and objectivates Enlightenment in this relative, relational existence. Besides this he offers man a kind of spiritual ideal, in which man can project him/herself as a being on the way to Enlightenment.

His function, both in Buddhist popular devotion as in the doctrinal development and experience, is therefore not to be underestimated. But also in the personal, intimate approach of the Dharma, the bodhisattva - on whatever level he is situated - is an important element.

BUDDHIST LOGIC

Buddhism has from the beginning emphasized a logical structure. Examples of this can be found in the structure of the (midwifery) talks and discourses of the Buddha.

The basic structure can be found in the logical *tetralemma*:

- A is true
- A is not true
- A is both true and not true
- A is neither true nor not true

This formulation, which is very often found back in the oldest texts, provides the 'key' to most 'typical Buddhist problems' towards their 'understanding' or their 'inconceivability' (e.g. the anatta-doctrine, the conception of sunyata, or the teaching of Totality within the Avatamsaka-teachings). What seems 'illogical' according to the binary logic (the so-called Aristotelian logic), becomes clear through the perspective of this tetralemma.

With its dissemination Buddhism unavoidably came into contact with other Indian spiritual currents. From this arose the necessity of having a set of polemic instruments at its disposal with which it could answer the argumentations of the formal-logically structured Hindu darsanas (especially Nyaya and Vaisesika).

In relation to this J. Takakusu says in his 'Essentials of Buddhist Philosophy': "Buddhist Logic is not a formal logic of thought, but is rather a logic of dispute or debate which lays stress on the investigation of cause, relations and possibility and is therefore an art of argumentation and refutation." We can see this need strongly represented in Nagarjuna, but even more decidedly with Vasubandhu, who by way of his view on the trayasatya (Three Truths) gave rise to the implementation of a clear Buddhist formal logic.

It is however Vasubandhu's disciple Dinnaga who is generally accepted as the factual founder of this logic. In his Nyaya-pravesa (also called Nyaya-mukha), 'Introduction to Logic', he explains the new lines of thought based on the 'knowledge of causality' (hetu-vidya). He supports his claims on the 'three forms of causality' (lingasya trini-rupani) by way of the 'nine necessitating causes' (hetu), in which he replaces the - until then - usual comparative method with a sharp method of deduction which expresses itself in new syllogistic formulations. His works are - except for the aforementioned Nyaya-pravesa and some Sanskrit fragments - mainly preserved in Chinese and Tibetan translations.

A next important step in Buddhist Logic was taken by Dharmakirti. Concerned about the decline of the Teaching in India, he searched for new structures of argumentation. In his works Pramana-varttika, Pramana-viniscaya, but especially in his Nyaya-bindu he points out that names and relations are only instituted by mind, whereas the sense-functions represent their objects of experience accurately, unless of course they are distorted and perverted.

KYOTO SCHOOL OF PHILOSOPHY

Ran-gaku or "Dutch Knowledge" developed during the Tokugawa Era, more precisely in the beginning of the 18 century. This form of imported science – in contradistinction to the revival of "National Science" (koku-gaku) – furthered rationalist thought in Japan. This led to a compromise, in which koku-gaku was seen as a superior (i.e. Confucianist) teaching necessary for the moral and social education of man, whereas ran-gaku, with subjects such as medicine, biology, astronomy, architecture, etc. was considered to be a 'practical', i.e. technical knowledge. The actual 'modern' period of Japan starts from 1868. At first, the Meiji regime aimed at a cooperation between the western forms of technology, science, and even 'knowledge' on the one hand, and the official State-Shinto thought (plus a large dose of Confucianism...) on the other, to thus establish the foundation for a modern, but national socio-moral and cultural life.

Young intellectuals however laid a greater emphasis on the imported philosophical systems than on the own Shinto-Confucianist heritage. From the 1870's onward their main interest went to August Comte, J. Stuart Mill, Darwin; in the 80's it extended to an interest in the French, e.g. Voltaire and Rousseau. In the 1890's it were however the German philosophers that occupied their main interest: Kant, Hegel, Schopenhauer – although also Nietzsche, Bergson, Tolstoi and William James were actively studied.

In most intellectual circles, however, it wasn't so much the "adoption" of foreign systems that was aimed at, but their comparison with familiar Buddhist and Confucianist values, towards which goal they used e.g. 'categorical' methods and criteria characteristic to western philosophy. This point of view did not lead to an imitation but to a more sharp and often more critical insight. Often, however, the Japanese intellectuals of the 2 half of the 19 century were presented with a superficial image of European and American philosophy. All this changed in the beginning of the 20 century thanks to the endeavor towards a synthesis of both eastern and western worlds of thought. Characteristic of this phenomenon is the publication of Hatano Seiichi's (1877-1950) study on Spinoza in 1904, which was – remarkably enough – written in German only to be translated in Japanese in 1910.

The breakthrough came with the informal foundation of the "Kyoto School of Philosophy" within the lap of the faculties of philosophy and religion of the Kyoto State University, mainly under the impulse of **Nishida Kitaro** (1870-1945), known as Japan's most important philosopher since the Meiji Restoration.

The Kyoto School is in the first place a renewed way of applying philosophy, "more of a philosophical ethos than a unified system of thought". As a basis for this we see:

1. a profound respect for the own religious traditions;
2. a definite openness towards that what western thought has to offer;
3. the intention of arriving at a synthesis of what the West has to offer (e.g. Christianity) and of the eastern heritage (e.g. Buddhism)

This basis can only be realized through a thorough, competent knowledge of both sides of the problem. It can not be characterized by missionary intentions or proselyte polemics, but should on the contrary move across contradictions and paradoxes, which is expressed by Nishida as a "self-identity of absolute contradictories".

Among the most important representatives of the Kyoto School we find – besides **Nishida** – **Tanabe Hajime** (1885-1962), **D. T. Suzuki** (1870-1966), **Nishitani Keiji** (1900-1990), **Takeuchi Yoshinori** (1913-..), and **Abe Masao** (1915-..).

For this essay on the Kyoto School of Philosophy we will limit ourselves to the two main currents: that of Nishida Kitaro, which is clearly inspired by Zen philosophy, and that of Tanabe Hajime, which is mainly based on Shinran (1173-1262: Founder of *Jodo-Shinshu*).

Nishida Kitaro

Through his Zen-experience, Nishida's thought is based on Prajñaparamita-literature and Madhyamika-philosophy. His remarkable point of view on the *topos* of Nothingness is directly derived from the intuition to which he gave the meaning of 'pure experience'.

Topos has – for Nishida – a broader significance than usual, e.g. in Plato's Timaeus or with Aristotle. Also the modern concept of 'force-field' or 'cosmic field' (Einstein) is said to have influenced Nishida. To approach his understanding of *topos*, we must keep in mind that our everyday word 'place' is neither a merely non-existing 'nothing' nor an existing 'something'. According to Jan Van Bragt *"it is more in the nature of what Jaspers calls an "encompassing" (Umgreifendes) that allows things to exist where they are: each on its own, and yet all together in a sort of oneness."*

Also the term "Nothingness" clearly refers to sunyata ('emptiness'), although also here Nishida gives a broader interpretation than is usual, namely a "no-thingness" (Undinglichkeit). His attitude is in the first place "to see the form of the formless and to hear the voice of the voiceless":

> *"By intuition (or seeing) I mean our way of seeing things in the world through which we see a 'being', but also our own act of seeing, as a shadow image of the Self-reflection of Nothingness – I mean the shadow of Self-reflection of Nothingness that fulfills its function by projecting itself on one point within its topos."*

To philosophically clarify the Topos-nature of Nothingness, Nishida introduces his three key-ideas of 'action-intuition', the 'Eternal Now' and the 'historical world in its identity of contradictories'.

1 *Action-intuition:*

Nishida here expressly refers to the Oriental methods of thought such as the Zen-koan and the art of Archery. Action-intuition is both the structure and the dynamic of all creative activity. Here there is a mutual process as e.g. with the cutting of a wooden image, whereby the sculptor sees anew and recreates his image with every move, in such a way that with every new 'seeing' of the form of the image, he is inspired to cut further. Thus, human creativity only becomes possible when the self-reflecting world expresses itself within the human being, which in its own turn expresses itself and reflects itself by way of its work in the mirror of the world. By way of this mutuality or interdependentness both the world and man realize their synthesis in the historical world.

2 *Eternal Now:*

The being-present of all things in the world is a "*presence in time*", namely in the present, in contradistinction to the past and the future. Only in the present one becomes self-conscious as an individual. This way of being-present-in-time is an immediate or direct event, out of which the endeavor for truth can start. In this, one's whole being is involved, but also the being of all other things in the world. Nonetheless, this kind of being-present is ephemeral and transient: "*it appears as being only to disappear again; and it disappears only to let a new being-present appear.*" Being and non-being are in their true structure interrelated to each other. Because of this the present is a unity of contradictory moments.

Although brief and ephemeral, the present envelops the totality of the time-experience, since past, present, and future all belong to that same present. It is in this way that the endless series of moments, from the incalculable past until the incalculable future, are dependent on the brief presence of the 'here-and-now'. The present is as a time-monad which contains in itself the whole width of past-present-future, despite the fact that it itself belongs to this series as an infinitely small part of the whole. From this follows that the present determines itself: it is 'the present of the present'. Out of this flows the time-experience, as it where from present to present. This characteristic of time explains the nature of man's direct (immediate) self-consciousness and feeling of freedom.

Yet, this experience of self-being and of freedom is closely tied to man's awareness of impermanence. How then is it possible that the fleeting moment can in itself contain the infinitely long series of time-moments? According to Nishida, this is possible because the present is rooted in the Eternal. The Eternal reflects itself and the focus of this self-reflection is the 'present-of-the-present'.

That the Eternal is topologically equal to the present is, according to Nishida, not a simple identification in the mystical sense of the word. Nishida's notion is more dialectic. According to him the fleeting present and the Eternal are on the one hand each others opposites; on the other hand however, one can interchange these both poles, since both are tied to each other through their ultimate self-identity. The Eternal, the Absolute-in-time as topos of Nothingness, can within itself summon each separate moment and bring it to life. The Eternal thus establishes each moment as a true (i.e. autonomous and self-determining) *individuum*: the present. Through this the Eternal and the present are interconnected in an identity of contradictories.

3 *The historical world in its identity of contradictories:*

The Creative Now is not only a synthesis in time, but also in space. The world itself is the self-reflection of the existence in which all *individua* are concluded. The world is the embodiment of the Eternal Self, or rather: Non-Self, since each individual existence in this body is only the manifestation of this individual. Each present has therefore the characteristic of a time-synthesis in space.

Because of this, time is determined in two ways: linear and spatial circular. Both time-dimensions converge at every time-moment, be it in an individual existence or in the entire world. This, thus, becomes a historical world, wherein time and space are intertwined; it is, in a sense, the same as the *religious world* since the Absolute Nothingness is the principle of both the historical world and religion. Since Absolute Nothingness is the life-principle in the world, it should be realized in the world. Its transcendence in relation to the world can only be realized through its immanence in the world. Through the unceasing consecutive manifestations of Absolute Nothingness in the world, the real historical world is unceasingly sanctified, i.e. religiously penetrated.

This can be explained by the double aspect that Nishida gives to his notion of Absolute Nothingness: on the one hand the Christian notion of Absolute Being, on the other hand the Buddhist vision of Absolute Enlightenment.

This does, however, not automatically mean that the world is the domain of religion. Nishida here makes a clear distinction between culture and religion. Religion should be regarded as being qualitatively different from the socio-cultural value-determining actions of humanity. The true ground of the world, however, is religious, just as our existence in the world is religious. But what does it mean when we say that we are religious? It is because we realize our restlessness, our brevity, that in our mind we discover the religious as factuality.

What is typical in Nishida's vision on religion is revealed in what he calls the *disjunction/conjunction* in the relationship between God and man. 'God' stands opposite to man as the divine Will stands opposite to the human will. To man, 'God' is a transcendence, and although he is immanent, man can not see him, can not meet him, can not immediately experience him. He is at the same time Absolute Being and Absolute Nothingness in his true identity of contradictories. In each moment in time and at each place in space he both is and is not, in the sense that his absence for the enlightened mind is the proof of his omnipresence.

Tanabe Hajime

Tanabe was originally a student of Nishida but because of his different outset – i.e. different from the Zen-experience – his thought was for a great part a reaction against Nishida. Tanabe was greatly influenced by the teaching of Shinran (1173-1262) and by the works and the life of Kiyozawa Manshi (1863-1903), who – mutatis mutandis – during the turn of the century fulfilled the role within Shin Buddhism that Kierkegaard had fulfilled within the Danish Lutheran Church.

According to Tanabe the only possibility to transcend the *noetic* (i.e. Metaphysics as speculative philosophy on the level of the subject/object relationship), is the undergoing of a total turning of the mind (J. e-shin), a *metanoia* in the "death-and-resurrection-experience". According to him, the true dialectic is neither the "and-and" speculative synthesis of Hegel, nor the "or-or" ethical concern of Kierkegaard; but the "neither-nor" double negation in our immediateness through the Compassionate activity of the

Absolute. Our awareness of 'sin', i.e. of our religious non-worth, means than at the same time the abolishment of 'sin' through the graceful activity of the Absolute (*zettai*), since 'God' or 'Buddha' is Absolute Nothingness, and therefore the power and mercy of absolute self-surrender.

For Tanabe the Absolute is only absolute as Nothingness. Absolute Nothingness is qualitatively different from the world and thus transcendent in relation to the relative world. The Love-Compassion of the Absolute is embodied in this world by the bodhisattva, the teacher who proclaims the message of the metanoic truth and who through his "fire" (i.e. his own experience of death-and-resurrection) ignites his disciples to action-entrusting. The Compassion of Absolute Nothingness is thus transmitted from teacher to disciple.

As mentioned before, Tanabe bases himself on Shinran's Kyogyoshinsho. The 'being born in the Pure Land' was already greatly demythologized by Shinran, who was convinced that the essential experience of death-and-resurrection was fulfilled at the moment of e-shin, of the metanoia that is the 'moment of shinjin', the 'settlement of birth', i.e. the samsaric aspect of Birth in the Pure Land, of which the nirvanic aspect – the fulfillment of Buddhahood (Absolute Truth) – remains shifted to "the other life".

Tanabe uses the image of the bodhisattva who makes all preparations to meet the Buddha, fulfills his path until the end and then goes and visits the Buddha in his room. He, however, discovers the Buddha's absence (the Buddha-room is after all emptiness) and realizes that at this moment the Buddha is in the world; therefore the bodhisattva returns to the world of suffering to work side by side with the Buddha. It is in and through this return that the bodhisattva becomes a Buddha, which in fact is a non-reachable goal because of its utter paradox: Buddhahood is after all a 'state' in which even the noble goal of becoming a Buddha is surpassed.

Against Nishida's action-intuition, Tanabe emphasizes action-entrusting. According to him, Nishida's topos still belongs to the domain of contemplative speculation. To him (as with Kierkegaard) religious truth in this life is fragmentary and certainly not a continuum. If this truth is a whole, than Being is and it would make no sense to call this Being 'Nothingness'. Absolute Truth – for Tanabe, Amida's Light – penetrates us in an intensive manner, not as an extensive totality. Tanabe uses the image of a figure-skater, who only keeps his balance on the ice as long as he is moving. In 'entrusting' there is always the presence of a certain anxiety and an existential uncertainty, but the more uncertainty there is, the more certain becomes our awareness of our limitation and our (karmic) awareness of 'sin' (i.e. our 'nothingness'), which can only be lifted through e-shin. The mind of entrusting, as the transformation of our nothingness to Absolute Nothingness, is – according to Tanabe – 'uncertain certainty'. It becomes established in the repetition of the Name, which is the decisive action. In the 'here-and-now' of this religious act there is also present the Absolute Truth, not so much as an eye-to-eye revelation, but as a veiled, i.e. hidden from our consciousness, Truth.

Nishida and Tanabe

1. Nishida emphasizes action-intuition; Tanabe emphasizes the meaning of action entrusting in the religious existence.
2. Action-intuition sees our existence as a creative element within the creative, historical world. Tanabe sees the dialectic only in function of the historical world.
3. Nishida places his creative element in each new moment, in such a way that the whole can continually be seen from a different perspective. To Tanabe, the historical world is at any moment and at any place a dead end street which has to be broken through with entrusting and determination. Nishida emphasizes the integrating aspect (each moment as integrated within the course of time), Tanabe emphasizes the infinity-aspect (mugen = infinite, unconditional light, infinite compassion, infinite wisdom).
4. The fundamental experience according to Nishida is the immediate realization of Absolute Nothingness as the Dharmakaya in Zen Buddhism. With Tanabe, the ethical standpoint dominates. It is out of his ethico-social concern (cfr. Kiyozawa Manshi) that he focuses on the study of religion, in an attempt to unite the truth of the Buddhist Zen and Pure Land traditions and the truth according to Christianity.

Despite these differences, both philosophers share a number of notions which became characteristic of the Kyoto School of Philosophy:

1. The absolute should be seen as Absolute Nothingness.
2. The essence and value of philosophical thought rest in our religious existence.
3. The representations of the Eternal Now and Nothingness as disjunction/ conjunction.

Chapter - 8

Buddhism in South Asia

South Asia, also known as **Southern Asia**, is a southern region of the Asian continent, which comprises the sub-Himalayan countries and, for some authorities, also includes the adjoining countries on the west and the east. It is surrounded (clockwise, from west to east) by Western Asia, Central Asia, Eastern Asia, and Southeastern Asia. South Asia consists of these following countries: India, Pakistan, Bangladesh, Bhutan, Sri Lanka, Maldives and Nepal.

BUDDHISM IN INDIA

Buddhism is a world religion, which arose in Bihar, India and is based on the teachings of Siddhartha Gautama, who is known as the Buddha (literally the *Enlightened One* or *Awakened One*). It flourished during the reign of Maurya Empire. Buddhism has spread through two main traditions; Theravada which extended south and east and now has widespread following in Southeast Asia, and Mahayana, which diffused first west, then north and later east throughout East Asia. Both traditions have since spread throughout the world.

Buddhism declined and disappeared from the land of it origin in around 13th century, but not without leaving a significant impact. Buddha is regarded as the 9th incarnation of Hindu god Vishnu. Buddhist practice still continue in Himalayan areas like Ladakh, Arunachal Pradesh and Sikkim. It has reemerged as a major faith in India in the past century.

Siddharth Gautam was the historical founder of Buddhism. Siddhartha Gautama was born as a Kshatriya prince in ancient India. His particular family of Sakya Kshatiryas were of Brahmin lineage as per their family name "Gautama". XIX c. scholars like Dr. Eitel connected it to the Brahmin Rishi Gautama. Lord Buddha is said to be a descendant of Brahmin Sage Angirasa in many Buddhist texts. For example, *"In the Pali Mahavagga "Angirasa" (in Pali Angirasa} occurs as a name of Buddha Gautama who evidently belonged to the Angirasa tribe..."*. Scholar Edward J. Thomas too connected Buddha with sages Gautama and Angirasa.

After asceticism and meditation, Siddhartha Gautama discovered the Buddhist

Middle Way—a path of moderation away from the extremes of self-indulgence and self-mortification.

Siddhartha Gautama attained enlightenment sitting under a pipal tree, now known as the Bodhi tree in Bodh Gaya. Gautama, from then on, was known as *"The Perfectly Self-Awakened One,"* the Samyaksambuddha.

Buddha found patronage in the ruler of Magadha, emperor Bimbisara. The emperor accepted Buddhism as personal faith and allowed the establishment of many Buddhist "Viharas." This eventually led to the renaming of the entire reigon as Bihar.

At the Deer Park near Vârânasî in northern India, Buddha set in motion the Wheel of Dharma by delivering his first sermon to the group of five companions with whom he had previously sought enlightenment. They, together with the Buddha, formed the first Sangha, the company of Buddhist monks, and hence, the first formation of Triple Gem (Buddha, Dharma and Sangha) was completed.

For the remaining years of his life, the Buddha is said to have traveled in the Gangetic Plain of Northeastern India and other reigons.

Buddha attained Parinirvana in the abandoned jungles of Kusinâra.

BUDDHIST MOVEMENT

The Buddha did not appoint a successor, and asked his followers to work for personal salvation. The teachings of the Buddha existed only in oral traditions. The Sangha held a number of Buddhist councils in order to reach consenseus on matters of Buddhist doctrine and practice.

According to the scriptures, a monk by the name of Mahakasyapa presided over the first Buddhist council held at Rajgir. Its purpose was to recite and agree on the Buddha's actual teachings and on monastic discipline. Some scholars consider this council fictitious.

The second Buddhist Council is said to have taken place at Vaishâli. Its purpose was to deal with questionable monastic practices like the use of money, the drinking of palm wine, and other irregularities; the council declared these practices unlawful.

What is commonly called the Third Buddhist Council was held at Pâtaliputra, and was allegedly called by Emperor Ashoka in the 3rd century BC. Organized by the monk Moggaliputta Tissa, it was held in order to rid the sangha of the large number of monks who had joined the order because of its royal patronage. Most scholars now believe this council was exclusively Theravada, and that the dispatch of missionaries to various countries at about this time was nothing to do with it.

What is often called the Fourth Buddhist council is generally believed to have been held under the patronage of emperor Kanishka at Jâlandhar, though the late Monseigneur Professor Lamotte considered it fictitious. It is generally believed to have been a council of the Sarvastivada school.

Following the Buddha's passing, many philosophical movements emerged within Buddhism. The first of these were the various Early Buddhist Schools (including Theravada). Later Mahayana Buddhism and Vajrayana Buddhism arose.

EARLY BUDDHIST SCHOOLS

The Early Buddhist Schools were the various schools in which pre-sectarian Buddhism split in the first few centuries after the passing away of the Buddha (in about the fifth century BC). These schools have in common an attitude to the scriptures, that doesn't accept the inclusion of the Mahayana Sutras as valid teachings of Gautama Buddha. It accepts the Tipitaka as the final recension of the teachings of the Buddha.

- Theravada is the single remaining representative of the Early Buddhist Schools of Indian Buddhism. Theravada is now practiced mainly in Sri Lanka, Myanmar, Thailand, Cambodia, and Laos.
- Another prominent Nikaya school was the Sarvastivada, and much of its doctrine was incorporated into Tibetan Buddhism. It included one of the main branches of Indian *Abhidharma* that was instrumental in the creation of the Yogacara doctrine. Its system of monastic rules *Vinaya* is still used in Tibetan Buddhism and has also been influential in monastic Chinese Buddhism.

MAHAYANA

The Mahayana branch of Buddhism popularized the concept of a *Bodhisattva* (literally *enlightened being* or "a Buddha-to-be") and the worship of the bodhisattvas. Bodhisattvas like Manjushri, Avalokiteshvara, Maitreya became the focus of popular devotional worship in the Mahayana sect. According to the Mahayana tradition, the key attributes of the bodhisattvas are compassion and kindness.

Mahayana Buddhism includes the following Indian schools:

- Madhyamaka (*Middle Way*), a Mahayâna tradition popularized by Nâgârjuna and Asvaghosa.
- Yogacara (*Consciousness Only*), founded by Asanga and Vasubandhu.

VAJRAYANA

A form of Indian Buddhism that emerged in the 4th century AD and later became widespread in Tibet, and Japan.

This school emerged from forest meditation traditions in northern India, in which the entire emphasis of teachings was on practice, using skillful means to attain the goal of enlightenment in one's present lifetime. This form is also known as Vajrayana (*the Diamond Vehicle*). Tantrism is an esoteric tradition. Its initiation ceremonies involve entry into a mandala, a mystic circle or symbolic map of the spiritual universe. Also central to Tantrism is the use of mudras and mantras. Vajrayana became the dominant form of

Buddhism in Tibet and was also transmitted through China to Japan, where it continues to be practiced by the Shingon sect.

It is generally accepted that the spread of Buddhism from India to Tibet and then to the wider regions of Central and East Asia took place mainly via the trade (and religious) route that went through the valley of Kathmandu, situated in present-day Nepal. The valley, forms the cradle of the Nepali state, and since the farthest point in historical time, has found itself under the cultural influence of the South Asian Hindu (and also Buddhist) civilization. However, being a distant outpost of Hinduism (and Buddhism), it was spared from the ravages of later conquests and social upheavals. Even after Buddhism died in the heartland, it survived in Kathmandu valley. Monastic records in the numerous monasteries show that till the mid-medieval period in Nepali history, Tibetan students regularly came there for learning Buddhism from the local spiritual masters. The Tibetan religious scripts Lantsha and Vartu are variants of the Rànjana system used by the Newars of Kathmandu. However, due to numerous social, economic and political factors prominent among which was declining patronage from the Hindu rulers, Buddhist monasticism in the valley died. By then Tibetan Buddhism had already gained prominence in the region.

Today, in the urban centres of Kathmandu valley, we still find Indian Mahayana Buddhism, modified through mixing with Vajrayana, practiced by the local Buddhist Newar population.

STRENGTHENING OF BUDDHISM IN INDIA

The flow between faiths was such that for hundreds of years, almost all Buddhist temples, including the ones at Ajanta, were built under the rule and patronage of Hindu kings.

ASHOKA AND THE MAURYAN EMPIRE

The Maurya empire reached its peak at the time of emperor Ashoka, who himself converted to Buddhism after the Battle of Kalinga. This heralded a long period of stability under the Buddhist emperor. The power of the empire was vast—ambassadors were sent to other countries to propagate Buddhism. Greek envoy Megasthenes describes the wealth of the Mauryan capital. Stupas, pillars and edicts on stone remain at Sanchi, Sarnath and Mathura, indicating the extent of the empire.

Emperor Ashoka the Great (304 BC–232 BC) was the ruler of the Maurya Empire from 273 BC to 232 BC.

Ashoka reigned over most of India after a series of military campaigns. Emperor Ashoka's kingdom stretched from South Asia and beyond, from present-day Afghanistan and parts of Persia in the west, to Bengal and Assam in the east, and as far south as Mysore.

According to legend, emperor Ashoka was overwhelmed by guilt after the conquest of Kalinga, following which he accepted Buddhism as personal faith with the help of his

Brahmin mentors Radhasvami and Manjushri. Ashoka established monuments marking several significant sites in the life of Shakyamuni Buddha, and according to Buddhist tradition was closely involved in the preservation and transmission of Buddhism. He used his position to propagate the relatively new philosophy to new heights, as far as ancient Rome and Egypt.

GRAECO-BACTRIANS, SAKAS AND INDO-PARTHIANS

Menander was the most famous king. He ruled from Taxila and later from Sagala (Sialkot). He rebuilt Taxila (Sirkap) and Pushkalavati. He became Buddhist and remembered in Buddhists records due to his discussions with a great Buddhist philosopher in the book *Milinda Panha.*

By 90 BCE Parthians took control of eastern Iran and around 50 BCE put an end to last remnants of Greek rule in Afghanistan. By around 7 CE an Indo-Parthian dynasty succeeded in taking control of Gandhara. Parthians continued to support Greek artistic traditions in Gandhara. The start of the Gandharan Greco-Buddhist art is dated to the period between 50 BCE and 75 CE.

KUSHAN EMPIRE

Kushan Empire under emperor Kanishka was known as the Kingdom of Gandhara. The Buddhist art spread outward from Gandhara to other parts of Asia. He greatly encouraged Buddhism. Before Kanishka Buddha was not represented in human form. In Gandhara Mahayana Buddhism flourished and Buddha was represented in human form.

This tower was reported by Fa-Hsien, Sun-Yun and Hsuan-Tsang. This structure was destroyed and rebuilt many times and remained in semi ruins until it was finally destroyed by Mahmud of Ghazni in 11th century.

DHARMA MASTERS

Indian shramanas propagated Buddhism in various regions, including East Asia and Central Asia.

In the Edicts of Ashoka, Ashoka mentions the Hellenistic kings of the period as a recipient of his Buddhist proselytism. Emissaries of Ashoka, such as Dharmaraksita, are described in Pali sources as leading Greek ("Yona") Buddhist monks, active in Buddhist proselytism (the Mahavamsa, XII).

Roman Historical accounts describe an embassy sent by the "Indian king Pandion (Pandya), also named Porus," to Caesar Augustus around the 1st century. The embassy was travelling with a diplomatic letter in Greek, and one of its members was a sramana who burned himself alive in Athens to demonstrate his faith. The event made a sensation and was described by Nicolaus of Damascus, who met the embassy at Antioch, and related by Strabo and Dio Cassius. A tomb was made to the sramana, still visible in the time of Plutarch, which bore the mention:

"ΖΑΡΜΑΝΟΧΗΓΑΣ ΓΝΔΟΣ ΑΠΟ ΒΑΡΓ□ΟΣΗΣ"

("The sramana master from Barygaza in India")

Lokaksema is the earliest known Buddhist monk to have translated Mahayana Buddhist scriptures into the Chinese language. Gandharan monks Jnanagupta and Prajna contributed through several important translations of Sanskrit sutras into Chinese language.

The Indian dhyana master Buddhabhadra was the founding abbot and patriarch of the Shaolin Temple. Buddhist monk and esoteric master from North India (6th Century CE), Bodhiruci is regarded as the patriarch of the Ti-Lun school. Bodhidharma (c. 6th century) was the Buddhist Bhikkhu traditionally credited as the founder of Zen Buddhism in China.

In 580, Indian monk Vinitaruci travelled to Vietnam. This, then, would be the first appearance of Vietnamese Zen, or Thien Buddhism.

Padmasambhava, in Sanskrit meaning *"lotus-born"*, is said to have brought Tantric Buddhism to Tibet in the 8th century. In Bhutan and Tibet he is better known as "Guru Rinpoche" (*"Precious Master"*) where followers of the Nyingma school regard him as the second Buddha. Shantarakshita, abbot of Nalanda and founder of the Yogachara-Madhyamika is said to have helped Padmasambhava establish Buddhism in Tibet.

Indian monk Atisha, holder of the *mind training* (Tib. lojong) teachings, is considered an indirect founder of the Geluk school of Tibetan Buddhism. Indian monks, such as Vajrabodhi, also travelled to Indonesia to propagate Buddhism.

DECLINE OF BUDDHISM IN INDIA

The **Decline of Buddhism in India**, in the land of its birth occurred for a variety of reasons, and happened even as it continued to flourish beyond the frontiers of India. Buddhism was established in the area of ancient Magadha and Kosala by Gautama Buddha in the 6th century BCE, in what is now modern Uttar Pradesh and Bihar. Buddhism, over the next 1500 years became the region's dominant belief system, spreading across the Indian sub-continent.

After the death of Gautama Buddha, Buddhism saw rapid expansion in its first century, especially in northern and central India. The Mauryan Emperor Ashoka (304-232 BCE) and later monarchs encouraged the expansion of Buddhism into Asia through religious ambassadors. Hindu monarchs endorsed the religion (viewing it as their own.) *National Geographic* reads, *"The flow between faiths was such that for hundreds of years, almost all Buddhist temples, including the ones at Ajanta, were built under the rule and patronage of Hindu kings."* Chinese scholars traveling through the region between the

5th and 8th centuries CE, such as Faxian, Xuanzang, I-ching, Hui-sheng, and Sung-Yun, began to speak of a decline of the Buddhist *sangha*, especially in the wake of the White Hun invasion. A continuing decline occurred after the fall of the Pala dynasty in the 12th century CE, continuing with the later destruction of monasteries by Muslim conquerors.

Buddhism was virtually extinct by the end of the 19th century. In recent times, Buddhism has seen a revival in India from the influence of Anagarika Dharmapala, Kripasaran Mahasthavir, Dr. B. R. Ambedkar and Tenzin Gyatso, the 14th Dalai Lama.

DECLINE OF BUDDHISM UNDER VARIOUS GOVERNMENTS

The Sungas

Following the Mauryans, Pusyamitra Sunga is linked in legend with the persecution of Buddhists and a resurgence of a form of Hinduism that forced Buddhism outwards to Kashmir, Gandhara and Bactria. There is some doubt as to whether he did or did not persecute Buddhists actively.

A Buddhist tradition holds him as having taken steps to check the spread of Buddhism as "the number one enemy of the sons of the Sakya's and a most cruel persecutor of the religion". The *Divyavadana* ascribes to him the razing of *stupas* and *viharas* built by Ashoka, the placing of a bounty of 100 dinaras upon the heads of Buddhist monks (*bhiksus*) and describes him as one who wanted to undo the work of Ashoka. This account has however been described as "exaggerated". Historian Romila Thapar writes that the Asokavadana legend is, in all probability, a "Buddhist version of Pusyamitra's attack of the Mauryas", and reflects the fact that, with the declining influence of Buddhism in the Imperial court, Buddhist monuments and institutions would receive less attention.

The accuracy of the Buddhist texts that record Pushyamitra's persecution of Buddhists has been debated by historians. The first accounts appear two centuries after Pushyamitra's reign in *Asokâvadâna* and the *Divyâvadâna*. Sir John Marshall states that it is possible that the original brick stupa built by Ashoka was destroyed by Pusyamitra and then restored by his successor Agnimitra. Archaeological evidence is scarce and uncertain. Following Ashoka's sponsorship of Buddhism, it is possible that Buddhist institutions fell on harder times under the Sungas but no evidence of active persecution has been noted.

The Sungas were patrons of Hinduism and their lack of royal patronage was also a setback to Buddhism, resulting in the splintering of Buddhism into many forces. Some of them were: the *Saravastivadins*, *Mahasargikas*, *Sthaviravadha*, and *Yogacara*. This resulted in a diversity of opinions and interpretations that led to a conflict between warring schools shortly after the fall of the Mauryans.

Traditional Hinduism is said by some writers to have competed in political and spiritual realm with Buddhism in the gangetic plains while Buddhism flourished in the realms of the Bactrian kings.

Contribution to Buddhism

However to many scholars, Sunga kings were seen as more amenable to Buddhism and as having contributed to the building of the stupa at Bharhut.

An inscription at Bodh Gaya at the Mahabodhi Temple records the construction of the temple as follows: *"The gift of Nagadevi the wife of King Brahmamitra"* So then this further means that the Sungas were in support of Buddhism. Another inscription reads: *"The gift of Kurangi, the mother of living sons and the wife of King Indragnimitra, son of Kosiki. The gift also of Srima of the royal palace shrine."*

Guptas

Buddhism saw a brief revival under the Guptas. By the 4th to 5th century Buddhism was already in decline in northern India, even as it was achieving multiple successes in Central Asia and along the Silk Road as far as China. It continued to prosper in Gandhara under the Shahi kingdom.

White Huns

Central Asian and North Western Indian Buddhism weakened in the 6th century following the White Hun invasion, who followed their own religions such as Tengri, Nestorian Christianity, and Manichean. Their Saivite King, Mihirakula (who ruled from 515 CE), suppressed Buddhism as well. He did this by destroying monasteries as far away as modern-day Allahabad, before his son reversed the policy.

Harsha

In the North and west the collapse of Harshavardana's kingdom gave rise to many smaller kingdoms. This led to the rise of the martial Rajputs clans across the gangetic plains. It also marked the end of Buddhist ruling clans, along with a sharp decline in royal patronage. This carried on until a revival under the Pala Empire in the Bengal region.

Buddhism in Southern India

In the south of India while there was no overt persecution of Buddhists at least two Pallava rulers Simhavarma and Trilochana are known to have destroyed Buddhist stupas and have had Hindu temples built over them. However, Bodhidharma, a patriarch of Zen Buddhism was a Brahmin prince from the Pallava dynasty.

Nagarjuna, the founder of Mahayana Buddhism, was a Brahmin from southern India.

The Satavahanas were worshipers of Buddha as well as other Hindu gods such as Krishna, Shiva, Gauri, Indra, the sun and moon. Under their reign Amaravati, the historian Durga Prasad notices that Buddha had been worshiped as a form of Vishnu.

Furthermore a vigorous Hindu revival of Vaishnavite Hinduism in the region led to a sharp decline of Buddhism.

Muhammad bin Qasim

In AD 711, Muhammad bin Qasim conquered the Sindh bringing Indian societies into contact with Islam. He succeeded partly because Dahir was an unpopular Hindu king that ruled over a Buddhist majority. Chach of Alor and his kin were regarded as usurpers of the earlier Buddhist Rai Dynasty. The forces of Muhammad bin Qasim defeated Raja Dahir in alliance with the Jats and other Buddhist governors. His campaign's success is ascribed to the support of Buddhists and the people of lower castes like Jats, Meds and Bhutto tribes.

The Chach Nama records a couple of instances of conversion of stupas to mosques such as at Nerun as well as the incorporation of the religious elite into the ruling administration such as the allocation of 3% of the government revenue was allocated to the Brahmins. As a whole, the non-Muslim populations of conquered territories were treated as People of the Book and granted Hindu and Buddhist religions the freedom to practice their faith in return for payment of the poll tax (jizya). They were then excused from military service or payment of the tax paid by Muslim subjects - Zakat. The jizya enforced was a graded tax, being heaviest on the elite and lightest on the poor.

While proslytization occurred, the social dynamics of Sind were no different from other Muslim regions such as Egypt, where conversion to Islam was slow and took centuries, and generally came from among the ranks of Buddhists.

Mahmud of Ghazni

By the 10th century Mahmud of Ghazni defeated the Hindu-Shahis, effectively removing Hindu influence and ending Buddhist self-governance across Central Asia, as well as the Punjab region. He demolished both stupas and temples during his numerous campaigns across North-Western India, but left those within his domains and Afghanistan alone, even as al-Biruni recorded Buddha as the prophet "Burxan".

Mahmud of Ghazni is said to have been an iconoclast. Hindu and Buddhist statues, shrines and temples were looted and destroyed, and many Buddhists had to take refuge in Tibet.

Palas

In the East under the Palas in Bengal, Mahayana Buddhism flourished and spread to Bhutan and Sikkim. The Palas created many temples and a distinctive school of Buddhist art. Mahayana Buddhism flourished under the Palas between the 8th and the 12th century, before it collapsed at the hands of the attacking Sena dynasty.

However some scholars believe that they were also Shaivaite judging by the image of Shiva and His ox on their coins and the etymology of their names. Art of Shiva also exists in temples such as the Melakadambur in Bengal where Nataraja and his bull are found.

They had also dedicated shrines to Vishnu. Figures of Vishnu were substantial in number in the Pala Era.

Other than figures of Buddha, Vishnu and Shiva there were also those of Sarasvati.

Muhammad of Ghor

Muhammad attacked the North-Western regions of the Indian subcontinent many times. Gujarat later fell to Muhammad of Ghor's armies in 1197. Muhammad of Ghor's armies destroyed many Buddhist structures, including the great Buddhist university of Nalanda.

In 1200 Muhammad Khilji, one of Qutb-ud-Din's generals destroyed monasteries fortified by the Sena armies, such as the one at Vikramshila. Many monuments of ancient Indian civilization were destroyed by the invading armies, including Buddhist sanctuaries near Benares. Buddhist monks who escaped the massacre fled to Nepal, Tibet and South India.

The Mongols

In 1215, Genghis Khan conquered Afghanistan and devastated the Muslim world. In 1227, after his death, his conquest was divided. Chagatai then established the Chagatai Khanate, where his son Arghun made Buddhism the state religion. At the same time, he came down harshly on Islam and demolished mosques to build many stupas. He was succeeded by his brother, and then his son Ghazan who converted to Islam and in 1295 changed the state religion. After his reign, and the splitting of the Chagatai Khanate, little mention of Buddhism or the stupas built by the Mongols can be found in Afghanistan and Central Asia.

Timur (Tamarlane)

Timur was a 14th-century warlord of Turco-Mongol descent , conqueror of much of Western and central Asia, and founder of the Timurid Empire.Timur destroyed Buddhist establishments and raided areas in which Buddhism had flourished.

Mughals

Mughal rule also contributed to the decline of Buddhism. They are reported to have destroyed many Hindu temples and Buddhist shrines alike or converted many sacred Hindu places into Muslim shrines and mosques. Mughal rulers like Aurangzeb were not only destroyed Buddhist temples and monasteries but also destroyed Hindu temples and replaced them with Islamic mosques.

IDEOLOGICAL AND FINANCIAL CAUSES

The period between the 400 BCE and 1000 CE saw gains by Hinduism at the expense of Buddhism. Some Hindu rulers resorted to military means in an effort to suppress Buddhism. However it is seen that the evolution of Hindu ideology influenced by Buddhisms was more important factor for the growth of Hinduism.

Hinduism became a more "intelligible and satisfying road to faith for many ordinary worshippers" because it now included not only an appeal to a personal god, but had also seen the development of an emotional facet with the composition of devotional hymns.

XUANZANG'S REPORT

Much of what we know about the state of Buddhism in the second half of the first millennium CE comes from the 7th century Chinese pilgrim Xuanzang, who traveled widely and documented his journey. Although he found many regions where Buddhism was still flourishing, he also found many where it had sharply and startlingly declined, giving way to Jainism and a Brahmanical order.

Xuanzang compliments the patronage of Harshavardana. He reported that Buddhism was popular in Kanyakubja (modern day Uttar Pradesh), where he noted "an equal number of Buddhists and heretics" and the presence of 100 monasteries and 10,000 bhikshus along with 200 "Deva" (Hindu) temples.. He found a similarly flourishing population in Udra (modern Orissa). He found a mixed population in Kosala, homeland of Nagarjuna, and in Andhra, and Dravida which today roughly correspond to the modern day Indian states of Andhra Pradesh and Tamil Nadu. In a region he calls Konkanapura, which may be Kolhapur in southern Maharashtra, he found great numbers of Buddhists coexisting with a similar number of non-Buddhists, and a similar situation in norther Maharashtra. In Sindh he finds a large Theravada population. He reports a fair number of Buddhists in what is now Pakistan.

In Dhanyakataka (today's Vijayawada), he found a striking decline, with Jainism and Shaivism ascendant. In Bihar, site of a number of important landmarks, he also found a striking decline and relatively few followers, with Hinduism and Jainism predominating. He also found relatively few Buddhists in Bengal, Kamarupa (modern Assam). He reported no Buddhist presence in Konyodha, few in Chulya (in the Tamil region), and few in Gujarat and Rajasthan, except in Valabhi, where he found a large Theravada population.

During the reign of the Chalukya dynasty, Xuanzang reported that numerous Buddhist stupas in regions previously ruled by Buddhist-sympathetic Andhras and Pallavas were "ruined" and "deserted".These regions came under the control of the Vaishnavite Eastern Chalukyas, who were not favorable to Buddhism and did not support the religion. Xuanzang's report also mentions that, in the 7th Century, Shashanka of the Kingdom of Gouda (Bengal), was expanding his influence in the region in the aftermath of the fall of the Gupta Empire. He is blamed by Xuanzhang and other Buddhist sources for the murder of Rajyavardhana, a Buddhist king of Thanesar. Xuanzang writes that Shashanka destroyed the Bodhi tree of enlightenment at Bodh Gaya and replaced Buddha statues with Shiva Lingams. However, it has been claimed that Xuanzhang had a Buddhist bias in favor of the buddhist rulers such as Harshavardhana and that his account may therefore be slanted.

PHILOSOPHICAL DIVERGENCE WITH ADI SHANKARA

In 9th century CE, Buddhist philosophers started to lose ground against the Advaitha philosophy of Adi Shankara. Shankara debated with Buddhist monks and raised issues with Buddhist philosophy. The resurgence of Hinduism with the ideas of Shankaracharya led to the reduction of royal patronage of the Buddhist monks. As political patronage failed, it came under increasing pressure from Hinduism and the revival movements of Adi Shankara. Shakyamuni Buddha eventually came to be venerated as a manifestation of the Hindu god Vishnu.

Literary evidences point towards an absorption of Buddhist elements by Hindu culture over a period of centuries. Anti-Buddhist propaganda was also reaching its peak during the 8th century when Shankara modeled his monastic order after the Buddhist Sangha. An upsurge of Hinduism had taken place in North India by the early eleventh century as illustrated by the influential Sanskrit drama *Prabodhacandrodaya* in the Chandela court; a devotion to Vishnu and an allegory to the defeat of Buddhism and Jainism. The population of North India had become predominantly Shaiva, Vaishnava or Shakta. By the 12th century a lay population of Buddhist hardly existed outside the monastic institutions and when it did penetrate the Indian peasant population it was hardly discernible as a distinct community. Buddhist monasteries were well-funded and life within was relatively easy. To avoid unwanted members, many monasteries became selective about whom they admitted, in some cases based on social class.

ISLAM

The Arabic invaders described Indian Pagans as But-parast, and idol-breakers as but-shikan. The word "but" is derived from Buddhism, but the Arabs used it for "Indian paganism" in general. When the Arabs arrived in Sind there were only glimpses of Buddhism nor any evidence of a provincial government in control of the Buddhists. During the seventh to thirteenth centuries when Islam arrived it replaced Buddhism as the great cosmopolitan trading religion in many places accompanied by a consolidation of the communal peasant religions of Hinduism. The Tibetan scholar of the seventeenth century Tarnatha writes that during the time of the Sena king *Stag-gzigs* (Turks) had begun to appear on horses and that monasteries had been fortified with troops stationed in them; however, they were overrun and monks at Uddandapura were massacred, the monastery razed and replaced by a new fort and further north-east Vikramshila was destroyed as well.

Hardly a contemporary evidence however exists on the destruction of Buddhist monasteries. Brief Muslim accounts and the one eye witness account of Dharmasmavim in wake of the conquest during the 1230s talks about abandoned viharas being used as camps by the Turukshahs. Later historical traditions such as Taranathas are mixed with legendary materials and summarized as "the Turukshah conquered the whole of Magadha and destroyed many monasteries and did much damage at Nalanda, such that many monks fled abroad" thereby bringing about a sudden demise of Buddhism with their destruction of the Viharas. Buddhism lingered longer in Iran than South Asia and was officially professed under fifty years of Mongol conquest. With the conversion of Ghazan to Islam in 1295, the backlash resulted in the destruction of many Buddhist places of worship and the further migration of monks into Kashmir.

Many places were destroyed and renamed. For example, Udantpur's monasteries were destroyed in 1197 by Mohammed-bin-Bakhtiyar and the town was renamed. Taranatha in his *History of Buddhism in India* (dpal dus kyi 'khor lo'i chos bskor gyi byung khungs nyer mkho) of 1608 C.E., gives an account of the last few centuries of Buddhism, mainly in Eastern india. His account suggests a considerable decline but not an extinction of Buddhism in India in his time.

SUFIS AND THE BHAKTI MOVEMENT

When Islam arrived in India, it sought conversion from, not assimilation to or integration with, the already present religions. Under Sufi influence, the pressures of caste, and with no political support structure left in place to resist social mores, many converted to Islam in the Bengal region.

After the Mongol invasions of Islamic lands across Central Asia, many Sufis also found themselves fleeing towards India and around the environs of Bengal. In Bengal, their influence, caste attitudes towards Buddhists, previous familiarity with converting Buddhists, a lack of Buddhist political power, Hinduism's resurgence through movements such as the Advaita and the bhakti movement, all contributed to a significant realignment of beliefs that relegated Buddhism in India to the peripheries.

SURVIVAL OF BUDDHISM IN INDIA

At the beginning of the modern era, Buddhism was very nearly extinct in mainstream Indian society. Some tribal peoples living in the territory of modern India did continue to practice Buddhism.

In Bengal, the Bauls still practice a syncretic form of Hinduism that was strongly influenced by Buddhism. There is also evidence of small communities of Indian Theravada Buddhists existing continuously in Bengal in the area of Chittagong hill tracts among the indigenous Chakma people up to the present. Though they are under increasing pressure from mostly Muslim Bengali settlers. There was genocide of the Chakma and Buddhists by Islamists in East Pakistan. The Chakma spiritual practices are a blend of Buddhism/Vaishnavism.

Buddhist institutions flourished in eastern India right until the Islamic invasion. Buddhism still survives among the Barua (though practicing Vaishnava/Hindu elements), a community of Bengali/Magadh descent that migrated to Chittagong region. Indian Buddhism also survives among Newars of Nepal.

Buddhism survived in Gilgit and Baltistan until 13-14th century, perhaps slightly longer in the nearby Swat Valley. In Ladakh region, adjacent to Kashmir valley, Tibetan Buddhism survives to this day. The historic prevalence and history of Tibetan Buddhism in the above mentioned Northern regions of Jammu and Kashmir is reported in the Rajatarangini of Kalhana written sometime during 1147–1149 CE.

In Tamilnadu and Kerala, Buddhism survived until 15-16th century. At Nagapattinam, in Tamil Nadu, Buddhist idols were cast and inscribed until this time, and the ruins of the Chudamani Vihara stood until they were destroyed by the Jesuits in 1867. In the South in some pockets, it may have survived even longer.

INFLUENCE OF HINDUISM

Hinduism became a more "intelligible and satisfying road to faith for many ordinary worshippers" because it now included not only an appeal to a personal god, but had also seen the development of an emotional facet with the composition of devotional hymns.

The period between the 400 CE and 1000 CE saw gains by Hinduism at the expense of Buddhism.

THE WHITE HUN INVASIONS

Chinese scholars traveling through the region between the 5th and 8th centuries CE, such as Faxian, Xuanzang, I-ching, Hui-sheng, and Sung-Yun, began to speak of a decline of the Buddhist *Sangha*, especially in the wake of the White Hun invasion.

TURKISH MUSLIM CONQUERORS

The Muslim conquest of the Indian subcontinent was the first great iconoclastic invasion into South Asia. The resulting occasional and sporadic destruction of temples did not affect Hinduism, but for Buddhism the destruction of the stupas has been attributed with a rapid and almost total disappearance from North India. Additionally purer forms of Indian Buddhism relied on patronage by kings and merchants and this change in rulership coupled with the economic integration with the Islamic world and thus the growing domination of long-distance trade by the Muslim merchant class eroded these sources of patronage resulting in an absorption into either Hinduism or Islam.

CAUSES WITHIN THE BUDDHIST TRADITION OF THE TIME

By the time the Muslims began conquering India in the twelfth century under the Ghurids, the number of monasteries had severely declined. Buddhism, which once had spread across the face of India, was a vital force confined to an ever-shrinking number of monasteries in the areas of its origins. Scholars believe that the monasteries at the time became detached from everyday life in India and that Indian Buddhism had no rituals or priests with the laymen relying on Brahmin priests for marriages and funerals.

REVIVAL OF BUDDHISM IN INDIA

On pilgrimage to Bodh Gaya in 1891, the Sri Lankan Buddhist leader Anagarika Dharmapala was shocked to find the temple in the hands of a Saivite priest, the Buddha image transformed into a Hindu icon and Buddhists barred from worship. The Buddhist revival then began in India, when he founded the Maha Bodhi Society. The organization's initial efforts were for the purpose of resuscitation of Buddhism in India and of restoring the ancient Buddhist shrines at Bodh Gaya, Sarnath and Kushinara. The Buddhist renaissance inaugurated by Anagarika Dharmapala through his Mahabodhi Movement is also described as "conservative" for it held the Muslim Rule in India responsible for the decay of Buddhism in India in the then current mood of Hindu-Buddhist brotherhood. The organization's initial efforts were to restore various Buddhist shrines that had been neglected under Hindu administration, and to open to the public various Buddhist sites and temples that had been destroyed in various periods of Muslim invasion.

Later in the 1950s Bhimrao Ramji Ambedkar pioneered the Dalit Buddhist movement in India. Dr. Ambedkar saw conversion to Islam and to Christianity as a factor contributing to the "denationalisation" of India. The revival movement of Buddhism in India underwent a major change when after publishing a series of books and articles arguing that Buddhism was the only way for the untouchables to gain equality, Ambedkar publicly converted on October 14, 1956 in Nagpur and then in turn led a mass-conversion ceremony for over 380,000 dalits. Many other such mass-conversion ceremonies organized since and has become a politically charged issue. Since Ambedkar's conversion, numerous similar many more people from different castes have converted to Buddhism. Many Dalits employ the term "Ambedkar(ite) Buddhism" to designate the Buddhist movement, which started with Ambedkar's conversion.

in 1959 Tenzin Gyatso, the 14th Dalai Lama transitioned from Tibet to India and set up the government of Tibet in Exile in Dharamsala, India, which is often referred to as "Little Lhasa." Tibetan exiles numbering several thousand have since settled in the town. Most of these exiles live in Upper Dharamsala, or McLeod Ganj, where they established monasteries, temples and schools. The town is sometimes known as "Little Lhasa", after the Tibetan capital city, and has become one of the centres of Buddhism in the world.

ANAGARIKA DHARMAPALA AND THE MAHA BODHI SOCIETY

Buddhist revival began in India in 1891, when the Sri Lankan Buddhist leader Anagarika Dharmapala founded the Maha Bodhi Society. Its activities expanded to involve the promotion of Buddhism in India. In June 1892, a meeting of Buddhists was organized at Darjeeling. Dharmapala spoke to the Tibetian Buddhists and presented a relic of the Buddha to be sent to the Dalai Lama.

Dharmapala built many viharas and temples in India, including the one at Sarnath, the place of Buddha's first sermon. He died in 1933, the same year he was ordained a bhikkhu.

BENGAL BUDDHIST ASSOCIATION

In 1892, Kripasaran Mahasthavir founded the Bengal Buddhist Association (Bauddha Dharmankur Sabha) in Calcutta. Kripasaran (1865–1926) was instrumental in uniting the Buddhist community of Bengal and North East India. He built other branches of the Bengal Buddhist Association at Shimla (1907), Lucknow (1907), Dibrugarh (1908), Ranchi (1915), Shillong (1918), Darjeeling (1919), Tatanagar Jamshedpur (1922), as well as in Sakpura, Satbaria, Noapara, Uninepura, Chittagong Hill Tracts Region of Chittagong area in present day Bangladesh.

TIBETAN BUDDHISM

Following Dalai Lama's departure from Tibet, Indian Prime Minister Jawaharlal Nehru offered to permit him and his followers to establish a "government-in-exile" in Dharamsala.

Tibetan exiles have settled in the town, numbering several thousand. Most of these exiles live in Upper Dharamsala, or McLeod Ganj, where they established monasteries, temples and schools. The town is sometimes known as "Little Lhasa", after the Tibetan capital city, and has become one of the centres of Buddhism in the world.

DALIT BUDDHIST MOVEMENT

The **Dalit Buddhist movement** in India began with support of Sri Lankan Buddhist monks. It received an impetus with B. R. Ambedkar's call for conversion of Dalits to Buddhism in the context of a caste based society that considered them to be a lower end of the hierarchy.

Buddhism was once dominant through much of India, it had however begun to decline by the 12th century. The Buddhist revival began in India in 1891, when the Sri Lankan Buddhist leader Anagarika Dharmapala founded the Maha Bodhi Society. The Maha Bodhi Society mainly attracted upper-caste people.

SOUTH INDIA

In 1890, Pandit C. Ayodhya Dasa (1845-1914), better known as Iyothee Thass founded the Sakya Buddhist Society (also known as Indian Buddhist Association). The first president of the Indian Buddhist Association was the German born American Paul Carus, the author of *The Gospel of Buddha* (1894).

Thass, a Tamil Siddha physician, was the pioneer of the Tamil Dalit movement. He argued that Tamil Dalits were originally Buddhists. He led a delegation of prominent Dalits to Henry Steel Olcott and asked for his help in the reestablishment of "Tamil Buddhism." Olcott helped Thass to visit Sri Lanka, where he received *diksha* from Bhikkhu Sumangala Nayake. After returning to India, Thass established the *Sakya Buddhist Society* in Madras with branches in many places including Karnataka. Thass established a weekly magazine called *Oru Paisa Tamizhan* ("One Paisa Tamilian") in Chennai in 1907, which served as a newsletter linking all the new branches of the Sakya Buddhist Society. The magazine discussed traditions and practices of Tamil Buddhism, new developments in the Buddhist world, and the Indian subcontinent's history from the Buddhist point of view.

Brahmananda Reddy, a Dalit leader of Andhra Pradesh, was also fascinated by Buddhism.

UTTAR PRADESH

In the early 20th century, the Barua Buddhists of Bengal under the leadership of Kripasaran Mahasthavir (1865-1926), founder of the Bengal Buddhist Association,

Calcutta (1892) established viharas in cities such as Lucknow, Hyderabad, Shillong and Jamshedpur.

In Lucknow, Bodhanand Mahastavir (1874-1952) advocated Buddhism for Dalits. Born Mukund Prakash in a Bengali Brahmin family, he was orphaned at a young age, and was then raised in Benaras by an aunt. He was initially attracted to Christianity, but became a Buddhist after a meeting with Buddhists monks from Ceylon at a Theosophical Conference in Benares. He later lived in Lucknow where he came in contact with Barua Buddhists, many of whom were employed as cooks by the British. In 1914, Prakash was ordained Bodhanand Mahastavir in Calcutta in the presence of Kripasaran Mahasthvir. He began preaching Buddhism in Lucknow. He founded the *Bharatiye Buddh Samiti* in 1916, and set up a vihara in 1928. In his book *Mula Bharatavasi Aur Arya* ("Original Inhabitants and Aryans"), Mahastavir stated that the shudras were the original inhabitants of India, who were enslaved by the Aryans.

Bodhanand Mahastavir wrote another book on Buddhist rituals called *Baudha Dvicharya*. His associate, Chandrika Prasad Jigyasu, founded the *Bahujan Kalyan Prakashan*. The two co-authored a book on the life and teaching of the Buddha.

Acharya Ishvardatt Medharthi (1900-1971) of Kanpur also supported the cause of the Dalits. He had studied Pali at Gurukul Kangri and Buddhist scripture was well known to him. He was initiated into Buddhism by Gyan Keto and the Lokanatha in 1937. Gyan Keto (1906-1984), born Peter Schoenfeldt was a German who arrived to Ceylon in 1936 and became a Buddhist. Although Medharthi heavily criticized the Indian caste system, he didn't criticize Hinduism. He claimed that the Dalits ("Adi Hindus") were the ancient rulers of India and had been trapped into slavery by the Aryan invaders. He also claimed that the sanatana dharma was the religion of "Adi Hindus", and tried to reconcile Buddhism with the Sant Mat.

Another Bhikkhu of Kanpur, Bhikshu Uttam, was a strong supporter of the Arya Samaj and the *Jat Pat Todak Mandal*, the anti-caste wing of the Arya Samaj.

B. R. AMBEDKAR

At the Yeola conference in 1935, prominent Dalit leader B. R. Ambedkar declared that he would not die a Hindu, saying that it perpetuates caste injustices. Ambedkar was approached by various leaders of different denominations and faiths. Meetings were held to discuss the question of Dalit religion and the pros and cons of conversion. On May 22, 1936, an "All Religious Conference" was held at Lucknow. It was attended by prominent Dalit leaders including Jagjivan Ram, though Ambedkar could not attend it. At the conference, Muslim, Christian, Sikh, and Buddhist representatives presented the tenets of their respective religions in an effort to win over Dalits.

Buddhist monk Lokanatha visited Ambedkar's residence at Dadar on June 10, 1936 and tried to persuade him to embrace Buddhism. Later in an interview to the Press, Lokanatha said that Ambedkar was impressed with Buddhism and that his own ambition was to convert all Dalits to Buddhism. In 1937, Lokanatha published a pamphlet *Buddhism Will Make You Free,* dedicated to the Depressed Classes of India from his press in Ceylon.

In early 1940s, Ambedkar visited Acharya Ishvardatt Medharthi's Buddhpuri school in Kanpur. Medharthi had earlier been initiated into Buddhism by Lokanatha, and by the mid-1940s, he had close contacts with Ambedkar. For a short while, Ambedkar also took Pali classes from Medharthi in Delhi.

Bodhananda Mahastvir and B. R. Ambedkar first met in 1926, at the "Indian Non-Brahmin Conference" convened by Shahu IV of Kolhapur. They met on two more occasions and for a short while in the 1940s, where they discussed dhamma. Mahastavir was objected to Dr Ambedkar's second marriage because his wife was a Brahmin. Later, his followers actively participated in Ambedkar's Republican Party of India.

AMBEDKAR'S CONVERSION

After publishing a series of books and articles arguing that Buddhism was the only way for the Untouchables to gain equality, Ambedkar publicly converted on October 14, 1956 in Nagpur. He took the three refuges and the Five Precepts from a Buddhist monk, Bhadant U Chandramani, in the traditional manner and then in his turn administered them to the 380,000 of his followers that were present. The conversion ceremony was attended by Medharthi, his main disciple Bhoj Dev Mudit, and Mahastvir Bodhanand's Sri Lankan successor, Bhante Pragyanand. Ambedkar would die less than two months later, just after finishing his definitive work on Buddhism.

Many Dalits employ the term "Ambedkar(ite) Buddhism" to designate the Buddhist movement, which started with Ambedkar's conversion.

DALIT BUDDHISM MOVEMENT AFTER AMBEDKAR'S DEATH

The Buddhist movement was somewhat hindered by Dr. Ambedkar's death so shortly after his conversion. It did not receive the immediate mass support from the Untouchable population that Ambedkar had hoped for. Division and lack of direction among the leaders of the Ambedkarite movement have been an additional impediment. According to the 2001 census, there are currently 7.95 million Buddhists in India, at least 5.83 million of whom are Buddhists in Maharashtra. This makes Buddhism the fifth-largest religion in India and 6% of the population of Maharashtra, but less than 1% of the overall population of India.

The Buddhist revival remains concentrated in two states: Ambedkar's native Maharashtra, and Uttar Pradesh — the land of Bodhanand Mahastavir, Acharya Medharthi and their associates.

DEVELOPMENTS IN UTTAR PRADESH

Acharya Medharthi retired from his Buddhapuri school in 1960, and shifted to an ashram in Haridwar. He turned to the Arya Samaj and conducted vedic yajnas all over

India. After his death, he was cremated according to Arya Samaj rites. His Buddhpuri school became embroiled in property disputes. His follower, Bhoj Dev Mudit, converted to Buddhism in 1968 and set up a school of his own.

Rajendranath Aherwar appeared as an important Dalit leader in Kanpur. He joined the Republican Party of India and converted to Buddhism along with his whole family in 1961. In 1967, he founded the Kanpur branch of "Bharatiya Buddh Mahasabha". He held regular meetings where he preached Buddhism, officiated at Buddhist weddings and life cycle ceremonies, and organized festivals on Dr. Ambedkar's Jayanti (birth day), Buddha Jayanti, Diksha Divas (the day Ambedkar converted), and Dr Ambedkar Paranirvan Divas (the day Ambedkar died).

The Dalit Buddhist movement in Kanpur gained impetus with the arrival of Dipankar, a Chamar bhikkhu, in 1980. Dipankar had come to Kanpur on a Buddhist mission and his first public appearance was scheduled at a mass conversion drive in 1981. The event was organized by Rahulan Ambawadekar, an RPI Dalit leader. In April 1981, Ambawadekar founded the Dalit Panthers (U.P. Branch) inspired by the Maharashtrian Dalit Panthers. The event met with severe criticism and opposition from Vishwa Hindu Parishad and was banned.

In 2002, Kanshi Ram, a popular out-caste political leader from a Sikh religious background, announced his intention to convert to Buddhism on October 14, 2006, the fiftieth anniversary of Ambedkar's conversion. He intended for 20,000,000 of his supporters to convert at the same time. Part of the significance of this plan was that Ram's followers include not only Untouchables, but persons from a variety of castes, who could significantly broaden Buddhism's support. However, he passed away October 9, 2006 after a lengthy illness; he was cremated as per Buddhist rituals.

Another popular Dalit leader, Bahujan Samaj Party chief Mayawati, has said that she and her followers will embrace Buddhism after the BSP gains control of the government.

MAHARASHTRA

Japanese-born Bhadant Nagarjun Surai Sasai is an important Buddhist leader in India. Susai came to India in 1966 and met Nichidatsu Fuji, whom he helped with the Peace Pagoda at Rajgir. He fell out with Fuji, however, and started home, but, by his own account, was stopped by a dream in which a figure resembling Nagarjuna appeared and said, "Go to Nagpur". In Nagpur, he met Wamanrao Godbole, the person who had organized the conversion ceremony for Dr. Ambedkar in 1956. Sasai claims that when he saw a photograph of Dr. Ambedkar at Godbole's home, he realized that it was Ambedkar who had appeared in his dream. At first, Nagpur folk considered Surai Sasai very strange. Then he began to greet them with "Jai Bhim" (victory to Ambedkar) and to build viharas. In 1987 a court case to deport him on the grounds that he had overstayed his visa was dismissed, and he was granted Indian citizenship. Sasai is one of the main leaders of the campaign to free the Mahabodhi Temple at Bodh Gaya from Hindu control.

VIPASSANA MOVEMENT

The Buddhist meditation tradition of Vipassana meditation is growing in popularity in India. Many institutions—both government and private sector—now offer courses for their employees. This form is mainly practiced by middle class Indians. This movement has spread to many other countries in Europe, America and Asia.

BUDDHISM IN SRI LANKA

Sri Lanka is the oldest continually Buddhist country, Theravada Buddhism being the major religion in the island since its official introduction in the 2nd century BC by Venerable Mahinda, the son of the Emperor Ashoka of India during the reign of King Devanampiya- Tissa. Later, the nun Sanghamitta, the daughter of Asoka, was said to have brought the southern branch of the original Bodhi tree, where it was planted at Anuradhapura. From that day up to the present, the Buddhists in Sri Lanka have paid and are paying the utmost reverence to this branch of the Bodhi Tree under the shade of which the Master achieved Enlightenment.

Monks from Sri Lanka have had an important role in spreading both Theravada and Mahayana throughout South-east Asia. It was in Sri Lanka, in the 1st century AD during the reign of King Vatta Gamini that the Buddhist monks assembled in Aloka-Vihara and wrote down the Tripitaka, the three basket of the Teachings, known as the Pali scriptures for the first time. It was Sri Lankan nuns who introduced the Sangha of nuns into China in 433AD. In the 16th century the Portuguese conquered Sri Lanka and savagely persecuted Buddhism as did the Dutch who followed them.

When the British won control at the beginning of the 19th century Buddhism was well into decline, a situation that encouraged the English missionaries that then began to flood the island. But against all expectations the monastic and lay community brought about a major revival from about 1860 onwards, a movement that went hand in hand with growing nationalism.

Since then Buddhism has flourished and Sri Lankan monks and expatriate lay people have been prominent in spreading Theravada Buddhism in Asia, the West and even in Africa.

Some of the most marvellous monuments in the Buddhist world belong to Sri Lanka, and her sculpture is closely associated with the early art of the Krishna valley and the later Pallava and Chola kings, owing to the close relationship that existed between south India and Sri Lanka.

Buddhism was introduced to Sri Lanka in 236 b.e. (cir. 250 BCE) and became the national religion of the Sinhalese from that date. It is, however, necessary for a proper study of the history of Buddhism in the island to consider the state of the island and its social and political developments and the culture and character of the people immediately preceding this period. This will enable us to get a clear understanding of the manner in which such a far-reaching revolution in the beliefs, manners, customs and character of a people was effected by the introduction of this new religion and the progress in literature, art and culture that has been manifested through its influence.

HISTORY OF BUDDHISM IN SRI LANKA

In order to understand and appreciate the history of early Buddhism in Sri Lanka we should have, as a background some general idea of the India of the third century B.C from where Buddhism come to Sri Lanka and also of the pre-Buddhist Sri Lanka to which it was introduced. When the Indian missionaries brought Buddhism to this Island they carried here with them not only the teaching of the Buddha but also the culture and civilisation of Buddhist India. Almost all Buddhist rites, ceremonies, festivals and observance of Sri Lanka were with slight local changes and modification, the continuation of Indian practice which the early Buddhist missionaries introduced into this country. It necessary there at the time of the advent of Buddhism to Sri Lanka.

Buddhism began as an intellectual and ethical moment in the sixth century B.C with the first sermon preached by the Buddha to the five ascetics at Isipathana near Benares.It spread gradually during the life-time of the Buddha along the gangetic valley and found its way into several kingdoms in north India between the vindhya mountains and the Himalayas Kings and ministers ,bankers and wealthy merchant ,brahmins and peasants became the followers of this new teaching which was a revolt again some of the accepted theories and practices of the day.

At the time of the Buddhas death about 483 B.C almost all the important states in North India seemed to have been deeply influenced by the new teaching. According to the Mahaparinibbna- sutta eight countries clammed, on various ground, a portion of the ashes of the Buddha,which shows that he had already gained many ardent devotees in these states. Yet there is no evidence to show that the teaching of the Buddha had been adopted as the state religion of these kingdoms till long after his death.

Immediately after the Buddhas death a council was held at Rajagaha during the rainy season under the patronage of Ajatasattu, king of Magadha, which Maha-kassapa as its president the mojstsenior of the disciples of the Buddha then alive.Its purpose was to decide and settle the authentic teaching of the Master. The Buddhas immediate deciples, like Ananda and Upali, were the principal protaganists in this great event.

About a century later, in the fourth century B.C during the time of King Kalasoka of pataliputta, a group of monks known under the generic name of Vajji bukkhus, residing at the Mahavana monastery in vesali raised ten new points of indulgence which perturbed the orthodox authorities. Under the guidance of Yasa, Revata and Sabbakami three leading theras of the day, a great council was held at Vasali and the ten joints raised by the Vajji bhikkus were condemned as false and heretic. The authentic and genuine teaching of the Master was defined for the second time.

After this second council the bhikkhus, who were condemned as unorthodox and heretic assembled elsewhere, held a rival council and inaugurated a new sect called

Mahasanghika (orMahasangiti),different from the theriya sect. The following century saw the rise of eighteen sects in all including the various schools of the theravada.

In the last years of the century B.C Chandragupta Maurya had founded and organised a large and powerful empire extending approximately from Afghanistan to Mysore. Territories which are even now outside the Government of India were part of the Indian Empire under Chandragupta.

The missionaries for the establishment of Buddhism were sent out to nine countries among which Sri Lanka was included. King Asokas own son Mahinda was entrusted with the task of establishing Buddhism in Sri Lanka. The emperor perhaps felt that his work would be most fruitful in this Island for Devanampriya-tissa the King of Sri Lanka had already expressed his friendship by sending ambassadors with valuable gift to the Indian emperor. Wherever they went the Indian Buddhist missionaries were successful. Even Greeks like Yonaka Dhammarakkhita become Buddhist bhikkhus but Sri Lanka was the most fertile of fields for the Buddhist activities of Asoka. So far as Edicts are concerned, Sri Lanka is mentioned as Tamraparni in Rock Edicts II and X!II and as the country already included by Asoka in the list of countries to which he despatches his Dutas or messengers to prosecute his scheme of Dharma Vijaya or Moral Conquest, thus by the time of these Edicts 9258-257 B.C Sri Lanka was already a sphere of Asokas missionary activities which according to Rock Edict II

In the third century B. C the capital of Sri Lanka was Anuradhapura. It was Pandukabhaya (377-307B.C) who developed the original Anuradhapura into real nagara or coty and he seems to have organised it very efficiently. Before Pandukabhaya there was nothing which could properly have been called a city in Sri Lanka. All centres of population were called gamas villages , but the words gama and nagara in the early part of the Mahavamsa are used indiscriminately both for village and city or town and do not help us to decide on the size and extent of place. Before Anuradhapura came into prominence there were other places like Tambapanni Vijitapura and Upatissagama which served as the seats of government for short periods. But from the time Anuradhapura was raised by Pandukabhaya to the eminence of a city in the latter part of the fourth century B.C it remained as the capital of Sri Lanka for about twelve centuries.

By the end of the third century B.C the architectural development of Anuradhapura seems to have reached a fairly high stage Pandukabhayas grand -uncle, Anuradha, who originally established the village of Anuradhagama calling it after his own name built for himself a house which was call Rajageha.

When Pandukabhkaya entered Anuradhapura, after the destruction of his enemies the old chief offered his house to his victorious grand-nephew. and went to live in another house. Pandukabaya is not reported to have built a place for his residence. But there is mention made of various buildings erected by Pandukabhaya in Anuradhapura and its suburbs. We are told also of a particular building called Ekathunika in Upati-sagama, the seat of government before Anuradhapura. This house which which as its name implies, stood on one pillar, was constructed by Pandukabhayas uncles for the specific purpose of imprisoning their sister citta in a futile attempt to prevent her from begetting a son. It was ventilated with windows (gavakkha).

All the same there seems to have been a few buildings in Anuradhapura even in the time of Devanampiya-Tiss could not,for instance,find a suitable house as residence for Mahinda. He hurriedly builds a house of mud and dries it with torch-fire. On account of the method adopted for drying it the wall became dark and the house was called Kalapasada-privana, Dark Residence. How the house built is not quite clear. But it is evident that there were no burnt brinks available for the purpose, at least locally or within easy reach.

Devanampiya-Tissa would never have offered such a residence as this to the grest royal missionary, son of Emperor Asoka and a visitor from India,if he had been in a position to provide more suitable accommodation.

It may be argued that Devanampiya-Tissa out of great respect did not wish to offer the holy man a house which had been occupied by others. But this does not seem likely, because Devanampiya-Tissa invited Mahinda, on the second day of his arrival to spend the night in a house in Mahameghavana and the latter consented. The house had undoubtedly been used by other people-at lease by the king and his queen and other members of royal family.

It would seem that there was no large hall in the city for a public gathering. When the townspeople desired to see and hear Mahinda, the king seeing that there was no room within the premises of the place, ordered the hall of the State Elephant to be cleansed and arranged for the purpose. It was here that the citizens assembled to listen to the royal visitor. As Mahindas audience grew bigger and bigger the venue had to be shifted from the Elephant hall to the bigger Nandana Garden outside the southern gate of the city, where open-air meetings were held in the royal park, thickly shaded, cool and covered with verdure.

These instances would show that there was a general lack of buildings in Anuradhapura at that time. It was only after the introduction of Buddhism that massive buildings like the Lohapasada began to rise in Sri Lanka. Although various religious buildings are said to have been built by Pandukabhaya there is no evidence of the existence of a single building spacious enough to accommodate large assemblies, this further indicates that either no public meetings were held, or if at all they were held in the open air. Perhaps it may be that it was only after the introduction of Buddhism that the people of Sri Lanka began to hold organised public gatherings for specific purposes such as listening to a religious discourse.

Sanitary conditions in Anuradhapura seem to have been of a high order. During Pandukabhayas time there were scavengers of the candala caste, 500 in number for cleaning the city ,2000 for cleaning the sewers; 150 for taking dead bodies away to the cemeteries and 150 as watchers. Pandukabhaya is reported to have created a new post called Nagara-guttika (guardian of city) for his uncle Abhaya, his predecessor, who was helpful both to Pandukabhaya and his mother. The duty of this officer was the administration of the government for the night time (ratti-rajjam). From that time onward there were Nagara-guttikas in the capital. This perhaps was the prototype of mayor in later time.

There were two parks near the capital. The Nandanavana (or jothivana as it called later) almost adjoined the city, just outside the southern gate. It was here that Mahinda delivered most of his sermons immediately after his arrival. The Mahamaghavana, which was laid out by Pandukabhayas son, Mutasiva was provided with fruit trees and flower trees.

This was neither too near nor too far from the city, and was situated outside the eastern gate of the city. There was in this park a pavilion (Raja-gaha Royal house) built for the use of the king. It was in this house or pavilion that Mahinda spent several days soon after his arrival. Within the park were beautiful tanks and pond. Mention is made of a little tank called Kakudhkavapi within the enclosure and also a beautiful pond called Murutta to the north of the royal pavilion.

Pandukabhaya built a tank to supply water to the city, although there was already a tank built by Anuradha, his grand uncle. Outside the city there was a general cemetery called Mahasusana laid out by Pandukabhaya, and there was also a place of execution.

The Candalas who were employed in the city, had their village known as Candalagama to the north-west of the general cemetery. This village seems to have had a population at least of about 2000 people during Pandukabhayas time, judging from the numbers given in the Mahavamsa To the north-east of this village there was a cemetery exclusively for candalas known as Nicasusana(Lover cemetery). Mention is made of a stable for horses assamandala, near the city during the time of Devanampiya-Tissa.There were also four suburbs, Dvaragam laid out by Pandukabhaya.

By the third century B.C practically the whole of Sri Lanka with the exception of the hilly country and the eastern coast, seems to have been populated though not very thickly perhaps. Almost all the habitable spots were were occupied. Henry Parker argues in favour of Mahagama and its surrounding villages as the first settlements of the early Aryans who landed here. Kirinda in the south according to him being the actual landing place. He says that all the early settlements of the leading chiefs were termed gama village and the capital became Mahagama the great village of the country.

Weather we agree with this suggestion or not there is no doubt that the area watered by the rivers Valaveganga, Kirindi-oya, Manik-ganga and Kumbukkan (modern kataragama).The representatives of these Ksatriyas were among the distinguished personages who attended the celebration held in honour of the Bodhi-branch brought from India by Sanghamitta.One of the first Bo-saplings was planted at Kajaragama.Devanampiya-Tissas brother, the vice-regent Mahanaga, in order to escape the dangerous consequence of the queens treachery, fled with his family from Anuradhapura to Ruhuna ,and ruled in Mahagama. The fact that Mahagama suggests that the Ksatriyas there were connected with the royal family at Anuradhapura. Throughout the history of Sri Lanka we find Ruhuna, the last refuge and sanctury of freedom. Whenever there was danger at Anuradhapura, either from foreign invasion or from internal conflicts, Kings, ministers, monks and others who desired freedom and protection took shelter in the South.

There was another settlement called Candanagama, hitherto unidentified, where too there were Ksatriyas. The representatives of these also were among those present at the celebrations of the Mahabodhi at Anuradhapura during Devanampriya-Tissas reign. One of the first Bo-saplings was planted here.

Mahanagas journey to Mahagama for safety shows that there was communication between Anuradpura and Mahagama. The road between these two places ran through centiyagiri (now Mihintale) Kacchakatittha (Magantota) or Vaddhamanakatittha (known also by the names Sahassatittha (dahastota) and Assamandalatittha) Mahiyangana(modern Aluthnuwara) Dihavapi and Guttahalaka (Buttala).This road also served always as a military route. There is no doubt that there were on this road many places of habitation though much of the road lay across desolate jungle (antaramagge agamakaranne).

Anuradhapura and the surrounding districts, within a radius of about 60 or 70 miles, seem to have been well populated. Pandukabhaya in his military campaign against his uncles, in order to subjugate the border districts (paccantagama) is reported to have withdraws as far south as Dolapabbata (supposed to be the modern Dolagalavela) in the Bintanna district. Thus at least the districts between Anuradhapura and Dolapabbata were well populated.

The districts to the west and north-west of Anuradhapura the area where some of the earliest villages were established, were also well populated. There were four road connecting the capital with four famous sea ports situated along the coast between north and west namely Mahatitta (mantai near Mannar) Jambukolapattna in the north, Gonagamapattana(of the eastern coast) and the sea port at the mouth of the Mahakandara river (probably in the north).The last three have not yet been definitely. The localities round these sea ports were without doubt inhabited and the four roads ran through many villages, great and small. It is said that when the Bodhi-branch was taken from jambukulapattana to Anuradhapura the procession halted at several places. Particular mention being made of village of a brahmana named Tivakka.

There was another settlement in Kalyani (modern Kalaniya) About a century after Devenampriya Tissa, in the second century B.C, we know definitely that there was a kingdom at Kalaniya. Duttha Gamanis mother, the daughter of king Tissa of Kalyani the famous Vihara-Mahadevi, came from this principality. The Rajavaliya says that Yatala

Tissa, the son of mahanaga, Devanamoriya_tissas brother who fled from Anuradhapura ruled in kalaniya and built the cetiya there. It is quite reasonable to assume that this principality was among the earliest settlements in Sri Lanka.

The Mahavamsa -Tika says that the early Aryans who came to this Island opened up new settlements in areas where water was easily available. These were mainly along the principal rivers of Sri Lanka. Anuradhagama and other early gamas (villages) such as Upatissa, Ujjeni, Uruvela and Vijita were on the rivers Kadambanadi Malvatu-oya, Gambhira-nadi and kala-oya .Then there were settlements along the Mahavali-ganga and the Amban-ganga,particularly round about Kacchakatittha (Magantota) In the south settlements were distributed among the four rivers Kumbukkan-oya, Manik-ganga(kappakandara) Kirindioya and Valave-Ganga. Another settlements was along the valley of the Kalani-ganga where there was no river water easily available, large reservoirs were built in order to make the settlement habitable. Thus there is reference quite early in history to tanks builts by Anuradha and Pandukabhaya.

EARLY TRADITIONS

According to the early chronicles relating the historical traditions of Sri Lanka, a prince named Vijaya and his followers who came from India and landed in Lanka on the day of the Parinibbaana of the Buddha were the first human inhabitants of this island. When they came the island was occupied by "yakkhas" (sprites, demons). "Yakkhas" and "naagas" are also said to have inhabited Lanka in the time of the Buddha. A legend relating the existence of a great civilization before this time, under a king named Raavana, is also current though the early chronicles make no mention of it.

The Vijaya legend of these chronicles is taken by modern historians as a poetic expression of the actual aryanization of Sri Lanka in about the sixth century BCE The term "yakkhas and naagas" may refer to the aborigines who occupied the island before their arrival. No traces of an advanced civilization, however, have yet been discovered to support the Raavana legend. Archaeologists have discovered chert and quartz implements and tools at various sites, believed to have been used by aborigines of Sri Lanka, and they indicate that these people were a primitive tribe who lived by hunting. These aborigines have not left traces of a strong political organization or an advanced culture. The present Veddas are believed to be their descendants.

COLONIZATION BY PRINCE VIJAYA AND HIS FOLLOWERS

Vijaya and his 700 followers are described in the Lankan chronicles as a set of adventurous young men who, when they were banished from their Indian homeland Laala (or Laata), came in search of new land for settlement. Other legends, some of which are even older, relating how the first aryan inhabitants came to settle down in Lanka are found in several Pali and Sanskrit works. Most of them show that the settlement of early aryan settlers is due to the enterprise of the pioneering merchant mariners who came to this island for pearls and precious stones. Historians thus do not lay much reliance on the details of the Vijayan legend but they accept Vijaya as the first traditional ruler of the newcomers — the Sinhalese.

Vijaya, who was a Kshatriya, landed in Lanka, according to the chronicles, on the day of the Parinibbaana of the Buddha. He allied himself with an aboriginal princess named Kuveni and married her and with her influence soon became the master of the country. Later he drove Kuveni away and obtained a princess from Maduraa whom he made his queen. Maidens of high birth came from the Pandyan kingdom as wives of his followers.

Vijaya ruled from his settlement Tambappanni and his ministers founded other settlements like Anuraadhagaama, Upatissagaama, Ujjeni, Uruvelaa and Vijitapura. Thus the earliest settlements that were founded in the time of King Vijaya were located along the river banks in the northwestern region of Lanka like the Malvatu-oya and the Kalaa-oya.

POLITICAL DEVELOPMENT AND SOCIAL ORGANIZATION AFTER VIJAYA

Vijaya died after a rule of 38 years. Since he had no son to succeed him, before his death he sent messengers to his brother Sumitta in Sihapura to come and rule here. Sumitta sent his youngest son Panduvaasudeva, since he himself was king of Sihapura and was also too old. Panduvaasudeva, Vijaya's nephew, arrived one year after Vijaya's death during which period the ministers of Vijaya ruled the country. When Panduvaasudeva came he brought with him 32 sons of ministers.

The early chronicles preserve an episode which connects the Sakka family of the Buddha with the sovereignty of Lanka from the time of King Panduvaasudeva. According to this account, Bhaddakaccaanaa, who also arrived in Lanka with 32 other maidens shortly after Panduvaasudeva arrived, was the daughter of Pandu Sakka, who himself was the son of Amitodana, an uncle of the Buddha.

Panduvaasudeva ruled for 30 years and was succeeded by his eldest son Abhaya, who ruled for 20 years. Abhaya's successor was Pandukaabhaya, the son of his sister Ummaadacitta. Pandukaabhaya was a great ruler in whose reign Anuraadhapura developed into a great city with well-marked boundaries. After a long reign of 70 years, Pandukaabhaya was succeeded by his son Mutasiva who ruled for 60 years. Mutasiva's second son, Devaanampiya Tissa, succeeded him in 250 BCE, that is, 236 years after the accession of Vijaya.

These 236 years could be reckoned as a separate period in the history of Sri Lanka for it formed the background for the offical introduction of Buddhism, which occurred during the opening years of the next ruler, King Devaanampiya Tissa. During this period the aryan colonists founded settlements along the fertile river banks almost throughout the island. They chose the river banks because they were mainly agriculturists. Thus the regions watered by the Malvatu-oya, Kalaa-oya, Valave-ganga, Kirindi-oya, Menik-ganga and Kumbukkan-oya, the Kelani-ganga and some regions around the Mahaveli-ganga soon became populated. Anuraadhapura became a well-organized city with boundaries marked, lakes dug and hospitals and other buildings constructed.3 In the south, Mahaagaama (Maagama), became the center of activity. The majority of the aboriginal inhabitants were absorbed into the new community through intermarriage while a few withdrew to the Malayadesa, the highlands.

PRE-BUDDHIST RELIGION IN SRI LANKA

It is evident from the chronicles relating the early history of Sri Lanka that before the introduction of Buddhism in the reign of King Devaanampiya Tissa (250-210 BCE) there was no single religion which was widely accepted as the national religion of the country. Nevertheless, there was a wide range of religious beliefs and practices, different from one another, and each individual seems to have freely observed his religion according to his belief.

A noteworthy feature of the pre-Buddhist religion of Sri Lanka is that it was a mixture of the aboriginal cults and the beliefs of the aryan newcomers.

The worship of yaksas and yaksinis was a widely prevalent aboriginal custom of pre-Buddhist Lanka. King Pandukaabhaya, the grandfather of Devaanampiya Tissa, provided shrines for many of these spirits and also gave them sacrificial offerings annually. Some of these yaksas and yaksinis mentioned by name are Kaalavela, Cittaraaja, Vessavana, Valavaamukhi and Cittaa. Vyaadhadeva, Kammaaradeva and Pacchimaraajini, though not known as yaksas and yaksinis, also belong to the same category of aboriginal spirits. Trees like the banyan and palmyrah were also connected with the cults of these spirits showing that tree-worship was also prevalent.

Many scholars agree that these yaksas and other non-human beings are none but the spirits of the dead relatives and tribal chiefs who, the people believed, were capable of helping friends and harming enemies. This belief, as is widely known, formed one of the main features of the primitive religion and is extant even today.

Accounts relating the pre-Buddhist history of Sri Lanka also show a considerable influence of the religious trends of India on the society of Lanka. Several niganthas (Jainas) such as Giri, Jotiya and Kumbhanda lived in the reign of Pandukaabhaya and hermitages were constructed for them and other ascetics like aajivakas, brahmans and the wandering mendicant monks. Five hundred families of heretical beliefs also lived near the city of Anuraadhapura. The brahmans occupied a high place in society and their religious beliefs were also respected. The worship of Siva too may have been prevalent.

The account in the *Mahaavamsa* of the settling of the adherents of various sects by King Pandukaabhaya does not specifically mention the presence of any adherents of Buddhism among them. But the work refers to three visits of the Buddha to Sri Lanka, a statement which, though not corroborated by other evidence, has not been disproved. Legendary accounts also claim that two stupas — the Mahiyangana and the Girihandu — were constructed before the introduction of Buddhism. Among the newcomers too there could have been some members who were acquainted with Buddhism, especially as Bhaddakaccaanaa, who arrived with 32 other maidens in the guise of nuns, was a close relative of the Buddha.

EMPEROR ASOKA AND BUDDHISM IN INDIA

Buddhism as a form of religious expression gained ascendency in India during this period. Emperor Asoka was crowned, according to the chronicles, in the year 218 of the Buddhist era (i.e., 268 BCE). Like his father Bindusaara and grandfather Candragupta, Asoka was a follower of the brahmanical faith at the beginning of his reign. In the early years of his reign he followed an expansionist policy and in the eighth year of his coronation he conquered Kaalinga, in the course of which 100,000 were slain and 150,000 taken prisoners. But the carnage of the Kaalinga war caused him much grief and the king was attracted towards the humanistic teachings of Buddhism. According to the Sri Lanka chronicles, it was a young novice named Nigrodha who converted Asoka.

After the conversion of this great emperor Buddhism flourished under his patronage. He inculcated the teachings of the Buddha and set up edicts of morality at numerous places of his vast empire so that his subjects would adhere to them and his successors might follow him. He himself followed those morals and set an example to the others. The king is reputed to have built 84,000 stupas. The monks were lavishly provided with their requisites.

The king even permitted his son Mahinda and daughter Sanghamittaa to join the Order when they were twenty and eighteen years of age respectively. These two illustrious disciples became noted for their piety, attainments, learning and profound knowledge of the Dhamma.

Vast numbers joined the Order in the reign of Asoka solely to share the benefits showered on it by the king, and such people were not only lax in their conduct, but also held doctrines counter to the teachings of the Buddha.

It was this dissenting element that led to the holding of the Third Buddhist Council under the patronage of King Asoka in order to purify the Buddhist religion (Saasana). It was at this Council held by a thousand theras (elders) under the leadership of Moggaliputta Tissa, at Paataliputta, that the Pali Canon of the Theravaada, as it exists today, was finally redacted.

At this Council was also taken, the important decision of sending missionaries to different regions to preach Buddhism and establish the Saasana there. Thus the thera Moggaliputta Tissa deputed Majjhantika Thera to Kaasmira-Gandhaara, Mahaadeva Thera to Mahisamandala, Rakkhita Thera to Vanavaasi, Yona-Dhammarakkhita Thera to Aparaantaka, Dhammarakkhita Thera to Mahaarattha, Mahaarakkhita Thera to Yonaloka, Majjhima Thera to Himavanta, theras So.na and Uttara to Suvannabhuumi, and Mahinda Thera with theras Itthiya, Uttiya, Sambala and Bhaddasaala to Lanka, saying unto the five theras: "Establish ye in the delightful land of Lanka the delightful religion of the Vanquisher."

THE MISSION TO SRI LANKA

Mahinda was thirty-two years old when he undertook the mission to Sri Lanka. He had adopted the religious life at the age of twenty, mastered the doctrines and attained the highest spiritual life, i.e., arahantship. Pondering on the fitting time to come to Lanka, he perceived that Mutasiva, the ruler at that time, was in his old age, and hence it was advisable to tarry until his son became ruler.

In the meantime Mahinda visited his relatives at Dakkhinaagiri and his mother at Vedisagiri along with his companions. His mother Devi, whom Asoka had married while he was yet a prince, was living at Vedisagiri at that time. Having stayed for six months at Dakkhinaagiri and a month at Vedisagiri, Mahinda perceived that the right time had come, for the old ruler was dead and his son Devaanampiya Tissa had become king.

Devaanampiya Tissa was the second son of Mutasiva. He was a friend of Asoka even before he became king but the two had not seen each other. The first thing that Devaanampiya Tissa did when he became king was to send envoys to Asoka, bearing costly presents. The envoys, when they returned, brought among other things the following message from Asoka:

"Aha.m Buddhañ ca Dhammañ ca Sanghañ ca sara.na.mgato upaasakatta.m vedesi.m Saakyaputtassa saasane tvamp'imaani ratanaani uttamaani naruttama citta.m pasaadayitvaana saddhaaya sara.na.m bhaja."

"I have taken refuge in the Buddha, his Doctrine and his Order, I have declared myself a lay-disciple in the religion of the Saakya son; seek then, O best of men, refuge in these best of gems, converting your mind with believing heart."

This message of Asoka was conveyed to King Devaanampiya Tissa in the month of Vesakha and it was the full-moon day of the following month Jettha (Sinh. Poson) that Mahinda fixed for his arrival in Sri Lanka. Among the companions of Mahinda were the theras Itthiya, Uttiya, Sambala and Bhaddasaala, the saamanera Sumana who was the son of Sanghamittaa, and the lay-disciple Bhanduka who was the son of a daughter of Devi's sister and had become an anaagaami (once-returner) on hearing a sermon of Mahinda preached to Devi.

ARRIVAL OF MAHINDA

Thus on the full-moon day of the month of Jettha in the year 236 b.e. (i.e., 250 BCE) Mahinda and his companions, departing from Vedisagiri, rose up in the air and alighted on the Silakuuta of the pleasant Missaka hill, presently Mihintale, eight miles east of Anuraadhapura. The thera alighted here for he had perceived that he would meet the king there on that day.

The first meeting of the king of Lanka and the thera Mahinda is graphically described in the chronicles of Sri Lanka. The full-moon day of Jettha was a day of national festival in Lanka. Men and women were engaged in amusing themselves. The king with a large party of followers went to Mihintale hills on a hunting expedition. There he saw the theras with shaven heads dressed in yellow robes, of dignified mien and distinguished appearance, who faced him and addressed him not as ordinary men addressing a king but as those to whom a king was their inferior. The conversation impressed the king and his immediate surrender to the wisdom and piety displayed by the thera was complete. Mahinda Thera in reply to the king's inquiry as to who they were and whence they had come, said:

"Samanaa mayam Mahaaraaja Dhammaraajassa saavakaa tav'eva anukampaaya Jambudiipaa idhaagataa."

"We are the disciples of the Lord of the Dhamma. In compassion towards you, Mahaaraaja, We have come here from India."

When he heard these words of the thera, the king laid aside his bow and arrow, and approaching the thera, exchanged greetings with him and sat down near him. Mahinda then had a conversation with the king, and realizing that the king was intelligent enough to comprehend the Dhamma, preached the Cuulahatthipadopama Sutta. At the end of the discourse the king and his retinue of forty thousand people embraced the new faith. Having invited the missionaries to the city the king left for his palace. Mahinda spent his first day in Sri Lanka at Mihintale where he solemnized the first ecclesiastical act by admitting to the Order the lay-follower Bhanduka who had accompanied him from India.

ENTRY INTO THE CAPITAL

On the invitation of the king, Mahinda and the other theras arrived at Anuraadhapura the following day. Going forward to meet the theras, the king respectfully led them into the palace where he himself served them with dainty food. After the meal Mahinda preached the Petavatthu, the Vimaanavatthu and the Sacca-samyutta to the royal household.

The people of the city who heard of the theras flocked near the palace-gate to see them and the king prepared a hall outside the palace so that the townspeople could see the theras. On this occasion Mahinda preached the Devaduuta Sutta (Majjhima Nikaya, No. 130).

This hall too was not spacious enough for the vast gathering and seats were prepared for the theras in the Nandana-garden in the royal park, where Mahinda preached the Baalapandita Sutta, (Majjhima Nikaya, No. 129).

In the evening the theras expressed their desire to go back to Mihintale. The king, who wished them to stay in his capital, granted to the Sangha the royal park Mahaamegha for their residence. The king himself marked the boundaries by plowing a furrow. Thus was established the Mahaavihaara which became the earliest celebrated center of the Buddhist religion. Having spent twenty-six days in the Mahaamegha Park, the thera returned to Mihintale for the rain-retreat (*vassa*). This was the beginning of the Cetiyagiri-vihaara, another great monastic institution of early Buddhist Sri Lanka.

SANGHAMITTAA AND WOMEN DISCIPLES

Many women of Sri Lanka, headed by Queen Anulaa, desired to enter the Order of disciples and thus it came about that emissaries led by the king's nephew Arittha were sent to Emperor Asoka to obtain the help of female disciples to enable the women of Lanka to obtain ordination.

Sanghamittaa, the sister of Mahinda Thera, who had entered the Order and had received ordination, was sent out to Lanka at the request of the king and the people and on the recommendation of Mahinda Thera.

The message sent by thera Mahinda to Emperor Asoka pleased him very much, for in it he realized that the mission to Lanka had been eminently successful and the king and the people of Lanka had accepted the new doctrine with enthusiasm.

ARRIVAL OF THE SACRED BO-TREE

Emperor Asoka decided on sending a token of the Great and Enlightened One to the land of Lanka and prepared a branch of the Sacred Bodhi Tree under which the Lord attained enlightenment. He planted the branch in a golden vessel and, when it had taken root, conveyed it to the ship, depositing it in the ship. He also sent a large number of attendants to accompany the tree. The chronicles mention that these were selected from the brahmans, nobles and householders and consisted of 64 families. Sanghamittaa Therii and her attendants embarked on the same ship as well as the ambassadors and messengers who came from Lanka.

The ship sailed from Taamralipti (Tamluk) and arrived at the port in Lanka in seven days. The port was known as Jambukola and was situated in the north of the island. The king of Lanka on hearing of the arrival of the ship had the road from Jambukola to the capital city of Anuraadhapura gaily decorated. He arrived in state and himself took charge of the Sacred Bodhi Tree. This tree was planted in the Mahaamegha garden of Anuraadhapura with great festivities and tended with honor and care. Up to this date it flourishes as one of the most sacred objects of veneration and worship for millions of Buddhists.

THE FIRM ESTABLISHMENT OF THE SAASANA

Arittha, the king's nephew who had obtained the king's permission to enter the

Order of monks on his return from India, did so with five hundred other men and all became arahants. With the ordination of Anulaa and the other women both the Bhikkhu-saasana and the Bhikkhuni-saasana were established in the island. Separate residences for monks and nuns were built by the king. The Thuupaaraama-cetiya enshrining the right collar-bone and other bodily relics of the Buddha was built, and the Sacred Bodhi Tree was planted for the devotion of the laity. When these acts of religious devotion were accomplished, the king asked Mahinda Thera whether the Saasana had been firmly established in the island, to which the latter replied that it had only been planted but would take firm root when a person born in Sri Lanka, of Sinhalese parents, studied the Vinaya in Sri Lanka and expounded it in Sri Lanka.

Arittha Thera had by this time become noted for his piety and his learning and on an appointed day, at a specially constructed preaching hall, in the presence of numerous theras, the king and the chiefs, Arittha Thera was invited to give a discourse on the Vinaya in the presence of the thera Mahaa Mahinda. And his exposition was so correct and pleasing that there was great rejoicing as the condition required for the firm establishment of the Saasana was fulfilled by him.

PROGRESS OF BUDDHISM IN LANKA

Devaanampiya Tissa ruled in Sri Lanka for forty years. It was in the first year of his reign that Buddhism was introduced and from that time the king worked for the progress of the new faith with great zeal. Apart from the Mahaavihaara, the Cetiyapabbatavihaara, the Thuuparaama and the Sacred Bodhi Tree, he established numerous other monasteries and several Buddhist monuments. The chronicles mention that he built monasteries a yojana from one another. Among these monuments the Isurumuni-vihaara and the Vessagiri-vihaara are important centers of worship to this day. He is also credited with the construction of the Pathamaka-cetiya, the Jambukola-vihaara and the Hatthaalhaka-vihaara, and the refectory.

Thousands of men and women joined the Order during his reign. The king not only built vihaaras for their residence but also provided them with their requisites. It was not only in the capital city that Buddhism spread in his reign but even in distant regions like Jambukola in the north and Kaajaragaama and Candanagaama in the south.

The remarkable success of Mahinda's mission and the rapid spread of the religion in a very short time were mainly due to the efforts of Mahinda and the unbounded patronage of King Devaanampiya Tissa. Apart from them the people of Lanka too were eminently ripe at this period for receiving and adopting the teachings of the Buddha. The people in the land were prosperous, their wants were few, and these were supplied by the fertile soil. There was prosperous trade, for merchants came from all lands to barter goods; their art was well developed, for in the leisure people enjoyed they were able to build cities and tanks, great and small, and to perform works both of utility and artistic value. Contentment reigned supreme. Where such conditions existed the people were ready to embrace new ideals that had the prospect of helping their culture and elating their thoughts and activities, and as such the new doctrine preached by Mahinda Thera fell on a fertile soil, where it soon rose to its full height. Hundreds of thousands of men and women rose to high spiritual attainments on hearing the new message and thus the Law of the Blessed One was firmly established.

THE PASSING AWAY OF MAHINDA AND SANGHAMITTAA

Both Mahinda and Sanghamitta survived Devaanampiya Tissa. Mahinda lived to the age of 80 years and Sanghamittaa to the age of 79 years. They spent nearly 48 years in the island. The former died in the eighth year and the latter in the ninth of the reign of King Uttiya, brother and successor of Devaanampiya Tissa. Uttiya performed their funerals with great honor and built stupas over their relics. The king himself died in the following year, 286 b.e., after a reign of ten years.

The hierarchy of the disciples was continued in pupilary succession. Arittha Thera succeeded Mahinda Thera; he was in turn succeeded by Isidatta, Kaalasumana, Diighanaama and Diighasumana.

INVASION OF TAMILS AND RESTORATION OF THE SAASANA BY KING DUTTHAGAAMANI

Twenty years after the death of Uttiya foreign usurpers from South India seized Anuraadhapura. Two of them, Sena and Guttika, reigned together for twenty-two years and another Tamil usurper, Elaara, reigned for forty-four years. The lack of interest of these Tamil rulers in the Buddhist faith and the vandalism of their supporters evidently retarded the progress of the religion. Furthermore, the Sinhalese rulers were not free to work for the religion during these periods of political unrest. Nevertheless, the people held strongly to their new religion and showed no signs of laxity.

It was a young prince from Maagama of the southeastern principality of Ruhuna who restored the lost glory of the Sinhalese and their religion. He was Abhaya, known to posterity by a nickname which means "disobedient," Dutthagaamani. He was a descendant of Mahaanaaga, who had established himself at Maagama when his older brother Devaanampiya Tissa was ruling at Anuraadhapura. Kaakavanna Tissa and Vihaaramahaadevi were his parents.

After a thorough preparation for war Dutthagaamani defeated and killed Elaara in battle and became the ruler of Anuraadhapura. Thus the sovereignty of the Sinhalese rulers of Anuraadhapura was once more established.

Dutthagaamani reigned for twenty-four years. The advancement of the Buddhist religion was his main concern. The Ruvanveli-saaya, the most celebrated stupa in Sri Lanka, was his greatest work. The magnificent edifice of nine storeys and nine hundred chambers, called the Lohapaasaada, "the Brazen Palace," was constructed by him for the use of the monks. Mirisaveti-daagaba was another of his works.

Dutthagamani was not only a supporter of Buddhism but was also a zealous follower himself. Many episodes in the Pali commentaries depict him as a pious monarch. Under his patronage there flourished several learned monks during his reign.

SOCIAL AND CULTURAL DEVELOPMENT DUE TO BUDDHISM

It is well to find out the social and cultural development of the Sinhalese during the two centuries following their acceptance of the Buddhist religion. We have many incidents and stories in the Sri Lanka chronicles from which a definite idea regarding these conditions can be inferred. For instance, the *Rasavaahinii*, a Pali work composed in the thirteenth century of the Christian era, contains over a hundred stories of the life of the people during this early period. According to these stories, among the Sinhalese there do not appear to have been any caste divisions. Brahmans are mentioned as living apart in their own villages, and they were more or less counted as foreign to the Sinhalese. The members of the royal families were held in a class by themselves, and those of such families who aspired to the kingdom had to marry a member of a royal family or at least from a Brahman family. The rest of the people were grihapatis (householders with settled abodes).

The Candalas (despised) were those without a fixed abode; they were despised on account of being tramps and vagrants with no fixed residence. In some cases the word Candala was used in a self-deprecatory manner in order to indicate unworthiness. There is the instance of Prince Sali, son of King Dutthagaamani, who fell in love with a village artisan's daughter, Devi (Asokamala). In addressing the prince she said that she was a Candali as she did not belong to a family into which a member of the royal family was allowed to marry. The two divisions of people merely appear to be those who had a fixed abode and those who had no fixed abode. There were at this time no special caste divisions for trades or occupations, for a householder or members of a family were, in general, expected to engage themselves in one of the three occupations, as traders, as artisans or as cultivators.

Prince Dighabhaya, when appointed as governor of Kasatota, required attendants and asked each chief family of a village to send one of its sons for service and sent a messenger to Sangha, the chief of the village. The chief called together his seven sons. The elder six asked him to send the youngest to the king's service as he was idling his time at home without engaging in any work. "We six are engaged in such occupations as trade, industries and cultivation and work hard at our occupations." Again, in another story, the father, a chief of a village, addressing his daughter regarding her husband, tells her that her husband is living in idleness, and like her brothers should engage himself in an occupation such as cultivation, industry and commerce. Thus it appears all trades were common, and the same family engaged in work as artisans, tradesmen and cultivators without distinction.

The religion of the Sinhalese during this period was purely and entirely Buddhist and the stories indicate much practical activity in religious affairs, both in endowment and maintenance of religious institutions and the practice of religious principles. The Orders of bhikkhus and bhikkhunis flourished during this period; a very large number of men and women entered the religious Orders. Some of the vihaaras (monasteries) had thousands residing in them. There were also large numbers who were practicing meditation in forests and rock caves. They were well supported by the laity. There were four classes of disciples: the novices (samanera), bhikkhus (fully ordained), theras (elders) and mahatheras (chief elders.) There are no Sangharajas (heads of the entire Sangha) mentioned in any of the stories and no interference by kings or ministers in appointment or in giving ranks to the members of the Order. The affairs of the Sangha were managed by the monks themselves under well established rules of the Vinaya.

There appear to have been large numbers of disciples who had attained to the state of arahant, i.e., saints who had gained emancipation. In addition practically every man or woman was an upaasaka or upasikaa, a devotee who regularly performed religious duties. The bhikkhus lived in their vihaaras during the rainy season and at other seasons traveled far and wide in the country, visiting villages, other viharas, and as pilgrims worshipping at shrines. Both laymen and bhikkhus are frequently mentioned as going on pilgrimages to Gaya in India to worship at the sacred Bodhi Tree there. These parties of pilgrims sometimes crossed over to Southern India and walked all the way to Gayaa, taking about six months on the journey; sometimes they went by sea and landed at Tamralipti at the mouth of the Ganges and reached Gayaa in half the time.

The canonical scriptures had not been committed to writing at this time though writing was known. The bhikkhus learned the Dhamma and many committed to memory the scriptures or parts of them, thus preserving the tradition by frequent rehearsal. That the art of writing was probably introduced to Sri Lanka only after the introduction of Buddhism seems deducible from the circumstance that so far, no pre-Buddhist writing, lithic or other, has been identified. The earliest lithic records date back to the time of King Uttiya, successor of Devanampiya Tissa.

The bhikkhus were the instructors of the people. This was practically a duty. The Dhamma was expounded individually on every occasion and sermons to congregations were also held from time to time. There is mention of the periodical expounding of the Dhamma at a temple. Each temple in a district sometimes took its turn once a year to preach the Ariyavamsa Sutta, which was continued each time for seven days; the gatherings on these occasions appear to be very large as in instances mentioned it is said that the crowds were so great that large numbers usually had to stand outside the hall for the whole night and listen to the Dhamma, the audience including bhikkhus and the laity. There is also mention of discourses by lay preachers well versed in the Dhamma employed by the king at halls of preaching.

It is not clearly stated whether brahmans who lived in brahman villages practiced their own religion. Mention is made of sannyasis or yogis who practiced asceticism and sometimes lived in cemeteries scantily clad, with bodies covered with ashes, and as the story says, pretending to be saints while at the same time they led sinful lives. There is no mention of brahman temples or places of worship.

Women had a very high status in society during this period. Practically in every strata of society the position of women showed no distinction from that of men. They freely took part in every activity of life and their influence is well marked. Their character is depicted in most favorable terms; they were gentle, courteous and good natured, hospitable, tender and intelligent, ever ready to help others, to preserve the honor of their families, devoted to religion and country with untrammelled freedom of action. The position of women is further seen from the fact that monogamy was a definite institution. There is no mention of any other form of marriage. Women had freedom to choose their husbands.

VATTAGAMANI ABHAYA

After the death of King Dutthagamani his younger brother Saddhatissa ruled for eight years and did a great deal for Buddhism. He was succeeded by his sons Thuulatthana, Lanjatissa, Khallata Naga and Vattagamani Abhaya, in succession.

The period of Vattagaamani Abhaya, also known as Valagambahu, is noteworthy in the history of early Buddhism in Sri Lanka. Five months after his accession to the throne, in 103 BCE a brahman named Tiya (or Tissa) from Ruhuna, South Lanka, revolted against him. At the same time a Tamil army led by seven Tamil chiefs landed at Mahatittha and waged war against the king. The Tamil army vanquished Tiya and defeated Vattagamani in battle after which the latter fled and lived in exile for fourteen years.

These fourteen years of Tamil domination were disastrous to the cause of Buddhism, especially because the country was also ravaged by an unprecedented famine during that period. Food was so scarce during that time that even cases of cannibalism are said to have occurred. Many thousands of monks and laymen died of starvation. The monasteries were deserted. The Mahavihaara of Anuradhapura was completely abandoned and the Mahaathuupa was neglected. Trees grew in the courtyards of vihaaras. 12,000 arahants from the Tissamahaarama and another 12,000 from the Cittalapabbata-vihara passed away in the forest due to lack of food. While thousands of monks died in the country, many left the country and went to India.

As a result of the death of most of the learned monks there was even the fear that some parts of the scriptures would be lost. The Mahaniddesa of the Sutta Pitaka, for instance, was on the verge of being lost, for this text was known by only one monk at that time. The monks, in their earnestness to preserve the teachings of the Buddha, subsisted on roots and leaves of trees and recited the scriptures, lest they should forget them. When they had the strength they sat down and recited and when they could no longer keep their bodies erect they lay down and continued their recitation. Thus they preserved the texts and the commentaries until the misery was over.

THE FIRST SCHISM

After Vattagaamani Abhaya regained the throne he demolished the monastery of a nigàntha (Jain ascetic) named Giri for having mocked him when he was fleeing. He built a Buddhist monastery called the Abhayagiri-vihara over it, which he presented to a monk named Kupikkala Maha Tissa who had helped the king in his exile. Later, the monks of the Mahavihara imposed the punishment of expulsion on Tissa on the charge of improper contact with lay families. Tissa's pupil Bahalamassu Tissa, who resented the punishment imposed upon his teacher, was likewise expelled from the Mahavihara. He then went away with a following of five hundred monks and lived at Abhayagiri-vihaara, refusing to return to the Mahavihaara. There was thus a group of monks who broke away from the Mahavihaara and lived separately in the Abhayagiri-vihara, but they did not yet disagree with each other either in the theory or the practice of the Dhamma.

The actual schism occurred only when monks of the Vajjiputta sect in India came to Sri Lanka and were received at the Abhayagiri, not long after Tissa and his followers occupied that monastery. Tissa and his followers liked the new monks and adopted their doctrines. Thenceforth they came to be known as the Dhammaruci sect, after the name of the great Indian monk who was the teacher of the newcomers to Abhayagiri. There was no official suppression of the new sect, presumably because the king was in their favor, but the Mahavihara monks opposed them as unorthodox and heretical. From this time the Abhayagiri existed as a separate sect opposed to the Mahavihara.

WRITING OF THE SACRED BOOKS

It is stated in the early chronicles that after the acceptance of Buddhism by the people in Lanka and after the formation of a hierarchy of disciples who were Sinhalese, a council was held under Mahinda Thera, where all the leading theras were present and the teachings were recited and authoritatively laid down, as was done in the third convocation held in India under the direction of Emperor Asoka. Theravaada was thus established in Sri Lanka and according to tradition and custom the various parts of the Tipitaka were learned by the members of the Order, committed to memory, and preserved as oral traditions. It was seen how, during the famine that broke out in the time of King Vattagamani Abhaya, a great strain was put on the continuance of this form of preserving the teachings of the Tipitaka. When conditions became normal, the members of the Order considered that they could lose the teachings if any similar calamity or calamities were to occur in the future, and they decided that the time had arrived for committing these teachings to writing so that they might be preserved for future generations. The advent of schisms about this time might also have weighed strongly in favor of this decision.

Thus the members of the Order assembled at the Mahavihara at Anuradhapura, took counsel together, and with the permission and encouragement of the king a convocation was held. The teachings were recited and scribes were engaged to commit to writing, on palm leaves, the Pali canonical texts (the Tipitaka) consisting of Vinaya, Sutta and Abhidhamma, and the Sinhalese commentaries. According to the *Nikaya Sangraha,* a Sinhalese work of the fourteenth century dealing with the history of the Buddhist order, after the convocation at the Mahavihaara at Anuradhapura, the selected number of reciters and scribes, 500 in all, went to Alulena (Aluvihaara) cave temple close to Matale, in the central province. There in retirement they completed the work assigned to them and thus for the first time brought out in book form the teachings of the Buddha.

THE GROWTH OF DISSENTIENT SCHOOLS

About two centuries after the formation of the Dhammaruci sect at the Abhayagiri-vihara, in the days of King Voharika Tissa (214-36 a.c.), the monks of the Abhayagiri-vihara adopted the Vaitulyavada. Thereupon the monks of the Mahavihara, having compared it with their own texts, rejected the Vaitulya doctrines as being opposed to traditional doctrine. The king, who had them examined by a learned minister named Kapila, burnt them and suppressed the Vaitulyavaadins.

Despite the suppression by Voharika Tissa, the Vaitulyavadins began to assert themselves again and a few years later, in the time of King Gothabhaya (Meghavanna Abhaya, 253-266 a.c.), the Dhammaruci monks of Abhayagiri again accepted Vaitulyavada. When this happened, about three hundred monks left the Abhayagiri-vihara to reside at the Dakkhinavihara, founding a new sect known as Sagaliya. The king, having assembled the bhikkhus of the five great monasteries of the Theriya Nikaya (Mahavihara Nikaya), had the Vaitulya books examined, ordered the books to be destroyed, and expelled the Vaitulya monks. Sixty of them left for the Chola country in South India.

The struggle did not end here, for the adherents of the new doctrine were firmly established in South India and they planned to undermine the Mahavihara Nikaya in Sri Lanka. With this object a very learned monk by the name of Sanghamitra came to Sri Lanka and obtained the post of tutor to the king's two sons. Sanghamitra gained considerable influence over the young pupil, Mahasena, and was able to instil into him the new doctrine and make him a follower of his views. When Mahasena ascended the throne, the opportunity looked forward to by the Vaitulyans came. The new king became a great supporter of his tutor and as such persecuted the Mahavihara monks. The king, at the instigation of Sanghamitra Thera, ordered that no one should give food to the monks of the Mahavihara. The Mahavihara, as a result, had to be abandoned for nine years. The supporters of Sanghamitra destroyed the buildings of the Mahavihara and carried away their material to construct new buildings for the Abhayagiri-vihara.

Two persons, a minister and a queen, came forward this time to suppress Vaitulyavada and save the Mahavihara. The minister, Meghavannabhaya by name, managed to persuade the king to rebuild the Mahavihara. The queen caused Sanghamitra to be put to death and burned the Vaitulya books.

But the king, who was yet favorable towards the followers of Sanghamitra, built and gave the Jetavana-vihara to a monk named Tissa. Tissa, who was later charged by the Mahavihara monks of a grave offense, was expelled from the Order. The monks of the Sagaliya sect at Dakkhina-vihara then came to reside in the Jetavana-vihaara. In the reign of Silakala (522-35) a Vaitulyan book called the *Dharmadhatu*, which was brought to Sri Lanka from India, was kept at the Jetavana-vihaara and venerated. Thus from this time the monks of Jetavana-vihara too became adherents of Vaitulyavada.

In the reign of King Aggabodhi I (575-608) a great monk and teacher named Jotipala, coming from India, so exposed the fallacies of the Vaitulya doctrines that in his day they fell into disrepute and disappeared from Sri Lanka. Since that time the monks of the Abhayagiri and Jetavana viharas who adhered to Vaitulyan doctrines, abandoned their pride and lived in submission to the monks of the Mahavihara.

Intercourse with India was so frequent that from time to time other unorthodox doctrines occasionally found favor with certain monks, but these had no marked effect on the general progress or the stability of the Mahavihara Nikaya.

For nearly three centuries after the time of Aggabodhi I the chronicles make no mention of the Vaitulyavada or any other heretical teaching, until in the reign of King Sena I (833-53) a monk of the Vaajraparvata Nikaya came to Sri Lanka from India and introduced Vajiriyavada, converting the king to his doctrines. It was at this time that teachings like the Ratnakuuta-sutra were also introduced to Sri Lanka and another heresy called Nilapata-darsana appeared. Sena II (853-87), who succeeded Sena I, managed to suppress these new doctrines. From his time until the Chola conquest in the early eleventh century there is no mention of any heretical sect in Sri Lanka. However, a survey of the religious monuments of that period clearly shows that their teachings survived side by side with the teachings of the Theravada.

THE NATURE OF THE NEW DOCTRINES

It is opportune here to enquire about the nature of the new doctrines as having been introduced into Sri Lanka from time to time since the first century a.c. It was the monks of the Vajjiputra sect in India who were the first to introduce a new teaching. The Vajjiputra sect is mentioned in the Sri Lanka chronicles as one of the groups that parted from the Theriya Nikaya after the Second Buddhist Council to form a new sect. They thus evidently held some views different from those of the orthodox teachings. Buddhaghosa mentions in the Pali commentaries that the Vajjiputrakas held the view that there is a persistent personal entity, which is opposed to the accepted theory of *anattaa* of the Theravada teachings. They also believed that arahants may fall away from their attainment.

These followers of the Vajjiputraka doctrines, residing at the Abhayagiri-vihaara, became adherents of the Vaitulya doctrines about two centuries afterwards, and until the beginning of the seventh century Vaitulyavada became closely associated with Abhayagiri-vihaara and Jetavana-vihara.

Like the Vajjiputra sect the Vaitulyavada is mentioned in the *Nikaaya Sangraha* as one of the sects that arose in India after the Second Buddhist Council. The *Nikaya Sangraha* also states that the Vaitulya Pitaka was composed by heretic brahmans called Vaitulyas who entered the Order in the time of King Asoka to destroy Buddhism. It has been noticed that the terms Vaitulya, Vaipulya and Vaidalya are commonly used as a designation for Mahaayana sutras and hence the term Vaitulyavaada is used in the Sri Lanka chronicles to denote Mahayanism in general without having a particular Buddhist school in view.

The Vaitulyavadins were considered even more heretical than the Vajjiputrakas. The Pali commentaries mention some of their heretical views. They held the view that the Buddha, having been born in the Tusita heaven, lived there and never came down to earth and it was only a created form that appeared among men. This created form and ânanda, who learned from it, preached the doctrine. They also held that nothing whatever given to the Order bears fruit, for the Sangha, which in the ultimate sense of the term meant only the path and fruitions, does not accept anything. According to them any human pair may enter upon sexual intercourse by mutual consent. The *Diipavamsa* used the term Vitandavada in place of Vaitulyavada and the Pali commentaries mention them as holding unorthodox views regarding the subtle points in the Dhamma, particularly the Abhidhamma.

Buddhaghosa also refers to the Vaitulyavaadins as Mahasuññavadins. The philosophy of the Mahaayaana as expounded by the great Mahaayana teacher Naagarjuna was Sunyavaada. Thus the fact that the first appearance of Vaitulyavada in Sri Lanka took place shortly after Naagarjuna's teachings spread in South India, and that Vaitulyavada is also identified with Sunyavada of Nagaarjuna, suggests that it was the teaching of Nagaarjuna that was received by the monks of Abhayagiri-vihaara in the days of Voharika Tissa.

The book called *Dharmadhatu*, which was brought to Lanka in the reign of Silakala, is described in the chronicles as a Vaitulyan book. The monks of the Abhayagiri-vihaara and the Jetavana-vihara are connected with the honors paid to it. It has become evident that a book named *Dharmadhatu* was known and held in high esteem in the tenth century in Lanka and it is quite probable that this book was a Mahayanistic treatise dealing with the doctrine of the three bodies of the Buddha found among the teachings of the Mahayana.

Vajiriyavada was introduced in the reign of King Sena I by a monk of the Vajraparvata Nikaya. Scholars have pointed out that the Vajiriyavadins are identical with the

Vajrayanists, a school of Buddhism which flourished in eastern India about this time and which was an exponent of the worst phases of Tantrism. The *Nikaaya Sangraha* describes their writings as "secret teachings" and the Guudhavinaya, i.e., the "secret Vinaya," is one of the compositions of the Vajrayanists.

The *Nikaaya Sangraha* mentions that about this time the Ratnakuta-sutra was introduced to Sri Lanka. In the Chinese Canon the second of the seven classes of the Mahaayaana-suutras is called the Ratnakuuta. The Niilapata-darsana, which was also introduced about this time, was also an extreme form of Tantrism. Blue has been a color often favored by Tantrists.

THE SACRED TOOTH RELIC

An important event in the early history of Buddhism in Sri Lanka is the arrival of Buddha's Tooth Relic, the left eye-tooth, from India about 805 b.e. (311 a.c.), during the time of King Sirimeghavanna, son and successor of King Mahaasena. Ever since this Sacred Tooth Relic was received in Sri Lanka it has been a national treasure of great value and a tangible token of the attachment of the Sinhalese to the doctrine of the Blessed Tathaagata. King Sirimeghavanna held a great festival for the Tooth Relic and decreed that it should be brought every year to the Abhayagiri-vihaara and the same ceremonial should be observed. Today it is enshrined in golden caskets in the Temple of the Tooth Relic (Dalada Maaligawa) in Kandy, which has become the center of devout pilgrims from all over the island and from Buddhist lands elsewhere.

Ancient customs and ceremonies are scrupulously kept up, offerings are made daily, and in honor of the Sacred Relic an annual festival lasting fourteen days is held in Kandy every year during August. The Perahera, or procession, on these occasions is conducted by the temple authorities with elephants, lights, music and dancers, and is witnessed by thousands of devotees. Chiefs in full ancient attire accompany the procession. Large tracts of land have been set apart as fees for services at this temple and the tenants of these lands have various services apportioned to them. The exhibition of the Sacred Relic itself takes place at rare intervals when tens of thousands of pilgrims find their way to the Temple to worship and view the Relic. A medieval chronicle, chiefly of the eastern part of the island, mentions the existence of the right eye-tooth and its enshrinement in Somavati Cetiya in pre-Christian times.

The Sacred Tooth Relic was in the possession of King Guhasiva of Kalinga before it was brought to Sri Lanka. When he was about to be defeated in battle he entrusted it to his daughter Hemamala, and she with her husband Dantakumara brought the Sacred Tooth to Lanka and handed it over to King Sirimeghavanna at Anuraadhapura. From this date the Sacred Tooth Relic became the care of the kings of Lanka, who built special temples for it. During the many vicissitudes of the fortunes of the kings of Lanka, the Sacred Relic was conveyed from place to place where the fortunes of the king happened to take him. Replicas of the Sacred Tooth were made at various times and were owned by princes claiming the throne. About the year 1071 King Anawrahta (Anuruddha) of

Burma sent various presents to King Vijayabahu I of Sri Lanka and in return received a duplicate of the Sacred Tooth Relic, which he received with great veneration, and a shrine was built for it in Burma.

The Portuguese, in one of their expeditions to Sri Lanka, claim to have captured the Sacred Tooth Relic at Jaffna in the year 1560. Jaffna was an outlying port away from the strongholds of Sinhalese kings and the relic said to have been found by the Portuguese in a temple at Jaffna appeared to be one of the several duplicates which had been made at various times. On this question Prof. Rhys Davids wrote in the *Academy* of September 1874: "Jaffna is an outlying and unimportant part of the Ceylon kingdom, not often under the power of the Sinhalese monarchs, and for some time before this it had been ruled by a petty chieftain; there is no mention of the Tooth brought by Dantakumara having been taken there — an event so unlikely and of such importance that it would certainly have been mentioned had it really occurred. We have every reason to believe therefore that the very Tooth referred to in the *Daañhavamsa* is preserved to this day in Kandy."

In 1815 the British occupied Kandy. As usual the Sacred Tooth Relic had been taken to the mountains for security and one of the earliest tasks of the Agent of the British Government in the Kandyan Province was to arrange for the bringing back of the Relic with due ceremony. The houses and streets of Kandy were decorated, the surface of the streets whitened, and the Relic was brought in a magnificent procession. In 1818 there was a rebellion in the Kandyan provinces and the Sacred Tooth Relic was taken away from Kandy and hidden in a forest. After the suppression of the rebellion the British were able to find the Sacred Tooth Relic and bring it back to Kandy. The Sacred Tooth Relic continued to be in the custody of the British Government till 1853, when by order of the Secretary of State for the Colonies, the charge was given over to the Diyawadana Nilame (lay custodian) and the chief monks of Malwatte and Asgiriya monasteries in Kandy.

BUDDHAGHOSA THERA AND THE COMPILATION OF THE PALI COMMENTARIES

The compilation of the Pali Atthakathaa (commentaries) by Buddhaghosa Thera is another important event in the annals of Sri Lanka, which marks the progress of Buddhism. As has already been stated, the Pitakas or the teachings of the Buddha which were being handed down orally were committed to writing in 397 b.e. (89 BCE) and the commentaries on these, composed in Sinhalese, were also committed to writing at this time. Since this period much by way of exegetical works in Sinhalese was added from time to time and during the next five hundred years literary activity progressed considerably. By about 896 b.e. (410 a.c.), when King Mahanama reigned at Anuradhapura, the fame of Buddhist literature in Sri Lanka was well recognized throughout India and tradition mentions Sinhalese Buddhist monks visiting India, China and other countries and introducing the literature produced in Sri Lanka. Monks from India and China also visited Anuraadhapura during this time to procure Buddhist books.

It was about this time that Buddhaghosa Thera came to Sri Lanka in the reign of King Mahanama (410-432). Mahanama succeeded to the throne 79 years after the death of King Sirimeghavanna, during whose reign the Sacred Tooth Relic was brought to Sri Lanka, and three rulers, namely Jetthatissa II, Buddhadasa and Upatissa I, reigned in between. The story of Buddhaghosa is given in detail both in the *Mahavamsa* and the Sinhalese works composed in later times. According to these sources Buddhaghosa was a brahman youth who was born in the vicinity of Buddha Gaya and became well known as an exponent of Veda and philosophy. He was such a proficient scholar that in his youth he was able to assert his knowledge among the great scholars of the time. He traveled from place to place, from one seat of learning to another, from one set of teachers to another, triumphantly asserting his knowledge and scholarship.

At a well-known Buddhist monastery at Tamluk, he met Revata Mahaathera, one well versed in the doctrines and philosophy of Buddhism. There he entered into discussions and found not a peer but one superior to him in knowledge and understanding. This made him join the Order of Buddhist monks as a pupil of Revata Mahathera. At this vihara he studied Buddhist philosophy diligently and produced a treatise on Buddhism, *Yanodaya;* he also planned to compose commentaries on the Abhidhamma and the suttas. His teacher at this stage advised him to go to Anuradhapura before undertaking this work, as he said that in Lanka were preserved not only the Tipitaka, the teachings of the Buddha himself, but also the Sinhalese commentaries and various expositions of the teachings which were very valuable and of high repute.

Buddhaghosa Thera proceeded to Sri Lanka and stayed at the Mahapadhanaghara of the Mahavihara. He then asked the monks at Anuraadhapura for access to books for the compilation of commentaries. The learned theras at Anuradhapura tested his knowledge and ability by setting him a thesis on which he compiled the well-known *Visuddhimagga.* They were so pleased with this work that he was given facilities for his projected work and books were placed at his disposal for the preparation of Pali commmentaries.

The old Sinhalese commentaries from which Buddhaghosa drew material for the compilation of his Pali commentaries are occasionally named in his works. The Maha (or Muula) Atthakatha occupied the foremost position among them while the Maha-paccari Atthakatha and the Kurundi Atthakatha were also important. These three major works probably contained exegetical material on all the three Pitakas. Apart from these there were other works like the Sankhepatthakatha, Vinayatthakatha, Abhidhamatthakatha and separate commentaries on the four âgamas or Nikayas, namely, the Diigha Nikaya Atthakatha, Majjhima Nikaya Atthakatha, Samyutta Nikaya Atthakatha, and the Anguttara Nikaya Atthakatha. References to numerous other sources like the Andhakatthakatha, the âcariya (or Teachers), and the Porana (or Ancient Masters) are also found in Buddhaghosa's works.

Utilizing the copious material of these commentaries and other sources, which sometimes contained conflicting views and contradictory assertions, Buddhaghosa compiled his Pali commentaries including all authoritative decisions, sometimes giving his own views but leaving out unnecessary details and repetitions as well as irrelevant matter. The first of such commentaries was the *Samantapasadika* on the Vinaya Pitaka. The *Kankhavitarani* on the Paatimokkha of the Vinaya Pitaka was compiled later. These books were followed by the commentaries on the four Nikaayas, the *Sumangalavilasini* on the Digha Nikaya, the *Papañca-suudani* on the Majjhima Nikaya, the *Saratthappakasini* on the Samyutta Nikaya, and the *Manorathapurani* on the Anguttara Nikaaya. The *Dhammapadañhakatha* on the Dhammapada, the *Jaatakañhakatha* on the Jaataka, and the *Paramatthajotikaa* on the Khuddaka Nikaaya, are also ascribed to him. On the books of the Abhidhamma Pitaka, Buddhaghosa compiled the *Aññhasalini* on the Dhammasangani, the *Sammohavinodani* on the Vibhanga, and the *Pañcappa-karanañhakatha* on the other five books.

The voluminous literature which Buddhaghosa produced exists to this day and is the basis for the explanation of many crucial points of Buddhist philosophy which without them would have been unintelligible. His commentaries become all the more important since the old Sinhalese commentaries gradually went out of vogue and were completely lost after the tenth century. Buddhaghosa's activities gave an impetus to the learning of Pali in Sri Lanka which resulted in the production of many other Pali commentaries and other literary works, and also established the pre-eminence of Sri Lanka as the home of Theravada Buddhism.

THE PALI CHRONICLES

Some time before and after the compilation of the Pali commentaries by Buddhaghosa two important literary works of a different type were produced in Sri Lanka. They are the *Dipavamsa* and the *Mahavamsa,* described in the foregoing pages either as the Sri Lanka chronicles or the Pali chronicles. These two works are the earliest extant literary records giving a continuous history of the activities of the kings of Sri Lanka from pre-Buddhistic times up to the end of the reign of King Mahasena. Both works are composed in Pali metrical verses.

The *Dipavamsa* is the earlier of these two chronicles. It is not a compilation of one individual author but is the outcome of several previous works to which additions have been made from time to time, taking its present form about the fourth century a.c. The chronicle does not name any author but it has been held by some scholars, from the abundant material it contains about nuns, that the *Dipavamsa* is a work compiled and continued by nuns from time to time.

The *Dipavamsa* consists of 22 chapters. They contain accounts of the three visits of the Buddha to Sri Lanka, the ancestry of the Buddha, the three Buddhist councils and the different Buddhist schools which arose after the Second Council, the activities of King Asoka, the colonization of Sri Lanka by Vijaya, his successors, the introduction of Buddhism in the reign of King Devanampiya Tissa and the activities of his successors, especially Dutthagamani, Vattagamani and Mahasena. The narrative ends with the reign of Mahasena (276-303).

The *Dipavamsa* has obtained its material from different sources of which the Sihala *Mahaavamsatthakatha* (also called the Sihalatthakatha or Poranatthakatha or merely Atthakatha) was pre-eminent. Besides this there were several other sources like the Uttaravihara Mahavamsa, Vinayatthakatha and the Dipavamsatthakatha. By these names were known the records collected and preserved in the Mahavihara and the other monasteries.

The *Mahavamsa*, which is the better work in its comprehensiveness, arrangement of facts and high literary standard, was compiled by a thera named Mahanama either in the late fifth century or the early sixth century A.C. It also covers the same period of history and its material is drawn from the same sources as the *Dipavamsa*, but it contains much more additional material presented in a better form.

The *Mahavamsa* contains 37 chapters in all. They deal mainly with the same events as those of the *Dipavamsa*, but there are much longer accounts and greater details of the activities of several kings such as Pandukabhaya and Dutthagamani and events like the establishment of Buddhism and the rise of new schools.

These two chronicles contain many myths and legends. Yet they are among the primary sources for the reconstruction of the early history of Sri Lanka for they contain a great deal of historical facts, especially in the narratives dealing with the period after the 2nd century BCE, corroborated by epigraphical, archaeological and other evidence.

The *Mahavamsa* has been continued in later times, at three stages, giving a connected history of the island up to modern times. This continuation of the chronicle, which is in three parts, is called the *Culavamsa*. The first part brings the history down to the twelfth century, the second part to the fourteenth century and the third part to modern times.

POLITICAL UNREST AND THE DECLINE OF BUDDHISM

The political situation in Sri Lanka from about the middle of the fifth century a.c. until the third quarter of the eleventh century a.c. was not favorable towards the progress of Buddhism. This period of Sri Lankan history is marked with continuous warfare between the reigning king and his rival claimants or the foreign invaders. Often when the reigning king was defeated in battle he fled to India and came back with a Tamil troop to regain his lost throne, and as a result the Tamils who thus settled down in Sri Lanka from time to time also became an important element even powerful enough to seize political power for themselves.

Such a political situation evidently did not give the rulers an opportunity to work for the religion and as a result the community and the monasteries were neglected. Some rulers like Aggabodhi III and Dathopatissa I even resorted to the evil practice of robbing monasteries of their gold images, precious gems and other valuables which had accumulated there for centuries, for the purpose of financing their military operations when the royal treasury had become empty. Dathopatissa I also removed the gold finial of the Thuparama and the gem-studded umbrella of the cetiya. Relic chambers of stupas were opened and valuable offerings were removed. Their Tamil soldiers were allowed to burn down monastic buildings like the Sacred Tooth Relic Temple and take away the valuables. The Pandya and the Chola invaders from South India who also attacked Sri Lanka several times during this period ransacked the monasteries and carried away vast treasures. These conditions necessarily worsened when Sri Lanka passed into the hands of the South Indian Cholas in 1017 and remained a part of the Chola empire until 1070.

Amidst this political unrest and the resultant religious decline several events important in the history of Buddhism in Sri Lanka occurred. In the reign of Moggallana I (495-512) the Sacred Hair Relic of the Buddha was brought to Sri Lanka from India and the king placed it in a crystal casket in an image house and held a great festival. The writing of the *Mahavamsa* by a Mahavihara monk is ascribed to the reign of his successor Kumara Dhaatusena (512-520). In the reign of Silaakala (522-535) the Mahayana book, the Dharmadhatu, was brought to Sri Lanka and in the reign of Aggabodhi I (575-608) the monk Jotipala defeats the Vaitulyavadins in a public controversy. Apart from these special events several rulers purified the Sasana and repaired the old and neglected monasteries. They also encouraged the recital of Dhamma.

VIJAYABAHU I AND THE REVIVAL OF BUDDHISM

In the year 1070 Vijayabahu I succeeded in defeating the Cholas and becoming the king of Sri Lanka. Residing at Polonnaruwa, which he made the capital of his kingdom, he turned his mind to the noble task of repairing the damage that had been inflicted upon the national religion by the invaders. The great religious edifices, the pirivenas and the monasteries which were in utter destruction were restored and new ones were built. But the greatest of his tasks was the restoration of ordination of monks. When he found that the five ordained monks required to carry out an ordination ceremony could not be found in the whole island, he sent an embassy to his friend and ally, King Anuruddha (i.e., Anawrahta) of Burma, soliciting his help in restoring the Sasana in Sri Lanka. King Anuruddha sent a number of eminent theras who re-established the Sasana in Sri Lanka and instructed a large number of monks in the three Pitakas and the commentaries. The king also brought about a reconciliation of the three Nikayas of the Mahavihara, Abhayagiri and Jetavana and restored their ancient monasteries to them. Thousands of laymen joined the Order.

The religious revival inaugurated by King Vijayabahu led to a great intellectual re-awakening and a large number of religious literary works in Pali and Sanskrit were written. King Vijayabahu also encouraged learned men to come and settle down in Sri Lanka and also induced his courtiers to engage in literary pursuits. These activities suffered temporarily with his death in 1110, but were revived after the accession of Paraakramabahu the Great in 1153.

REVIVAL OF BUDDHISM UNDER PARAAKRAMABAHU THE GREAT

King Paraakramabahu the Great (1153-1186) ascended the throne after a great struggle with rival claimants and even after his accession he had to suppress many rebellions. Being a great leader of men he was able to restore order and even carry his prowess as a conqueror to foreign lands including South India and Burma. He rebuilt the city of Polonnaruwa. King Paraakramabahu also undertook the restoration of the ancient capital city of Anuradhapura which had been neglected and abandoned after the Cholas had captured and devastated it about a century and a half earlier. The four great thuupas were overgrown with trees, and bears and panthers dwelt there. The king restored all the important monuments at Anuradhapura and the entire Mihintale monastery.

But the most important task which the king performed for the establishment of the Saasana was its purification and the unification of the Sangha. In spite of the activities of King Vijayabahu I there were by this time members of Sangha who were unfit to lead the monastic life. Some of the monks are said to have even supported wives and children. With a learned thera named Maha Kassapa of Udumbaragiri Vihara (Dimbulagala near Polonnaruwa) at its head, the king convened a Council of the leading monks of the dissentient schools and was convinced that the teachings of the Mahavihara were correct and their claims were in keeping with the Dhamma. Consequently with great care and patience, the king made investigations into the members of the schismatic schools. Many of the unworthy monks were persuaded to leave the Order and those who were not open to persuasion were expelled. Some monks were made to return to the status of novices. After that the three fraternities of the Mahavihara, the Abhayagiri-vihara and the Jetavana-vihara remained united.

Subsequent to this purification of the Sangha the king, with the assistance of the leading monks, proclaimed a code of regulations for the guidance of the bhikkhus. After the proclamation of that code the internal discipline of the Sangha was in the hands of the monks themselves and the king acted only when a necessity arose. The code of regulations enforced by King Parakramabaahu became a royal proclamation. It gave directions for the proper observance of the Vinaya rules and dealt with the procedure that should be followed by his subjects who had become or who wished to become lay pupils, novices and subsequently ordained monks. The king also caused this proclamation to be engraved on the rock surface of the Uttararama, presently known as Gal-vihara, which exists to this day. It is now known as Polonnaru-katikavata or the Parakramabahu-katikavata.

The great interest taken by the king in the affairs of the religion coupled with internal peace and prosperity brought about a revival of Buddhist learning which created a rich literature during this period.

COMPILATION OF RELIGIOUS TREATISES

It has been mentioned earlier that Buddhaghosa Thera compiled the Pali commentaries to many of the texts of the Tipitaka in the early part of the fifth century.

Buddhaghosa was, however, not able to compile commentaries to all the books of the Tipitaka due perhaps to the fact that the illness of his teacher Revata in India caused him to leave Sri Lanka before he finished the entire work. Fortunately, there were several other scholars who took up the work left undone by Buddhaghosa, and in the succeeding years they compiled commentaries to the rest of the texts of the Pali Canon.

Thus the commentator Dhammapala Thera compiled the commentaries to the Udaana, Itivuttaka, Vimanavatthu, Petavatthu, Theragatha, Therigatha and Cariyapitaka of the Khuddaka Nikaya; all these commentaries are known by the name *Paramatthadipani*: Upasena Thera compiled the *Saddhammappajjotika* on the Niddesa. Mahaanama Thera compiled the *Saddhammappakaasini* on the Patisambhidaamagga, and Buddhadatta Thera compiled the *Madhuratthavilaasini* on the Buddhavamsa. The author of the Visuddhajanavilaasini, which is the commentary on the Apadana, is not known. Of these commentators Buddhadatta was a contemporary of Buddhaghosa; Upasena and Mahanama flourished about the latter part of the sixth century, and Dhammapala about the latter part of the tenth century.

The political disturbances from the time of King Dhatusena until the reign of Vijayabahu I greatly hampered literary activities and as a result only a few religious works were composed during this period. About the end of the tenth century, a thera named Khema wrote an expository work on the Abhidhamma, called the *Paramatthadipani*. To the same period belongs also the Pali *Mahaabodhivamsa*, which gives primarily the history of the Sacred Bodhi Tree at Anuraadhapura and the ceremonies connected with it. A poem entitled *Anaagatavamsa* on the future Buddha Metteyya is also ascribed to this period. To the tenth or the early part of the eleventh century belongs a Pali poem of 98 stanzas, called the Telakañahagatha, in the form of religious exhortations of a great elder named Kalyaniya Thera, who was condemned to be cast into a cauldron of boiling oil.

King Vijayabahu I, in whose reign occurred a great intellectual re-awakening, was himself a great patron of literature and a scholar of high repute. Many Sinhalese works including a Sinhalese translation of the Dhammasangani are attributed to him but not one of them exists today. About this time a monk named Anuruddha composed the *Anuruddhasataka*, the *Abhidhammattha-sangaha*, the *Namaruupa-pariccheda* and the *Paramattha-vinicchaya*. The first is a Buddhist devotional poem of 101 stanzas, in elegant Sanskrit. The second work is a compendium on the teachings of the Abhidhamma and is held in high esteem by all Buddhists of the southern school. The third and fourth are two short works in verse on the Abhidhamma, giving the reader a general idea of the subjects dealt with in the Abhidhamma Pitaka.

The reign of King Parakramabahu the Great ushered in another great epoch of literary activity. Three great scholarly monks flourished in his reign, namely, Maha Kassapa of Dimbulagala Vihara, Moggallana Thera and Sariputta Thera. Maha Kassapa was the author of a Sinhalese paraphrase (*sanne*) to the *Samantapaasadika*, which is now lost. He is also reputed to have written a sub-commentary to the *Abhidhammattha-sangaha*. It is probable that he was also the author of several other works such as the *Mohavicchedani*, which is a treatise on the Abhidhamma, and *Vimativinodani*, which is a commentary on the Vinaya. Moggallana, a contemporary of Maha Kassapa, was the author of the Pali grammar, *Moggallana Vyaakarana*. He is also credited with the authorship of the *Abhidhanappadipika*, which is the only ancient Pali dictionary in Sri Lanka.

Saariputta was the most prominent scholar of the reign of Paraakramabaahu the Great. A clever Sanskrit scholar as he was, Saariputta compiled two works on Sanskrit grammar. Another work by him, the *Vinayasangaha*, was a summary of the Vinaya Pitaka. This work was known by several titles and was widely known in Burma. On this work Saariputta himself wrote a sub-commentary (*ñika*) and a Sinhalese paraphrase. The most comprehensive and therefore important work of Saariputta is the masterly sub-commentary called the *Saratthadipani*, which he composed on Buddhaghosa's commentary on the Vinaya, the *Samantapaasadika*. The immense and valuable information it contains shows that his knowledge was extensive and profound even as that of the great commentator Buddhaghosa.

He further wrote a Sinhalese paraphrase to the *Abhidhammattha-sangaha* of Anuruddha Thera and this paraphrase is still held in high esteem by modern scholars. Sariputta is also credited with the authorship of two other ñikayas, the *Saratthamañjuusa* on the *Manorathapurani* and the *Linatthappakasini* on the *Papañcasuudani*, which are commentaries on the Anguttara and Majjhima Nikayas, respectively, by Buddhaghosa. To this period also belong the ñiikaas on the other three Nikayas of the Sutta Pitaka, collectively known as the *Saratthamañjusa-ñika*.

It should be mentioned here that the ñikayas named above formed one of the major groups of Pali literature compiled during this period. As described in the *Saddhamma-sangaha*, a Pali work of the 14th century, Maha Kassapa and a large congregation of monks who assembled at the Jetavana Vihara at Polonnaruwa decided to compose exegetical commentaries since the existing sub-commentaries on the old Atthakathas were unintelligible. Acting on this decision they compiled ñiikaas, namely, the *Saratthadipani* on the Vinaya Pitaka, the *Saratthamañjusa* in four parts on the first four Nikayas of the Sutta Pitaka, and the *Paramatthadipani* in three parts on the Abhidhamma Pitaka.

These ñikayas or sub-commentaries were works containing expositions of points in the Atthakathas compiled by Buddhaghosa and other commentators, which needed further elucidation for their correct interpretation. There were ñikayas compiled from time to time subsequent to the compilation of the commentaries, and what the council headed by Maha Kassapa performed was the bringing of these various ñiikaas together and making a synthetic summary of them. Though the *Saddhamma-sangaha* does not give any prominence to the part played by Saariputta at this council, it is well known that several ñikayas were compiled either by him or under his supervision.

Several religious works written in Sinhalese also belong to this period. The Sinhalese exegetical works on which the Pali commentaries were based were preserved in the Mahaavihara as late as the tenth century. Likewise there were the collections of Jaataka stories and the stories connected with the verses of the Dhammapada, in the Sinhalese language. A collection of stories from which the Pali *Rasavaahini* drew material and a work called the *Sihalañhakatha Mahavamsa,* on which the Pali chronicles were based, also existed in Sinhalese. None of these works is now extant. Several Sinhalese religio-literary works which were composed in or about the twelfth century are popular even today. Among them are the *Sasadavata,* which is a poem on the Sasa Jaataka; the *Muvadevdavata,* which is a poem on the Makhaadeva Jataka; and the *Kavsilumina,* which is a poem on Kusa Jataka. Gurulugomi's *Amavatura* and *Dharmapradipikava* and Vidyacakravarti's *Butsarana* are also generally ascribed to the twelfth century.

DECLINE OF BUDDHISM AFTER PARAKRAMABAAHU I AND RESTORATION BY PARAAKRAMABAHU II

After the death of Parakramabahu the Great there was much internal disturbance in the country caused by rival claimants to the throne and invasions by foreigners. As a result Buddhism was on the decline again. Parakramabahu's immediate successor, Vijayabahu II, promoted trade and religious relations between Burma and Sri Lanka but was slain after a year's rule by a usurper. The usurper was, however, slain five days later by Nissankamalla, who thereafter reigned for nine years (1187-96). Nissankamalla was a great benefactor of Buddhism. He built several notable religious edifices in Polonnaruwa, his capital. Some of these, like the Ruvanveli-dagaba (now called Rankot-vehera), the beautiful Vatadage, the Sacred Tooth Relic Temple (Hetadaage), and the Nissankalata-mandapa exist to this day. He made occasional tours in his kingdom, visiting places of religious significance like the Sumanakuuta (Sri Paada, or as called by the English, Adam's Peak) and the Dambulu-vihara. He built alms-houses at several important places and purified the Sasana by expelling corrupt bhikkhus from the Order.

The period of two decades that followed the death of King Nissankamalla was one of the most disturbed periods in Sri Lanka, during which time occurred several assassinations of rulers and invasions by foreigners. In 1214 a foreigner named Megha invaded, defeated the Sinhalese ruler and reigned for 36 years (1215-51). His reign was one of the most disastrous for Buddhism, for he plundered the monasteries and made them over to his soldiers to dwell in. The people were persecuted by torture and were forced to adopt a different faith. He also destroyed libraries containing many valuable books. The situation was temporarily saved by Parakramabahu II, who ruled from Dambadeniya from 1236 while Magha was still dominating north Lanka. Parakramabahu II, who was a ruler of great learning, earned for himself the title Kalikala Sahitya Sarvajña Pandita.

He made efforts to restore the Sasana by bringing over monks from the Chola country in South India and holding a festival to admit monks to the higher ordination. He established several monasteries and pirivenas and encouraged learning. The king also held a great council of monks under the leadership of the great thera Aranyaka Medhankara and purified the Sasana. Subsequently, like Parakramabahu I, he formulated rules for the proper conduct of the monks, the code of these rules being known by the name Dambadeni Katikavata. At Palabatgala he constructed a great monastery for the hermit-monks who were full of virtue and were able to undergo strict austerities. Two succeeding kings, Vijayabahu IV (1270-72) and Parakramabahu III (1287-93), took much interest in maintaining Buddhism and consolidating the efforts of their predecessor.

THE LITERARY REVIVAL

The religious revival brought about by Parakramabahu II continued until about the fifteenth century, though there was not much political stability in the country during that period. The outstanding feature of the period is the compilation of a large number of religio-literary works. Parakramabaahu II himself obtained teachers from India to teach Lankan monks. He persuaded his younger brother Bhuvanekabaahu to become a scholar and be a teacher to many thousands of elders. The king's minister Devapatiraaja was a great patron of learning. To Parakramabahu II is ascribed the authorship of the Sinhalese translations to the *Visuddhimagga* and the *Vinaya Vinicchaya,* the Sinhalese poem *Kavsilumina,* the masterpiece of Sinhalese poetry, based on the Kusa Jataka, and the Sinhalese prose work *Dalada-sirita.* In the reign of Parakramabahu II lived the thera Dharmakirti who was the author of the Pali poem Daathaavamsa and the first part of the *Cutavamsa.*

The *Thupavamsa* on the erection of stuupas in Lanka, the *Hattha-vanagalla-vihara-vamsa* on the history of the ancient vihara at Attanagalla, the *Rasavahini* which is a collection of stories about ancient India and Sri Lanka, the *Samantakuta-vanana* on the Buddha's visit to Sumanakuta (Adam's Peak), the *Kesadhatuvamsa* on the history of the hair-relics of the Buddha, the *Parami-mahasataka* on the ten perfections (*paraamitaa*), the *Saddhamma-Sangha* which gives an account of the history and development of Buddhism in Lanka, are several of the religious works of merit composed in Pali from the time of Parakramabahu II until the fifteenth century.

A large number of Sinhalese works on religious subjects too belongs to this period. The *Saddharmaratnavali,* which narrates the stories of the Pali Dhammapadatthakatha in Sinhalese, the *Puujavalii* which relates the honor and offerings received by the Buddha, the *Pansiya-panas-jaataka* based on the Pali Jaataka commentary, the Sinhala *Bodhivamsa* on the history of the Bodhi Tree, the *Elu-Attanagaluvamsa* which is a translation of the Pali work, the *Saddharmaalankara,* based on the Pali *Rasavaahini,* the *Guttilakavyaya* based on the Guttila Jaataka, the *Kaavyasekharaya,* based on the Sattubhatta Jaataka, the *Budugunaalankaraya,* which narrates the dispelling of the calamity in Vesaali by the Buddha, and the *Loveda-sangarava,* containing religious instructions for the laity, are the standard works among them.

EMBASSY FROM BURMA TO OBTAIN ORDINATION

As a result of this religious revival, the reputation of the Sangha in Sri Lanka became so well established that in the year 1476 King Dhammaceti of Burma decided to send twenty-two selected bhikkhus to Lanka to obtain ordination and bring back to Burma the traditions of Lanka. He sent these bhikkhus with numerous presents in charge of two ministers, Citraduta and Raamaduta. They came in two ships. The first ship with eleven bhikkhus and their attendants, in charge of the minister Citraduta, arrived in Colombo and the other ship in charge of Raamaduta with eleven bhikkhus and attendants arrived at Weligama on the southern coast of Lanka. These deputations were received with due ceremony and given a cordial reception by King Buvanekabahu VI (1470-78), who reigned at Kotte (Jayawardhanapura), six miles from Colombo.

The king of Burma sent the following message to the chief theras of Lanka: "My Lords, I am sending many articles to be offered to the Sacred Tooth Relic, etc. and I request you to make an endeavor to offer these to the Sacred Tooth Relic. May the noble ones obtain facilities for the twenty-two bhikkhus and their pupils and the two ministers, Citraduta and Ramaduta, who are attending on these bhikkhus to assist them in worshiping, honoring and viewing the Sacred Tooth Relic if they are so fortunate as to get an opportunity to do so; after which may the Noble Ones be pleased with their endeavor to enable the twenty-two bhikkhus and their pupils to be ordained in the community of succession from Mahavihara fraternity founded by the great thera Mahinda by selecting such bhikkhus who hold an established high reputation and giving the ordination of Upasampada in the Sima (ordination hall) in the river Kalyani, which has been made sacred by its association with our Great Lord."

The request made by the king of Burma was duly granted, the bhikkhus were ordained in the Sima in the Kalyani River. The minister Raamaduta with twenty bhikkhus and thirty-three pupils, duly ordained, returned to Burma. The other minister, Citraduta, and his party of bhikkhus were shipwrecked and six of these bhikkhus met with their death. The remaining ones reached their country.

ESTABLISHMENT OF MAHAVIHARAVAMSA IN BURMA

In Burma King Dhammaceti built an ordination hall, known as Kalyani Sima, and the bhikkhus ordained there went by the name of Kalyanivamsa. At a later period ordination of this Nikaya was carried to Siam from Burma. The connection with Burma at this period has an important bearing on the fortunes of Buddhism in Sri Lanka, for through these embassies the books that existed in Lanka were taken to Burma, Siam and Cambodia and the Mahavihara Nikaya was established in these countries. This helped Lanka to reobtain the books and the ordination at a subsequent period, when ordination had disappeared in the island and the books were lost.

THE ARRIVAL OF THE PORTUGUESE AND THE PERSECUTION OF BUDDHISM

The political stability that was maintained by Parakramabahu II and his successors until about the fifteenth century began to weaken by the end of that century. At this time the Sinhalese king who ruled at Kotte was the head of a very small territory. The interior regions of the country were in the hands of several petty chiefs who did not care about the religion or the welfare of the people. The Moors on the other hand controlled the trade of the coastal regions. Economically too the country had sunk to such a very low level that by this time Sri Lanka had become dependent on India even for food.

Such was the condition when the Portuguese, who were engaged in discoveries and conquests in the East and were in pursuit of Eastern trade, landed in Lanka in 1505, when Vira Parakramabahu VIII (1484-1508) was ruling at Kotte. The Portuguese promised him military aid against his rivals and great riches from the trade which they proposed to establish. They then gained a foothold in Lanka by erecting a fortress on the rocky beach in Colombo and establishing many trading settlements. Before long the entire coastal region passed into the hands of the Portuguese and the kings of Kotte were entirely at the mercy of their allies. They even made several assaults on the interior of the country in order to become masters of the whole island.

The Portuguese arrived in Colombo in 1505 and, gradually occupying all maritime provinces, remained in their possession up to 1658. The Lanka chronicles as well as the records of their friendly historians describe them as cruel, inhuman, rapacious, bigoted and savage persecutors of Buddhism in their endeavor to impose their own faith — Roman Catholicism — on the people of Sri Lanka.

A few decades after the arrival of the Portuguese, King Bhuvanekabahu VI (1534-1551), who ruled at Kotte, sought the assistance of his allies, the Portuguese, to ensure the succession of his grandson Dharmapala to the throne. For this purpose an ivory image of Dharmapala was sent to Portugal where a coronation of the effigy was held by the Portuguese emperor. When the Sinhalese ambassadors returned they were accompanied by a party of Franciscans who, under the direction of the Portuguese emperor and with the permission of the king of Kotte, preached the Christian Gospel in Lanka. Thus for the first time Christian communities were organized in the maritime provinces of Lanka. Dharmapala, who had become a baptized Christian under the name of Don Juan Dharmapala, as an expression of thankfulness to the Portuguese gave them a deed of gift (*sannas*) after his accession, transferring to them the Daladaa Maaligawa (i.e., the Temple of the Tooth), the temple at Kelaniya and all the temple revenues in the island for the maintenance of the missionary establishments.

Thus there was the necessary assistance given to the Portuguese by the rulers of Kotte to suppress the national religion of the Sinhalese and propagate their own religion — Catholicism. With this support they set about their task. In their conversions they adopted two distinct methods, namely, inducement by offices and other temporal favors, and brutal punishment where inducement failed. People who wished to obtain high offices under them and who wished to earn the goodwill of those in power readily adopted the new faith and took up new Biblical names. Others who hesitated to give up their national faith and showed resistance were brutally punished.

There are lurid accounts of men thrown into rivers to be eaten by crocodiles, babies spitted on the soldiers' pikes and held up before the parents, or crushed between millstones before the eyes of their mothers who later were to be tortured to death. Those who dared to worship in public or wear the yellow robe were put to death. Buddhist monasteries and institutions were destroyed and their treasures looted. Libraries were set on fire. Thus did the period of Portuguese rule become one of the darkest periods of Buddhism in Sri Lanka.

PERSECUTION OF BUDDHISM BY RAJASINHA I

The Portuguese were not the only enemies of Buddhism at this period. King Rajasinha I (1581-1592), who was the son of Mayadunne, a brother of Bhuvenekabahu VI, ruled from Sitawaka when the Portuguese were holding power at Kotte. A gallant leader as he was, Rajasinha succeeded in gaining the confidence of the Sinhalese who opposed the Portuguese rule and winning several battles against the Portuguese, the battle at Mulleriyawa being the most famous. But, as the chronicles mention, his popularity was shortlived. The foolish king, in his thirst for power, slew his old father with his own hands. Later, being seized with the fear of his crime, Rajasinha sought the advice of the monks for setting himself free from the sin. When the monks explained to him that it was too great a crime to be absolved, the king was provoked to anger.

He then became a follower of the Saivites, in whose advice he took refuge, and became an enemy of Buddhism. The chief Buddhist elder was stoned to death, and many other monks were buried neck-deep in the earth and their heads plowed off. Some others were put to the sword. The sacred edifices and the monasteries were pulled down, and the sacred books were reduced to ashes. The lands which had been endowed in earlier times to the monastic establishments were taken away and Sri Pada, the Sacred Footprint of the Buddha on Adam's Peak, was handed over to the Saivites. Those monks who managed to escape from the king's wrath disrobed themselves and fled.

VIMALA DHARMASURIYA'S ATTEMPT AT RESTORING BUDDHISM

In 1592, the year in which Rajasinha died, a Sinhalese ruler, Vimala Dharmasuriya I, ascended the throne of the hill capital, Kandy, and ruled for twelve years. Though he had been educated by the Portuguese and was originally favored by them, the king soon after his accession turned against them out of his love for the country and the religion.

Vimala Dharmasuriya I was a great patron of Buddhism of that time. After his wars with the Portuguese he set his heart on repairing the damage done by Rajasinha. Several Buddhist monuments were restored. Finding that there was hardly a single monk left in the country who was properly ordained, Vimala Dharmasuriya sent an embassy to the country of Arakan (now part of Burma) to obtain monks to restore ordination in Sri Lanka. The mission was successful; several monks led by the elders Nandicakka and Candavisala came to Kandy and in the year 1597 an ordination ceremony was held in the Udakukkhepa Sima at Getambe, near Kandy, many men of noble families entering the Order on this occasion. The king also built a storeyed pavilion and, bringing back the Sacred Tooth Relic from the Delgamuvihara where it was hidden, deposited it in the pavilion. The control of Sri Pada was taken from the Saivites and handed over to the Buddhist monks.

SUCCESSORS OF VIMALA DHARMASURIYA I AND THE ARRIVAL OF THE DUTCH IN SRI LANKA

Vimala Dharmasuriya was succeeded on the throne of Kandy by Senarat, a man zealous in religious works. In his reign the Portuguese invaded Kandy and the king carried away the Sacred Tooth Relic to Mahiyangana for safety. Senarat's son and successor Rajasinha II (1634-1687) was a great warrior but was not zealous. In his reign ended the Portuguese rule in the maritime provinces of Lanka, a feat which the king accomplished with the aid of the Dutch in June 1658.

It was as early as 1602 that the Dutch visited the court of Kandy, in the reign of Vimala Dharmasuriya I, seeking an alliance. In 1612 a treaty was agreed upon between the Dutch and King Senarat, the then king of Kandy, and in accordance with this agreement, in 1638 Rajasinha II sought Dutch assistance against the Portuguese. From that time the two European nations fought each other until in 1658 the Portuguese were expelled from the country and the Dutch came to occupy those regions which formerly were occupied by the Portuguese. They remained in possession until 1796, in which year they were ousted by the British.

The Dutch, whose religion was Protestant Christianity, followed a policy which was in marked contrast to that of the Portuguese. Extension of commerce was their main concern and since peace was essential to achieve this end, they even endured with subdued humbleness and patience whatever insult and provocation came from the Sinhalese. They even assisted the Sinhalese in two embassies to Siam which were sent to obtain monks to establish higher ordination in Sri Lanka.

The Dutch, however, had an established system of education throughout their territories. The school building was both church and school, the schoolmaster was both teacher and representative of the religion. Services were held regularly at these places; births and marriages were registered according to Christian rites. When the agent of the Church was so disposed, he was able to get those who did not attend church punished for the alleged offense. All civil rights and inheritance depended on a person's church affiliation. No person who was not a Christian could hold even a minor office under government, no person who was not a Christian could get married legally or register the birth of a child.

There was, however, one redeeming feature of this system. The organization was so extensive that they had to employ Sinhalese as their teachers and agents of religion. The vast majority of these Protestant agents were at heart Buddhists; they were Christians only in the sense of their office. The people themselves followed this plan: they were Buddhists inwardly but were officially Christians, for the purpose of registering their marriages, the births of their children, for holding office, etc. Thus the efforts of the Dutch in the propagation of their religion did not affect Buddhism much. On the other hand the Portuguese, where they had priests and where they had established churches under the direct control of these priests, were able to look after the congregations and gradually established their religion in such centers. Most of them were zealous and earnest in their duties and took a genuine interest in the welfare of their flocks.

VIMALA DHARMASURIYA II AND HIS SUCCESSORS

When the Dutch were occupying the maritime provinces, several Sinhalese rulers of the Kandyan kingdom made attempts to restore Buddhism. One of them was Vimala Dharmasuriya II (1687-1706), son and successor of Rajasinha II. He constructed a three-storeyed pavilion for the Sacred Tooth Relic. The king also made a pilgrimage to Sumanakuta (Adam's Peak) on foot. Seeing that the state of the Order of monks was unsatisfactory again to such an extent that not more than five ordained monks were found in the whole country, the king sent an embassy to Arakan and obtained monks for an ordination ceremony. With the help of these monks an ordination ceremony was held at Gẹtambe, at the place where a similar ceremony had been held formerly in the reign of Vimala Dharmasuriya I. At this ceremony thirty-three novices were given higher ordination and another one hundred and twenty persons were admitted to the Order.

Vimala Dharmasuriya II was succeeded by his son Sri Viraparakrama Narendrasinha (1706-1739), a just ruler, mindful of the welfare of the religion. He constructed a two-storeyed building for the Sacred Tooth Relic, provided the monks with their requisites, and induced several members of the laity to enter the Order. However, during his reign many a monk had resorted to scandalous practices.

His successor Sri Vijaya Rajasinha (1739-1747), also a pious ruler, induced many a young person to join the Order and also held several religious festivals. He spent money on getting religious books written, caused preaching halls to be constructed at several places, and took measures to educate the people in the doctrine. Discovering that the Order of the Sangha was almost extinct in the island, he sent two missions to Siam, with the help of the Dutch who lent a ship for the voyage. The first expedition proved disastrous due to shipwreck, and before the second mission returned the king died. Thus his attempt to restore higher ordination failed.

THE REIGN OF KIRTI SRI RAAJASINHA

Sri Vijaya Rajasinha was succeeded by King Kirti Sri Rajasinha, whose reign proved to be one of the most inspiring periods for Buddhism in that century. At the time of his accession the Order of monks had sunk to very low levels of degeneracy. There was not a single monk in the whole island who had received the higher ordination. There were plenty of novices (i.e., saamaneras), but apart from a few skillful and pious ones among them the majority were leading a life unbecoming to monks. They set aside the study of Dhamma and Vinaya and resorted to the study of astrology, medicine and devil worship, led scandalous lives and engaged in cultivation of land and in trade. The older saamaneras ordained only the sons of their relatives so that they could obtain the immense wealth which the generations of kings and ministers had dedicated to the service of the Order.

Kirti Sri Rajasinha was determined to set right this state of affairs. With the aid of the Dutch who gave a vessel for the voyage, the king sent an embassy to King Dhammika of Siam and re-established the higher ordination in Sri Lanka. Several hundreds were ordained and education was fostered. The king also proclaimed a code of conduct (*katikaavata*) for the guidance of the monks.

VELIVITA SRI SARANANKARA

In all these religious activities of King Kirti Sri Rajasinha he was inspired and guided by a great personality, a saamanera who was distinguished for his piety, enthusiasm, learning and determination. He was Velivita Pindapatika Sri Saranankara. Born in 1698 at Velivita, a village near Kandy, he became a novice at the age of sixteen as a pupil of an elder samanera called Suriyagoda. With great effort and devotion he studied the Pali language and the doctrine, for which purpose he traveled from place to place in search of books and tutors. Later he went about preaching the Dhamma, thus encouraging others to rise up for the welfare of the religion. These activities of Saranankara Samanera soon made him popular as a teacher of great renown who devoted his life to his own welfare and that of others, a poet, preacher and controversialist.

Apart from his skill as a scholar he was also known for his austere practices. When he went round the country learning or preaching, he depended for his sustenance on the ancient practice of a bhikkhu, called *pindapata,* gathering his food from house to house in his almsbowl. For this he became known as Pindapatika Saranankara. When King Vimala Dharmasuriya II reigned he was a samanera, but his sincere devotion had pleased the king so much that he made a gilt casket set with seven hundred gems and presented it to Saranankara Saamanera, with many books. This king also provided the monk with the requisites and induced him to write several literary works.

When King Sri Vijaya Rajasinha came to the throne it was at the request of Saranankara Samanera that the king sent two embassies to Siam. In the reign of King Kirti Sri Rajasinha, Saranankara Samanera offered his fullest cooperation in his activities in the revival of Buddhism and the king depended upon the samanera for guidance, advice and inspiration. He urged the king to send the embassy to Siam and himself wrote the messages that were taken to the Siamese king and the Sangharaaja of that country. The king's ministers who constituted the embassy were chosen on his advice and this mission was successful mainly due to his exertions. After the return of the embassy Saranankara Samanera was given higher ordination and was appointed Sangharaja of Sri Lanka, the highest office conferred on a monk.

The activities of Saranankara Thera not only restored the higher ordination and the purity of the Sangha but also brought about a literary revival as a result of the impetus given by him to the study of the Pali language and the Buddha's teachings.

Saranankara Thera himself compiled several important religious works such as the *Munigunalankara,* a Sinhalese poem in praise of the Buddha, the *Sarartha Sangraha,* a treatise on various doctrinal teachings in Buddhism. *Abhisambodhi-alankara,* a Pali poem in a hundred stanzas on the life of the Buddha from the time of Dipankara up to his enlightenment, the *Madhurartha Prakasani,* which is a Sinhalese commentarial paraphrase to the Pali *Mahabodhivamsa,* and the *Rupamala,* a work on Pali grammar. Several others who were pupils of Saranankara Thera also composed many literary works. The great monk died in 1778 a.c. at the age of 81.

The successors of Sri Saranankara Thera are known as belonging to the Syamopaali Nikaya, now popularly called the Siyam (Syama) Nikaya. Only those who belonged to what was regarded as the highest caste could obtain higher ordination in that Nikaya. In the year 1799 a samanera named Ambagahapitiya Yanavimalatissa, who did not belong to that caste, went to Amarapura in Burma to obtain higher ordination and on his return he established the Amarapura Nikaya in 1803. Subsequently, in 1863 Ambagahawatte Sri Saranankara Thera established the Ramañña Nikaya. These three Nikayas exist up to this day, with no doctrinal differences between them.

THE ARRIVAL OF THE BRITISH AND THE END OF SINHALESE RULE IN SRI LANKA

King Kirti Sri Rajasinha, whose reign, as was seen above, was one of the most fruitful for the cause of Buddhism, was succeeded by his brother Rajaadhi Rajasinha. A scholar of Pali, Sanskrit and Sinhalese as he was, the king himself composed the beautiful Sinhalese poem *Asadisa-daa-kava* and worked for the religion by taking necessary steps to preserve the purity of the Saasana. His nephew, Sri Vikrama Rajasinha, was the next and last king of Lanka. This ruler, who was in constant fear of the intrigues of his Adigar Pilima Talawe and his allies, had recourse to intoxicating drinks, hoping thus to forget his sorrows, and tortured all his enemies with appalling cruelty. There was general unrest in the kingdom and these conditions were evidently not conducive to the progress of Buddhism.

It was in 1796, during the reign of Rajadhi Rajasinha, that the Dutch, who were defeated in battle, surrendered their territories to the British colony and Sir Frederick North was sent as the first British governor.

Before long North realized that the opportunity would come soon for them to possess the whole island, for Pilima Talawe, the Adigar of King Sri Vikrama Rajasinha of Kandy, disclosed his plans to ruin the king to the British governor himself. However, this plan of Pilima Talawe was revealed to the king, and the Adigar was beheaded in 1812. Ehelepola, who became the next Adigar, was detected in an attempt to organize a general rebellion against the king, and as punishment, the king tortured his wife and children cruelly. Subsequently the king punished all whom he suspected and as a result, unrest and disorder became the order of the day.

In these circumstances, Ehelepola appealed to the British for help. In January 1815 a British army marched to the capital city of Kandy and took the Sinhalese king captive. On the 2nd of March 1815, at a solemn assembly of the Kandyan chiefs and the monks, the king was deposed and his dominions were vested in the British Crown. Thus ended the glamour of the Kingdom of Kandy which had withstood the invasions and attacks of the Portuguese and the Dutch and for some time the English. Thus ended too the line of the Buddhist kings of Lanka who for 2301 years, from the accession of Vijaya in 486 BCE, brought glory and fame to their country and religion.

THE BRITISH ATTITUDE TOWARDS BUDDHISM

The British occupied the low-country of Lanka in 1796 and the Kandyan territories in 1815. These territories remained in their hands until 1948, in which year Sri Lanka regained her independence.

Mention has already been made of the solemn assembly of the 2nd of March 1815 held in Kandy. At this assembly a treaty was signed between the British rulers and the Kandyan chiefs, by which the chiefs handed over the country to the British and the British promised to safeguard Buddhism, declaring its rites and ceremonies sacred and inviolate.

The inclusion of this clause referring to Buddhism in the very treaty by which the chiefs handed over the country to the British is very significant. On the one hand, it indicates how concerned the Sinhalese leaders were about the future of Buddhism even in the hour of their misfortune. On the other hand, the British had obviously considered that its omission would bring disastrous results.

However, the British attitude towards Buddhism soon caused dissatisfaction among the Sinhalese chiefs. The chiefs and the Buddhist monks realized that the British had no desire to respect the clause of the treaty relating to Buddhism, and that they were keen to convert the people to their own faith.

During the early years after the signing of the treaty the British governor took part in the annual ceremonies connected with the Sacred Tooth Relic and appointed the chief theras, as had been done by the Sinhalese kings in former times. This created resentment on the part of the Christian missionaries in Sri Lanka and the Christian authorities in England, and soon both practices were dropped, severing whatever connection they had with Buddhism. From 1847 the bhikkhus were required to elect and appoint their own chiefs and in 1853 the British government handed over the Tooth Relic from their custody to the Diyawadana Nilame and the chief monks of the Malwatte and the Asgiriya monasteries.

While thus violating the treaty of 1815 the British rulers even prohibited the Buddhists from enjoying some of the privileges that were granted to the followers of the Christian faith. Thus, for instance, even as late as 1805 no child could be legally registered without previous baptism by a Christian minister, and the clergy did not solemnize the marriage of unbaptized individuals. Further, only those who adopted the Christian faith were favored with government employment. This attitude of the British made vast numbers of Buddhists adopt the new faith without any understanding of its teachings. These people saw in Christianity "not only happiness in the world which is to come, but, what was more important to them, the promise of this life as well!"

Some of the British governors in their attempt to disrupt the Buddhist organization even tried to bring about disunity between the monks and the laity and also to win over some of the leading Buddhist monks to their side. For they realized that the monks were the main obstacle to their conversions and that as long as the monks and the laity remained united their attempts would not meet with great success.

Lastly, the British rulers gave all possible support to the Christian missionaries to carry out their educational and missionary activities.

THE CHRISTIAN MISSIONARY ACTIVITIES

From the beginning of the period of British rule several Christian missionary bodies engaged themselves actively in missionary activities in Sri Lanka. The Baptists had already started their activities in 1792. They were followed by the Wesleyan Methodists in 1814, the Americans in 1816, and the Church of England in 1818. These missionary bodies received every encouragement and assistance from the government.

The establishment of missionary schools in various parts of the island was one of the principal undertakings of these missionary bodies. These schools were manned and managed by the missionary societies with the assistance of the British government and were partly financed by public funds. The schools attracted large numbers of Buddhist children because they were the centers where young men were trained for high government offices. Hitherto the temple had been the village school and the monks were the instructors of the village children in secular learning as well as in spiritual wisdom. But under the British government temple education could not provide the learning necessary for government employment. Thus the Buddhist parents who wished to see their children in high government offices willingly sent them to the new missionary schools.

In these schools the children were molded according to the requirements of the missionary bodies. The authorities did not insist that one should become a Christian before admission, but each student was required to learn the Christian religion and to participate in the morning and evening religious services in the school. They had no opportunity of participating in their own religious observances. Almost every school had its own church. The lessons imparted to these children were arranged with a view to undermining their Buddhist religion. The teaching of the Buddha was criticized and condemned and the Buddhist practices were ridiculed. Buddhism was held up as a religion of the vulgar masses as opposed to the Christianity of civilized people.

This disparagement in course of time naturally had its expected result. People gradually began to give up their national faith for the new faith which they were trained to think of as more refined and cultured. It now became the fashion to adopt the Christian faith and Christian names and customs. Even those who did not embrace Christianity became indifferent to their own religion. When they grew up they did not even mind their conversion to any religion.

The missionaries also did not neglect the education of the girls. Convents were opened up with boarding facilities and in them the girls were brought up and educated with the utmost care until they were married in due time, with the sanction of the Christian guardians.

MOHOTTIWATTE GUNAANANDA THERA AND THE BUDDHIST RE-AWAKENING

When the Christian missionaries were thus active in towns and villages propagating their gospel and converting the Buddhists to their faith, the Buddhist monks were not able enough to offer much resistance. When the villagers assembled in the temple on Poya (*uposatha*) days, they attempted to refute the arguments of the Christian preachers in the course of their sermons, but this method was not very effective.

It was at this time, about 1860, that a young Buddhist saamanera named Mohottiwatte Gunaananda appeared on the scene and challenged the Christian missionaries to meet him in open-debate. This young novice had obtained his early education in Christian schools and had thus studied the Christian scriptures and was also well versed in the Buddha's teachings. He went from village to village making public speeches and held meetings in several Christian strongholds, often challenging the Christian clergy to face him in open debate. Soon he earned a great reputation for his eloquence and people flocked in thousands to hear him.

The Christian clergy at first took no notice of the challenge of this monk, but later, quite confident of their success they accepted the challenge. This resulted in three public controversies, one at Udanvita in 1866, another at Gampola in 1871 and the last at Panadura in 1873.

The Panadura controversy, which lasted for a week, was the most important of them all. It was the culmination of his efforts and it led to a Buddhist reawakening. The controversy was to take place in the presence of leading Sinhalese Christians and Buddhists. Rules were laid down so that the meeting could be held in a fair manner. The leading English newspaper of the time, *The Ceylon Times*, sent a special representative to report the proceedings. A complete report of all the speeches corrected by the speakers themselves was published in English day by day.

The controversy ended with victory for the Buddhists. The Buddhist orator not only replied effectively to the fallacies of the Christian speakers, but also enlightened them on the principles and tenets of the Buddhist doctrine. When the Christians retired from the debate defeated, the Buddhists were overjoyed. Festivities were held in every temple to mark their triumph and the effigy of Gunaananda Thera was carried in procession in every village.

The triumph of the Buddhists over their Christian adversaries at the Panadura controversy flushed into their veins vigor and enthusiasm to work for the recovery of their lost glory.

COLONEL OLCOTT AND BUDDHIST ACTIVITIES

An American scholar named Dr. Peebles, who happened to be in Sri Lanka on a visit about the time of this Panadura controversy, was so impressed with it that he published its proceedings in book form on his return to America. The attention of Colonel Henry Steele Olcott was first drawn towards Buddhism by this report of the controversy which he happened to read in a public library in America. Olcott was an American by birth who had spent his early life as a very successful farmer and a colonel of both the army and the navy. At an early age of 43 years in 1875 he gave up all worldly fortunes and together with Madame Blavatsky formed the Theosophical Society for the quest of truth in all religions. Having read the reports of the Panadura controversy, he realized the importance of the teachings of the Buddha and in 1880 he came over to Lanka along with Madame Blavatsky to gain a first-hand knowledge of Buddhism. When his studies soon convinced him of the teachings of the Buddha, he embraced Buddhism and worked for the upliftment of the Buddhists in Lanka.

Olcott showed the Buddhist leaders of Sri Lanka that if Buddhism was to raise its head against the Christian missionary activities, they should open up Buddhist schools to educate their children. Under his guidance and leadership, and with the support of all the leading Buddhist monks, the lay Buddhist leaders in Sri Lanka at that time founded the Buddhist Theosophical Society on 17th June 1880. The primary objects of the society were the establishment of Buddhist schools, and the bringing together of Buddhist workers in a cooperative body without distinction of caste or position for the purpose of promoting the welfare of the Buddhists of Lanka.

At the time of Olcott's arrival there were only three Buddhist schools in Sri Lanka which obtained government grants, one at Dodanduwa, another at Panadura, and the third at Bandaragama. In 1897, twelve years after the establishment of the society, there were 25 boys' schools, 11 girls' schools, and 10 mixed schools founded by the society. In 1903 there were 174 schools under the management of the society with an attendance of about 30,000 children. In 1940 the number of schools had risen to 429.

Olcott and his supporters went from village to village appealing to the people to donate subscriptions for the maintenance of these schools, and funds were readily forthcoming. Several leading educationists of his day made his educational plans a great success. Mention should be made among them of C. W. Leadbeater, Bowles Daly, F. L. Woodward, A. E. Bultjens and Mrs. M. M. Higgins. Mrs. Higgins was particularly responsible for the successful education of the Buddhist girls. The leading Buddhist schools of the present day such as Ananda and Nalanda Colleges in Colombo, Dharmaraja in Kandy, Mahinda in Galle, Dharmasoka in Ambalangoda, Visakha in Bambalapitiya, and Museus in Colombo are outstanding examples of the success of his efforts.

Olcott pointed out to the Sinhalese Buddhist leaders of his time that they should have their own publications to give publicity to Buddhist and national opinion. For this purpose the Buddhist Theosophical Society started the Sinhalese newspaper, *Sarasavisandarasa*, in December 1880, and later its English supplement, *The Buddhist*, now a monthly of the YMBA, Colombo. Colonel Olcott worked hard to win back for the Sinhalese their lost rights. It was as a result of his efforts that the Buddhists of Lanka gained freedom to hold their Buddhist processions and that the full-moon day of Vesak was declared a public holiday. The present Buddhist flag is also a creation of Olcott which he appealed to the Buddhists to hoist on all important Buddhist occasions. His efforts also resulted in the appointment of Buddhist registrars of marriages.

Of the Panadura controversy and the consequent arrival of Colonel Olcott, it could justly be said that these two events jointly closed down a dark period in Lankan Buddhism and ushered in a new bright era.

This noble personality who awakened the Sinhalese Buddhists and showed them the path on which they should proceed passed away in 1907 while he was in India.

OTHER ACTIVITIES OF THE BUDDHIST RENAISSANCE MOVEMENT

Apart from meeting the Christian opponents in open debate, Mohottivatte Gunaananda Thera and his companions had planned other devices to counteract the anti-Buddhist propaganda of the Christian missionaries and revive the Buddhist faith in the country. One of these devices was the establishment of a printing press whereby they could reply to the criticisms of the Christians and also publish books for the study of Buddhism.

Thus the first press, controlled by Sinhalese Buddhists, was established in 1862 under the name of Lankopakaara Press. It was a donation by the king of Siam. In the same year Mohottivatte Gunaananda Thera established the Sarvajña-saasanaabhivurddhi-daayaka Press at Kotahena, near Colombo. Consequently the Lakrivikirana Press was established in 1863 and the Lankabhinavavisruta Press in 1864.

In the meantime learned monks of the period, with the assistance of lay followers, brought about a revival of Buddhist learning. Pioneers among them were the venerable Hikkaduve Sri Sumangala, who founded the Vidyodaya Pirivena of Maligakanda in Colombo in 1874 and the venerable Ratmalaane Sri Dhammaaloka, who founded the Vidyaalankara Pirivena of Peliyagoda in Colombo in 1875. In these two great centers of learning a vast number of monks and lay people received education and in a short time the fame of these two pirivenas spread even in foreign countries.

The scholars whom these two centers produced opened up other pirivenas in different parts of the country and also contributed to Buddhistic studies by compiling and editing numerous books. It was also about this time that devoted scholars from foreign countries who happened to be in Sri Lanka evinced a great interest in Buddhism, its culture and literature, and created an interest in their kinsmen in the West through their valuable treatises. Turner, Tennant, Childers, Rhys Davids and Geiger were but a few among them.

ANAGARIKA DHARMAPALA AND THE BUDDHIST CULTURAL REVIVAL

A different type of revivalistic activity was carried out by a group of lay Buddhist leaders just at this time, the foremost of this group being Anagaarika Dharmapaala. The fame of this great personality lies in his successful effort of reforming the Buddhist society in Sri Lanka, which had fallen into a very low moral state, and also in his activities in India for the purpose of reviving Buddhism in that country and for winning back the Buddhist sacred places there for their rightful owners, the Buddhists. We are presently concerned only with his social reformation in Sri Lanka.

Anagaarika Dharmapaala, formerly known as David Hewavitarana, was born in 1864 as the eldest son of a leading businessman in Colombo who had migrated to the capital city from Matara in south Lanka. The father, mother and the grandfather of the child were devoted Buddhists who were close associates of the venerable Hikkaduve Sri Sumangala Thera. At home the child was thus brought up in a Buddhist environment though he received his education in Christian schools. Those were the days when Mohottiwatte Gunaananda Thera was engaged in verbal battles against the Christian missionary activities, and young Dharmapaala had not only listened to the orations of the great speaker with much inspiration, but also had become a favorite of the monks by his constant visits to the temple at Kotahena. When Colonel Olcott and Madame Blavatsky arrived in Lanka in 1880, Dharmapaala, then a youth of 16 years, naturally became a great favorite of the two foreigners through his association with Gunaananda Thera.

The speeches and activities of Colonel Olcott greatly inspired the young enthusiast. In 1883, consequent upon a brutal assault on a Buddhist procession by a Catholic mob at Kotahena, Dharmapaala left his Catholic school and in the following year became a member of the Buddhist Theosophical Society in Colombo, of which his grandfather was the president. At the age of 20 Dharmapaala obtained permission from his father to leave home and lead a celibate life as he wished to devote all his time to the welfare of the Saasana. From that time he stayed at the headquarters of the Buddhist Theosophical Society.

In 1886 when Colonel Olcott returned to Sri Lanka after a short stay abroad and planned to go round the country addressing public gatherings and collecting money for the Buddhist Educational Fund, Anagaarika Dharmapaala joined him as his interpreter. For this purpose he obtained leave from the Education Department where he was working as a junior clerk and subsequently vacated his post in order to dedicate all his life to the good of the religion.

As the interpreter of Colonel Olcott, Dharmapaala gained immense experience as a speaker. He now traveled throughout the country with or without his companion, Olcott.

Those were the days when the Buddhists of Lanka were reluctant to declare themselves Buddhists, for Buddhism was considered to be the faith of the unurbanized masses. It was the fashion at that time to become a Christian, to study English and other allied subjects, to adopt a foreign name and to imitate the dress of the foreigners and their customs and manners. Buddhism and Buddhist culture were subjected to ridicule and were the heritage of villagers in the interior.

Anagaarika Dharmapaala was the foremost among those who rose against this mentality of the Buddhists. Through his public speeches and numerous articles in newspapers and journals he vehemently opposed the habit of imitating foreigners in religion, names and customs. He emphatically pointed out that this tendency to imitate was a clear manifestation of a lack of the primary element of self-esteem. In keeping with his preaching he himself changed his name from David to Dharmapaala. The people listened to his sermons and attentively read his articles in journals and newspapers and were convinced of the truth of his philosophy. Gradually there came about a cultural revival. The people began to take pride in their religion, their language and their customs.

Above all, several younger men of his time joined the Buddhist forward movement to guide the destinies of future generations of Buddhists in Sri Lanka.

This great personality, who indefatigably gave his services for the revival of Buddhism in Lanka, India and other parts of the world, in his last days entered the Order as the venerable Devamitta Dhammapaala Thera. He passed away in the year 1933, while he was in India. To perpetuate his memory Sri Lanka and India celebrated his birth centenary in 1964-65.

BUDDHISM IN SRI LANKA IN THE FIRST HALF OF THE TWENTIETH CENTURY

The leading men in the Buddhist community at the beginning of the twentieth century were inspired by the activities of Anagaarika Dharmapaala and they formed into organized bodies for the promotion of the Buddhist revivalistic movement. Among them were great personalities such as Sir D. B. Jayatillake, F. R. Somnayake, Valisinha Harishchandra and W. A. de Silva. To them the Buddhist revival was the national revival. These prominent men, whose names have gone into history, became active members of leading Buddhist associations like the Buddhist Theosophical Society (founded 1880), the Colombo Young Men's Buddhist Association (1898), the Maha Bodhi Society (1891), and the Ceylon Buddhist Congress (1918), and worked with remarkable success to achieve the aims and objects of those organizations. Through such organizations these Buddhist leaders were able to unite and bring together all Buddhists in Sri Lanka, to inspire them to be active, to collect funds for educational and other religious purposes, to give the Buddhist children a sound religious and secular education, to do a great deal of social work and to raise the spiritual and moral standard of the people.

A great deal of literary work was produced during this period. The Vidyodaya and the Vidyalankara Pirivenas and their affiliated institutions, which numbered about 200, had produced many scholars who edited several canonical and commentarial works in the early twentieth century. Simon Hewavitarana, the youngest brother of Anagaarika Dharmapaala, had left a large legacy which was to be used for the printing and publishing of Pali books, and this greatly facilitated the production of books at this time. From about 1930 many modern scholars, both monks and laymen, have edited and published many more texts of Pali Buddhism and have also compiled several secondary works on the different aspects of Buddhism. To name these scholars and their publications is not necessary since they and their works are very well known.

A great enthusiasm was also created for the rebuilding of ancient Buddhist shrines in the old capitals of Sri Lanka. The Ruwanveli Dagaba was the first to receive attention. The other shrines too were renovated one by one and today the old city of Anuraadhapura has once more become a sacred city with the Catholic Church and the commercial sites which were in the city being moved to other places.

Sri Lanka has not only reorganized her Buddhist activities within the country but has also taken a leading part in sending *Dhammadutas*, "messengers of the Dhamma," abroad. In 1950 the World Fellowship of Buddhists was set up in order to bring all Buddhist countries together, and several conferences were held in the subsequent years.

It is a very significant fact that this revival of Buddhism in the twentieth century was accelerated towards the middle of that century as a result of the Sinhalese Buddhist leaders of the time gaining control of the reins of government. Ultimately in 1948 Sri Lanka regained its independence after a period of British rule of 133 years. The Buddhist leaders who worked indefatigably for the cause of Buddhism were also the Sinhalese national leaders who led the struggle for liberation from foreign rule. It was therefore to be expected that when these leaders gained national freedom and took over the reins of government from the British rulers, they were mindful of their national faith and its culture and therefore took the necessary steps to set things right so that Buddhism would once more receive its rightful place.

THE BUDDHA JAYANTI AND AFTER

In the year 1956, on the 23rd of May, which was the Vesak full-moon day of that year, the Buddhists in Sri Lanka and other parts of the world celebrated the Buddha Jayanti. That was the 2500th anniversary of the Buddha's Parinibbaana, a day specially significant to the Buddhists the world over on account of the tradition that it constitutes half the life-span of the Saasana and that from that year the Dhamma would flourish and spread far and wide.

The history of Buddhism in Sri Lanka from the closing years of the last century has clear indications that the prophecy, as far as Lanka is concerned, is coming true. In other parts of the world too it is seen that more and more people who were not Buddhists by birth are becoming interested in Buddhism.

The government of Sri Lanka, on its part, undertook numerous activities in commemoration of the Buddha Jayanti. A committee of leading Buddhist monks and laymen was appointed to advise the government on all matters relating to the Buddha Jayanti celebrations. Arrangements were made to translate the Tripitaka into Sinhalese and compile an *Encyclopaedia of Buddhism* in English and one in Sinhalese as well. It was also decided to compile other books dealing with the biography of the Buddha, his teachings and the history of Buddhism. The completion of the renovation of the Daladaa Maaligawa (the Temple of the Tooth) in Kandy, before the Buddha Jayanti and to aid the reconstruction of the Mahiyangana Thupa were among its other undertakings. A substantial grant was also given to the organization which was handling the construction work of a Sanghaaraama for the Buddhist monks at the University of Ceylon, Peradeniya. Arrangements were made to hold a World Buddhist Conference in Colombo in the following year.

From the Buddha Jayanti year it was noticeable that the Buddhists in Lanka applied themselves more keenly to the practice of morality taught in Buddhism while showing interest in the celebration of Buddhist festivals. More and more people observe the eight precepts on the Poya days and young children are given a sound religious education. The government on its part has given the necessary encouragement for this religious re-establishment. In January 1959 the Vidyodaya and the Vidyaalankaara Pirivenas were made two universities. The private Buddhist and Christian schools were taken over in December 1960 and are now managed by the government. The four Poya days of the month (i.e., full and new moon, and the two quarter moon days) were made the weekend holidays in 1966, instead of Sundays as in previous times. It has also been planned to start a new Bhikkhu University in Anuraadhapura.

Sri Lanka has today about 6.5 million Buddhists, which is about sixty-five percent of her total population. There are nearly 6,000 Buddhist monasteries all over the island with approximately 15,000 monks. Almost all the monasteries in the island have their Dhamma schools where Buddhist children are given religious instruction on the Poya days (previously on Sundays). The Colombo Young Men's Buddhist Association conducts an island-wide examination annually for the pupils of these Dhamma schools. The children are provided with free books, by the Ministry of Cultural Affairs and prizes are given to those who pass these examinations, including one on the Dhammapada, and this association spends annually a large sum of money on the religious education of children. In 1956-57, 163,180 children sat for the Dhamma examination.

The foregoing account will tell the reader of the vicissitudes that this great religion, Buddhism, had to face during its history of over 2,000 years in this isle of Sri Lanka. It had its tidal ebb and flow. During the four centuries of foreign domination Buddhism withstood all the assaults that almost crushed it. Since Sri Lanka gained its independence in 1948, there has been a revival of the Buddhist religion and culture in the country, and this reawakening was particularly noticeable when the Buddha Jayanti was celebrated in 1956.

The progress achieved since the eighties of the last century may well be called remarkable. Yet, to the Buddhists of Lanka, this should not be a cause of complacency, for which there is no room in a world of change. It remains the duty of the present generation and the coming ones to preserve and strengthen these achievements against the corrosive forces of a materialist age, and to work devotedly so that the Buddha's message of Wisdom and Compassion may take still firmer and deeper roots in Lanka and also spread its beneficial influence over the world.

BUDDHISM IN BHUTAN

Mahayan Buddhism is the state religion of Bhutan, and Buddhists comprise 98% of its population. Although originating in Tibetan Buddhism, the Buddhism practiced in Bhutan differs significantly in its rituals, liturgy, and monastic organization. The state religion has long been supported financially by the government through annual subsidies to monasteries, shrines, monks, and nuns. In the modern era, support of the state religion during the reign of Jigme Dorji Wangchuck includes the manufacture of 10,000 gilded bronze images of the Buddha, publication of elegant calligraphied editions of the 108-volume Kangyur (Collection of the Words of the Buddha) and the 225-volume Tengyur (Collection of Commentaries), and the construction of numerous *chorten* (stupas) throughout the country. Guaranteed representation in the National Assembly and the Royal Advisory Council, Buddhists constitute the majority of society and are assured an influential voice in public policy.

In 1989 some 1,000 monks (*lam*, or *gelong*, novices) belonged to the Central Monastic Body in Thimphu and Punakha, and some 4,000 monks belonged to district monastic bodies. The hierarchy was headed by the Je Khenpo, who was assisted by four *lonpon* or masters, each in charge of religious tradition, liturgy, lexicography, or logic. The *lonpon*, one of whom, the Dorji Lonpon, normally succeeded the current Je Khenpo, had under them religious administrators and junior monastic officials in charge of art, music, and other areas. Gelugpa monks were celibate, but Nyingmapa's consist of not only monks but also householders, allowing them to marry, raise families, and work in secular occupations while performing liturgical functions in temples and homes. In all, there were some 12,000 monks in Bhutan in the late 1980s. There were also active congregations of nuns, but no figures were readily available. The majority of Bhutan's Buddhists are adherents of the Drukpa subsect of the Kargyupa (literally, oral transmission) school, one of the four major schools of Tibetan Buddhism.

Since July 2002, Menjong Chöthün Tshogpa, currently a nationwide non-profit organization in Bhutan, has been formed by the Supreme Dharma King or His Holiness of Bhutan mainly to preserve the indigenous Buddha's Teachings as their age-old culture and tradition. Subsequently His Eminence Trizin Tsering Rimpoche has been enthroned as the chairman by His Holiness Truku Jigme Chödrag Rinpoche 70th Kyabje Dorjechang (Supreme Dharma King) of Bhutan himself since June 2003.

Later in 2004, His Eminence Trizin Tsering Rimpoche founded the Buddha Dordenma Image Foundation, under the patron of His Holiness of Bhutan, with an aim to fulfill a former prophecy in a term of Guru Padmasambhava to bestow blessings on world peace and glorious happiness through the currently running Buddha Dordenma Project.

THE SHABDRUNG

Prior to 1907, the highest Buddhist leader in Bhutan was the Shabdrung, a tulku who is seen as the reincarnation of Bhutan's founder. His formal activity to benefit all sentient beings is destined to occur in seven lives, each with his own prophecy.

Since the community has an utmost respect and devotion to the Shabdrung, many illegitimate parties capitalize on this move by posing themselves as the Shabdrung. Some even sell their sons by claiming the babies as the Shabdrung. In the early years, real Shabdrung could prove anything that he said. His true power had been witnessed by people from all walks of life - including the ordinary, the dead, and even the blind. In the recent years, however, fake Shabdrung has given claims to myriad things with none proved to be true. It is outright obvious that these moves are aimed at commercial benefit.

MONASTERIES

Monasteries and convents are common in Bhutan. Both monks and nuns keep their heads shaved and wear distinguishing maroon robes. Their days are spent in study and meditation but also in the performance of rituals honoring various bodhisattvas, praying for the dead, and seeking the intercession of bodhisattvas on behalf of the ill. Some of their prayers involved chants and singing accompanied by conch shell trumpets, trumpets made from human thighbones, metal horns up to three meters long, large standing drums and cymbals, hand bells, temple bells, gongs, and wooden sticks. Such monastic music and singing, not normally heard by the general public, has been reported to have "great virility" and to be more melodious than its Tibetan monotone counterparts.

BUILDINGS AND OBJECTS

To bring Buddhism to the people, numerous symbols and structures are employed. Religious monuments, prayer walls, prayer flags, and sacred mantras carved in stone hillsides are prevalent. Among the religious monuments are chorten, the Bhutanese version of the Indian stupa. They range from simple rectangular "house" chorten to complex edifices with ornate steps, doors, domes, and spires. Some are decorated with the Buddha's eyes that see in all directions simultaneously. These earth, brick, or stone structures commemorate deceased kings, Buddhist saints, venerable monks, and other notables, and sometimes they serve as reliquaries. Prayer walls are made of laid or piled stone and inscribed with Tantric prayers. Prayers printed with woodblocks on cloth are made into tall, narrow, colorful prayer flags, which are then mounted on long poles and placed both at holy sites and at dangerous locations to ward off demons and to benefit the spirits of the dead. To help propagate the faith, itinerant monks travel from village to village carrying portable shrines with many small doors, which open to reveal statues and images of the Buddha, bodhisattavas, and notable lamas.

BUDDHISM IN NEPAL

Buddhism in Nepal dates from the birth of Siddharta Gautama himself. Legend has it that many bodhisattvas and previous Buddhas also visited the land. Monuments to these Buddhas can still be seen. Early Buddhist history is difficult to document, but we know that Nepal became a great meeting point for Indian and Tibetan Buddhist teachers. Nagarjuna, the great Madhyamika master, and many other great practitioners visited, lived, and taught in Nepal. Stone inscriptions and colophons provide clear evidence that a strong lineage of Mahasanghika Bhiksunis existed in the seventh century. The country became a repository of Buddhist Sanskrit literature and famous for its production of fine Buddhist art.

Many famous temples have been erected throughout Nepal. Although many ancient temples were destroyed by earthquakes in 1355 and 1934, many important religious structures still survive. The ancient stupas of Swayambhu and Bodhnath are regarded as most sacred. Buddhism in Nepal includes Theravada, Mahayana and Vajrayana traditions. The rulers of Nepal have primarily been Hindu, but have supported the development of Buddhism over the centuries. The Tibetan Mahayana tradition is the most popular in northern Nepal, with approximately 3000 monasteries. Newar Vajrayana Buddhism is a widespread religious system in the Kathmandu Valley with an elaborate tradition of ritual. Since the early 40s some Nepalese have turned to Theravada practice based on the Pali canon, stressing the rational aspects of Buddhism over ritual. Most Theravada monasteries are located in the Kathmandu Valley. There are approximately 100 monks and 150 nuns, mostly belonging to the Newar community. Newars with the Shakya surname trace their lineage to the family of Shakyamuni Buddha.

The Great Stupa of Svayambhunath stands on a hill to the west of Kathmandu. Its name means "The self created, Self-existent Buddha." The myth of its origin is also the myth of the valley's origin. It tells the story of the primordial Buddha's enlightenment and the spread of Buddhism in Nepal.

This most sacred site has always been the most important power place for local Buddhists and for pilgrims from all over the world. It is considered to be the most powerful shrine in the Himalayas.

Indian Buddhism began to penetrate the mountain passes into Nepal in perhaps the 4th or 5th century AD, although its influence has always been mainly confined to the Kathmandu Valley and the western part of the country. With the destruction of Buddhism in India in the 13th century, Tibet, Nepal's powerful neighbour to the north, began to influence the country's religious development. However, the Tantric Buddhism that resulted became increasingly corrupt and fused with Hinduism, the predominant religion, and the two became and remain even today almost indistinguishable.

In the 1930s the first Nepalese ordained as Theravada monks in India, but Nepal's Hindu ruler's refused to allow them to return to the country and imprisoned those who did. With the change of government in 1950 and the coming of religious freedom, Theravada Buddhism has begun to steadily gain support. Since 1959 Tibetan refugees have also established themselves in the country and their presence has helped to some extent to revive traditional Nepalese Buddhism.

Until recently, nuns in Nepal took ten precepts and did not have access to full ordination. In 1988 a group of nuns went to Los Angeles, California to receive full ordination as bhikkhunis. In 1998 other Nepali nuns received bhikkhuni ordination in China and Bodhgaya, India. In 1999 in Lumbini, Bhikkhuni Dhammavati organised the first siksmana ordination to be held in Nepal in 1000 years.

Buddhist influences are evident in the culture of Nepal because Buddha was born in a part of Ancient India within the borders of present-day Nepal and his clan Shakya moved to Kathmandu valley and have incorporated into Newars. Nepal has strong Buddhist background and has played role in spread of Buddhism to Tibet. Nepalese princess Bhrikuti played a significant role in development of Buddhism in Tibet and Far East. Tibetan Buddhist architecture has long been influenced by Nepalese artists and sculptors like Araniko. The sacred Buddhist texts in Mahayana Buddhism are mainly written in Ranjana script (the script of Newars) or scripts like Lantsa which are derived fron Ranjana.

In the Tibeto-Burman tribes, Tibetan Buddhism is the most widely practised form. Newar practice Newar variant of Vajrayana Buddhism and Theravada Buddhism. Many Buddhist groups are also influenced by Hinduism.

Buddhism is the dominant religion of the thinly-populated northern areas, which are inhabited by Tibetan-related peoples, namely the Sherpa, Lopa, Manangi, Thakali, Lhomi, Dolpa and Nyimba. They constitute a small minority of the country's population.

Ethnic groups that live in central Nepal, such as Gurung, Lepcha, Tamang, Magar, Newar, Yakkha, Thami and Chepang, are also followers of Buddhism. These ethnic groups have larger populations compared to their northern neighbours. They came under the influence of Hinduism due to their close contacts with the Hindu castes. In turn, many of them eventually adopted Hinduism and have been largely integrated into the caste system.

The Kirant tribes, especially the Limbu and the Rai, have also adopted Tibetan Buddhist practises from their Buddhist neighbours. The Jirel, which is considered a Kirata tribe, have also adopted Tibetan Buddhism.

BUDDHISM DURING PRE-LICCHAVI PERIOD (BEFORE 400)

Shakya clans of Lumbini

Buddha was born in Lumbini (which is now in Nepal). According to Tripitaka, he visited his father's kingdom and converted his family and clan to Buddhism. The Shakya clans later moved to Kathmandu valley and helped establish Buddhism there.

Kathmandu valley

Buddha visited Kathmandu valley during the reign of Kirat king Jitedasti.

Emperor Ashoka from India put up a pillar at Lumbini, the birthplace of the Buddha in the 2nd century BC. It is also believed that Ashoka went to Patan and had four stupas built there. It is believed that his daughter Charumati established the village of Chabahil, which is located between Kathmandu and Bodhnath. There is a stupa and monastery in Chabahil that are said to date back to her time.

It is said that upon the expansion of the Mauryan dynasty into the Terai plains in Nepal, Buddhism was adopted by the ancestors of the Tharu and flourished until the resurgent Licchavi repelled its adherents in AD 200. But, in fact, the Tharu are the remnants of ancient Sakya, Koliya, Mourya and many other ancient tribes. Thus, obviously, Buddhism in Nepal has been flourishing since Buddha's time if we consider ancient Kapilvastu and Devdah in Nepal.

BUDDHISM DURING THE LICCHAVI PERIOD (400-750)

The Licchavi period saw the flourishing of both Hinduism and Buddhism in Nepal. Excellent examples of Buddhist art of the period are the half-sunken Buddha in Pashupatinath, the sleeping Vishnu in Budhanilkantha, and the statue of Buddha and the various representations of Vishnu in Changu Narayan.

Ancient Buddhist texts claim that Mulasarvasti Vadavinaya (better known as the Shakyas of Kapilvastu, Bhikshu Ananda, and the Baniyas of Sravasti) came to Nepal, then known as Newal, from Tibet.

Another Buddhist text, the Manjushrimula Kalpa, mentioned Manadeva as the King of Nepal Mandala. Researchers believe the Mulasarvastivadavinaya was written in the 2nd century CE, and that the Manjushriulakalpa was written during Manadeva's reign. The Swayambhu Purana, the ancient Buddhist Purana text, and a Licchavi inscription all mentioned Nepal Mandala.

Buddhist inscriptions and chronicles and Tibetan sources also record a few tantric Buddhist deities, namely Aksyobhya, Amitabha, Vajrayogini, Vajrabhairava, Usnisavijaya and Samantabhadra. Strong influence from Animist cults resulted in belief in Buddhist deities such as the Pancaraksas.

Religious tolerance and syncretism were stressed during the Licchavi period. King Manadeva paid homage at both Hindu and Buddhist sites. His family subsequently found expression for their beliefs in various different religions.

The worship of the Caitya and the Rath Jatra cart festival of Avalokitesvara were introduced around this period. Many ancient sites in the Kathmandu Valley were identified with major Buddhist Caityas, such as Swayambhu Mahacaitya, Boudnanath Stupa, Kathmandu and the four "Ashoka" stupas of Patan, and another two hundred stone caityas dating from the Licchavi Period, were testified to the widespread antiquity of caitya worship.

It is possible that this practice, in its earliest incarnation, was related to the worship of stones, which may have originated in the early, rival Kirata inhabitants of the Valley, prior to the Licchavis. According to one of the earliest Licchavi inscriptions, Caitya worship ordinarily consisted of ritual circumambulation of the caitya and offering standard items such as incense, colored powder, oil lamps and ablutions. At times, the inscriptions indicate, it could even involve resurfacing an existing Caitya and covering the new surface with many elaborate paintings.

Caitya worship was an important factor in bringing more of the proto-Newar tribal inhabitants into the Buddhist fold, as it was a devotional practice designed for the general public. Thus, the masses probably began practicing the cart festival of Avalokitesvara/ Matsyendranath (Bungakya) during the latter half of the seventh century A.D.

This festival was celebrated by hundreds or even thousands of people, who helped to construct and transport a huge, wheeled cart that bore the image of Avalokitesvara for several days or weeks along a specific route. The introduction of this festival must have been an instant success among the majority of the Kathmandu Valley population. This strengthened Buddhism's standing in relation to the other Hindu and Animist faiths of the Valley at the time.

Forty stone inscriptions made some mention of Buddhism throughout the Licchavi period. Most of the references are concerned with monasticism. However, almost nothing is known about the day-to-day life in the Vihara monasteries or how they functioned administratively.

The names of the fifteen Buddhist monasteries are known, and it is clear from the context in which some of these are named that they are among the most important religious sites of that time. It is not known for certain what schools of Buddhism were most prominent at the time. But the strongest early influences (aside from an even earlier probable substratum of Pali Buddhism) probably came from the Mahasanghika, Sammitiya and the Sarvastivada schools. The Makhyamaka and Yogacara schools were thought to be more influential in the later period with the emergence and growth of the Vajrayana school.

Inscriptional evidence also proves that there was a string of traditional methods of making religious gifts. These offerings were used for earning blessing and making merit, and the women of the Buddhist seem to have taken the lead in offering these gifts. Strikingly, parallel points within the Buddhist cave contain inscriptions of Maharastra, which predated the Licchvi Nepal. The references in the Licchavi inscriptions to the Mahayana and Vajrayana will be mentioned below in connection with Buddhist art and notable Buddhist figures of the Licchavi period.

BUDDHISM DURING THE THAKURI PERIOD (600-1200)

The first Thaukri king, Amsuvarma, married his daughter Bhrikuti to the ruler of Tibet, King Songtsen Gampo. According to legend, she received the begging bowl of the Buddha as part of her wedding dowry. It is believed that she introduced Buddhism into Tibet. she is also believed as a reincarnation of the Green Tara of Tibetan Buddhism, who is seen in many Buddhist Thangkas. Thakuri period is known as the golden time for Buddhism.

BUDDHISM DURING THE MALLA DYNASTY (1200-1769)

The Malla dynasty saw to the golden period of the syncretism of Hindu and Buddhist art forms by the Newar. The Paubha, the Newari counterpart of the Tibetan Buddhist Thangka, flourished in this period.

BUDDHISM DURING THE SHAH DYNASTY (1769-1846)

The Shah dynasty saw the decline of Buddhism in Nepal where it eventually merged with Hinduism as the Hindu Gurkha rose to prominence. In the north, the Mustang kingdom ruled by the Buddhist Lopa and the Thakali saw to the flourishing of Vajrayana (Tibetan Buddhism) in the North.

BUDDHISM DURING THE RANA DYNASTY (1846-1951)

Modern Newar Buddhist practises in Nepal have largely been absorbed into mainstream Hinduism, although certain distinct practises, artforms and castes do remain. In the north, people of Tibetan origin continued to be the much-unchanged practises of Tibetan Buddhism, especially in the case of the Nyimba of Northwest Nepal. On the other hand, the Thakali, who had traditionally played an important role in the Nepali society but yet retained Tibetan Buddhism, have begun to embrace Hinduism as well in the recent years.

SHAH DYNASTY (1951-2006)

After the overthrown of Rana dynasty in 1951, Buddhism gradually developed in the country. Theravadin Buddhism played a great significance role for the Buddhist revival campaign in modern Nepal since 1920s. This revival movement has changed Buddhism from ethnic-religion of some ethnic groups and castes into beyond the caste and ethnic religion in Nepal. Presently, there are three main Buddhist schools; Tibetan Buddhism, Newar Buddhism and Theravada Buddhism.

Tourism is another important factor for promoting Nepali Buddhism to the world. Every year, Kathmandu can receive more than 10,000 travellers from all over the world just to visit the Boudhanath and the Swayambhunath stupas. These are the remarkable and significant architect, which only found in Nepal. Apart from these two main Buddhist monuments there are hundreds of Buddhist monuments every corner of streets of Kathmandu and some other main cities of Nepal.

END OF SHAH DYANASTY (2006-PRESENT)

Nepal became a secular country in 2006. All religion got equal opportunities to propagate according to their belief. Thus, the role the Buddhist tradition played, is playing and will play to smoothly run social, strengthen it and extend it widely from the narrow frontiers is a great thing worth appreciating.

BUDDHISM IN BANGLADESH

Bangladesh was once the cradle of Buddhism still bearing trances in the various architectural remains of temples and monasteries with large number of Buddha image, relics, copper and stone plates discovered at different times from various parts of the country.

There is difference of opinion among researchers as regards spread of Buddhism in Bangladesh. Much currency is given to the theory that the teaching of Buddha propagated during the lifetime of Buddha since he himself came to Bangladesh (*Samatata)* on a visit while preaching his new thoughts. Fa-Hien (5th Century), Hieun-Tsang (middle of the 7th century), It-Sing (end of the 7th century) and others in their travel accounts referred that Buddha came to the *Pundra-Bardhan* (northern part of Bangladesh). He preached his principles also at *Samatata* (south-eastern part of Bengal) presently Chittagong, Noakhali Kamasbama (now Murshidabad West Bengal).

The Chinese travelers saw hundreds of monasteries and centers of Theravada and Mahayana Schools in these parts of Bangladesh and as well as in the West Bengal of India. The description in ancient Buddhist literature like Anguttara-nikaya, Samjutta-nikaya, Divyabadana, Asokabadana and Avadana-kalpalata also testify the truth of the above. The names of two prominent disciples of the Buddha, 'Bangisha' and 'Bangantaputta' show that they might have derived their names from Bangala (Bangladesh). The copper plates, stone inscription found at Mahasthagar (*Bogra*), *Paharpur, Sumpuri mahavihara* (*Rajshahi*), *Mainamati (Comilla)* and *Ashrafpur* (Dhaka) were dated between 6th-10th Centuries. Very recently similar evidence discovered at *Salimpur* and *Barauthan* in Chittagong were dated between 10th-13th Centuries, speak highly of flourishing state of Buddhism in ancient Bangladesh. The epigraphic findings and antiquities reveal hitherto unknown facts and cover wide area of information besides the Holy Scriptures and other religio-philosophical writings. Plenty of legends, folk-lore, popular devotional songs, tales relating to Buddhist life and teaching of Buddha as well as other followers and devotees of Buddha are spread over the interior of Bangladesh, enriching over the historical findings.

The Chinese traveler Fa-Hien visited India during the time of Chandra Gupta Vikramaditya of Gupta dynasty. He records that there were twenty- two Buddhist monasteries at *Tamralipi*. Buddhism was in a flourishing condition in *Samatata* and in capital itself there were 2000 monks and thirty monasteries. Hiuen-Tsang states that Gautama Buddha stayed for sometime at *Vasu Vihara*, which was situated on the outskirts of *Pundravardhana*. At the close of the 7th Century AD the Chinese pilgrim Sheng Chi visited *Samatata*, the capital city of *Vangrastra*. He described that as many as 4000 monks lived in *Samatata*, Buddhism was a predominant religion in the then Bengal. King Rajarajabhatha was a strong supporter of the Three Jewels (ti-ratana).

The rich ruins of *Trikutaka Vasu* at *Mahasthangarh (Bogra)*, *Jagaddal Somapuri mahavihara* at *Paharpur (Rajshahi)*, *Salbana* and *Banakastupa Vihara (Comilla)*, *Vikrampuri* and *Dhammarajika Vihara* at *Vikrampur (Dhaka)* and *Chakrashala Vihara* at *Hiaidgaon* and *Pandit Vihara* at Chittagong were the glaring examples of seat of learning and Buddhist civilization. The ruins of *Pandit Vihara* are believed to be lying buried under the Deyang hills on the bank of the river *Karnaphuly* just on the other side of *Patenga* Airport, Chittagong.

The National Museum of Dhaka has a big hall reserved for Buddhist historical objects and contains unique sculptures in stone, metal and wood. The terracotta figures from *Paharpur Monastery (Rajshahi)* arouse great popular interest. A few words can be added here on *Vikrampur Vihara*, which is only a few miles away from *Vikrampur*, the oldest historically recorded city in the neighborhood of Dhaka. It was an important place during the hey-day of *Pala* rulers of Bengal. According to some historians, the name *Vikrampur* is derived from the title *Vikramaditya*, said to have been assumed by *Dharmapaladeva*, the second and the greatest of the *Pala* dynasty who built a Buddhist monastery there.

After the death of Buddha in 646/647 AD his empire fell to pieces and independent kings established themselves in Bengal. For some centuries, knowledge about East Bengal (Bangladesh) remains scanty after the death of *Sasanka* in 639 AD for about a century from 650 AD to 750 AD. But certain amount of information has been derived from inscribed copper plates was to record their grant of land, but they are also of historical value. Preambles of these grants mention the king or chief in whose time the grant was made and record his ancestry. One local dynasty, that of the *Khadgas* are mentioned in a plate found in the Dhaka district at *Ashrafpur*. These kings were Buddhists and their capital was *Karmanta*. Which N. K._Bhattasali, late Curator of the Dhaka Museum, identified with *Kamta* 14 miles west of Comilla. In the 10th and 11th century there was another line of local ruler, also Buddhist by religion, who bear the name of Chandra and had their capital at *Vikrampur* in the Dhaka district. Knowledge of their existence is due to the discovery of copper plate grants at Idirpur and *Kedarpur* in this district, as well as at *Rampal*, the old capital of *Vikrampur* in Dhaka.

At any rate, there can be little doubt about the fact that a portion or the district of Dhaka was included in the ancient kingdom of *Brahmaputra* valley of *Kamrup*. A passage in the *Jogini Tantra* distinctly states that the southern boundary of that Kingdom was the junction of the river *Brahmputra* and the Lakshya, where the town of *Narayangonj* is located today. The early traditions that have come down speak that Dhaka and some of the neighboring districts were originally under the sway of Buddhist King. The numerous Viharas scattered all over the country were meant not only for monastic way of teaching but also for imparting lessons on subjects like arts, crafts, astronomy, geography, agriculture, herbal medicines, pottery and so on. Thousands of monks and students used to reside in these viharas for equipping themselves with different skills and knowledge, in addition to their scriptural lessons.

Ancient religious writings speak of '*Vanga*' (Benga/Bangladesh) which was later described by Kalidas, the great poet of the 5th Century A.D. as the territory situated within the *Gangetic* basin. According to Lama Taranath (b. 1573 AD), the Chandra dynasty ruled over 'Bangla' between the 6th and 8th Century AD. *Savar* (Dhaka) inscriptions speak of one king Harish Chandra who belong to a family of *Desabala Buddha*, six copper plates discover from *Faridpur* speak of Maharajadhiraj Sena Chandra Deva with head quarter at '*Suvarna Vihara*' flourishing in the 6th century AD.

According to O'malley, this *Vanga* or *Vangla* or Bengal was incorporated in the empire of Harsha. We have brief account of this part of the country from the pen of Chinese pilgrim, Hiuen-Tsang who traveled in different parts of India from 630-643 AD when Harsha was at the height of his power. According to his account, *Samatata* corresponded to the ancient *Vanga*, a low-lying country bordering the sea, rich in crops, flowers and fruits. The climate was soft, the manner of the people was agreeable. The inhabitants were of small stature and of dark complexion but diligent in acquisition of learning. There were about thirty Buddhist Monasteries with some 3000 priests and thirty Brahaminical temples. He also writes that it is interesting to observe that adherents of orthodox Hinduism, Buddhism and Jainism lived side by side apparently peacefully. This was Bangladesh depicted through the pen of Hieun-Tsang. Another version says that *Samatata* was the capital of South and East of Bengal before the 7th century AD Chinese traveler Hieun-Tsang recorded that *Pundra-Bardhan*, *Samatata*, and *Tamralipi* were in a very flourishing state of condition. According to '*Tamra Sasana*' found at *Ashrafpur* (Dhaka), much information has come to light that *Khadga* dynasty ruled here.

In pre-Muslim period the present Dhaka district was included in the administrative unit of *Vanga* which at times used to be identified with *Samatata* and *Harikela*. Since Hieun-Tsang noticed *Asoka Stupas* in *Samatata*, *Mayurya* rule in the district cannot be denied. Ruins of *stupas* built by Asoka in the village *Dhamrai* (Dhaka) still stands as a witness of supposed to have derived its name from *Dharmarajika*. The historians Jatindra Nath Bose corroborated this view.

The nomenclature itself has a significant background. *Savar*, not far from Dhaka was visited by Buddha according to Buddhist literature and was confirmed by the Bengal historian J. N. Bose. It has mount created by King Asoka. In course of time the place has been known as *Dharmarajika* which again turned into *Dhammarajika*. Like the ruins in

Dhaka district bearing theatrics of rich Buddhist culture another district, *Dinajpur* (northern part of Bangladesh) also bears evidence of Buddhism, highly patronized by the ruler themselves. The *Pala* kings were princes of *Gaur*, a name that seems to have applied rather to the whole province, of which *Dinajpur* formed the principal part. The founder of this dynasty appears to have come from Western India and had become Buddhist. Francis Buchanan (Hamilton) while describing of education in the district of *Dinajpur* in the beginning the state of 19th century still found the traces of Buddhism there. He wrote, "the only vocabulary used in *Dinajpur* is the *Omarkosh or Omorsinghe*, whom the *Pandit* as usual considers a person belonging to the sect of Buddha. Since Buddhism flourished there in the court of *Vikram*".

Buddhism has traveled a long way under the patronage of series of ruling dynasties—Chandra (7th century), Pala (8th-11th century), Deva (9th-13th century), and the Barman (11th-12th century). These dynasties patronized Buddhism successively for nearly seven hundred years when Buddhism, specially its Mahayana sect, found a golden era in Bangladesh. Bangladesh has produced a larger number of Buddhist scholars who were not only known for disseminating religious doctrines and ideology as teachers of different Viharas but also contributed to the development of creative arts. These glorious sons of ancient Bangladesh like Santarakkita, a professor of *Nalanda University*; Atisha Dipankara Srijnana, a world famous saint and philosopher; Pandit Shilabhadra, the Principal of *Nalanda University*; Pandit Prajnabhadra alias 'Tilopa' the Principal of *Pandit Vihara University* and other scholars made many contribution to the progress of mankind. The Siddhacharyas (saint scholars) of ancient Bengal like Luipa, Kanupa, Ariyapa or Haripa who were engaged in teaching in Viharas used to compose mystical lyrics or songs known as *Charyapadas* which marked the creation of Bengali language more than one thousand year ago.

In eastern Indian (presently Bangladesh) Buddhism and its art under the *Palas* and *Senas* (AD. 730-1197) gradually assimilated with *Saivism* and *Vaisnavism*. The last great center of Buddhism in the Sub-continent was at *Nalanda* in *Bihar* (India). Later, Buddhism gradually began to assimilate with Hinduism in India and almost disappeared with the advent of Muslim era.

Travelers and tourists from Indian Sub-continent and Bengal walked thousand of miles and even crossed the mighty Himalayas with the message of love and compassion. The renowned Buddhist saint scholar Atisha_Dipankara Srijnana who more than 1500 years after Buddha preached his teachings beyond India provides the best example. About Atisha there are many verses found in local Bengali literature. Such as:

"He crossed the mountain
Covered with perilous frost
He is the Atisha of Bengal
Who lit the light of learning in Tibet"

The details of life of this great saint Atisha is not yet fully known. So far brought to light about him, he was a celebrated scholar, a linguist, philosopher having a good knowledge of herbal medicine. He was born in the year 980/982 AD in the village of *Bajrojogini* in *Vikrampur* (Dhaka). Atisha in his memoir written Tibetan language mentioned about his place of birth which tallies with some other historians also. Professor Jogendra Nath Gupta recorded this village *'Bajrojogini'* at Atisha's birthplace. During this time Bangladesh was under the Palas, when Buddhist religion was established on firm footing in Vanga and Vihara. His parents were Kalyana Sri and Prabhabati. He was the second son of his parents. He was known as Chandragarva in his childhood.

He got his early lessons at *Bajrashan Vihara*, near *Ashrafpur*, Dhaka. He was ordained as at the age of nineteen by *Mahasanghanayaka* of *Odantpuri Vihara*, under Acharya Shilarakkita, who gave his name Dipankara Srijnana. Later, he became famous as teacher of the *Vikramsila* monastery in *Magadha*. During this period, *Magadha* was in Bengal. Atisha, at the age of thirty-one took *Upasanpada* from Acharya_Dharmarakkita of *Magadha*. At the age of forty-three he left *Vikramsila Vihara* and went to *Magadha*. The great Pala King Dharma Pala founded this Vihara at the end of English century.

Atisha stated for Tibet in 1040 AD on the invitation of the king of Tibet. He was the founder of KADAMPA tradition in Tibet. Atisha died in Tibet at the Nathang Monastery near Lhasa in 1055 AD. A number of his writings are enshrined in the volumes of Tanjur. In fact Atisha is the title given by the Tibet of king meaning 'the best', that the best of the Dipankaras. With the assistance of the Government brought the sacred ashes of the saint were bought from China in 1978 to Bangladesh. The ashes are preserved at the *Dhammarajika Buddhist Monastery*, Dhaka and will be enshrined in the memorial for veneration.

After the 12th century, militants Brahmanism and other opposing forces in the sub-Chittagong challenged Buddhism. This was popularly called as *'Thakurgarh'*. Chittagong, Comilla and parts of Bangladesh were still carrying on the legacy of Mahayana school of Buddhism. Though they came directly in contact with rites and rituals of Tantric forms of Mahayana they did not surrender their original Theravada doctrines. The support came several times under the rule of *Arakenese* Kings from 2nd century to 15th century. These *Arakanese* kings were followers of Theravada Buddhism. Thus Theravada Buddhism came to prevail again in the mainstream of Bangladesh largely through the *Arakanese* influence. Particularly as a result of reformation movement pioneered by Sangharaja Saramedha of *Arakan* in mid-nineteenth century in Chittagong, Buddhist populated Chittagong Hill Tracts and other region continent and was finally wiped out from its birthplace. Lama Taranath however added that the reason of the decline of Buddhism emerged from within the creed itself.

At this declining state of Buddhism, a group of orthodox Buddhists from *Vaishali, Magadha* (now *Bihar* and *Uttar Pradesh*, India) migrated to further East through *Assam* to Chittagong and settled there with the help of local Buddhist rulers. By the all kinds of support of Sangharaja Saramedha the Buddhist people of Chittagong constructed a *Bhikkhu sima* (Ordination place for monk) at Hanchantar-ghona of *Mahamuni Pahartali.* Latter on the old form of *Sangha* reform in *Theravada (Sangharaj)* by the leadership of the then Sangharaj Saramedha which we can see present day in Bangladesh.

BRIEF HISTORY OF BUDDHISM IN BANGLADESH

Bangladesh (historical Bengal) has a unique place in the history of Buddhism, mainly for two reasons. Firstly, Bengal was the last stronghold of Indian Buddhism where it could survive as a socio-cultural force until the 12th century, despite its disappearance from other parts of the Indian subcontinent. Secondly, it is generally believed that Bengal was the home of a form of Buddhism, namely, the Tantric Buddhism. Tantric Buddhism is a later development in Bengal and therefore it remains to be seen what specific factors are responsible for turning the pure form of Buddhism into tantricism and whether the mystic and esoteric practices in the Buddhism of Bangladesh are of distinctively Bengali origin.

Early origins

In the early days of Buddhism, many kings and rulers like Bimbisara, Ashoka, Kanishka patronized the spread of Buddha's teaching. This continued until the Palas and Chandras of Bengal in the 12th century. Of course, Buddhism faced hostility from some of the rulers, but throughout the first millennium and beyond, Buddhism thrived in Bengal.

It is possible that Buddhism entered Bengal before Asoka's time. After attaining enlightenment, the Buddha is said to have delivered his first sermon at Saranath and then moved to Magadha, Kosala, Vaishali and other places within what was known as Majjhimadesha or Madhyadesha. In the Divyavadana, the eastern boundary of the Majjhimadesha is said to have extended as far as Pundravardhana (North Bengal). Furthermore, the Buddha is said to have received considerable support from King Bimbisara of Magadha who not only dedicated Venuvana as a residence for monks, but also remained his close friend and a great patron of his Dhamma throughout his life. Since Bengal was adjacent to Magadha, it is possible that the Buddha had visited parts of Bangladesh as suggested by Hiuen Tsang, who notes that Asoka had erected stupas at various places in Bengal and Orissa to commemorate these visits.

Asoka's Reign and the Post-Maurya Period Epigraphic and other sources reveal that Buddhism had established a powerful footing in Bengal during Asoka's reign. The discovery of a Mauryan inscription in Brahmi characters at Mahasthangarh in the district of Bogra bearing the name Pudanagala (Pundranagara) and the recovery of many Mauryan coins and other artifacts dating from the fourth and third centuries BC suggest that the Gangetic delta was under the control of the Mauryan empire. The Chinese traveller, I-tsing, is said to have noticed Asoka's stupas near tamralipti (Tamluk) and Karnasuvarna (modern Burdwan and Murshidabad districts) in current West Bengal, in Pundravardhana

(North Bengal) and in Samatata (Bangladesh). The port of Tamralipti to the west of the Bhagirathi-Hooghli river, in particular, played an important role during Asoka's rule. It was from here, according to Mahavangsa, that the Buddhist mission from Asoka's capital city, Pataliputra, sailed for Sri Lanka to spread the message of the Buddha.

Post-Mauryan period

With the decline of the Maurya Empire, Buddhism lost the royal patronage which it once enjoyed. Pusyamitra, after killing his master, Brhadratha, declared himself the emperor and ascended the throne of Magadha. He founded the Sunga dynasty in the 2nd century BC. With the resurgence of the Sungas, Buddhism met with its first major setback. Buddhism, once a thriving religion, declined in the absence of the royal patronage, as also because of the unfavourable attitude of the Sunga kings towards Buddhism and the Sangha.

Contrary to this position, some Indian scholars are of the view that the orthodox Sunga kings were not intolerant towards Buddhism, and that Buddhism continued to prosper even during the time of the Sunga kings. During the Sunga period, Buddhism was in existence in Bengal, and this can also be inferred from a terracotta tablet that was found at a place called Tamralipti. This terracotta tablet is currently on exhibit at the Asutosh Museum, University of Calcutta.

The Kushana period (around 1st century) gave further impetus to Buddhism when Kanishka raised Buddhism to the status of the state religion , erected stupas and chaityas, built monasteries and, like Asoka, sent missions abroad. The discovery of Buddha images, copper and gold coins and inscriptions, belonging to this period, indicate the flourishing status of Buddhism during the reign of Kaniska.

Gupta dynasty

Kings of the Gupta dynasty were devout adherents of a Hindu faith, sometimes called as *Parama Bhagavatas*, and they patronized and revived Hinduism, but they also possessed a tolerant outlook which allowed Buddhism to flourish. In the meantime, rise of the two powerful Hindu cults of Saivism and Vaisnavism, brought Buddhism closer to Hinduism. In its spiritual nihilism, Buddhism was approximated to the Bhakti movements so much so that, by the middle of the 6th century, the Buddha was accepted as an avatar of Vishnu.

According to Chinese sources, Maharaja Gupta, also known as Shri Gupta, the first ruler of the Gupta dynasty, built a Buddhist temple and offered it to Buddhist monks from China along with a gift of twenty four villages. This temple is believed to have remained a sacred place till the 7th century. Samudra Gupta, although a devout worshipper of Vishnu, also proved to be a great patron of Buddhism. It was during his reign that cultural relations between India and Ceylon were established. His teacher and guide, the celebrated Buddhist scholar Vasubandhu, was appointed minister, and, with the permission of the Ceylonese King Meghavanna, a monastery was built at Bodh Gaya for the monks and pilgrims of Ceylon. Chandra Gupta II who, like his father Samudra Gupta, was a devout Vaisnava by faith, gave full freedom to the practice of other faiths in his empire.

Fa Xian's account

During his visit to Bengal, Fa Xian is said to have travelled eastward along the course of the Ganges river, and during his journey, he came across Buddhist stupas and monks at several places. In a place named Tamralipti, Fa Xian is said to have spent two years, and visited twenty-two monasteries, inhabited by monks who lived in accordance with the Buddhist Vinaya.

Archaeological evidences also support Fa Xian's account about the thriving state of Buddhism in the Gupta period. An inscription found at Gunaigarh near Comilla, bearing the year 188 of the Gupta era (corresponding to 506 or 507 of the Christian era), records a gift of land by Maharaja Vainya Gupta in favour of the Buddhist Avaivarttika Sangha of the Mahayana sect. The Sangha, founded by the Acharya Shantideva and housed in a monastery called *Ashrama Vihara,* was dedicated to Avalokiteshvara. The inscription also refers to other Buddhist monasteries, one of which was known as *Raja Vihara,* which literally translates into *Royal Vihara.* Two Buddhist sculptures, a standing image of the Buddha found at Biharail in Rajshahi district and a gold-plated bronze image of Manjushri discovered at Balai Dhap mound at Mahasthana in Bogra, also bear testimony to the flourishing state of Buddhism during the rule of the Gupta kings.

Both the Hinayana and Mahayana sects of Buddhism flourished during the Gupta period. A number of Buddhist inscriptions, seals, images and manuscripts in Gupta characters, discovered at various archaeological excavations sites, testify to the thriving state of the early Hinayana schools, namely, the Sarvastivadins, the Sammatiyas (or the Vatsiputriyas) and Sthavirvadins. Gradually, Hinayana lost its hold, and Mahayana took ascendancy over Hinayana. Mahayana, with its ultra-altruistic principles, its scope for devotion and worship, and its opening of the state of Bodhisattvahood began to capture the imagination of common people, and acquired the status of an important religious movement. As Mahayana grew popular, Bodhisattvas such as Manjusri, Avalokitesvara and the goddess Prajnaparamita rose to occupy important positions. The *Adi Buddha* and Amitabha Buddha also received special attention. Worship of Bodhisattva images along with the image of the Buddha turned into a common practice. The Mahayanists are said to have revered the Prajna texts just as the Hinayanists revered their Vinaya and Abhidharma books. The Mahayanists are also said to have practised spells (dharanis) for religious purposes.

Hiuen Tsang visited India in the 7th century and visited almost all the major places associated with Buddhism in Bangladesh. According to him, there were six or seven Buddhist monasteries at Kajangala near Rajmahal, housing over three hundred monks. In the northern part of the country, he also claimed to have seen a belvedere built of stone and brick, with a broad and high base, artistic ornamentation and distinct carved images of the Buddha and the devas. At Pundravardhana he is said to have found twenty Buddhist monasteries with more than 3,000 monks who practised both Hinayana and Mahayana. The magnificent Po-shi-po, with spacious halls and storeyed chambers, occupied by over 700 monks, was located in the vicinity of the capital of Pundravardhana. There is also mention of a temple with an image of Avalokitesvara not far from this establishment, which attracted visitors from far and near.

Fa Xian visited India in the 5th century, and found that some of the old Buddhist centres like Kapilavastu and Saraswati were in a neglected and ruinous state, while Pataliputra, Mathura, Bodh Gaya, Sarnath and Nalanda were flourishing as active centres of Buddhism. The great monastery of Nalanda, which was founded by Kumara Gupta Mahendraditya, rose to prominence in the Gupta period and in course of time turned into a university and became the greatest centre of Buddhist learning in Asia. From an early date, the Buddhists of Bengal were closely linked with this great institution, although it was situated in Magadha. Prior to Hiuen Tsang's visit to Nalanda, Acharya Dharmapala had been the high priest of its monastery. He was succeeded by his disciple Acharya shilabhadra, a scion of a Brahmana king of Samatata. It was under Shilabhadra's guidance that Hiuen Tsang studied Buddhist philosophy, including the vedas and Sangkhya Shastras, for five years. Not only scholars from Bengal but also its kings, the Guptas, the Palas etc., contributed to the development of the great institutions at Nalanda.

Post-Gupta Period

During the post-Gupta period, Harsavardhana gave Buddhism a new impetus. But, in the 7th century, Shashanka came to the throne, who is claimed to have been hostile to Buddhism. According to Hiuen Tsang's account, Shashanka ordered the extermination of the Buddhist monks in and around Kushinagar; he cut down the holy Bodhi tree of Bodh Gaya and threw into the Ganges a sacred stone bearing the footprints of the Buddha. He is also said to have removed a Buddha image from a temple close to the Bodhi tree and replaced it with an image of Hindu god Lord Shiva.

Contrary to this, the reign of Emperor Harsavardhana (606-647) was one of resurgence and renewed progress and development. Despite being a worshipper of Shiva and Surya, Harsavardhana had great leanings towards Buddhism, and his elder brother, Rajyavardhana, and sister Rajyashri both were being devout Buddhists. Harsa was at first a follower of the Hinayana sect, but, in later life, became an ardent follower of Mahayana. Some of his notable contributions to the cause of Buddhism include erecting stupas on the banks of the Ganges, building monasteries at places sacred to Buddhism, and forbidding the slaying of animals. Another of his important contributions to Buddhism was his convening regularly the quinquennial convocation in which he gave away in religious alms everything he possessed. Harsa used to summon Buddhist monks once a year for religious discussions. Harsa was specially attached to Nalanda and extended help liberally.

After Harsavardhana, the Khadga dynasty is said to be the first Buddhist dynasty to rule an independent Bengal between the 7th and 8th centuries AD. The discovery of two copperplates, one at Ashrafpur, 30 miles north-east of Dhaka and another at Deulbari, 14 miles south of Comilla, gives valuable information about this royal dynasty. These copperplates mention the names of three kings, Khadgodyama, Jatakhadga and Devakhadga, and include the names of the queen and the son of Devakhadga, Prabhavati and Rajaraja or Rajarajabhata. I-tsing's account notes that as many as fifty-six Buddhist priests from China visited India and its neighbouring areas in the latter half of the 7th century AD. One of these monks, Sheng-chi, who visited Samatata, mentions Rajabhata as its king and describes him as an ardent worshipper of the three gems (*Triratna*), that is, the Buddha, Dhamma and Sangha. There were 30 monasteries with more that 4,000 monks in Samatata alone during the pilgrim's visit. It is clear from all these that during the reign of the Khadga kings, Buddhism continued to flourish in Bengal during the 7th century AD.

Pala Dynasty

The Pala Dynasty ruled Bengal from 8th to 12th century, and this period is regarded as the golden age of Buddhism in Bengal. The Pala rulers were devout Buddhists (*Parama-saugata*), and were also equally sympathetic to other religious faiths. Palas invoked the Buddha at the beginning of their official records and proceedings. Under the royal patronage of the Pala kings, Buddhism and all institutions associated with Buddhism continuously flourished and thrived in Bengal for four centuries under the patronage of the Pala kings. During the same period, Buddhism was almost wiped out in other parts of the Indian subcontinent, and at the same time, it also became a dominant force in neighbouring regions, extending its influence to Tibet in the north and the Malaya peninsula in the south.

Archaeological and epigraphic discoveries indicate the generous support of the Pala rulers towards Buddhism, and instances of the Palas' patronage of Buddhism are numerous. According to Tibetan Buddhist tradition, King Gopala (750-770) built a monastery at Nalanda and established many schools for dissemination of Buddhist principles. According to Taranatha, many distinguished Buddhist teachers flourished during the reign of King Gopala, prominent among them were Danashila, Vishesamitra, Sura and Prajavarman. The Odantapuri Vihara was an example of rare architectural beauty. The famous Sam-ye monastery of Tibet is believed to have been built on the model of this great Vihara.

King Dharmapala (770-781) continued the religious policy of his father, and he also extended liberal support to Buddhist establishments. He founded the famous Vikramshila Vihara on a hill top on the bank of the Ganges river in Magadha. This Vihara soon rose to prominence as an international centre of learning and emerged as a university, second only to Nalanda. Vikramshila University maintained contact with Tibet and several Tibetan scholars participated in the affairs of the university throughout the rule of the Pala dynasty. Several of Vikramashila scholars, who once numbered 3000 in the 12th century, composed numerous books in Sanskrit, and also translated them into Tibetan. The curricula of the university included logic, metaphysics, grammar, tantras, and rituals. Importantly, the reigning monarch of the land awarded degrees to the students.

A monastery, built by King Dharmapala at Somapura Rajshahi district, and now better known as the Somapura Mahavihara (Naogaon) and which became a model for many such monasteries in South-east Asia, stands as a magnificent testament to the Pala patronage of Buddhism. King Dharmapala is also said to have established at least fifty religious schools designed to teach Buddhist philosophy, and to study Prajnaparamita in particular. He was a great patron of the Buddhist writer, Haribhadra, and, during his reign, as in his father's, many distinguished Buddhist teachers, such as Purnavardhana, Prabhakara, Kalyanagupta, Sagaramegha, Bhuddhajapada, flourished.

Under King Devapala (810-850), the Pala empire reached the zenith of its glory, and Bengal became a paramount power. King Devapala is said to have granted an endowment of five villages for the upkeep of a monastery founded by King Balaputradeva of Java, Sumatra and Malaya. Not only did he complete the Somapura establishment, he also showed keen interest in the well-being of the Vikramshila Vihara. Mahipala I, the ninth king of the Pala dynasty and rightly called the founder of the second Pala empire, is responsible for the revival of the past glory of the Buddhist establishments. He repaired the Buddhist monuments at Nalanda and constructed two new temples at Bodh Gaya. Many famous monasteries were built during the Pala period of which mention may be made of Jagaddala, Traikutaka, Pandita, Devikota, Pattikeraka, Sannagara, Phullahari and Vikramapuri.

Chandra Dynasty

Buddhism flourished during the reign of the Chandra dynasty in Harikela (eastern and southern parts of Bengal). The discovery of a large Buddha stupa, Salbana Vihara and other inscriptions at the Mainamati hills, four miles to the west of Comilla, still bears testimony to the condition of Buddhism during the Chandra kings. According to Tibetan sources, Buddhist tantricism flourished under the Chandra rule. The famous Buddhist scholar of Vikramapura, Atisha Dipankara Srijnana, is believed to be related to the Chandra dynasty.

The Pala Kingdom was not only the last stronghold of dying Buddhism in India, it was also responsible for the rise of Tantric Buddhism. This new phase of Mahayana Buddhism has been variously designated by Charles Eliot and others as 'late', 'degenerate', and 'corrupt'. Such allegations are based on the assumption that when Buddhism entered Bengal, it gradually came under the powerful influence of tantric beliefs and practices, including what are known as sexo-yogic practices, which made it fall away from the purity of its early form and eventually develop into what came to be known as esoteric or magical Buddhism.

Professor Trevor Ling opines that in Bengal from the time of Asoka to the Pala period, both the Hinayana and Mahayana, not the tantric, forms of Buddhism were practised. He describes the classical pattern of Buddhism as a three-cornered relationship between Sanga, king and people and emphasizes that the Buddhism of the Pala period was a true representative example of this classical pattern. Trevor Ling and many others believe that the Pala rule in Bengal heralded an era of progress in culture, religion, education, literature, art and sculpture. Amongst other achievements of the Palas, Ling has particularly mentioned their active patronage of Bangla language and literature. It was in a popular new language, a proto-Bangla form, that the Buddhist poets composed what are known to be the first poems of Bangla literature, the famous charyapada, a Tantric work of twenty-three Buddhist Tantrikists known as Siddhas.

Decline and revival

The Sena Dynasty gained prominence after the decline of the Palas. The Senas were orthodox followers of Saivaism or Vaisnavism. Under them, the royal support for Buddhism ended. As a consequence, Buddhism soon began to decline and disintegrate. The biggest factor of course was the advent of Islam through the subsequent defeat of the Sena dynasty at the hands of the Turkish invader Bakhtiyar Khalji, whose forces vandalized and destroyed several Buddhist universities, including Nalanda and Vikramshila. After that, many of the surviving Buddhist monks fled to Nepal, Tibet or Bhutan. The Buddhist laity were either converted to Islam or were integrated into the fold of Hinduism. Buddhism, as a separate entity, was almost extinct, surviving in many debased forms of popular practices such as dharma thakur puja or the puja of Jagannath.

The decline of Buddhism, however, did not result in its total disappearance from the land of its birth, and it continued to survive in various forms of popular worship, rites and rituals until its resurgence in modern India. With its rediscovery in its parent country, the traditions of Buddhism were significantly recognized so that the Asokan pillar, the sacred Wheel of Law (Dharmachakra) and the Singhanada sculpture from Saranatha are now a part of Indian national life and heritage. The renewal of Buddhism in India today is attributed to Dr BR Ambedkar, the architect of the Indian Constitution, who led the mass conversion of millions of untouchables or 'Scheduled Castes' to Buddhism in 1956. In Bengal, however, the revival of Buddhism seems to have taken place centuries before Dr BR Ambedkar's introduction of the neo-Buddhist movement in Maharastra and other places. In the districts of Chittagong and the Chittagong Hill Tracts, the south-eastern parts of Bangladesh, a Buddhist minority had been practising Theravada long before the Moghuls and the British arrived in Bengal. In course of time, these Buddhists reformed their Sangha and in 1887 founded the Chittagong Buddhist Association, believed to be the first Buddhist society to be formed in the South Asian sub-continent.

BUDDHISM IN PRACTICE

There are several monasteries in the Chittagong Hills area, and in most Buddhist villages there is a school (kyong) where boys live and learn to read Burmese and some

Pali (an ancient Buddhist scriptural language). It is common for men who have finished their schooling to return at regular intervals for periods of residence in the school. The local Buddhist shrine is often an important center of village life.

Essentially tolerant, Buddhism outside the monastic retreats has absorbed and adapted indigenous popular creeds and cults of the regions to which it has spread. In most areas religious ritual focuses on the image of the Buddha, and the major festivals observed by Buddhists in Bangladesh commemorate the important events of his life. Although doctrinal Buddhism rejects the worship of gods and preserves the memory of the Buddha as an enlightened man, popular Buddhism contains a pantheon of gods and lesser deities headed by the Buddha.

The Ministry of Religious Affairs provides assistance for the maintenance of Buddhist places of worship and relics. The ancient monasteries at Paharpur (in Rajshahi Region) and Mainamati (in Comilla Region), dating from the seventh to ninth century A.D., are considered unique for their size and setting and are maintained as state-protected monuments.

THE BUDDHIST COMMUNITY OF BANGLADESH

The mid-19th Century was a turning point in the religious history of the Buddhists of Chittagong which in fact was the home of Buddhism in the then Bengal and undivided India. In that very dark age, the Buddhists were steeped in deep superstitions. The Sangharaj of neighboring Arakan most Venerable Saramedha Mahathero came on a chance to visit Chittagong in 1856. He was shocked to see the condition of Buddhism with Tantric rituals and worship of false gods and goddesses. The Sangharaja Sramedha again visited Chittagong and Chittagong Hill Tracts in 1864 and took upon himself the task of reforming the prevailing Buddhism in accordance with Dhamma and Binaya of the Tripitaka.

He faced a tough time but he succeeded in having the support of Rani Kalaindi, the ruler of the Chakma dynasty of the Chittagong Hill Tracts and some leading figures in Chittagong during his Theravada reformation movement. Beside the Bangalee Buddhists in the plains of the Chittagong district, a large number of Buddhists in the hilly regions of the Chittagong Hill Tracts are mainly Chakma, believed to be of Tibetan-Thai origin having emigrated here from a place called Champak nagar (city). Another group of Buddhists are the Bomangs who are settlers of neighbouring Arakan several hundred years ago. All these three groups bound together by common bond of Theravada Buddhism were inspired by the reformation of Sangaraj Saramedha in the mid-19th Century, particularly with patronage and impetus from Chakma Rani Kalaindi Devi who had harbored the reformist Sangharaj for a long time.

The lamp of Saddhamma was enkindled by the Theravada religious reformation movement launched by Sangharaj Saramedha. Monks and laity were inspired by his illuminating discourses and finally discarded Tantric practices and a lot of other superstitions alien to Buddhism. Monks were given fresh ordination on attaining the age of 20 and initiated into the Theravada monastic disciplines laid down in the Binaya. The reformation movement electrified the entire Buddhist community. As a result, more than 95 per cent of total number of Buddhist monks in Chittagong, Chittagong Hill Tracts and other Buddhist-populated regions came under the fold of the newly reformed Theravada Buddhist Sangha.

The Buddhist community during the days of British rule sought to assert social, religious and cultural existence. One important event was the holding of a big Buddhist Conference in 1938 in Hoara para (suburb) village of Chittagong on the occasion of birth anniversary of Most Venerable Aggasara Mahathero who was an eminent religious personality. During the British rule the Buddhists called for a separate identity for themselves as a religious community. Two Buddhist leaders – Dr. Arbinda Barua, Barister-at-Law and Rai Bahadur Dhirendra Lal Barua were nominated members of Bengal Legislative Assembly in Calcutta in the Forties to represent the cause of the Buddhists. In 1947 at the time of independence from the British rule, the Indian Sub-continent was partitioned into India and Pakistan. Buddhist populated regions like Chittagong and Chittagong Hill Tracts were included in Pakistan. The Buddhists identified themselves with the new State.

A well known Buddhist leader and lawyer late Phani Bhusan Barua who was also the President of the then Pakistan Buddhist Association was nominated as member of the Advisory Committee of the Pakistan Constituent Assembly for framing the National Constitution. Later in 1954 an educationist late Mr. Sudhangsu Bimal Barua was elected as member of the then East Pakistan Legislative Assembly. From the Chittagong Hill Tracts Raja Tridiv Roy, the then Chakma Chief of the Chittagong Hill Tracts was also elected as member of the Legislative Assembly. Mr. Maung Shwe Prue Chowdhury, Bomang Chief of the Hill Tracts was elected as member of the Legislative Assembly and later became a Cabinet Minister. During the Pakistan period an organisation name as East Pakistan Bouddha Kristi Prachar Sangha was founded in 1949/50 which later was turned into all Pakistan organisation. Most Venerable Visuddhananda Mahathero has been President since 1950 till now of the Sangha, now named Bangladesh Bouddha Kristi Prachar Sangha.

During the Pakistan period the first Buddhist Monastery in the capital city was established in Dhaka for which the government had made a gift of five acres of plot of land for the entire Buddhist community. A very dynamic and talented social worker with sharp intellect, Deva Priya Barua, popularly known as D.P. Barua infused a new direction in the Bouddha Kristi Prachar Sangha of which he was the Secretary General for 16 consecutive years from 1961 to 1977 while Most Venerable Visuddhananda Mahathero and later Most Venerable Joytipal Mahathero had been the President. During the Sixties D.P. Barua made outstanding contribution in the emergence of the Sangha with its national and international identity as well as socio-cultural activities of the Buddhist community including establishment of the Monastery in Dhaka known as Dhammarajika

Bihar. Two other temples in the capital city recently established are International Buddhist Monastery founded by the Most Venerable Santapada Mahathero, former President of ABCP and Secretary General of Sangharaj Bhikkhu Sangha and »Sakyamuni Bihar« established by the Buddhists of Chittagong Hill Tracts living in Dhaka.

During the war of liberation of Bangladesh in 1971, Ven. Joytipal Mahathero together with Ven. Santapada Mahathero and some others made significant contribution in mobilizing world opinion in favor of Bangladesh struggle for independence in a crucial phase of our national existence. Ven. Joytipal visited Sri Lanka, Thailand and Japan in August 1971 to mobilise Buddhist public opinion in favor of Bangladesh struggle.

Buddhist organizations of Bangladesh have maintained link with international fraternity of Buddhists. Those affiliated with the World Fellowship of Buddhists are, Bangladesh Buddhist Association with headquarters at Chittagong Monastery, Bangladesh Bouddha Kristi Prachar Sangha with head office in the Dhammarajika Bihar and a youth organization, Bangladesh Bouddha Juva Parishad, the Youngmen's Buddhist Association. A new organization named Bangladesh Buddhist Federation has come into being in recent times. In 1975 the National Center of the Asian Buddhist Conference for peace was established in Bangladesh. That year Ven. Jyotipal Mahathero and Mr. D.P Barua were invited to attend the Executive Council meeting of the ABCP held in Moscow.

This was followed by their visit to the ABCP headquaters in Ulan Bator, Mongolia. The outcome of the visit led to the founding of the ABCP National center in Bangladesh as a broad-based forum of Buddhists working for peace and harmony based on the teachings of Buddha. In 1980/81 Most Venerable Jyotipal spent nearly a year in Bipasana meditation in Buddha Gaya and on his return to Bangladesh, he decided to concentrate solely in meditation and Dhamma by relinquishing himself from activities of organizational responsibilities. Mr. D.P. Barua, Secretary General with his deep commitment as well as dynamism in organizational work carried on for sometime as acting Head of ABCP National Center under directive from the ABCP Headquarters, Ulan Bator and played crucial role in revitalizing the National Center. Most Venerable Santapada Mahathero, Vice-President of the ABCP National Center and Secretary General of the Bangladesh Supreme Sangha Council for 20 consecutive years who enjoyed pre-eminent position in the Buddhist community was unanimously elected President of the ABCP National Center in early 1981. He worked relentlessly for the cause till death cut short his life in 1987.

The Supreme Patriarch of the Buddhists and the most respected Sangaraja of Bangladesh, most Venerable Shilankar Mahathero was elected as the President of the ABCP National Center. Today the large number of monks and laity under his leadership have been working for the Dhamma and peace in Bangladesh. The Buddhist community today is making endeavors to forge ahead in their religious, social and cultural activities. At the head of the religious fraternity is the Eighth Sangharaj, the Most Venerable

Sangharaj Shilankar Mahathero who resides in the monastic headquarters at Shantidham Bihar.

BUDDHISM IN PAKISTAN AND MALDIVES

PAKISTAN

Buddhists live both in Pakistani controlled Kashmir and in Indian occupied Kashmir to the east of the Line of Control. Mostly Ladakhi and ethnically related to Tibetans (plus a few Indo-Aryan Dards), a rough dividing line between Islamic culture and Buddhist culture can be drawn through Mulbekh and Shergol in the Indus valley (to the east of Kargil) and well to the west of Leh, the Nun Kun massif and Rangdum Buddhist monastery at the head of the Suru river valley (a tributary of the Indus) on the Indian side of the line of control.

MALDIVES

Buddhism came to the **Maldives** at the time of Emperor Ashoka's expansion and became the dominant religion of the people of the Maldives until the 12th century AD.

Western interest in the archaeological remains of early cultures on the Maldives began with the work of H. C. P. Bell, a British commissioner of the Ceylon Civil Service. Bell was shipwrecked on the islands in 1879, and returned several times to investigate ancient Buddhist ruins. He studied the ancient mounds, called *havitta* or *ustubu* (these names are derived from chaitiya or stupa) by the Maldivians, which are found on many of the atolls.

Although Bell mentioned that the ancient Maldivians followed Theravada Buddhism, many local Buddhist archaeological remains now in the Malé Museum display in fact Mahayana and Vajrayana iconography.

According to a legend of the Maldivian Folklore, a prince named Koimala from India or Sri Lanka entered the Maldives from the North (Ihavandhu) and became the first king from the House of Theemuge. Prior to that the Maldives had been settled by people of Dravidian origin from the nearest coasts, like the group today known as the Giravaaru who claim ancestry from ancient Tamils. It is unlikely that the Giraavaru islanders were the only early settlers in the Maldives. The importance they have been given is because they are mentioned in the legend about the establishment of the capital and kingly rule in Malé. The Giraavaru people were just one of the island communities predating Buddhism and the arrival of a Northern Kingly dynasty and the establishment of centralized political and administrative institutions.

The ancient Maldivian Kings promoted Buddhism and the first Maldive writings and artistic achievements in the form of highly developed sculpture and architecture are from that period. The conversion to Islam is mentioned in the ancient edicts written in copper plates from the end of the 12th century AD. There is also a locally well-known legend about a foreign saint (Persian or Moroccan according to the versions) who subdued a demon known as Rannamaari.

Over the centuries, the islands have been visited and their development influenced by sailors and traders from countries on the Arabian Sea and the Bay of Bengal. Until relatively recent times, Mappila pirates from the Malabar Coast – present-day Kerala state in India – harassed the islands.

Chapter - 9

Buddhism in Modern Century

Buddhism has spread and developed not only in the land of its birth, but in many other lands as well. Why does Buddhism present such an attractive religious option to so many different cultures? Buddhism is no different from other religions in claiming to possess the means by which to attain that most cherished of human goals—eternal peace. Where Buddhism differs is in its acceptance of a number of alternate methods by which to attain this goal, each suited to different temperaments and conditions. Buddhism developed a sophisticated worldview very early. At the core of this worldview is what later Western philosophers would define as *angst,* that vague feeling of uneasiness and separateness from the world that often tinges life. This inherent element of human existence, say the Buddhists, is an inevitable part of life that is caused by life's intrinsic instability.

This concept that the universe is unstable is reminiscent of modern physics. The ancient Buddhist philosophers saw the world not as a stable, material, entity, but rather as a constantly changing cloud of interactive forces. The Buddhist analysis of the unsatisfactory and unstable nature of existence is the foundation of a whole way of life. That way of life is based not only on the Buddhist understanding of the nature of reality, but also on their understanding of human fate and the factors that affect it. For the Buddhist, human existence is not a brief excursion between birth and death. It extends endlessly through time and space (for the Buddhists believe that there are an almost limitless number of alternate worlds to this one), and the human being can look forward only to an infinite series of rebirths either in this world or elsewhere.

The driving force behind these lives is *karma,* the iron law of cause and effect that meant that good actions will have good results and evil actions evil ones. This means that there is no hope to be had outside of one's self. Human beings are, in the deepest sense, on their own. No supernatural agency exists that can deliver a person from the round of birth and death. Teachers can only point in the direction that one should go. No amount of personal material success can allow you to buy your way out. This bleak picture is relieved by only one thing. The Buddha has discovered a way out, a way to *Nirvana.*

However, different groups of Buddhists interpret this basic Buddhist message in different ways in order to fit differing circumstances.

THERAVADA: THE LIFE OF DISCIPLINE AND THE PRODUCTION OF MERIT

Of the many schools of Buddhism which still exist, the one that is closest to the Buddhism of the Buddha is the Theravada school. Now found only in Sri Lanka, Burma, Thailand, Laos, and Cambodia, the Theravada school holds to the oldest collection of Buddhist scripture—the Pali Canon. If we are to look for a simple phrase to sum up Theravada Buddhism's philosophy of spiritual practice, it would be personal effort. Central to the Buddha's revelatory experience was the realization that release from rebirth came from personal effort. There was no god who could save you, no teacher who could present you with the truth. It was only through personal effort that the nature of reality could be understood and the cycle of birth and death broken. Thus salvation, in the broadest sense of the term, needed to be acquired through the disciplining of the mind and body.

In some theravadin countries, one becomes a monk for as long as the individual chooses to remain in the order. In other countries, the decision to ordain is permanent (or at least intended to be so). In either case, the process of becoming a monk is a two-fold one. The first part of this process is called *pabbajja* or going forth. In a reenactment of the Buddha's renunciation of his home, the aspiring monk "goes forth" from the life of a householder to that of a member of the *Sangha*. There is no set age at which this ceremony takes place. Often parents decide to have one of their sons ordained at an early age. This is seen as having two benefits. One is to the new monk's family, who gain merit from his ordination and the second is to the young monk himself. In times past, the monkhood was often the only way to gain the education that led to high government position. Even today, many boys are ordained by their parents in order to receive an education.

The ordination ceremony itself is relatively simple. It takes place at a time that is usually determined through consulting the candidate's horoscope. In addition, the young novice's new status is announced to the gods and local spirits. The candidate has his head shaved and takes a ritual bath. After this, he takes the Three Refuges and is presented with a set of robes and other things used by monks in their daily life. He is now an official member of the Buddhist Order, and it is from this date that his seniority in the Buddhist Order is calculated. What follows is a period of learning under the supervision of a senior monk. After several years of training, but not before his twentieth birthday, the novice may request the second step in the ordination process. This is the rite of *upasampada*. This ceremony marks the novice's full acceptance into the *Sangha*. After this, the monk may serve as a preceptor to younger monks. He may also serve as a member of monastic government. If a monk should choose to leave the Buddhist Order, he simply does so. There is no formal ceremony involved.

From the Buddha's point of view, the most important way to employ one's incarnation as a human being, itself a very rare event, was to strive for Enlightenment. Since this was a very difficult undertaking, it came to be regarded as a fulltime job for people specializing in religion. The first thing that the Buddha did when he began to preach was to establish a set of rules which aspirants to Enlightenment needed to follow. These rules, known collectively as the *Vinaya* or Discipline, covered all aspects of the disciple's life. It still forms the framework within which the modern Buddhist monk lives out his life. These regulations lay out what food the monk can eat and when, what clothes he can wear, who he can have sex with, and many other aspects of his life great and small. Those who follow these rules become known as *bhikkhus* and, in the case of women, *bhikkhunis*. Collectively they make up the *Sangha,* the Buddhist Order, which is the personification of the Buddha's teaching.

It is natural, therefore, that the professional monks and nuns in the *Sangha* came to wield considerable influence in early Buddhist society. While changes in other schools of Buddhism resulted in the *Sangha* being less influential, Theravada Buddhism still gives the monk a very prominent role in society. This is somewhat surprising given the fact that the monks are supposed to have little actual interaction with lay people. As the religion grew, however, this stance modified somewhat. Some monks, termed forest monks, continued to hold to the traditional Buddhist monastic ideal of separation from the laity. Other monks, indeed the majority of modern monks, came to be regarded as village monks. These monks lived on the periphery of the village, and acted as school teachers and local religious advisors to the laity. These were the monks who ministered to everyday people.

Unlike other religions, or other forms of Buddhism for that matter, Theravadin religious rituals for the laity are distinctly austere. Lay groups meet on the day of the new moon and that of the full moon each lunar month. At this meeting, which generally has a monk in attendance, they renew their allegiance to the Buddhist lifestyle by publicly reciting the **Three Refuges** and accepting the **Five Precepts**. They then listen to the monk preach a sermon, which is usually of a formal rather than a spontaneous nature. After this, they may indulge in a brief period of meditation. Seasonal festivals have much the same character and center on events in the life of the Buddha.

From one standpoint, there does not seem to be much here of a religious nature. But this is something of a mistake which arises from a misunderstanding of the religious functions appropriate to different segments of society. For the Theravadin Buddhist, religious exercises such as meditation are not the province of the lay person, they are activities generally reserved for monks. The cultivation of insight, hold these Buddhist lay people, is a fulltime job and one which cannot easily be accomplished in the hurly-burly of the modern world. Thus if one wishes to undertake this type of training, one must dedicate oneself to it completely and renounce the world as the Buddha had done. By so doing, one earns tremendous merit and should therefore be treated with the profoundest respect. In Theravada countries today, it is not unusual to see grandmothers on the bus get up and give their seats to teenage monks. In a paradoxical way, the renouncing of the world gives the monk an elevated status within it.

To understand this, we need to understand the essence of lay Buddhism in Theravada countries. Lay persons can, of course, always become monks. But most choose to remain in the estate of life to which they were born. But this does not mean that they lack religious sentiments, nor that they do not participate in their tradition. Rather, they follow the path laid out for lay persons—the path of merit *(punya)*.

The lack of Buddhist nuns in present-day Theravada countries reflects an historical accident rather than deliberate sexism. Indeed, women still play a very effective, if unofficial, religious role in these countries. Moreover, a movement is strengthening to reintroduce the ordination of nuns in the Theravada countries. Nuns still exist in Mahayana and Vajrayana Buddhism.

Sangha and the laity are two halves of a single entity. The monks need the lay people to supply them with food, clothing, and the other prerequisites of life. The laity, on the other hand, need the monks as moral exemplars and a means of generating merit. But what is the point of this merit?

Here again we come back to the question of *karma* and rebirth. If one knows that one is going to be reborn, and that one's favorable rebirth is dependent on good actions, it is only prudent to accumulate as great a stock of good actions as possible. Within Theravadin culture, this is seen as being accomplished through *dana,* or giving. This giving is seen as being most effective when its recipients are monks. What has evolved is a symbiotic religious relationship that benefits both sides. Moreover, merit has other uses as well.

While Theravadins do not believe that gods can lead them to ultimate freedom, they are still seen as having their uses. When one needs help with the crops, sickness, love, and so forth, it is useless to consult the Buddha and his monks, since these worldly problems are not their area of concern. The gods can help, but they need to be coerced. This is done through the transfer of merit. Since Buddhists do not see the gods as immortal, only very longlived, they believe that the gods will be reborn just as they will. This being the case, the gods need merit as well if they are to be reborn in a good condition. But the nature of being a god makes it impossible, for a variety of reasons, to generate such merit. Thus the gods are dependent on human beings in that they can acquire merit only if it is transferred to them by humans. This the Theravadin Buddhists are happy to do in return for worldly considerations.

The emphasis placed on meditation for monks means that they spend much of their time separate from ordinary practitioners. But this is not always the case. On the great Buddhist holidays, the two groups interact. In general, Buddhist festivals are structured around events from the life of the Buddha. Moreover, since they developed within the context of agricultural societies, they also tend to bear some relationship to the cycle of planting and harvest. Other festivals, such as the beginning of the New Year, vary from one society to another.

In Theravada countries, regular fortnightly days based on the appearance of the full and the new moons are set aside for religious observance. These days, called *poya* days, correspond loosely to the European or American Sunday. On these days, lay persons observe the Five Precepts of not lying, killing, stealing, practicing inappropriate sexual acts, or taking drugs or liquor. Lay people often spend the day in religious pursuits such as going to hear a sermon delivered by a monk and practicing a small amount of meditation. This is the general pattern followed on all religious holidays, which occur on the *poya* days of particular months. *Poya* days are not celebrated in non-Theravada Buddhist countries.

For the Theravada Buddhist, the most important celebration of the year is the full moon day of May, known as *Wesak*. The birth, Enlightenment, and death of the Buddha are all believed to have happened on this day (albeit in different years). Another important festival falls on the full moon day of June. This marks the beginning of the three month long Rain Retreat (sometimes called the Buddhist Lent). At this time, the monks withdraw from society in order to practice meditation more intensively. Lay persons also attempt to adhere more strictly to Buddhist principles during this period. This period ends with *Kathina,* where lay persons bring the monks new robes and other necessities of life.

Some festivals are practiced only in certain areas. For example, the festival of *Poson* celebrates the bringing of Buddhist teachings to Sri Lanka in the second century B.C.E. Likewise the observance of *Esala* takes place only in Sri Lanka. It is marked by a huge parade in Kandy, called the *Esala Perihara,* at which time the holy tooth relic of the Buddha is displayed. In other Theravada countries, other local festivals take place as well. While these festivals are serious events, they are also enjoyable occasions.

ZEN: THE WAY OF EMPTINESS

Zen Buddhism stands in sharp contrast to Theravada Buddhism, both geographically and ideologically. The original home of Zen was India, but it was not until it was carried to China, and then to Korea and Japan, that it reached its fullest potential. The course which Zen initially followed was different from that of most other schools of Buddhism. These schools tended to congregate in monasteries which came to acquire more and more property over the centuries. Thus the monks found themselves in a peculiar position. Individually they were as poor as the Buddha's original followers. Collectively, however, they were often rich beyond the dreams of avarice. Increasingly, they sank these funds into large buildings, elaborately adorned and richly furnished. While this impressed outsiders, there was a growing feeling among some of the monks that such frills were dangerous distractions from the essential business of gaining release from the cycle of life and death. These new intellectual currents were to affect the development and orientation of Zen.

Philosophically, the essence of Zen is that all beings are already enlightened. They simply do not know it yet. The goal of Zen, therefore, is to awaken people to their own spiritual nature. This is accomplished, not through book learning or intellectual activities, but through meditation. Zen meditation is designed to overcome the rational, dualistic mind and to lead the practitioner to the unifying ground of existence which we all share. This can be done in one of two ways. In the Soto school of Zen, the practitioner "just sits," since this school believes that the very act of concentrated meditation is in itself sufficient to lead to Enlightenment. For the Rinzai sect, the process is a bit more complex. This school uses short paradoxical questions known as *koans* as a means of shocking individuals out of their dualistic thinking. Some of these *koans,* such as "what is the sound of one hand clapping" or "does a dog have the Buddha nature," have become famous even outside the Buddhist tradition.

This meditative training, along with Zen's emphasis on simplicity, might lead one to think that Zen has done away with the more ritualistic side of Buddhism. Indeed, it was this assumption that first attracted many American and European converts just after World War II. But this is not in fact the case. Zen was influenced by the wishes of its patrons, the wealthy and powerful ruling classes of Japan. These classes, who often saw religion and government as two sides of the same coin, were often more interested in Zen monks' perceived ability to perform powerful protective rituals than in the philosophical and meditative practices that they advocated. While this type of activity found its fullest expression in other Buddhist schools such as Shingon, all of the Japanese Buddhist schools were to some extent tinged with this ritualistic emphasis.

Consequently, ritual had, and still has, an important place in Zen Buddhism. In the monasteries and temples there is usually a morning and an evening service presided over by either the abbot, in the case of a monastery, or the chief priest of the temple. Lay persons can attend these ceremonies, but except for the great Buddhist holidays, they tend to be for religious specialists only. Fruit, flowers, and incense are offered to the Buddha and the major *Bodhisattvas* such as Manjusri and Avalokitesvara at these ceremonies. Various texts are chanted, particularly the Heart Sutra, a brief scripture that encapsulates the philosophical teachings of Zen. At these services, the officiants often wear gorgeous embroidered silk robes that seem very far removed from the austere life preached by Zen. All of this comes as something of a shock to American and European practitioners who have learned their Zen from books and not from living teachers.

As in the Theravada Buddhist countries, the monks and the lay people come together to celebrate important religious dates. But Mahayana Buddhist religious holidays often vary from those of Theravada countries. In Japan, the largest Mahayana country, the Japanese Buddhists do not celebrate the birth, Enlightenment, and death of the Buddha on the same day as their Theravada cousins in Sri Lanka and Southeast Asia. The Buddha's birth *(Hana Matsuri)* is celebrated on 8 April, his enlightenment *(Nehan)* on 15 February, and his death *(Rohatsu)* on 8 December. *Rohatsu* marks a period of one week of intensive meditation. Of particular importance to Japanese Buddhists is the four day festival of

Obon which starts on 13 July. This festival commemorates the release of the mother of one of the Buddha's disciples from one of the Buddhist hells. In Japan, it has become a festival of remembrance of one's deceased ancestors. Some festivals are strictly of importance to Zen practitioners. In October is celebrated the festival commemorating Bodhidharma, the first teacher to bring Zen from India to China. Great Japanese Zen teachers are honored as well. Rinzai Zenji is remembered on 10 January, Daito Zenji on 22 November, Dogen Zenji on 28 August, and Keizan Zenji on 15 August. Pure Land practitioners honor their founder, Shinran, on 21 May.

VAJRAYANA: THE WAY OF RITUAL MYSTICISM

Sometime around 500 C.E., another set of religious developments was taking place in India. It was at this time that both Hinduism and Buddhism began to exhibit those traits that we now term Tantra. Tantra seems to have been an attempt to develop a new form of practice which was more dynamic than the static meditations of earlier Buddhism. In the process, a radical new form of Buddhism emerged. Vajrayana Buddhism starts from somewhat different premises than other forms of Buddhism. This difference is not so much one of philosophy as it is of methodology. Vajrayana Buddhism, far from dismissing the body as a means of achieving Enlightenment, embraces it.

Consequently, the Vajrayana Buddhist monk's training is somewhat different from that of the Theravadin or Zen monk. The essence of Theravada training is the perfection of meditation through monastic regulations and the knowledge of the Pali scriptures. The essence of Zen training is the perfection of meditation through self-discipline. The essence of Vajrayana training is perfection of meditation through ritual practice. But this emphasis on ritual performance comes relatively late in the monk's career. First, he is required to undergo a long period of scriptural study in order to prepare for his ritual studies. Tantric practices are seen as extremely effective in leading the practitioner to *Nirvana,* but they are extremely dangerous as well. To approach them without intense preparation is not wise and can lead to reincarnation in one of the numerous Buddhist hells. It is for this reason that lay people tend to avoid Tantric practice, leaving its use to religious specialists.

Tantra is not something that can be done on one's own. It can be learned only at the feet of a guru who has himself traveled the path that the practitioner wishes to follow, and who can guide him or her by experience. Indeed, the guru is seen as being of such great importance that he is often venerated as a deity in his own right. Many of these highly developed gurus are seen as being able to reincarnate over and over again at will. Under the guidance of an experienced guru, the novice enters the Tantric path.

This begins with the preliminary practices. These practices may vary from school to school, but they have certain common elements. The practitioner must make 100,000 prostrations. He or she will perform 100,000 repetitions of various ritual offerings and repetitions of formulas designed to purify and focus his or her mind. But it must be remembered that none of these practices are actually Tantric in themselves! These practices, which necessarily take years and beyond which many people never go, are designed to test the would-be Tantric practitioner and purify him or her for the work ahead. This being said, the practices are also thought to have value in themselves, and many people, particularly lay persons, perform these rites without any thought of progressing beyond them to the actual study of Tantra, which is generally seen as the preserve of the monks and nuns. Such practitioners see these practices as bearing fruit in some future existence.

Having completed these preliminary practices, the student is now ready to be initiated by his or her guru. This ritual, the *abhiseka,* is central to the student's study. Without it, even if one had access to the Tantric texts, one's study would be in vain. The *abhiseka* not only authorizes a person's practice, it empowers it as well. Perhaps more importantly, it places the student in the "family" of those who use the particular text or texts named in the ritual. This qualifies the practitioner to receive the oral teachings that have passed down from teacher to student concerning the meaning of the text. This is very important. In modern society, we believe that texts should be self-explanatory. But in the Tantric traditions, the text was seen as far too dangerous to be clearly explained in itself. The knowledge contained in the text could cause real damage. As a result, the texts were often written in confusing and enigmatic language sometimes called twilight language. This meant that the texts themselves were not the primary vehicle for transmitting the teaching, but rather served as a sort of memory aid for the teachers and students in the study of the much more important oral tradition.

It is at the time of the *abhiseka* as well that the student receives his or her *mantra* and the *mandala* of his *yidam.* Vajrayana Buddhists appear to believe in a vast pantheon of gods and goddesses. But for the practitioner of Tantra, these deities are not so much actual existing entities as what we would call archetypal symbols for psychological processes and neuroses. As such, they provide the practitioner with a way of interacting with factors in his or her own mind that might otherwise only exist at an unconscious level, and thus be inaccessible in other ways. At the time of initiation, the guru, who is experienced with such questions, selects a *yidam* for the student to work with. Likewise, he shows the student the appropriate *mantra* for that deity. This *mantra,* usually of Sanskrit origin, encapsulates the essence of the *yidam* in a short phrase which the student can meditate on at all times and in all places in daily life. Through it, the student maintains a constant spiritual connection with his or her inner self.

The *mandala* is used in more formal religious practice. It is a very complex drawing which in effect unites the universe, in all its complexities, with the student. Through the *mandala,* a sacred space is created which unites the two. The *mandala* becomes a sort of sacred road map that describes the journey of the student to the "palace" of the *yidam.* By ritually and meditatively following this map, and overcoming the various obstacles that confront him or her, the student moves closer to the ultimate goal of uniting with the *yidam.* Such union is the culmination of the student's practice. Through it, he or she comes to recognize his or her identity with Ultimate Reality and thus achieves release from the cycle of birth and death.

Rituals of this nature, such as the Kalachakra ritual, are not tied to the Buddhist year with its recurring religious holidays. The Tibetan calendar is lunar and so the days on which festivals occur can vary quite widely. The Tibetans celebrate the birth of the Buddha on the ninth day of the fourth month of the year. They celebrate his Enlightenment and death on the fifteenth day of the fourth month. On the fourth day of the first month, the Tibetans begin to celebrate *Monlam Chenmo,* which goes on for some three weeks. On the fifteenth day of the fifth month, offerings are made to local gods and goddesses who are believed to be the protectors of the Buddhist teachings. Of particular interest to the majority Gelugpa sect are the festival of the death of its founder Je Tsongkhapa on the twenty-fifth day of the tenth month and the birthday of the present Dalai Lama which is celebrated on 6 July of the Western calendar.

PURE LAND: THE SAVING GRACE OF AMIDABUTSU

All of the paths that we have discussed up to this point are very difficult for the lay person to follow. They require that the practitioner leave society, and that he or she spend long hours in meditation or ritual practice in order to achieve the desired goal of Enlightenment. For the vast majority of people, this is neither an attractive nor a possible alternative to life in the world. Family and social obligations do not allow it. What hope, then, does Buddhism hold out for such people? Was supporting monks or engaging in preparatory practices the most to which they could aspire? Were they required, in effect, to postpone any hope of Enlightenment until a future incarnation? This question arose early in the history of Buddhism, and the answers that evolved were to give birth to perhaps the most widespread of the Buddhist schools—the Pure Land School.

The roots of the Pure Land lie in India. New ideas associated with the Mahayana school started to develop there sometime around 100 B.C.E. One of these new ideas was the concept that the universe that we inhabit was only one of many world systems. In the Buddhist scriptures, we read that near the end of his life the Buddha was strolling through the forest one day when he casually mentioned to his attendant Ananda that, if someone should ask him, a Buddha could live on in the world indefinitely. Unfortunately, Ananda was not the quickest of the Buddha's disciples and he failed to take the hint. Undaunted, the Buddha repeated himself. Again Ananda failed to make the appropriate request. The Buddha tried one more time and when Ananda still did not ask him to remain in the world, promptly informed him that he would soon die.

For Buddhists, the death of the Buddha marks the beginning of the decline of the power of the Buddha's message in our world. As time goes on and we become more remote in time from the period of the Buddha, the moral condition of the world continues to decline. Indeed, many Buddhists believe that it has declined so much that in the current age it is impossible to reach Enlightenment. However, not all world systems were like ours. The main reason for this was that each of these worlds had its own Buddha, and that the Buddhas who had incarnated in those worlds had not died as had the Buddha of our world.

This came to affect the whole goal of religious practice. For the Theravadins, the decline of this world meant that the most that they could aim for was a favorable rebirth in a future time when a new Buddha, Maitreya, will appear on earth to rejuvenate the Buddhist faith. But many Mahayana Buddhists had a more immediate possibility—rebirth in a different, purer universe. These universes came to be known collectively as the Pure Land. The Buddhas who had established Buddhism in these worlds had been gifted with disciples who were somewhat quicker on the uptake than poor Ananda. Consequently, these Buddhas continue to live forever. As a result, their worlds not only did not decay as our own had, but actually improved to the degree that, from our perspective, they were paradises. In fact, they were so perfect that anyone being born into such a world was inevitably able to progress spiritually to the point that they would achieve Enlightenment in the course of one lifetime.

The goal of Buddhists in this world, as the Pure Land Buddhists envisioned it, was to be reborn in one of these Pure Land worlds. However, there was a problem. Pure Land Buddhists believed that our world was so corrupt that nothing we could do on our own would be sufficient to ensure our rebirth in the Pure Land. Fortunately, human beings had super-natural allies in the Buddhas who ruled these lands, the Dhyani Buddhas. The most famous of these was Amitabha or, as he was called in Japan, Amidabutsu. Like all Buddhas and *Bodhisattvas,* Amitabha had taken a vow that he would save all intelligent beings. In his case, this meant he would aid anyone who called upon him with perfect faith to be reborn in his Pure Land. This would assure that person's achieving Enlightenment in their next birth.

At one stroke, this concept breathed new life into Buddhism. Meditation, ritual, and text study could be practiced only by those who could afford the large outlay of time that these methods demanded. This meant that they were open only to those who had either renounced the world or were independently wealthy. But the basic tenet of Pure Land, that salvation depended on faith more than works, meant that common people, tradesmen, and peasants could now enter fully into Buddhist practice.

There now arose a series of devotional exercises and literature aimed toward the class of people who had up to now been more or less relegated to the role of support staff to the monks and nuns. While the peasants could and did continue to gain merit through giving, they could also aspire to salvation through the aid of supernatural beings. Through the constant repetition of short formulas and prayers, the lower classes could both work and pray at the same time. This, coupled with pilgrimages to sacred sites whenever possible and the support of the monks became characteristic of the followers of the Pure Land path.

Pure Land never seems to have been a large school in India, but when it spread to East Asia its progress accelerated rapidly. Part of the reason for this was that both China and Japan produced many gifted preachers. Unfortunately, their championing of Pure Land doctrine was often seen as subversive by the ecclesiastical and lay authorities, who from time to time persecuted them. All of this only served to reinforce in the minds of the common people the idea that Pure Land Buddhism was the Buddhism of the people, whereas other forms of Buddhism were the Buddhism of the upper class. Consequently, Pure Land Buddhism spread extremely widely throughout the lower strata of society in China and Japan. It is not surprising, therefore, to find that Pure Land Buddhism was the first Buddhism to reach America as people from these classes emigrated in search of a better life.

BUDDHISM AND THE CHALLENGE OF THE MODERN WORLD

Buddhism has had a long and interesting history but it would be unwise to assume that its glories are all in the past or that it is no longer a dynamic religion. Buddhism has been forced to adapt itself to the swiftly changing conditions of the modern world. In some cases, the transition has gone smoothly. In others, however, the tensions between Buddhism and modern ideologies have not been resolved without severe difficulties.

BUDDHISM AND NATIONAL IDENTITY IN SRI LANKA

Buddhism has a long history in Sri Lanka, and the religion swiftly became an established part of the culture of the Indo-European Sinhala people. Buddhism continued to solidify its hold on the Sinhala consciousness for several centuries. Indeed, it is in Sri Lanka that the scriptures of the Theravada school were first committed to writing in the first century B.C.E. It should be noted, however, that other schools of Buddhism flourished here as well. The Theravada school of Buddhism did not become the official religion of Sri Lanka until the time of Parakkama-Bahu I (reigned 1153-86 C.E.).

But it was during this time as well that the steady progress of Buddhism was interrupted by political upheaval. Sri Lanka began to experience the recurring invasion of the northern part of the island by Dravidian speaking Tamil peoples from South India. These invaders were, by and large, Hindus who felt no compulsion to support the Buddhist religious establishment. As their influence waxed and waned through the centuries, so too did the fortunes of Buddhism in Sri Lanka. It is no surprise, therefore, that Buddhism came more and more to be associated with the Indo-European speaking Sinhala group, just as Hinduism came to be associated with the Dravidian speaking Tamils.

This association became explicit during the reign of King Dutugamuna (101-77 B.C.E.). It was during his reign that the Sinhala people regained control of much of the northern section of the island that had previously been wrested from them by a Tamil invader. In order to do so, Dutugamuna raised the standard of religious war, casting the conflict in terms of righteous Buddhist Sinhalas regaining their homeland from unrighteous Hindu Tamils. This was a pattern of rhetoric which was to be intensified and consolidated by subsequent kings until it became an article of faith within Sinhala culture. Thus a tension was created which was to bear such bitter fruit in Sri Lanka in our own time.

This pattern was further reinforced with the arrival of the European powers in the early 1600s. Driven by a mixture of commercial ambition and religious fervor, the European powers were to play an increasingly important role not only in Sri Lanka, but throughout all of Asia. The Portuguese were the first such colonial power in Sri Lanka. Conditioned by centuries of warfare against the Muslims in the Iberian peninsula during the period known as the Reconquista, they had come to associate their colonial expansion with the expansion of their own austere form of the Roman Catholic faith. Fiercely intolerant of all other religious expression, they carried on a vigorous program of eradication of Buddhist and Hindu religious sites, and of conversion (often forced) to Roman Catholicism. The Portuguese were soon displaced by the Dutch who promptly imposed their own Protestant religious preferences on the region. They in turn were followed by the British who were primarily interested in trade and felt that this interest was best served through the pursuit of a policy of religious toleration.

As colonial expansion increased, the political power of the Sinhala (and Tamil) peoples decreased until the only indigenous independent state was the kingdom of Kandy in the hilly center of the island. It was inevitable, given the religious prejudices exhibited by the invading European colonial powers, that the Kandyan kingdom was perceived as the guardian of Sri Lankan Buddhism. Moreover, Buddhism and political independence came to be intimately linked in the Sri Lankan mind just as it had in years past. This link became very important in the postcolonial period for the direction that Buddhism has taken in Sri Lanka.

THE MODERN SRI LANKAN EXPERIENCE

During the colonial period, Sri Lanka had seen its full share of Christian missionary activity. But the Buddhist *Sangha* had always been able to maintain much of its dominant position. Since most colonial activity was confined to the coastal regions of the island, the kingdom of Kandy protected from intrusion by its surrounding palisade of mountains, remained a haven for traditional Sri Lankan life and culture and a lavish supporter of institutional Buddhism. All of this changed with the advent of the British. In 1815, with the memory of the threat of French and Dutch ships disrupting their lines of communication with their eastern colonies still fresh in their minds, the British proceeded to eliminate the Kandyan kingdom.

With the disappearance of this last official protector, the Buddhists found that they now served a new master who did not understand their ancient traditions. At first, this seemed to present no great problem. The British rulers of South Asia had no interest in the religious lives of their subjects. Motivated by the ledger rather than the Bible, they were satisfied if they received their duties and taxes. But events back in Great Britain were to change the colonial government's easygoing attitudes to religion.

One of the major causes of this shift of opinion was a wave of evangelical fervor which had swept through the country. Many influential people now believed that Britain had a moral responsibility to its colonial subjects. Given the tenor of the times, this meant that every effort should be made to bring the indigenous populations within the fold of Christianity. This left the British colonial government in Sri Lanka (and elsewhere) in a paradoxical position. On the one hand, they believed that the indigenous people would indeed be better off as Christians. On the other hand, they were bound by promises that they had given religious authorities in Sri Lanka at the time of the Kandyan conquest. Buddhism had become very much a state religion. Its growth in Sri Lanka was such that the king (or the government acting in his stead) held control of the monasteries' financial assets and served as the judge in interfactional disputes. When the Kandyan kingdom had been dissolved, these functions were taken over by the British who pledged to support the Buddhist religion as had its native predecessor.

But as the clamor for increased missionary activity in Sri Lanka increased, the colonial government found it harder and harder to fulfill this pledge. When the older generation of sympathetic administrators died or retired, their replacements felt less and less bound to honor this obligation. By 1840, missionary activity was in full swing. By 1860, with the tacit aid of the government, Buddhism was being forced more and more on the defensive. It is not surprising, therefore, that it is during this period that we see a change in Buddhist attitudes away from peaceful coexistence with the Christians, and toward a confrontational counterattack on the missionaries and their religion.

The initial impetus for this came from a rather peculiar source. Colonel Henry Olcott was an American Civil War hero who had become a follower of H.P. Blavatsky and one of the founders of a new religious movement called Theosophy that incorporated into itself many ideas taken from Hinduism and Buddhism. Convinced of the spiritual value of Eastern thought, he had sailed to India and Sri Lanka in 1880 to study it in its natural environment. Appalled by the inroads the Christian missionaries were making in Sri Lanka, he launched a successful campaign to organize Buddhist opposition to the new religion. This included the foundation of lay Buddhist organizations, Buddhist schools, and an organized refutation of the Christian missionary position. In due time, he passed the torch to his protégé, David Hewavitarne, who is better known to history by his religious name—Anagarika Dharmapala (1864-1933).

Dharmapala did more to revitalize Sri Lankan Buddhism than any other single person in modern history. Nor did his efforts stop at the coast of Sri Lanka. Deeply distressed by the fact that the Buddhist holy places in northern India were in the hands of Hindus, he organized the formation of the Maha Bodhi Society to purchase and refurbish them. In the process, the sites once again became centers of pilgrimage for Buddhists from all over the world and this marked the beginning of the revival of Buddhism in the land of its birth. In Sri Lanka, Dharmapala, who never became a monk of the Buddhist Order despite living like one all of his life, began to support the formation of lay Buddhist groups for the practice of meditation. Since Buddhist meditation had traditionally been the preserve of the monks, this new trend toward lay involvement in religion brought Buddhism more and more into the public arena.

As the agitation for political freedom escalated, it became apparent to the politicians that Buddhism still greatly influenced the Sinhalese peasant population. A good example of how far they were willing to go to exploit this can be seen in the career of S.W.R.D. Bandaranaike. Bandaranaike had been raised an Anglican, but he adopted the religion of his ancestors as a useful adjunct to his rising civil service career. Bandaranaike had even proposed before independence that the proper language for studying Buddhism was not Pali or Sinhalese (the language of the majority of the population), but English! However, sometime between then and his election as Prime Minister in 1956, he had become a born-again Buddhist.

It was at this point that he and others like him came to present Buddhism as the normative religion of Sri Lanka. Needless to say, this did not sit well with the more than 20 percent of the island's people who were not Buddhists. The Christians, and to a far greater degree the Hindu Tamil speakers of the north and northeastern parts of the island, found themselves increasingly politically isolated as politicians exploited sectarian differences. With this increased emphasis on religious differences, rioting broke out as the government began a deliberate shift toward isolationist policies. The legislation that began to be passed disenfranchised English in favor of Sinhalese, abolished the state mandated quotas that guaranteed the Tamils a significant share in educational institutions and the government, and started to promote Buddhism at the expense of other religions.

The results are still with us. Sri Lanka has suffered for more than a decade with a smoldering and bitter civil war which has often been waged through the appeal of both sides to religious principles. Nor does it appear that this will end any time soon. Not only does the government periodically mount military operations against Hindu strongholds in the northern and eastern parts of the island, but the Hindus retaliate with a campaign of terrorism in the Sinhalese-held parts of Sri Lanka. The tragedy of Sri Lanka is that Buddhism, one of the world's most pacific religions, has become a rallying point for violence and intolerance. Sadly, this is the case not only in Sri Lanka, but elsewhere in the Buddhist world as well.

BUDDHISM AND COLONIALISM IN SOUTHEAST ASIA

We can see similar forces at work in Southeast Asia. The countries now known as Indonesia, the Philippines, Malaysia, Vietnam, Cambodia, Thailand, Laos, and Burma (Myanmar) had for many years been influenced by cultural currents emanating from India and, to a somewhat lesser extent, China. A number of historians in the earlier part of this century saw Buddhism (and Hinduism) as being carried into Southeast Asia on a wave of cultural imperialism. While it is true that the indigenous cultures of the region found these religions and other aspects of Indian and Chinese culture appealing, and so incorporated them into their own cultural traditions, it would be unwise to see this as an uncritical process or one resulting from outside pressure. These cultures appear to have absorbed these new religious forms on their own terms, and they seem to have modified these new traditions in such a manner as to have them become, to all intents and purposes, indigenous religions in their own right. Buddhism presents a good example of this. Chinese records show that Buddhism was established on the coastline of Vietnam at a very early period, but the exact dates of its coming to the region are unknown. Yet it may very well be that it is from this region, as well as from Central Asia, that Buddhism first penetrated China. In any event, it is clear that Buddhism and Hinduism had traveled along the maritime trade routes to Southeast Asia at a very early date, probably starting in the second century B.C.E. But it was Hinduism that first attracted royal patronage in the region, and it is for this reason that we have very little archeological evidence to trace the development of Buddhism here.

All of this changes around 1000 C.E. After this date, Buddhism increasingly becomes the official religion of the growing nation states of Southeast Asia. In these areas, the more conservative Theravadin school based on the Sri Lankan model was the form of choice. By c. 1300 C.E., Burma, Thailand, Laos, and Cambodia had become Theravada Buddhist countries. The practice of linking Buddhism with the state which had come to be a distinctive feature of Sri Lankan Buddhism was widespread here as well, partially as a result of local conditions and partially due to the fact that Buddhist leaders in this area saw Sri Lanka as the senior center of their religion. In any case, Buddhism flourished and was nurtured by royal patronage.

All of this changed as the European powers extended their sway over the region. This was, however, a relatively late development. The earliest colonizers, the Portuguese and the Spanish who came to Southeast Asia in the late fifteenth century, did not at first attempt to totally dominate the region. They were satisfied with controlling the relatively small areas around their trading ports. Thus, despite the fact that they saw colonization and religious conversion as the same thing, they only affected small areas of the Philippines and Indonesia. More concerted were the nineteenth-century efforts of the Dutch in Indonesia, the French in Vietnam, Cambodia, and Laos, and the British in Burma, Malaysia, and Singapore.

Among the first to receive the unwelcome attention of the Europeans was Burma. In an escalating series of wars, the British progressively incorporated more and more of Burma into their Indian empire. By 1880, the old state of Burma had effectively ceased to exist. The French began their colonial efforts in Southeast Asia at about the same time. Supposedly in order to protect Roman Catholic missionaries in Vietnam, the French began a series of aggressive wars which gobbled up more and more Vietnamese territory. Although they tolerated the existence of a Vietnamese emperor up to 1954, by 1900 the French controlled not only Vietnam but Cambodia and Laos as well. Thus the only part of Buddhist Southeast Asia that remained independent was Thailand, and that only because neither the British to the west nor the French to the east would allow the other to possess it. As in Sri Lanka, Buddhism came to be intimately linked with the concept of nationhood in the popular mind, and would have a role to play in the region's fight to regain its independence.

BUDDHISM AND THE RETREAT FROM THE MODERN WORLD IN SOUTHEAST ASIA

The situation in mainland Southeast Asia displays a number of similarities with that of Sri Lanka. In Burma, Theravada Buddhism was the religious faith of the Burman ethnic group which made up some 75 percent of the total population of the country. It is not surprising, therefore, that the struggle to escape the colonial grasp of Great Britain was in some degree associated with the resurgence of Buddhism in the same way that it had been in Sri Lanka. In 1906, the Young Men's Buddhist Association was formed and this organization provided the leadership that was to lead the country to independence in 1948. But the Burma that was created at this time was by no means a monolithic Burman state. Some 25 percent of its population was of other ethnic stock, and many of these peoples had been heavily influenced by European missionaries and become Christian.

It is not difficult to understand why these constituent groups of the Burman state were hesitant to support any institution which would bolster Burman domination. Their fears were not decreased by the appointment of U Nu as prime minister of the new Burmese Federation. U Nu was a pious Buddhist to whom being Burmese and being Buddhist were identical. His vision of Burma's future was one associated with a sort of Buddhist Socialism. This led to an insurrection of the Karens, who were mostly Christian and wanted their own state. Early Karen victories in the early 1950s led to the appointment of Ne Win as the commander of the government forces. This was to be a momentous appointment.

Meanwhile, U Nu sponsored a Buddhist religious revival in hopes of promoting unity in the country. In 1956, Burma hosted an international conference of Buddhist luminaries to celebrate the 2500th birthday of the Buddha. This did not calm the anxiety of the minority groups who feared Burman domination, and increasingly, these groups, who tended to live in the mountainous marginal land that surrounded the fertile rice-producing river valleys, sought to gain autonomy from the central government. This, in turn, drove the government to place more and more power into the hands of the military. In 1958, the military under the command of General Ne Win took control of the country. An abortive attempt was made to return to civilian rule in 1960. It was at this time that the Burmese constitution was amended to make Buddhism the official religion of the country. But civilian government proved once again ineffectual, and in 1962, Ne Win took up the reins of power again, and they have remained in military hands to the present day.

At the same time, the military closed Burma off from interaction with the rest of the world. Except for brief periods of relative openness, Burma still remains one of the most isolated countries on earth. The resulting political climate has been one of unremitting oppression. All critics of the regime have been silenced either by intimidation or assassination. Nor have the Buddhist monks been exempt from such treatment.

Consequently, the state-supported Buddhist Order has become little more than a government department. On the other hand, many dissident monks have joined resistance groups that oppose the government, and are very active in the struggle to return Burma to a democratic system of government.

The Buddhist relationship to the state was one of the key factors in the recent history of Vietnam as well, but in a some-what different fashion. When the French had gained control of the area now known as Vietnam, Cambodia, and Laos in the late nineteenth century, they realized that they were going to need indigenous personnel in their administration. They turned to the relatively small number of Vietnamese who had converted to Christianity. When the region gained its independence, it was natural that the government be turned over to individuals with the experience to run it. Thus the Roman Catholic Vietnamese, who represented no more than 10 percent of the population, came to control the lives of the numerically much superior Buddhists.

In time the Buddhists, under the directions of activist monks, began to demonstrate for a restoration of Buddhist civil rights. The Catholic minority tried to hold on to power, but after a series of spectacular martyrdoms in which Buddhist monks calmly poured gasoline over their bodies and burned themselves to death, the Catholic government was deposed. Subsequent events, such as the Indochinese wars and the Communist takeover of Vietnam, curtailed but did not completely suppress Buddhism. Despite repression by the Communist government of Vietnam, the religion is still very much in evidence both in Vietnam and abroad among the immigrant communities of Europe and the United States.

Buddhism had been an honored part of Cambodian life for many centuries when that country resumed its independence in 1953. But in 1975, it suffered a blow from which it may never recover. In that year, the new masters of Cambodia, the Khmer Rouge, decided that in order to renovate Cambodian society they were going to have to eliminate all elements of society which did not lead directly to a socialist state. They proceeded to deport to the countryside and kill many of the country's educated elite. This included most of the Buddhist monks. In a brief reign of terror, some 15 centuries of Buddhist culture were almost completely eradicated. Only a few monks managed to flee the country in time. As a result, Cambodian Buddhist culture was kept alive in such diverse places as Long Beach, California, Lowell, Massachusetts, and Paris by a handful of monks. Today, attempts are being made to renovate Cambodian Buddhism in its homeland, but so much tradition has been lost and destroyed that it is questionable whether it will ever be restored to its former grandeur.

STATE PERSECUTION OF BUDDHISM IN CHINA

In China, the situation was somewhat different. Despite great initial successes, Buddhism was always suspect to the Confucian ruling class which continued to dominate Chinese government. Buddhism, as they saw it, undermined traditional Chinese family values, and donations to the various Chinese schools of Buddhism reduced the tax base. It is not surprising, therefore, that Buddhism was periodically persecuted in China. As time went on, these persecutions took their toll. While among the peasants Buddhism continued to command a faithful following, it did so more on the strength of its supposed magical potency than because of a deep devotion to its metaphysical principles.

Consequently, when the Chinese reasserted themselves politically, they did so intellectually as well. New forms of Confucianism came to dominate Chinese thinking. Buddhism became more and more a rural religion practiced by the politically disenfranchised, and it never regained the intellectual stature which it had enjoyed in the seventh and eighth centuries C.E. But it would be unwise to conclude from this that Chinese Buddhist philosophical thought disappeared entirely. China's efforts to exclude foreign invaders and to reestablish its political unity drew a number of young monks into the struggle for modernity. Although they were never a majority of the *Sangha* and were often disapproved of by the official leaders of the Buddhist community they were to have an effect on the modern development of Buddhism in China.

The most famous of these young monks was T'ai-hsu (1890-1947). He founded schools, promoted the study of Buddhist languages other than Chinese, and advocated the idea of a world federation of Buddhists. These efforts were beginning to bear fruit when China was taken over by the Communists. They saw the Buddhist monks and nuns as parasites who were draining the vitality of the Chinese people. In 1951, they confiscated most of the monastic lands and returned young monks and nuns to the lay state. In 1953, the Chinese Buddhist Association was formed to bring the Buddhist community under government control. Periodic campaigns of repression such as the Red Guard movement further weakened Buddhism in China. While Buddhism has lost much of its strength as a result of these persecutions, it still persists in China and will likely continue to do so in the forseeable future.

BUDDHISM IN MODERN KOREA AND JAPAN

Buddhism in Korea and Japan has been closely linked for many centuries. Indeed, it was often Buddhist monks from Korea who provided the link between Chinese and Japanese culture. By 1000 C.E., Son, a school of Zen Buddhism, had become the most popular form of Buddhism in Korea. Unfortunately, Buddhism was repressed by the rigidly Confucian Yi dynasty of kings (1392-1910). Strangely enough, it was the Japanese conquest of Korea in 1910 that marked the revival of Buddhist fortunes.

Although the Japanese allowed a resurgence of Buddhism in Korea, they attempted to force its development along Japanese models that were often quite different from indigenous Korean ones. This led to friction that eventually resulted in the formation of a unified Korean Buddhism in 1935. After World War II (1939-45) and the Korean War (1950-53), Buddhism was effectively eliminated in North Korea and to some extent curtailed in South Korea. However, Korean Buddhism continues to prosper despite these difficulties not only at home but also abroad.

Buddhism in Japan was to have its own share of difficulties in the modern period. During the period after the Meiji Restoration of 1868, Buddhism was ignored in favor of state-supported Shinto that glorified the Emperor. It was during this period that Buddhist clerical celibacy was made illegal with the result that today Japanese Buddhism is one of the few forms of Buddhism that allows a married clergy. It was during this period as well that Japanese Buddhism adopted many innovations from the West such as Sunday Schools, meditation clubs, young people's organizations, and, in some cases, the outward trappings of Protestant ritual and dress. Another interesting development in modern Japanese Buddhism has been the rise of new lay Buddhist organizations such as Soka Gakkai and Rissho-koseikai. These new organizations have done away with the old organizational principles of Buddhism and replaced them with aggressive new methods that more traditional Buddhists find somewhat upsetting. On the whole, Japanese Buddhism has become a dynamic part of the national life. Moreover, a number of Japanese schools are finding fertile ground in Europe and America for their ideas and practices.

BUDDHISM AND THE DESTRUCTION OF A CULTURE IN TIBET

For many centuries, Tibet was viewed by China as a province of the Chinese empire. Satisfied with formal submission and the ritual exchange of gifts, China was content to allow the country to be governed by the great monastic orders as it had been for many centuries. All of this changed, however, when the Communists came to power in 1950. Dissatisfied with the traditional arrangements and anxious to secure its borders, the new Chinese government attempted to rule more directly. In order to do this, and consistent with their own atheistic ideology, they occupied the country, moved to suppress the monasteries, and disenfranchised the Buddhist religion.

In 1959, the Tibetan people rebelled. It was at this time that the present Dalai Lama fled Tibet and settled in India. The Chinese then embarked on a reign of terror designed to completely eradicate Tibetan Buddhism. Temples were looted, monasteries razed, monks tortured and killed, scriptures burnt: But extinguishing the Buddhist faith in Tibet proved to be more difficult than the Chinese Communists imagined. Monks began to make the long trek across the Himalayas into India carrying with them the invaluable texts of their faith. As they gathered in India, they reconstituted the ruined monastic colleges and began to teach a new generation of young novices the complex rites and rituals of Tibetan Buddhism.

Meanwhile, the Dalai Lama became an eloquent and charismatic spokesman for his country and his faith. By bringing his country's difficulties to world attention, he helped to popularize Tibetan Buddhism. Many Westerners, attracted by the rich and vibrant nature of the tradition, began to support Tibetan efforts to preserve their cultural heritage. While the politics of the Chinese occupation of Tibet have yet to be resolved, it can safely be said that Tibetan Buddhism has managed to weather the storm. Through the courage and persistence of present-day practitioners, it will be preserved and passed on intact to future generations.

PLANTING NEW FLOWERS: BUDDHISM IN EUROPE AND THE UNITED STATES

Buddhism is so much a part of modern culture, at least on a superficial level, that it is hard to imagine that as little as 200 years ago people in the West had almost no idea of the nature of this religion. It was not until the European powers began to carve out their colonial empires in South and Southeast Asia, and meddle in the affairs of the East Asian nations, that they began to pay attention to the indigenous belief systems of the conquered peoples. But generally this attention had little or nothing to do with the intrinsic worth of these systems. Rather, these early administrators saw religion as a means of social control. As time progressed, however, some Europeans came to appreciate Buddhism and the other Asian religions in their own right. As they began to master the classical languages of Asia, such as Sanskrit, Chinese, Japanese, and Pali, European scholars began to piece together what was to them a new and fascinating universe of thought.

This group of scholars tended to emerge from the lower ranks of the colonial administrators who spent most of their days dealing with the administrative problems of the common people over whom they ruled. Since there were very few other Europeans to socialize with, these officers often took up study of the local culture. A good example of this was the case of T.W. Rhys-Davids (1843-1922). An administrator in Sri Lanka, he spent his leisure hours learning Pali, the sacred language of Theravada Buddhism. What he found astonished him. The Buddhism that began to emerge from the texts was not the (seemingly) superstitious religion that surrounded him, but rather an elegant, subtle philosophy that resonated with the logical, scientific thought that was coming to dominate European thinking. He became so enthusiastic about his studies that he founded the Pali Text Society with the intention of editing the entire Pali canon and translating it into English. This is a goal that the Society (which still exists) has very nearly achieved.

The next major change in Buddhist-European relations came in 1879, when Sir Edwin Arnold published his famous epic poem, *The Light of Asia*. This was a retelling in English verse of the life of the Buddha, not from an academic standpoint but from that of someone who appreciated Buddhist teaching as religious expression. Soon after this, Helen P. Blavatsky, a Russian, and Henry Steele Olcott, an American, two founders of the religious movement known as Theosophy, traveled to India and Sri Lanka to study Eastern thought. In Sri Lanka, they participated in a ceremony that formally accepted them into the Buddhist faith. Although their understanding of Buddhism was somewhat peculiar, these new converts were enthusiastic.

But the Theosophists were on the tip of the iceberg, so to speak. From around 1850 onward, Europe and the United States began to enter a period of religious crisis. Increasingly, intellectuals (and those who fancied themselves intellectuals) were becoming dissatisfied with Christianity. Some took issue with the idea that the Bible gave a complete and accurate picture of the origins of humanity and the physical world. Others took issue with Christian claims to the exclusive possession of the means of salvation in this world and the next. Many others simply wanted to replace what they thought of as mere superstition with a more scientific worldview. For many, Buddhism's "sudden" appearance on the intellectual horizon offered an answer to their dilemma.

But these early enthusiasts in Europe and America tended to misunderstand Buddhism. As we have seen, Buddhism does not suggest that more powerful beings than humans do not exist. Rather, it simply asserts that their influence is limited and that *ultimate* salvation lies elsewhere. Early European and American adherents to Buddhism tended to interpret Buddhism as being completely atheistic and self-oriented. This was certainly not the case for many, if not most, Buddhists. It is not surprising, therefore, that early converts to Buddhism tended toward Theravada Buddhism where "supernatural" elements seem to be the least pronounced. When Europeans began to investigate Buddhism seriously in the middle of the last century, they were very attracted to the Pali scriptures of this school of Buddhism. This was because they saw modern European thinking embodied in these ancient works.

As we have seen, this is not precisely the way in which Theravada Buddhism has been played out in its indigenous setting. But this early European viewpoint has just enough truth in it to have made Theravada Buddhism an attractive option to many European and American seekers who could not accept an otherworldly component to their spiritual quest. The first of these converts to actually be ordained as a Buddhist monk was Allen Bennett (1872-1925) who was ordained in Burma. He was soon followed by a number of other Britons and Germans who embraced the monastic lifestyle. But it was not until after World War II that other forms of Buddhism began to make their way into European and American society.

The war itself was the major contributing factor to this new renaissance of European and American interest in Buddhism. The war brought Europeans and Americans into contact with other Buddhist countries such as China and Japan. Buddhism from these countries had already made a small beachhead in Hawaii and the West Coast of America. Unfortunately racism tended to keep these immigrant communities separated from the main-stream of American life. All of this changed after the war.

The first of the great Buddhist invasions of North America was the Zen craze that swept 1950s America. Zen had come to America with the attendance of the Japanese monk Soyen Shaku (1859-1919) at the great World Farliament of Religions held in Chicago in 1893. Meeting there with the enthusiastic publisher of religious materials, Paul Carus, this monk agreed to sent one of his disciples to help Carus with the translation of Japanese Zen Buddhist texts. This disciple was to spend much of his life introducing Zen to the West. His name was D.T. Suzuki (1870-1966).

Other Zen masters were to follow Suzuki to America in the period before World War II, and they soon gathered small groups of enthusiastic American disciples. But it was the Beatnik generation that emerged after the war which took Zen to its heart. Writers from this movement, such as Jack Kerouac, Gary Snyder, and Allan Ginsberg, became ardent publicists for Zen (at least as they understood it). Alan Watts (1915-73), a wandering Jack of All Religions, also preached the gospel of Zen to an appreciative audience of youthful enthusiasts (mainly in California) during the late 1950s and 1960s.

This initial groundwork led to an influx of Zen teachers into America in the decades that followed, These teachers established Zen training facilities that taught Zen in the oldfashioned, rigorous Japanese manner. While something of a shock to an earlier generation of seekers who saw Zen as a "do your own thing" sort of religion, the Zen now in America has, as a result of this second wave of teachers, come more into line with traditional expressions of the religion. Indeed, a number of Americans have been recognized as Zen masters in their own right. It might even be said that there is a new type of Zen, American Zen, emerging under their guidance.

Nor should the contributions of the Chinese and Korean Zen schools be forgotten. In California, Zen Master Hsuan Hua (1908-) founded the Sino-American Buddhist Association and the Gold Mountain Dhyana Monastery where the training is very traditional and very rigorous. Other teachers, such as Sheng Yen Chang, are also spreading the teachings of Chinese Zen to America. Likewise, Korean masters such as Soen Sa Nim (1927-) are revealing the treasures of the lesser known Korean tradition. Soen Sa Nim established the increasingly popular Kwan Um school (named for Kuan-yin, the *Bodhisattva* of compassion) in 1972. He was preceded in 1967 by Samu Sunim with his Toronto-based Zen Lotus Society.

Just as World War II marked the beginning of the penetration of Zen into America, the Indochinese wars of the late 1960s and 70s mark the beginning of a new appreciation of Theravada Buddhism. During this period, American armed forces serving in Vietnam used the neighboring country of Thailand as a rest and recreation spot. Here they came in contact with Theravada Buddhism. Likewise, the increased American presence in Southeast Asia led to a growing number of Peace Corps volunteers being sent to the more stable countries in the region. All of this resulted in an heightened awareness of Theravada.

At this time as well, a number of people such as the American meditation teachers Jack Kornfield and Joel Goldstein went to these countries, and to Sri Lanka, to study and even to be ordained as Buddhist monks under such great contemporary Theravadin teachers as Ajahn Chah in Thailand and Taungpulu Sayadaw in Burma. Eventually, many of them returned to Europe and America, either to reenter lay life, or to teach as ordained monks. The Theravada Buddhism that they taught, however, was somewhat different in nature from that of the countries in which they had trained. There, lay persons did not, by and large, meditate—that was something which was done by monks. But in America and Europe, this was to become the primary religious activity of monks and lay persons alike.

On the other hand, many traditional lay activities associated with Theravada Buddhism in its home countries did not find a home among Europeans or Americans. The people most drawn to Theravada Buddhism were often persons who were not comfortable with traditional religion, particularly its institutional and supernatural aspects. Just as had been the case earlier in the century, it was the perception of Theravada Buddhism as an "atheistic" and "scientific" philosophy, rather than a religion in the traditional sense of the term, that was attractive to this new set of followers. As a consequence, many of the more devotional aspects of Theravada Buddhism were not adopted by these practitioners.

But for many people, the austere meditative practices of the Zen and Theravada varieties were unappealing. These people were looking for a more colorful Buddhism than these two traditions provided. For them, the answer to their search for religious meaning lay in Vajrayana Buddhism. This form of Buddhist expression was the least known of the Buddhist schools and the one which was the last to come to the West. Content to remain isolated in its Tibetan homeland, Vajrayana Buddhism might have remained unappreciated by outsiders had it not been for the national catastrophe which overtook it in 1950.

Right from the first, those Tibetan monks who had left Tibet for India were faced with a severe problem. The Chinese were systematically destroying their entire religious culture. Horrible stories emerged, most of which are unfortunately all too true. They told of monasteries burned, monks tortured and killed, and priceless works of art smashed. These activities became even more pronounced in the late 1960s during the Chinese Cultural Revolution. The Tibetan monks needed to find a way in which to preserve their cultural tradition. Replacing their depleted numbers was no real problem. Tibetans continued to enter the religious life, as many still do today. But how to support these monks now that the great Tibetan monasteries and their holdings were gone? What could be done to replace their texts, many of which were unique to the Tibetan tradition? The answer, the Tibetans swiftly discovered, lay in the West.

Thus in the 1960s Tibetan monks began to teach in the West. The most famous of these early missionaries was Chogyam Trungpa (1939-87), a *tulku* of the Kagyu order. He established the first Tibetan *gonpa* (monastery) outside of Asia, Samye Ling, in Dumfriesshire, Scotland in 1967. From this humble beginning, Trungpa created the far-flung Vajradhatu organization dedicated to propagating Kagyu Tibetan Buddhism in the West. After a serious car crash from which he never completely recovered, Trungpa married and left Britain for the United States. The more numerous Gelugpa school was somewhat slower in sending out feelers to Europe and the New World. The first teachers of this school to gain disciples in the West were Thubten Yeshe (1935-84) and his disciple Zopa Rimpoche (1946-) who founded the Foundation for the Preservation of the Mahayana Tradition in 1971 and Wisdom Publications, a well-respected publishing house now based in Boston.

But it was in the United States that Tibetan Buddhism really flourished. In 1951, a group of Kalmyks, fleeing from their former homes in postwar Russia, were allowed to settle in New Jersey. Since the Kalmyks had been for many centuries followers of Tibetan

Buddhism, it was here that the first Tibetan Buddhist temple in America was established, presided over by the Gelugpa monk Geshe Wangal (1901-83). This led to the first formal teaching of Tibetan and Tibetan Buddhism in America when, in 1967, Geshe Wangal's disciple, Geshe Sopa (1923-), was invited by the great Canadian Buddhologist Richard Robinson to join the faculty of the newly established Buddhist Studies Program at the University of Wisconsin. Geshe Sopa, in turn, arranged for the Dalai Lama to come to the United States in 1981, and in that year the Dalai Lama presided over a Kalachakra Initiation which some 12,000 people were said to have attended.

In 1970, Chogyam Trungpa, wearied by constant internal struggles in his European organization, migrated to the United States. At Boulder, Colorado, he established a new international Vajradhatu organization. He was succeeded as head of this organization by his American disciple Osel Tendzin (1945-90) whose profligate lifestyle and subsequent death from AIDS underscored the dangers in the unquestioning obedience to the guru taught by the Tibetan tradition. More orthodox in his approach was the Gelugpa master Kalu Rinpoche (1905-89) whose saintly personality and rigorous traditional approach to Tibetan Buddhist training began to produce the first group of authentically trained Western Vajrayana monks qualified to run their own training establishments.

It was in America as well that Nyingma Tibetan Buddhism found a new lease of life. In 1969, Tarthang Tulku established the Tibetan Nyingma Institute in Berkeley, California. He was soon followed by other notable teachers of the school, including its supreme head Dudjom Rinpoche (1904-87). One of Tarthang Tulku's major projects was to edit and publish the enormous corpus of Nyingma scriptures, a goal that is currently well on the way to completion. This, along with other similar ventures such as Wisdom Publications, has ensured that the immensely rich scriptural tradition of Tibetan Buddhism will be preserved for future generations.

Finally, a word must be said concerning the fortunes of Pure Land Buddhism. This school of Buddhism has been part of the American scene since the mid-nineteenth century when Chinese and Japanese workmen began to be brought to the United States to work on the railroad and in the cane fields of Hawaii. Over the years, it has acquired many trappings reminiscent of Protestant Christianity, not only in the West but even in the lands of its birth. By and large, it has remained in the Asian community. Most non-Asians who are attracted to Buddhism are drawn to the radical difference of its core message from that of Christianity and Judaism. Thus Pure Land Buddhism, with its many apparent similarities to these traditions, does not seem as appealing as more exotic forms of Buddhism. Nevertheless, its traditional followers are still numerous, particularly the Japanese school of Jodo Shin-shu, under the title of the Buddhist Churches of America.

BUDDHISM IN THE TWENTY-FIRST CENTURY

Buddhism is no different from other world religions in that it faces challenges in the modern world as well as opportunities. The twentieth century has not been kind to

Buddhism. Large areas of the Buddhist world have disappeared due to political and social changes. A good example of this is China, where Buddhism had once been widespread. After the Communists took power, Buddhism (and all other religions) was systematically suppressed so that it is difficult today to discern how many Buddhists still remain in that huge country. As we have seen, the Communists carried their dislike of Buddhism to Tibet in 1951 where they attempted to stamp out Buddhism entirely, often by extraordinarily violent means. Likewise during the hideous excesses of the Khmer Rouge in Cambodia between 1975 and 1979, virtually the entire Buddhist monastic Order was murdered along with perhaps as much as half of the entire population of this Theravadin Buddhist country Many estimate that at the end of this period, out of an initial 80,000 monks, only a few hundred managed to survive. In China, Cambodia, and Tibet, temples were destroyed, scriptures burned, and valuable pieces of Buddhist art sold to the highest bidder.

Terrible as this overt attempt to destroy Buddhism has been, it is eclipsed by a more concerted and subtler assault on the *Cultural Synthesis in Western Buddhism.*

One of the notable features of the developing Buddhism in the West is the degree to which women teachers have taken a leading role in transmitting the teachings. While women have never been excluded from Buddhism, the male-oriented nature of most Asian societies has assigned them a subordinate role in religious matters. In the West, this is not the case. Indeed, many of the pioneers of Buddhist scholarship, such as Mrs. Caroline Rhys-Davids (1858-1942) and I.B. Horner (1896-1981), are still remembered as notable scholars. However, it is as religious teachers that Western women have come into their own.

One particularly interesting example of this was Jiyu Kennett Roshi (Peggy Teresa Nancy Kennett, 1924-96). British by birth, Kennett Roshi trained first in Western music at London's Trinity College of Music. Increasingly dissatisfied with the life of the Western world, she began to study Buddhism. One of the first women to receive the approval of Japanese and Korean Zen masters, she was authorized by them to teach. In 1969, she traveled to the United States and founded Shasta Abbey in northern California. Since then, her organization, the Order of Buddhist Contemplatives, has founded a number of other monasteries and temples.

One might assume from this that Shasta Abbey would be a faithful recreation of a Japanese monastery, but this is not the case. Kennett Roshi decided early in her career that Buddhism needed to be adapted to the particular conditions of the West. For her, trained as she was in classical Western art and music, this meant taking Western forms and imbuing them with a Buddhist spirit. Hence one finds at Shasta Abbey that the monks and nuns wear robes that resemble those worn by Christian religious orders. Likewise, the music of the various services is based on Gregorian plainchant, not on Eastern musical models. One might rightly ask if this is the proper way to go about adapting Buddhism to the West, given the fact that these forms no longer resonate with the bulk of the population. Nevertheless, Kennett Roshi's attempts to place Buddhist spirituality within a traditional Western context shows the dynamic spirit of American Buddhism, and suggests paths for future development.

This has come through the medium of Western culture. Smuggled in on the backs of Mickey Mouse and Michael Jackson, the Western gospel of consumerism is entirely at odds with Buddhist values which preach simplicity, tranquility, and turning away from the relentless acquisition of goods. But the Coca-Colonization of Asian societies has left them awash in rock videos, Western nightclubs, and expensive electronic consumer goods. While certainly not bad in themselves, these things sound a not-so-subtle counterpoint to the traditional Buddhist values of simplicity and disengagement with the world of the senses.

They do this by replacing Buddhist ideals with their own vision of the nature of human happiness as the pursuit of "stuff": the idea, as one sardonic philosopher has observed, that "the person who dies with the most toys wins." Along with these cultural values comes the worldview that supports them. This Western scientific worldview, with its discounting of religious values and its emphasis on the material here and now, has had a powerful effect on many of the Buddhist countries' educated classes. These groups have in many cases rejected Buddhism, equating it with the superstitions of the rural agriculturalists. This too has had an adverse effect on Buddhism.

Need we fear, therefore, that Buddhism, like so many religions before it, will disappear? The answer to this is that such an event is very unlikely. Over the centuries, Buddhism has shown itself to be highly adaptable to new cultural conditions. As we have seen, it spread from its original home in India throughout most of Asia, coping with new cultures and new languages as it encountered them. In the process, it became an integral part of these cultures. Even now, it is changing and adapting. The Buddhism that came to America and Europe from various Asian cultures is being reconceptualized and revitalized in such a manner as to make it uniquely a part of these cultures.

Likewise, Buddhism is adapting to the changing environment in its homelands as well. Whereas for many years it was seen as being outside the normal flow of secular society, Buddhist groups whose main concern centers on secular social problems are now springing up. A good example of this is currently taking place in Thailand. The Thais are in the process of transforming their economy from an agricultural one to a more industrial model. Unfortunately, as the European experience with the Industrial Revolution showed Westerners, this change is often accompanied by a fearful cost in the quality of human life. Thailand is finding this out. A particularly severe example of this is the ecological problems the country is now facing. Large tracts of land are being deforested as their trees feed the demand for wood products in Japan and elsewhere. This, in turn, is resulting in other problems such as erosion. In order to combat this, Buddhist groups headed by monks are addressing environmental concerns stemming from the country's rapid industrialization. Using nonviolent but innovative techniques such as ordaining trees (even Westernized Thais still hold the *Sangha* in respect and would not cut down an "ordained" tree), these groups are lobbying for saner use of natural resources based on the Buddhist respect for the integrity of all living beings.

In Sri Lanka, monastic organizations are becoming more involved in community health and other social issues in the many tiny villages which dot the island. Traditionally associating with lay persons only to teach and preach, many Buddhist monks are now concerning themselves with more mundane problems. Two good examples of this are Venerable Pandita Walgowwagoda Wimalabuddho Thero of Sri Wardhanaramaya monastery and Venerable Medagama Dhammananda Thero of Asgiri Mahavihara monastery in Kandy.

Pandita Wimalabuddho is a member of the highest council of the Buddhist church in Sri Lanka, but his interests extend beyond purely spiritual matters. One of the programs that he has been instrumental in supporting has been a joint program with Japanese Buddhist organizations to combat eye diseases in rural areas. These diseases, which if left untreated cause blindness, have always been a problem in the humid tropical climate of the island. Their treatment, which involves the simple application of antibiotic ointment, while relatively cheap is still beyond the means of the average poor farmer even if he or she understood the mechanics of the disease. Through the generosity of Japanese Buddhists, these antibiotics are being sent to Sri Lanka and are being distributed to the villages.

Nor is this the only example of Buddhist engagement with contemporary problems in Sri Lanka. Venerable Dhammananda represents a change which is sweeping through the Buddhist *Sangha*. A young, well educated man, Ven. Dhammananda was not content to remain in Sri Lanka but traveled to Taiwan to experience Buddhism in that setting. On returning to Sri Lanka, he began to work with lay people on a variety of social issues. He is emblematic of a change of attitude among younger Buddhist monks as a whole, namely that Buddhism demands engagement with the world, not retreat from it. Nor is this attitude restricted to religious specialists. In Sri Lanka the *Sarvodaya* Movement has been formed by Buddhist lay persons in order to address the socioeconomic problems found in the countryside. All of this heralds a new day in the relationship of Buddhism to its environment in this ancient society.

This reorientation of Buddhism is not happening in traditionally Buddhist countries alone. In the United States, Buddhist teachers and lay persons are a persuasive voice in many areas of social concern. A good example of this is Buddhist work with AIDS sufferers. When the AIDS epidemic first burst on the American scene, it appeared to be a disease almost exclusively associated with homosexual men. Since homosexual behavior was condemned by traditional Christianity and therefore poorly understood or appreciated by the bulk of the American public, AIDS patients were often isolated from traditional spiritual caregivers. Moreover, as the epidemic spread to intravenous drug users, this stereotypical association of "sin" and AIDS became even more widespread.

Among the first religious groups to go against this prevailing tendency were the American Buddhists. Since Buddhism, by and large, did not have the concept of sin and did not condemn homosexuality per se, AIDS was not seen as being disgraceful or a just punishment. Rather, it was regarded as just another example of the painful nature of existence, and those suffering from it as fellow beings in need of compassionate treatment. Thus, practicing Buddhists, both gay and straight, were in the fore-front of caregiving to AIDS patients. Needless to say, such actions, along with other similar activities such as aiding the homeless, have greatly enhanced the religion's reputation in the United States and Europe.

THE TIMELESS MESSAGE OF THE BUDDHA

What are the factors which contribute to this continuing appeal of Buddhism, and more particularly its growing appeal to Europeans and Americans? The simplest answer lies in the fact that the problems which Buddhism first addressed some 2500 years ago are still with us today more or less unchanged. People still question the nature of life and its ultimate meaning. People still wonder why the good suffer and the evil go unpunished. People still ponder the unstoppable forces of nature and their relationship to human existence. For many of these searchers, the Buddhist analysis of reality and its practical program for achieving transcendence from the pains of human life are very appealing. But other religions, such as Islam, Christianity, and Hinduism, offer answers to these questions as well. What is unique in Buddhism?

One of the features of Buddhism which is attractive to many people, especially people raised in the scientific milieu of Western society, is that Buddhism does away with the idea of the "supernatural," a split between this world and some unseen, totally other, reality. The universe, says the Buddhist, is a vast system of processes, not things.

For the Buddhist, one can no more change the inexorable laws of cause and effect than one can hope to repeal the law of gravity. Such a viewpoint is extremely attractive to the Western mind which has been nurtured on scientific principles. Whereas other religions depend on the unproven (and perhaps unprovable) concept of a supreme deity, Buddhism has no such needs. Moreover, Buddhist presuppositions seem to proceed much more easily from the generally accepted laws of physics, which increasingly seem to support many Buddhist contentions about the nature of the universe, than do theistic presuppositions. In many ways, Buddhist principles such as cause and effects seem merely to be physical laws applied to the metaphysical realm. Thus for many people Buddhism is an increasingly acceptable religious option because it is so "nonreligious," lacking many of the features that Westerners deem essential to religion such as that of a supreme deity.

Another reason that Buddhism maintains its popularity is that it tends toward individual rather than corporate expressions of religiosity. Among the Western religions, the core religious actions are defined as taking place in community. The believing Christian or Jew is enjoined to attend weekly services in association with his or her fellow believers.

Buddhism, on the other hand, sees religious activity to consist of personal actions. The individual has, of course, opportunities to associate with and take comfort from the community of believers, but he or she can be just as good a Buddhist without ever encountering another coreligionist. It is the interior work of the individual that matters.

In the increasingly individualistic societies of Europe and America, this is a distinct advantage, particularly as demands on the individual's time increase and the stately seasonal cycles of ritual which mark Judaism and Christianity, geared as they are to the slow pace of agricultural societies, become increasingly impractical in a 24 hours a day, seven days a week industrial world.

Moreover the individual can practice as much or as little ritualism as he or she chooses. Whereas the bulk of Western religious activity takes place within the context of formal ritual, Buddhists can practice their religion without any recourse to ritual whatsoever if they choose (although very few people in a traditionally Buddhist country would choose to do so). On the other hand, those who do wish to support their meditation practice with more formal rituals can do so easily. There is a ritual style to suit all tastes in Buddhism, ranging from the relatively austere ritualism of Theravada to the ornate and complex ritualism of Tibetan Buddhism.

This appreciation of the personal in Buddhism plays out in other ways as well. Buddhism lacks much of the institutionalized prejudice that exists in other religions. Thus people of differing races, genders, sexual orientation, and lifestyles find a supportive atmosphere in Buddhism which they do not find in the Western religions. This is not to say that Buddhism is entirely free of the prejudices that assail other religions—such things as the present troubles in Sri Lanka are ample proof of that. Rather it is to say that there is no scriptural or institutional warrant for such prejudice, and indeed, much scriptural condemnation of such behavior. No Buddhist will be able to advance on the spiritual path through persecution of other religions, quite the contrary in fact.

Another appealing Buddhist trait is its long history of using everyday vernacular language rather than a sacred language understood by only a few specialists. This means that the scriptures of the religion are readily available to all of its members for study and reflection. This is not to say that the Buddhist scriptures are all of uniform quality or importance. But there is no privileged ritual language in Buddhism. The scriptures are seen as being just as authoritative in translation as they are in the original languages. In addition, the lack of a mediating priesthood means that each individual Buddhist possesses an equal potential for achieving realization of Ultimate Reality without needing to depend on another.

But perhaps the greatest strength of Buddhism is its commitment to peace. In a world that has had two major world wars and innumerable smaller conflicts in the last hundred years, the Buddhist call to peace and human reconciliation is particularly compelling. Buddhist leaders such as the Vietnamese monk Thich Nhat Hanh and the Dalai Lama are regularly nominated for the highest awards as a result of their activities on behalf of peace. Nor do these leaders preach a message of reconciliation between humans alone. They are also active in crusading on behalf of the mute inhabitants of our planet, demanding that we treat other species and the environment in general with the same respect that we wish for ourselves. In this, they offer a clear alternative to the prevailing human paradigm of exploitation, both of one another and of the earth.

There can be little doubt, therefore, that Buddhism will continue to remain a compelling advocate for a gentler world. As long as the problems that mark human existence persist, Buddhism will always find people in every generation for whom its message of hope, peace, and compassion still resonates. It will continue to offer such individuals a way of coping with life's many disappointments and tragedies, and an alternate model of human interaction with the world at large. For these people, Buddhism will always be the religion of many paths, but one goal—the goal of peace.

Chapter - 10

Buddhism
Spreading to the West

Although Buddhism spread throughout Asia it remained virtually unknown in the West until modern times. The early missions sent by the emperor Ashoka to the West did not bear fruit. Knowledge of Buddhism has come through three main channels: Western scholars; the work of philosophers, writers and artists; and the arrival of Asian immigrants who have brought various forms of Buddhism with them to Europe, North America and Australia.

The 'come and see for yourself ' attitude of Buddhism attracts many Westerners. They are not asked to believe in anything, but to follow the Buddha's advice of testing ideas first. With the growth of easy travel and communications, the West has been able to find out more about Buddhism in this century than in all the time before. The informality and emphasis on practice of Buddhism appeals to many Westerners.

THE INFLUENCE OF BUDDHISM

Buddhist attitudes of peace, mindfulness and care for all living creatures have come to be the concern of many groups in the West. Buddhist believe that all things should be looked after: the earth, plants, birds, insects and animals. This is close to the feeling among many people in recent years that the human race should stop polluting the atmosphere and destroying the surface of the earth by cutting down forests.

BUDDHISM TRAVELS WEST

Although the Buddha's teachings have been known in countries throughout Asia for over 2,500 years, very few people in Europe or America would have known what the word 'Buddhist' meant unless they had been born in the last 50 years.

Over a century ago people from France, the Netherlands, Great Britain, and other European countries began to travel in the Far East. Many of them returned with Eastern ideas, and so Europeans began to hear about Buddhism.

More recently, Buddhist people have moved to the West. Many of them have been refugees from conflict. Many Tibetans, for example, fled from their country after the Chinese takeover in 1959. The wars in Indochina in the 1950s and 1960s led many Vietnamese people to move to and settle in Europe, Australia and America. Other Buddhists from countries such as Thailand have established businesses in the larger Western cities. They have all brought their Buddhist beliefs to their new homes, and helped to set up Buddhist centres.

INTRODUCTION OF BUDDHISM TO EUROPE

In the eighteenth century onwards, a number of Buddhist texts were brought to Europe by people who had visited the colonies in the East. These texts aroused the interest of some European scholars who then began to study them.

Around the middle of the nineteenth century, a few Buddhist texts were translated into European languages. Thus Buddhist teaching came to be known to the European scholars. A few of them who were influenced by Buddhism, introduced Buddhist ideas into their own writings. Later, more and better European translations of Buddhist texts were made by the early part of the twentieth century, a large number of Buddhist texts had already been translated into English, French and German. This includes virtually the entire collection of Theravada scriptures as well as a number of important Mahayana texts.

GROWTH OF BUDDHISM IN EUROPE

Before the beginning of the twentieth century, the study of Buddhism was confined mainly to scholars and there was not much practice of the teachings. Later, this pattern began to change. A number of Europeans felt that merely reading about Buddhism was not enough, so they travelled to the East to acquire firsthand knowledge of the Buddhist practices and to experience the monastic life.

In addition, Buddhist organisations were founded in the major cities of Europe. One of these, the Buddhist Society of London, was established in 1924. It is the oldest and one of the largest Buddhist organisations in Europe. These organisations helped the growth of interest in Buddhism through their meditation sessions, lectures and circulation of Buddhist literature.

By the early part of the twentieth century, a number of the Europeans, who had travelled to the East to study Buddhism, had returned. Some of them had become monks and they inspired and strengthened the Buddhist circles in Europe. They were soon joined by Buddhist monks from Sri Lanka and other Buddhist countries in Asia. In recent years, there has been a marked growth of interest in Buddhism in Europe. The membership of existing Buddhist societies has increased and many new Buddhist centres have been established. Their members include large numbers of professionals and scholars. Today, the major Buddhist traditions of Asia such as Theravada, Pure Land,

Ch'an (or Zen), Vajrayana and Nichiren Shoshu, have a sizeable number of followers in Europe.

INTRODUCTION OF BUDDHISM TO AMERICA

As in Europe, scholars in America became acquainted with a number of Buddhist ideas in the nineteenth century. Some of the oldest universities in America had departments of oriental studies where scholars studied Buddhist texts.

During the second half of the nineteenth century, Chinese immigrants settled in Hawaii and California. These immigrants brought a number of Mahayana Buddhist practices with them and built numerous temples. The Japanese Buddhist immigrant who arrived later, not only built temples but also invited over to America, the Japanese monks who belonged to the various Mahayana Buddhist sects. However, Buddhist activities remained largely confined to these immigrant communities.

At the end of the nineteenth century, two outstanding Buddhist spokesmen, Dharmapala from Sri Lanka and Soyen Shaku, a Zen master from Japan, attended the World Parliament of Religions in Chicago. Their inspiring speeches on Buddhism impressed their audience and helped to establish a foothold for the Theravada and Zen Buddhist traditions in America. During this period, the Theosophical Society, which teaches the unity of all religions, also helped to spread some elements of Buddhist teachings in America.

GROWTH OF BUDDHISM IN AMERICA

It was not until the second half of the twentieth century that Buddhist ideas reached a wider section of the American society. American servicemen returning from East Asia after the Second World War and Korean War, brought with them an interest in Asian culture which included Nichiren Shoshu and Zen Buddhism. The latter gained considerable popularity in the nineteen-sixties among literary and artistic groups in America and this helped to popularise Buddhism. When Tibetan refugees began arriving in America after 1959, they brought with them Vajrayana Buddhism. Soon it gained a substantial following there. During the postwar period, academic interest grew. Many new departments of Buddhist studies were established in the American universities.

AT WESTERN BUDDHIST CENTRES

The basis of Buddhist practice in the West, as in the East, is meditation, and people may sit on cushions with their legs folded and hands in their laps. The photograph on the left was taken during a ten-day retreat at the Blue Mountains Insight Meditation Centre, Australia, with a western monk as the Teacher.

The students practised intensive sitting meditation and meditative walking, with a daily interview; received personal instruction and listened to an evening talk. Some groups will also do some chanting, and make offerings to the Buddha image in its shrine. A Theravadin group will be very quiet and peaceful. They may form themselves into lines to give food to the monks in the morning and expect to hear a talk during the day.

A Tibetan group can be more active, chanting, asking questions and ringing bells. Japanese Zen groups are more restrained and spend a lot of time in meditation or zazen. The activities at Buddhist centres allow people to find ways of understanding Buddhism. Today, there exist numerous Buddhist centres spread across Australia, New Zealand, Europe, North and South America. Virtually all the major Buddhist traditions are represented and continue to attract the interest of Westerners in all walks of life.

BUDDHISM IN THE WEST

Occasional intersections between Western civilization and the Buddhist world have been occurring for thousands of years. Alexander the Great's conquest of much of Central Asia set the stage for contacts between the civilizations of Greece and India.

In the latter half of the 19th century, Buddhism (along with many other religions and philosophies) came to the attention of Western intellectuals. The first English translation of the *Tibetan Book of the Dead* was published in 1927 and the reprint of 1935 carried a commentary from C.G. Jung. The book is said to have attracted many westerners to Tibetan Buddhism.

The first Buddhists to arrive in the United States were Chinese and Japanese immigrants who established many temples mainly for their own purposes of worship. In 1959 Suzuki Roshi (a Japanese teacher) arrived in San Francisco. At the time of Suzuki's arrival, Zen had become a hot topic amongst some groups in the United States, especially beatniks. In 1965, monks from Sri Lanka established the Washington Buddhist Vihara in Washington, D.C., the first Theravada monastic community in the United States. In the 1970s, interest in Tibetan Buddhism grew dramatically.

Today, Buddhism is practiced by large numbers of people in the Americas, Europe and Oceania. Buddhism has become the fastest-growing religion in Australia and some other Western nations. Many Hollywood movies with Buddhist themes, such as *Kundun*, *Little Buddha* and *Seven Years in Tibet*, have had considerable commercial success.

GRECO-BUDDHISM

Greco-Buddhism, sometimes spelt Graeco-Buddhism, refers to the cultural syncretism between Hellenistic culture and Buddhism, which developed between the 4th century BCE and the 5th century CE in the area covered by modern Afghanistan, Pakistan and north-western border regions of modern India namely western portions of Jammu and Kashmir. It was a cultural consequence of a long chain of interactions begun by Greek forays into India from the time of Alexander the Great, carried further by the establishment of Indo-Greek rule in the area for some centuries, and extended during flourishing of the Hellenized empire of the Kushans. Greco-Buddhism influenced the artistic (and perhaps the conceptual) development of Buddhism, particularly Mahayana Buddhism, before Buddhism was adopted in Central and Northeastern Asia, from the 1st century CE, ultimately spreading to China, Korea and Japan.

The interaction between Hellenistic Greece and Buddhism started when Alexander the Great conquered the Achaemenid Empire and further regions of Central Asia in 334 BCE, crossing the Indus and Jhelum rivers, and going as far as the Beas, thus establishing direct contact with India, the birthplace of Buddhism.

Alexander founded several cities in his new territories in the areas of the Oxus and Bactria, and Greek settlements further extended to the Khyber Pass, Gandhara and the Punjab. These regions correspond to a unique geographical passageway between the Himalayas and the Hindu Kush mountains, through which most of the interaction between India and Central Asia took place, generating intense cultural exchange and trade.

Following Alexander's death on June 10, 323 BCE, the *Diadochoi* (successors) founded their own kingdoms in Asia Minor and Central Asia. General Seleucus set up the Seleucid Kingdom, which extended as far as India. Later, the Eastern part of the Seleucid Kingdom broke away to form the Greco-Bactrian Kingdom (3rd–2nd century BCE), followed by the Indo-Greek Kingdom (2nd–1st century BCE), and later the Kushan Empire (1st–3rd century CE).

The interaction of Greek and Buddhist cultures operated over several centuries until it ended in the 5th century CE with the invasions of the White Huns, and later the expansion of Islam.

Religious interactions

The length of the Greek presence in Central Asia and northern India provided opportunities for interaction, not only on the artistic, but also on the religious plane.

Alexander the Great in Bactria and India (331-325 BCE)

When Alexander conquered the Bactrian and Gandharan regions, these areas may already have been under Buddhist influence. According to a legend preserved in Pali, the language of the Theravada canon, two merchant brothers from Bactria, named Tapassu and Bhallika, visited the Buddha and became his disciples. They then returned to Bactria and built temples to the Buddha (Foltz).

In 326 BCE, Alexander invaded India. King Ambhi, ruler of Taxila, surrendered his city, a notable center of Buddhist faith, to Alexander. Alexander fought an epic battle against Porus, a ruler of a region in the Punjab in the Battle of Hydaspes in 326 BC.

Several philosophers, such as Pyrrho, Anaxarchus and Onesicritus, are said to have been selected by Alexander to accompany him in his eastern campaigns. During the 18 months they were in India, they were able to interact with Indian religious men, generally described as Gymnosophists ("naked philosophers"). Pyrrho (360-270 BCE), returned to Greece and became the first Skeptic and the founder of the school named Pyrrhonism. The Greek biographer Diogenes Laertius explained that Pyrrho's equanimity and detachment from the world were acquired in India. Few of his sayings are directly known, but they are clearly reminiscent of eastern, possibly Buddhist, thought:

"Nothing really exists, but human life is governed by convention"

"Nothing is in itself more this than that" (Diogenes Laertius IX.61)

Another of these philosophers, Onesicritus, a Cynic, is said by Strabo to have learnt in India the following precepts:

"That nothing that happens to a man is bad or good, opinions being merely dreams"

"That the best philosophy [is] that which liberates the mind from [both] pleasure and grief"

These contacts initiated the first direct interactions between Greek culture and Indian religions, which were to continue and expand for several more centuries.

The Mauryan empire (322–183 BCE)

The Indian emperor Chandragupta, founder of the Mauryan dynasty, re-conquered around 322 BCE the northwest Indian territory that had been lost to Alexander the Great. However, contacts were kept with his Greek neighbours in the Seleucid Empire. Seleucid king Seleucus I came to a marital agreement as part of a peace treaty, and several Greeks, such as the historian Megasthenes, resided at the Mauryan court.

Chandragupta's grandson Ashoka converted to the Buddhist faith and became a great proselytizer in the line of the traditional Pali canon of Theravada Buddhism, insisting on non-violence to humans and animals (ahimsa), and general precepts regulating the life of lay people.

According to the Edicts of Ashoka, set in stone, some of them written in Greek, he sent Buddhist emissaries to the Greek lands in Asia and as far as the Mediterranean. The edicts name each of the rulers of the Hellenic world at the time:

"The conquest by Dharma has been won here, on the borders, and even six hundred yojanas (4,000 miles) away, where the Greek king Antiochos (Antiyoga) rules, and beyond there where the four kings named Ptolemy (Turamaya), Antigonos (Antikini), Magas (Maka) and Alexander (Alikasu[n]dara) rule, likewise in the south among the Cholas, the Pandyas, and as far as Tamraparni." (Rock Edict Nb.13).

Ashoka also claims he converted to Buddhism Greek populations within his realm:

"Here in the king's domain among the Greeks, the Kambojas, the Nabhakas, the Nabhapamkits, the Bhojas, the Pitinikas, the Andhras and the Palidas, everywhere people are following Beloved-of-the-Gods' instructions in Dharma." Rock Edict Nb13 (S. Dhammika).

Finally, some of the emissaries of Ashoka, such as the famous Dharmaraksita, are described in Pali sources as leading Greek ("Yona") Buddhist monks, active in Buddhist proselytism (the Mahavamsa, XII).

The Greek presence in Bactria (325 to 125 BCE)

Alexander had established in Bactria several cities (Ai-Khanoum, Begram) and an administration that were to last more than two centuries under the Seleucids and the Greco-Bactrians, all the time in direct contact with Indian territory. The Greeks sent ambassadors to the court of the Mauryan empire, such as the historian Megasthenes under Chandragupta Maurya, and later Deimakos under his son Bindusara, who reported extensively on the civilization of the Indians. Megasthenes sent detailed reports on Indian religions, which were circulated and quoted throughout the Classical world for centuries:

> *"Megasthenes makes a different division of the philosophers, saying that they are of two kinds, one of which he calls the Brachmanes, and the other the Sarmanes..."*
> Strabo XV. 1. 58-60

The Greco-Bactrians maintained a strong Hellenistic culture at the door of India during the rule of the Mauryan empire in India, as exemplified by the archaeological site of Ai-Khanoum. When the Mauryan empire was toppled by the Sungas around 180 BCE, the Greco-Bactrians expanded into India, where they established the Indo-Greek kingdom, under which Buddhism was able to flourish.

The Indo-Greek kingdom and Buddhism (180 BCE –10 CE)

The Greco-Bactrians conquered parts of northern India from 180 BCE, whence they are known as the Indo-Greeks. They controlled various areas of the northern Indian territory until 10 CE.

Buddhism prospered under the Indo-Greek kings, and it has been suggested that their invasion of India was intended to protect the Buddhist faith from the religious persecutions of the new Indian dynasty of the Sungas (185–73 BCE) which had overthrown the Mauryans.

Coinage

The coins of the Indo-Greek king Menander (reigned 160 to 135 BCE), found from Afghanistan to central India, bear the inscription "Saviour King Menander" in Greek on the front. Several Indo-Greek kings after Menander, such as Zoilos I, Strato I, Heliokles II, Theophilos, Peukolaos, Menander II and Archebios display on their coins the title of "Maharajasa Dharmika" (lit. "King of the Dharma") in the Prakrit language and in the Kharoshthi script.

Some of the coins of Menander I and Menander II incorporate the Buddhist symbol of the eight-spoked wheel, associated with the Greek symbols of victory, either the palm of victory, or the victory wreath handed over by the goddess Nike. According to the Milinda Pañha, at the end of his reign Menander I became a Buddhist arhat, a fact also echoed by Plutarch, who explains that his relics were shared and enshrined.The ubiquitous symbol of the elephant in Indo-Greek coinage may also have been associated with Buddhism, as suggested by the parallel between coins of Antialcidas and Menander II, where the elephant in the coins of Antialcidas holds the same relationship to Zeus and Nike as the Buddhist wheel on the coins of Menander II. When the zoroastrian Indo-Parthians invaded northern India in the 1st century CE, they adopted a large part of the symbolism of Indo-Greek coinage, but refrained from ever using the elephant, suggesting that its meaning was not merely geographical.

Finally, after the reign of Menander I, several Indo-Greek rulers, such as Amyntas, King Nicias, Peukolaos, Hermaeus, Hippostratos and Menander II, depicted themselves or their Greek deities forming with the right hand a benediction gesture identical to the Buddhist vitarka mudra (thumb and index joined together, with other fingers extended), which in Buddhism signifies the transmission of Buddha's teaching.

Cities

According to Ptolemy, Greek cities were founded by the Greco-Bactrians in northern Pakistan. Menander established his capital in Sagala, today's Sialkot in Punjab, one of the centers of the blossoming Buddhist culture. A large Greek city built by Demetrius and rebuilt by Menander has been excavated at the archaeological site of Sirkap near Taxila, where Buddhist stupas were standing side-by-side with Hindu and Greek temples, indicating religious tolerance and syncretism.

Scriptures

Evidence of direct religious interaction between Greek and Buddhist thought during the period include the Milinda Panha, a Buddhist discourse in the platonic style, held between king Menander and the Buddhist monk Nagasena.

Also the Mahavamsa records that during Menander's reign, "a Greek ("Yona") Buddhist head monk" named Mahadharmaraksita (literally translated as 'Great Teacher/ Preserver of the Dharma') led 30,000 Buddhist monks from "the Greek city of Alexandria" (possibly Alexandria-of-the-Caucasus, around 150km north of today's Kabul in Afghanistan), to Sri Lanka for the dedication of a stupa, indicating that Buddhism flourished in Menander's territory and that Greeks took a very active part in it.

Several Buddhist dedications by Greeks in India are recorded, such as that of the Greek meridarch (civil governor of a province) named Theodorus, describing in Kharoshthi how he enshrined relics of the Buddha. The inscriptions were found on a vase inside a stupa, dated to the reign of Menander or one his successors in the 1st century BCE:

"Theudorena meridarkhena pratithavida ime sarira sakamunisa bhagavato bahu-jana-stitiye":

"The meridarch Theodorus has enshrined relics of Lord Shakyamuni, for the welfare of the mass of the people"
(Swât relic vase inscription of the Meridarkh Theodoros)

This inscription represents one of the first known mention of the Buddha as a deity, using the Indian bhakti word Bhagavat ("Lord", "All-embracing personal deity"), suggesting the emergence of Mahayana doctrines in Buddhism.

Finally, Buddhist tradition recognizes Menander as one of the great benefactors of the faith, together with Asoka and Kanishka.

Buddhist manuscripts in cursive Greek have been found in Afghanistan, praising various Buddhas and including mentions of the Mahayana Lokesvara-raja Buddha (λωγοασφαροραζοβοδδο). These manuscripts have been dated later than the 2nd century CE. (Nicholas Sims-Williams, "A Bactrian Buddhist Manuscript").

Some elements of the Mahayana movement may have begun around the 1st century BCE in northwestern India, at the time and place of these interactions. According to most scholars, the main sutras of Mahayana were written after 100 BCE, when sectarian conflicts arose among Nikaya Buddhist sects regarding the humanity or super-humanity of the Buddha and questions of metaphysical essentialism, on which Greek thought may have had some influence: "It may have been a Greek-influenced and Greek-carried form of Buddhism that passed north and east along the Silk Road".

The Kushan empire (1st–3rd century CE)

The Kushans, one of the five tribes of the Yuezhi confederation settled in Bactria since around 125 BCE when they displaced the Greco-Bactrians, invaded the northern parts of Pakistan and India from around 1 CE.

By that time they had already been in contact with Greek culture and the Indo-Greek kingdoms for more than a century. They used the Greek script to write their language, as exemplified by their coins and their adoption of the Greek alphabet. The absorption of Greek historical and mythological culture is suggested by Kushan sculptures representing Dionysiac scenes or even the story of the Trojan horse and it is probable that Greek communities remained under Kushan rule.

The Kushan king Kanishka, who honored Zoroastrian, Greek and Brahmanic deities as well as the Buddha and was famous for his religious syncretism, convened the Fourth Buddhist Council around 100 CE in Kashmir in order to redact the Sarvastivadin canon. Some of Kanishka's coins bear the earliest representations of the Buddha on a coin (around 120 CE), in Hellenistic style and with the word "Boddo" in Greek script.

Kanishka also had the original Gandhari vernacular, or Prakrit, Mahayana Buddhist texts translated into the high literary language of Sanskrit, "a turning point in the evolution of the Buddhist literary canon" (Foltz, Religions on the Silk Road)

The "Kanishka casket", dated to the first year of Kanishka's reign in 127 CE, was signed by a Greek artist named *Agesilas*, who oversaw work at Kanishka's stupas (caitya), confirming the direct involvement of Greeks with Buddhist realizations at such a late date.

The new syncretic form of Buddhism expanded fully into Eastern Asia soon after these events. The Kushan monk Lokaksema visited the Han Chinese court at Loyang in 178 CE, and worked there for ten years to make the first known translations of Mahayana texts into Chinese. The new faith later spread into Korea and Japan, and was itself at the origin of Zen.

Artistic influences

Numerous works of Greco-Buddhist art display the intermixing of Greek and Buddhist influences, around such creation centers as Gandhara. The subject matter of Gandharan art was definitely Buddhist, while most motifs were of Western Asiatic or Hellenistic origin.

The anthropomorphic representation of the Buddha

Although there is still some debate, the first anthropomorphic representations of the Buddha himself are often considered a result of the Greco-Buddhist interaction. Before this innovation, Buddhist art was "aniconic": the Buddha was only represented through his symbols (an empty throne, the Bodhi tree, the Buddha's footprints, the prayer wheel).

This reluctance towards anthropomorphic representations of the Buddha, and the sophisticated development of aniconic symbols to avoid it (even in narrative scenes where other human figures would appear), seem to be connected to one of the Buddha's sayings, reported in the Digha Nikaya, that discouraged representations of himself after the extinction of his body.

Probably not feeling bound by these restrictions, and because of "their cult of form, the Greeks were the first to attempt a sculptural representation of the Buddha". In many parts of the Ancient World, the Greeks did develop syncretic divinities, that could become a common religious focus for populations with different traditions: a well-known example is the syncretic God Sarapis, introduced by Ptolemy I in Egypt, which combined aspects of Greek and Egyptian Gods. In India as well, it was only natural for the Greeks to create a single common divinity by combining the image of a Greek God-King (The Sun-God Apollo, or possibly the deified founder of the Indo-Greek Kingdom, Demetrius), with the traditional attributes of the Buddha.

Many of the stylistic elements in the representations of the Buddha point to Greek influence: the Greco-Roman toga-like wavy robe covering both shoulders (more exactly, its lighter version, the Greek *himation*), the contrapposto stance of the upright figures, the stylicized Mediterranean curly hair and topknot (ushnisha) apparently derived from the style of the Belvedere Apollo (330 BCE), and the measured quality of the faces, all rendered with strong artistic realism. A large quantity of sculptures combining Buddhist and purely Hellenistic styles and iconography were excavated at the Gandharan site of Hadda. The 'curly hair' of Buddha is described in the famous list of 32 external characteristics of a Great Being (mahapurusa) that we find all along the Buddhist sutras. The curly hair, with the curls turning to the right is first described in the Pali canon of the Smaller Vehicle of Buddhism; we find the same description in e.g. the "Dasasahasrika Prajnaparamita".

Greek artists were most probably the authors of these early representations of the Buddha, in particular the standing statues, which display "a realistic treatment of the folds and on some even a hint of modelled volume that characterizes the best Greek work. This is Classical or Hellenistic Greek, not archaizing Greek transmitted by Persia or Bactria, nor distinctively Roman".

The Greek stylistic influence on the representation of the Buddha, through its idealistic realism, also permitted a very accessible, understandable and attractive visualization of the ultimate state of enlightenment described by Buddhism, allowing it reach a wider audience: "One of the distinguishing features of the Gandharan school of art that emerged in north-west India is that it has been clearly influenced by the naturalism of the Classical Greek style. Thus, while these images still convey the inner peace that results from putting the Buddha's doctrine into practice, they also give us an impression of people who walked and talked, etc. and slept much as we do. I feel this is very important. These figures are inspiring because they do not only depict the goal, but also the sense that people like us can achieve it if we try" (The Dalai Lama)

During the following centuries, this anthropomorphic representation of the Buddha defined the canon of Buddhist art, but progressively evolved to incorporate more Indian and Asian elements.

A Hellenized Buddhist pantheon

Several other Buddhist deities may have been influenced by Greek gods. For example, Herakles with a lion-skin (the protector deity of Demetrius I) "served as an artistic model for Vajrapani, a protector of the Buddha" (Foltz, "Religions and the Silk Road"). In Japan, this expression further translated into the wrath-filled and muscular Niô guardian gods of the Buddha, standing today at the entrance of many Buddhist temples.

According to Katsumi Tanabe, professor at Chûô University, Japan (in "Alexander the Great. East-West cultural contact from Greece to Japan"), besides Vajrapani, Greek influence also appears in several other gods of the Mahayana pantheon, such as the Japanese Wind God Fujin inspired from the Greek Boreas through the Greco-Buddhist Wardo, or the mother deity Hariti inspired by Tyche.

In addition, forms such as garland-bearing cherubs, vine scrolls, and such semi-human creatures as the centaur and triton, are part of the repertory of Hellenistic art introduced by Greco-Roman artists in the service of the Kushan court.

Greco-Buddhism and the rise of the Mahayana

The geographical, cultural and historical context of the rise of Mahayana Buddhism during the 1st century BCE in northwestern India, all point to intense multi-cultural influences: "Key formative influences on the early development of the Mahayana and Pure Land movements, which became so much part of East Asian civilization, are to be sought in Buddhism's earlier encounters along the Silk Road" (Foltz, Religions on the Silk Road). As Mahayana Buddhism emerged, it received "influences from popular Hindu devotional cults (bhakti), Persian and Greco-Roman theologies which filtered into India from the northwest" (Tom Lowenstein, p63).

Conceptual influences

Mahayana is an inclusive faith characterized by the adoption of new texts, in addition to the traditional Pali canon, and a shift in the understanding of Buddhism. It goes beyond the traditional Theravada ideal of the release from suffering (dukkha) and personal enlightenment of the arhats, to elevate the Buddha to a God-like status, and to create a pantheon of quasi-divine Bodhisattvas devoting themselves to personal excellence, ultimate knowledge and the salvation of humanity. These concepts, together with the sophisticated philosophical system of the Mahayana faith, may have been influenced by the interaction of Greek and Buddhist thought:

The Buddha as an idealized man-go

The Buddha was elevated to a man-god status, represented in idealized human form: "One might regard the classical influence as including the general idea of representing a man-god in this purely human form, which was of course well familiar in the West, and it is very likely that the example of westerners' treatment of their gods was indeed an important factor in the innovation... The Buddha, the man-god, is in many ways far more like a Greek god than any other eastern deity, no less for the narrative cycle of his story and appearance of his standing figure than for his humanity".

The supra-mundane understanding of the Buddha and Bodhisattvas may have been a consequence of the Greek's tendency to deify their rulers in the wake of Alexander's reign: "The god-king concept brought by Alexander (...) may have fed into the developing bodhisattva concept, which involved the portrayal of the Buddha in Gandharan art with the face of the sun god, Apollo" (McEvilley, "The Shape of Ancient Thought").

The Bodhisattva as a Universal ideal of excellence

Lamotte (1954) controversially suggests (though countered by Conze (1973) and others) that Greek influence was present in the definition of the Bodhisattva ideal in the oldest Mahayana text, the "Perfection of Wisdom" or *prajñâ pâramitâ* literature, that developed between the 1st century BCE and the 1st century CE. These texts in particular redefine Buddhism around the universal Bodhisattva ideal, and its six central virtues of generosity, morality, patience, effort, meditation and, first and foremost, wisdom.

Philosophical influences

The close association between Greeks and Buddhism probably led to exchanges on the philosophical plane as well. Many of the early Mahayana theories of reality and knowledge can be related to Greek philosophical schools of thought. Mahayana Buddhism has been described as the "form of Buddhism which (regardless of how Hinduized its later forms became) seems to have originated in the Greco-Buddhist communities of India, through a conflation of the Greek Democritean-Sophistic-Skeptical tradition with the rudimentary and unformalized empirical and skeptical elements already present in early Buddhism" (McEvilly, "The Shape of Ancient Thought", p503).

- In the Prajnaparamita, the rejection of the reality of passing phenomena as "empty, false and fleeting" can also be found in Greek Pyrrhonism.
- The perception of ultimate reality was, for the Cynics as well as for the Madyamikas and Zen teachers after them, only accessible through a non-conceptual and non-verbal approach (Greek Phronesis), which alone allowed to get rid of ordinary conceptions.
- The mental attitude of equanimity and dispassionate outlook in front of events was also characteristic of the Cynics and Stoics, who called it "Apatheia"
- Nagarjuna's dialectic developed in the Madhyamika can be paralleled to the Greek dialectical tradition.

Cynicism, Madhyamika and Zen

Numerous parallels exist between the Greek philosophy of the Cynics and, several centuries later, the Buddhist philosophy of the Madhyamika and Zen. The Cynics denied the relevancy of human conventions and opinions (described as *typhos*, literally "smoke" or "mist", a metaphor for "illusion" or "error"), including verbal expressions, in favor of the raw experience of reality. They stressed the independence from externals to achieve happiness ("Happiness is not pleasure, for which we need external, but virtue, which is complete without external" 3rd epistole of Crates). Similarly the Prajnaparamita, precursor of the Madhyamika, explained that all things are like foam, or bubbles, "empty, false, and fleeting", and that "only the negation of all views can lead to enlightenment" (Nâgârjuna, MK XIII.8). In order to evade the world of illusion, the Cynics recommended the discipline and struggle ("askçsis kai machç") of philosophy, the practice of "autarkia" (self-rule), and a lifestyle exemplified by Diogenes, which, like Buddhist monks, renounced earthly possessions. These conceptions, in combination with the idea of "philanthropia" (universal loving kindness, of which Crates, the student of Diogenes, was the best proponent), are strikingly reminiscent of Buddhist Prajna (wisdom) and Karuna (compassion).

Greco-Persian cosmological influences

A popular figure in Greco-Buddhist art, the future Buddha Maitreya, has sometimes been linked to the Iranian yazata (Zoroastrian divinity) Mièra who was also adopted as a figure in a Greco-Roman syncretistic cult under the name of Mithras. Maitreya is the fifth Buddha of the present world-age, who will appear at some undefined future epoch. According to Foltz, he "echoes the qualities of the Zoroastrian Saoshyant and the Christian Messiah". However, in character and function, Maitreya does not much resemble either Mitra, Mièra or Mithras; his name is more obviously derived from the Sanskrit *maitrî* "kindliness", equivalent to Pali *mettâ*; the Pali (and probably older) form of his name, Metteyya, does not closely resemble the name Mièra.

The Buddha Amitâbha (literally meaning "infinite radiance") with his paradisiacal "Pure Land" in the West, according to Foltz, "seems to be understood as the Iranian god of light, equated with the sun". This view is however not in accordance with the view taken of Amitâbha by present-day Pure Land Buddhists, in which Amitâbha is neither "equated with the sun" nor, strictly speaking, a god.

Gandharan proselytism

Buddhist monks from the region of Gandhara, where Greco-Buddhism was most influential, played a key role in the development and the transmission of Buddhist ideas in the direction of northern Asia.

- Kushan monks, such as Lokaksema (c. 178 CE), travelled to the Chinese capital of Loyang, where they became the first translators of Mahayana Buddhist scriptures into Chinese. Central Asian and East Asian Buddhist monks appear to have maintained strong exchanges until around the 10th century, as indicated by frescos from the Tarim Basin.
- Two half-brothers from Gandhara, Asanga and Vasubandhu (4th century), created the Yogacara or "Mind-only" school of Mahayana Buddhism, which through one of its major texts, the Lankavatara Sutra, became a founding block of Mahayana, and particularly Zen, philosophy.
- In 485 CE, according to the Chinese historic treatise Liang Shu, five monks from Gandhara travelled to the country of Fusang ("The country of the extreme East" beyond the sea, probably eastern Japan, although some historians suggest the American Continent), where they introduced Buddhism:

"Fusang is located to the east of China, 20,000 *li* (1,500 kilometers) east of the state of *Da Han* (itself east of the state of *Wa* in modern Kyûshû, Japan). In former times, the people of Fusang knew nothing of the Buddhist religion, but in the second year of Da Ming of the Song dynasty (485 CE), five monks from Kipin (Kabul region of Gandhara) travelled by ship to Fusang. They propagated Buddhist doctrine, circulated scriptures and drawings, and advised the people to relinquish worldly attachments. As a results the customs of Fusang changed"

Bodhidharma, the founder of Zen, is described as a Central Asian Buddhist monk in the first Chinese references to him (Yan Xuan-Zhi, 547 CE), although later Chinese traditions describe him as coming from South India.

Intellectual influences in Asia

Through art and religion, the influence of Greco-Buddhism on the cultural make-up of East Asian countries, especially China, Korea and Japan, may have extended further into the intellectual area. At the same time as Greco-Buddhist art and Mahayana schools of thought such as Dhyana were transmitted to East Asia, central concepts of Hellenic culture such as virtue, excellence or quality may have been adopted by the cultures of Korea and Japan after a long diffusion among the Hellenized cities of Central Asia, to become a key part of their warrior and work ethics.

Greco-Buddhism and the West

In the direction of the West, the Greco-Buddhist syncretism may also have had some formative influence on the religions of the Mediterranean Basin.

Exchanges

Intense westward physical exchange at that time along the Silk Road is confirmed by the Roman craze for silk from the 1st century BCE to the point that the Senate issued, in vain, several edicts to prohibit the wearing of silk, on economic and moral grounds. This is attested by at least three significant authors:

- Strabo (64/ 63 BCE–c. 24 CE).
- Seneca the Younger (c. 3 BCE–65 CE).
- Pliny the Elder (23–79 CE).

The aforementioned Strabo and Plutarch (c. 45–125 CE) wrote about king Menander, confirming that information was circulating throughout the Hellenistic world.

Buddhism and Christianity

Although the philosophical systems of Buddhism and Christianity have evolved in rather different ways, the moral precepts advocated by Buddhism from the time of Ashoka through his edicts do have some similarities with the Christian moral precepts developed more than two centuries later: respect for life, respect for the weak, rejection of violence, pardon to sinners, tolerance.

One theory is that these similarities may indicate the propagation of Buddhist ideals into the Western World, with the Greeks acting as intermediaries and religious syncretists.

> "Scholars have often considered the possibility that Buddhism influenced the early development of Christianity. They have drawn attention to many parallels concerning the births, lives, doctrines, and deaths of the Buddha and Jesus" (Bentley, "Old World Encounters").

The story of the birth of the Buddha was well known in the West, and possibly influenced the story of the birth of Jesus: Saint Jerome (4th century CE) mentions the birth of the Buddha, who he says "was born from the side of a virgin". Also a fragment of Archelaos of Carrha (278 CE) mentions the Buddha's virgin-birth.

Early 3rd-4th century Christian writers such as Hippolytus and Epiphanius write about a Scythianus, who visited India around 50 AD from where he brought "the doctrine of the Two Principles". According to these writers, Scythianus' pupil Terebinthus presented himself as a "Buddha" ("he called himself Buddas" Cyril of Jerusalem). Terebinthus went to Palestine and Judaea where he met the Apostles ("becoming known and condemned" Isaia), and ultimately settled in Babylon, where he transmitted his teachings to Mani, thereby creating the foundation of what could be called Persian syncretic Buddhism, Manicheism. One of the greatest thinkers and saints of western Christianity, Augustine of Hippo was originally a Manichean.

In the 2nd century CE, the Christian dogmatist Clement of Alexandria recognized Bactrian Buddhists (Sramanas) and Indian Gymnosophists for their influence on Greek thought:

> *"Thus philosophy, a thing of the highest utility, flourished in antiquity among the barbarians, shedding its light over the nations. And afterwards it came to Greece. First in its ranks were the prophets of the Egyptians; and the Chaldeans among the Assyrians; and the Druids among the Gauls; and the Sramanas among the Bactrians and the philosophers of the Celts; and the Magi of the Persians, who foretold the Saviour's birth, and came into the land of Judaea guided by a star. The Indian gymnosophists are also in the number, and the other barbarian philosophers. And of these there are two classes, some of them called Sramanas and others Brahmins."* (Clement of Alexandria "The Stromata, or Miscellanies").

The main Greek cities of the Middle-East happen to have played a key role in the development of Christianity, such as Antioch and especially Alexandria, and "it was later in this very place that some of the most active centers of Christianity were established" (Robert Linssen, "Zen living").

BUDDHISM AND THE ROMAN WORLD

Several instances of interaction between Buddhism and the Roman world are documented by Classical and early Christian writers.

Pandion embassy

Roman historical accounts describe an embassy sent by the "Indian king Pandion (Pandya), also named Porus," to Caesar Augustus around 13 CE. The embassy was travelling with a diplomatic letter in Greek, and one of its members was a sramana who burned himself alive in Athens to demonstrate his faith. The event made a sensation and was described by Nicolaus of Damascus, who met the embassy at Antioch, and related by Strabo and Dio Cassius. A tomb was made to the sramana, still visible in the time of Plutarch.

These accounts at least indicate that Indian religious men (Sramanas, to which the

Buddhists belonged, as opposed to Hindu Brahmanas) were circulating in the Levant during the time of Jesus.

Western knowledge of Buddhism

Some knowledge of Buddhism existed quite early in the West. In the 2nd century CE, Clement of Alexandria, the father of Christian dogmatism, wrote about the Buddha:

"Among the Indians are those philosophers also who follow the precepts of Boutta, whom they honour as a god on account of his extraordinary sanctity." — *Clement of Alexandria, Stromata (Miscellanies)*

He also recognized Bactrian Buddhists (Sramanas) and Indian Gymnosophists for their influence on Greek thought:

"Thus philosophy, a thing of the highest utility, flourished in antiquity among the barbarians, shedding its light over the nations. And afterwards it came to Greece. First in its ranks were the prophets of the Egyptians; and the Chaldeans among the Assyrians; and the Druids among the Gauls; and the Sramanas among the Bactrians; and the philosophers of the Celts; and the Magi of the Persians, who foretold the Saviour's birth, and came into the land of Judaea guided by a star. The Indian gymnosophists are also in the number, and the other barbarian philosophers. And of these there are two classes, some of them called Sramanas, and others Brahmins." — *Clement of Alexandria, Stromata (Miscellanies)*

The story of the birth of the Buddha was also known: a fragment of Archelaos of Carrha (278 CE) mentions the Buddha's virgin-birth, and Saint Jerome (4th century CE) mentions the birth of the Buddha, who he says "was born from the side of a virgin". Queen Maya came to bear the Buddha after receiving a prophetic dream in which she foresaw the descent of the Bodhisattva (Buddha-to-be) from the Tucita heaven into her womb. This story has some parallels with the story of Jesus being conceived in connection with the visitation of the Holy Spirit to the Virgin Mary.

Buddhism and Gnosticism

Early 3rd century–4th century Christian writers such as Hippolytus and Epiphanius write about a Scythianus, who visited India around 50 CE from where he brought "the doctrine of the Two Principles". According to Cyril of Jerusalem, Scythianus' pupil Terebinthus presented himself as a "Buddha" ("He called himself Buddas"). Terebinthus went to Palestine and Judaea ("becoming known and condemned"), and ultimately settled in Babylon, where he transmitted his teachings to Mani, thereby creating the foundation of Manichaeism:

"But Terebinthus, his disciple in this wicked error, inherited his money and books and heresy, and came to Palestine, and becoming known and condemned in Judæa he resolved to pass into Persia: but lest he should be recognised there also by his name he changed it and called himself Buddas."

In the 3rd century, the Syrian writer and Christian Gnostic theologian Bar Daisan described his exchanges with the religious missions of holy men from India (Greek: Σαρμαναίοι, Sramanas), passing through Syria on their way to Elagabalus or another Severan dynasty Roman Emperor. His accounts were quoted by Porphyry and Stobaeus.

Finally, from the 3rd century to the 12th century, some Gnostic religions such as Manichaeism, which combined Christian, Hebrew and Buddhist influences (Mani, the founder of the religion, resided for some time in Kushan lands), spread throughout the Old World, to Gaul and Great Britain in the West, and to China in the East. Some leading Christian theologians such as Augustine of Hippo were Manichaeans before converting to orthodox Christianity.

Such exchanges, many more of which may have gone unrecorded, suggest that Buddhism may have had some influence on early Christianity: "Scholars have often considered the possibility that Buddhism influenced the early development of Christianity. They have drawn attention to many parallels concerning the births, lives, doctrines, and deaths of the Buddha and Jesus" (Bentley, "Old World Encounters")

MEDIEVAL CONTACTS

An account of Buddha's life was translated in to Greek, and widely circulated to Christians as the story of Barlaam and Josaphat. By the 1300s this story of Josaphat had become so popular that he was venerated as a saint.

The next direct encounter between Europeans and Buddhism happened in Medieval times when the Franciscan friar William of Rubruck was sent on an embassy to the Mongol court of Mongke by the French king Saint Louis in 1253. The contact happened in Cailac (today's Qayaliq in Kazakhstan), and William originally thought they were wayward Christians (Foltz, "Religions of the Silk Road").

Buddhism and Western Intellectuals

In the latter half of the 19th century, Buddhism (along with many other religions and philosophies) came to the attention of Western intellectuals. These included the pessimistic German philosopher Schopenhauer, who encountered Buddhism, and Eastern thought in general, after having devised a philosophical system of considerable compatibility. The American philosopher Henry David Thoreau translated a Buddhist sutra from French into English.

There are frequent comparisons between Buddhism and the German philosopher Friedrich Nietzsche, who praised Buddhism in his 1895 work *The Anti-Christ*, calling it "a hundred times more realistic than Christianity". Theologist David Loy argues that there is "a deep resonance between them" as "both emphasise the centrality of humans in a godless cosmos and neither looks to any external being or power for their respective solutions to the problem of existence".

The first English translation of the *Tibetan Book of the Dead* was published in 1927 and the reprint of 1935 carried a commentary from none other than C.G. Jung. The book is said to have attracted many westerners to Tibetan Buddhism. Jung also provided the forward for the 1935 publication of D.T. Suzuki's Introduction to Zen Buddhism.

Western spiritual seekers were attracted to what they saw as the exotic and mystical tone of the Asian traditions, and created esoteric societies such as the Theosophical Society of H.P. Blavatsky. The Buddhist Society, London was founded by Theosophist Christmas Humphreys in 1924. At first Western Buddhology was hampered by poor translations (often translations of translations), but soon Western scholars such as Max Müller began to learn Asian languages and translate Asian texts. During the 20th century the German writer Hermann Hesse showed great interest in Eastern religions, writing a book entitled *Siddhartha*. It must also be noted that there are significant differences between the finer points of Theosophical and Buddhist Philosophy, in particular regarding the common doctorine of reincarnation, which on the surface might at first be overlooked by the interested westener.

American beat generation poet Jack Kerouac became a well-known literary Buddhist, for his roman-a-clef *The Dharma Bums* and other works. Also influential was Alan Watts, who wrote several books on Zen and Buddhism. The cultural re-evaluations of the hippie generation in the late 1960s and early 1970s led to a re-discovery of Buddhism, which seemed to promise a more methodical path to happiness than Christianity and a way out of the perceived spiritual bankruptcy and complexity of Western life.

Buddhists Arrive in the West

The first Buddhists to arrive in the United States were Chinese. Hired as cheap labor for the railroads and other expanding industries, they established temples in their settlements along the rail lines. At about the same time, immigrants from Japan began tc arrive as laborers on Hawaiian plantations and central-California farms. In 1899, they established the Buddhist Missions of North America, later renamed the Buddhist Churches of America.

In 1959, Suzuki Roshi (a Japanese teacher) arrived in San Francisco. At the time of Suzuki's arrival, Zen had become a hot topic amongst some groups in the United States, especially beatniks. Suzuki Roshi's classes were filled with those wanting to learn more about Buddhism, and the presence of a Zen master inspired the students.

In 1965 Philip Kapleau traveled to Rochester, NY with the permission of his teacher, Haku'un Yasutani to form the Rochester Zen Center. At this time there were few if any American citizens that had trained in Japan with ordained Buddhist teachers. Kapleau had spent 13 years (1952-1965) and over 20 sesshin before being allowed to come back and open his own center. During his time in Japan after World War II, Kapleau wrote his seminal work; The Three Pillars of Zen.

In 1965, monks from Sri Lanka established the Washington Buddhist Vihara in Washington, D.C., the first Theravada monastic community in the United States. The Vihara was quite accessible to English-speakers, and Vipassana meditation was part of it activities. However, the direct influence of the Vipassana movement would not reach the U.S. until a group of Americans returned there in the early 1970s after studying with Vipassana masters in Asia.

In the 1970s, interest in Tibetan Buddhism grew dramatically. This was fuelled in part by the 'shangri-la' view of this country and also because Western media agencies are largely sympathetic with the 'Tibetan Cause'. All four of the main Tibetan Buddhist schools became well known.

Tibetan lamas such as the Karmapa (Rangjung Rigpe Dorje), Chögyam Trungpa Rinpoche, Geshe Wangyal, Geshe Lhundub Sopa, Dezhung Rinpoche, Sermey Khensur Lobsang Tharchin, Tarthang Tulku, Lama Yeshe and Thubten Zopa Rinpoche all established teaching centers in the West from the 1970s.

Perhaps the most widely visible Buddhist teacher in the west is the much-travelled Tenzin Gyatso, the current Dalai Lama, who first visited the United States in 1979. As the exiled political leader of Tibet, he is now a popular cause célèbre in the west. His early life was depicted in glowing terms in Hollywood films such as *Kundun* and *Seven Years in Tibet*. He has attracted celebrity religious followers such as Richard Gere and Adam Yauch.

In addition to this a number of Americans who had served in the Korean or Vietnam Wars stayed out in Asia for a period, seeking to understand both the horror they had witnessed and its context. A few of these were eventually ordained as monks in the Theravadan tradition, and upon returning home became influential meditation teachers establishing such centres as the Insight Meditation Society in America. Another contributing factor in the flowering of Buddhist thought in the West was the popularity of Zen amongst the counter-culture poets and activists of the 60's, due to the writings of Alan Watts, D.T. Suzuki and Philip Kapleau.

Historically, Buddhism has absorbed elements of the culture of the countries in which it is practiced. This can be seen in the artistic style of Buddha statues; a Chinese statue looks different to a Thai, which differs from a Sri Lankan, and similarly across most Asian countries. Different local customs are included also, and may influence the form of rituals and ceremonies.

There is a general distinction between Buddhism brought to the West by Asian immigrants, which may be Mahayana or a traditional East Asian mix, and Buddhism as practiced by converts, which is often Zen, Pure Land, Indian Vipassana or Tibetan Buddhism. Some Western Buddhists are actually non-denominational and accept teachings from a variety of different sects, which is far less frequent in Asia.

The largest Buddhist temple in the Southern Hemisphere is Nan Tien Ssu (translated as "Southern Paradise Temple"), situated at Wollongong, Australia. It is operated by the Fo Guang Shan Order, founded in Taiwan, and around 2003 the Grand Master, Venerable Hsing Yun, asked for that temple and Buddhist practice there to be operated by Australians within about thirty years.

Western Buddhism Today

Today, Buddhism is practiced by large numbers of people in the Americas, Europe and Oceania. Buddhism has become a growing religion in Australia and some other Western nations.

For the most part, Western Buddhism is identical to Buddhism in East Asia, borrowing Asian practices such as the sangha and meditation (although most Asian Buddhist rituals are not borrowed). Western Buddhism, however, also has its roots in the Western concepts of freethought and secular humanism.

The Foundation for the Preservation of the Mahayana Tradition (FPMT) is a network of Buddhist centers focusing on traditional Tibetan Buddhism. Founded in 1975 by Lamas Thubten Yeshe and Thubten Zopa Rinpoche, who began teaching Buddhism to Western students in Nepal, the FPMT has grown to encompass more than 142 teaching centers in 32 countries.

A feature of Buddhism in the West today is the emergence of other groups which, even though they draw on traditional Buddhism, are in fact an attempt at creating a new style of Buddhist practice. Controversial lama Chögyam Trungpa, the founder of the Shambhala meditation movement, claimed in his teachings that his intention was to strip the ethnic baggage away from traditional methods of working with the mind and to deliver the essence of those teachings to his western students. Chögyam Trungpa also founded Naropa University in Boulder, Colorado in 1974.

Another example of a school evolving new idioms for the transmission of the dharma is the Friends of the Western Buddhist Order (FWBO), founded by Sangharakshita in 1967.

Commercialization of Buddhism

Buddhist practitioners in the West are catered for by a minor industry that has grown up around them, providing such items as charm boxes, meditation cushions, and ritual implements. Shakya has criticized this industry as the publication of Buddhist books has uprooted small forests and consequently killed thousands of insects. And many Hollywood movies such as *Kundun, Little Buddha* and *Seven Years in Tibet* have had considerable commercial success.

BUDDHISM IN THE UNITED STATES OF AMERICA

Buddhism is a religion with millions of followers in the United States, including traditionally Buddhist Asian Americans as well as non-Asians, many of whom are converts.

The U.S. presents a strikingly new and different environment for Buddhists, leading to a unique history and a continuing process of development as Buddhism and America come to grips with each other.

BUDDHISM AND THE WEST

Occasional intersections between Western civilization and the Buddhist world have been occurring for thousands of years. Perhaps the most significant of these began in 334 BC, early in the history of Buddhism, when the Macedonian king Alexander the Great conquered most of Central Asia. The Seleucids and successive kingdoms established an important Hellenistic influence in the area, which interacted with the Buddhism that had been introduced from India to produce Greco-Buddhism.

In the Christian era, Buddhist ideas would periodically filter into Europe via the Middle East. A notable example is the story of Barlaam and Josaphat, folk heroes who were canonized by the Roman Catholic Church and whose story is believed to be an altered account of the life of Siddhartha Gautama, translated from Persian to Arabic to Greek. The first direct encounter between European Christians and Buddhists to be recorded was in 1253 when the king of France sent William of Rubruck as an ambassador to the court of the Mongol Empire. Later, in the 17th century, a group of Mongols practicing Tibetan Buddhism established Kalmykia, the only Buddhist nation in Europe, at the eastern edge of the continent.

BUDDHISM IN THE NEW WORLD

The above examples produced very little real religious interaction, the European settlers who come to colonize the America had virtually no exposure to Buddhism. This almost complete isolation last largely undisturbed until the 19th century, when significant numbers of immigrants from East Asia began to arrive in the New World. In the United States, the first immigrants from China entered around 1820, but they began to arrive in large numbers following the California Gold Rush of 1849. The first Buddhist temple in America was built in 1853 in San Francisco by the Sze Yap Company, a Chinese American fraternal society. Another society, the Ning Yeong Company, built a second in 1854; by 1875, there were eight such temples, and by 1900 there were approximately 400 Chinese temples on the west coast of the United States, most of them containing at least some Buddhist elements. These temples were often the subject of suspicion and ignorance by the rest of the population, and were dismissively referred to as *joss houses*.

The Chinese Exclusion Act of 1882 curtailed the growth of the Chinese American population, but large-scale immigration from Japan began in the late 1880s and from Korea around 1903. In both cases, immigration was at first limited primarily to Hawaii. Populations from other Asian Buddhist countries followed, and in each case, the new communities established Buddhist temples and organizations. For instance, the first Japanese temple in Hawaii was built in 1896 near Paauhau by the Honpa Hongwanji branch of Jodo Shinshu. In 1898, Japanese missionaries and immigrants established a Young Men's Buddhist Association, and the Rev. Sôryû Kagahi was dispatched from Japan to be the first Buddhist missionary in Hawaii. The first Japanese Buddhist temple in the continental U.S. was built in San Francisco in 1899, and the first in Canada was built at the Ishikawa Hotel in Vancouver in 1905. The first Buddhist clergy to take up residence in the continental U.S. were Shuye Sonoda and Kakuryo Nishimjima, missionaries from Japan who arrived in 1899.

At about the same time that Asian immigrants were first starting to arrive in America, some American intellectuals were beginning to come to terms with Buddhism, based primarily on information reaching them from British colonial possessions in India and East Asia. The Englishmen William Jones and Charles Wilkins had done pioneering work translating Sanskrit texts into English. The American Transcendentalists and associated persons, in particular Henry David Thoreau took an interest in Hindu and Buddhist philosophy. In 1844, *The Dial*, a small literary publication edited by Thoreau and Ralph Waldo Emerson, published the first English version of a portion of the Lotus Sutra; it had been translated by Elizabeth Palmer Peabody from a French version recently completed by Eugène Burnouf (this translation is often attributed to Thoreau himself, but this appears to be erroneous). His Indian readings may have influenced his later experiments in simple living: at one point in *Walden* he wrote: "I realized what the Orientals meant by contemplation and the forsaking of works." The poet Walt Whitman also admitted to an influence of Indian religion on his writings.

The first prominent American to publicly convert to Buddhism was Henry Steel Olcott. Olcott, a former U.S. army colonel during the Civil War, had grown increasingly interested in reports of supernatural phenomena that were popular in the late 19th century. In 1875, he, along with Helena Blavatsky and William Quan Judge founded the Theosophical Society, which was dedicated to the study of the occult and was partly influenced by Hindu and Buddhist scriptures. The group's leaders believed or claimed to believe that they were in contact, via visions and messages, with a secret order of adepts referred to as the "Himalayan Brotherhood" or "the Masters". In 1879, Olcott and Blavatsky travelled to India and then, in 1880, to Sri Lanka, where they were met enthusiastically by local Buddhists, who saw them as allies against an aggressive Christian missionary movement. On May 25 of that year, Olcott and Blavatsky took the pancasila vows of a lay Buddhist before a monk and a large crowd of onlookers. Although most of the Theosophists appear to have counted themselves as Buddhists, they held idiosyncratic beliefs that separated them from all known Buddhist traditions; only Olcott was enthusiastic about following mainstream Buddhism. He would return to Sri Lanka on two further occasions, where he worked to promote Buddhist education, and also visited Japan and Burma. Olcott authored a *Buddhist Catechism*, stating his view of the basic tenets of the religion.

A series of new publications greatly increased public knowledge of Buddhism in 19th century America. In 1879, Edwin Arnold, an English aristocrat, published *The Light of Asia,* an epic poem he had written about the life and teachings of the Buddha, expounded with much wealth of local color and not a little felicity of versification. The book became immensely popular in the United States, going through eighty editions and selling more than 500,000 copies. Dr. Paul Carus, a German American philosopher and theologian, was at work on a more scholarly prose treatment of the same subject. Carus was the director of Open Court Publishing Company, an academic publishing house specializing in philosophy, science, and religion, and editor of *The Monist*, a journal with a similar focus, both based in La Salle, Illinois. In 1894, Carus published *The Gospel of the Buddha,* which was compiled from a variety of Asian texts and, true to its name, presented the Buddha's story in a form resembling the Christian Gospels.

Perhaps the most significant event in the 19th century history of Buddhism in America was the Parliament of the World's Religions, held in Chicago in 1893. Although most of the delegates to the Parliament were Christians of various denominations, the Buddhist nations of China, Japan, Thailand, and Sri Lanka sent representatives. Buddhist delegates included Soyen Shaku, a Japanese Zen abbott; Zenshiro Noguchi, a Japanese translator; Anagarika Dharmapala, a Sri Lankan associate of H. S. Olcott's; and Chandradat Chudhadharn, a brother of King Chulalongkorn of Thailand. Paul Carus also attended as an observer. The Parliament provided the first major public forum from which Buddhists could address themselves directly to the Western public; Dharmapala was particularly effective in this role because he spoke fluent English.

A few days after the end of the Parliament, in a brief ceremony conducted by Anagarika Dharmapala, Charles T. Strauss, a New York businessman of Jewish descent, became, it is believed, the first person to formally convert to Buddhism on American soil. A few fledgling attempts at establishing a Buddhism for Americans followed. One of the most interesting, in fact, had initially appeared prior to the Parliament, met with little fanfare, in 1887: *The Buddhist Ray*, a Santa Cruz, California-based magazine published and edited by Phillangi Dasa, born Herman Carl (or Carl Herman) Veetering (or Vettering), a recluse about whom little is known. The *Ray*'s tone was, in the words of Rick Fields, "ironic, light, saucy, self-assured ... one-hundred-percent American Buddhist" (Fields, 1981), which was by all means a novel development in that time and place. It ceased publication in 1894. Elsewhere, six white San Franciscans, working with Japanese Jodo Shinshu missionaries, established the Dharma Sangha of Buddha in 1900 and began publishing a bimonthly magazine, *The Light of Dharma.* In Illinois, Paul Carus wrote further books about Buddhism and attempted setting portions of Buddhist scripture to Western classical music.

THE EARLY 20TH CENTURY

In the first half of the 20th century, it would prove to be Buddhist teachers from Japan who played the most active role in disseminating Buddhism to the American public, perhaps because Japan was the most developed and self-confident Buddhist country at the time. In 1905, Soyen Shaku was invited to stay in the United States by a

Mr. and Mrs. Russell, a wealthy American couple. He lived for nine months in their home near San Francisco, where he established a small zendo in their home and gave regular zazen lessons, making him the first Zen Buddhist priest to teach in North America. This short sojourn eventually produced an effect on American Buddhism that continues to the present. Shortly after Shaku settled in to his erstwhile home, he was followed by Nyogen Senzaki, a young monk from Shaku's home temple in Japan. Senzaki briefly worked for the Russell family and then, expressing his desire to stay in America, he was reportedly advised by Shaku to spend seventeen years as an ordinary worker before teaching Buddhism. Thus, it was in 1922 that Senzaki first rented a hall and gave an English talk on a paper by Soyen Shaku; his periodic talks at different locations became known as the "floating zendo". In 1931, he established a permanent sitting hall in Los Angeles, where he would teach until his death in 1958.

Another Zen teacher, Sokatsu Shaku, one of Soyen Shaku's senior students, arrived in late 1906. Although he stayed only a few years and had limited contact with the English-speaking public, one of his disciples, Shigetsu Sasaki, made a permanent home. Sasaki, better known under his monastic name Sokei-an, spent a few years wandering the west coast of the United States, at one point living among American Indians near Seattle, and reached New York City in 1916. After completing his training and being ordained in 1928, he returned to New York to teach. In 1931, his small group incorporated as the Buddhist Society of America, later renamed the First Zen Institute of America. By the late 1930s, one of his most active supporters was Ruth Fuller Everett, a British socialite and the mother-in-law of Alan Watts. Shortly before Sokei-an's death in 1945, he and Everett would wed, at which point she took the name Ruth Fuller Sasaki.

In 1914, under the leadership of Koyu Uchida, who succeeded Shuye Sonoda as the head of Jodo Shinshu missionary effort in North America, several Japanese Buddhist congregations formed the Buddhist Mission of North America (BMNA). This organization would later form the basis of the Buddhist Churches of America, currently the largest and most influential ethnic-based Buddhist organization in the U.S. The BMNA focused primarily on social and cultural activities for and ministering to Japanese American communities. In the late 1920s, it first began to develop programs to train English-speaking priests, for the benefit of the growing number of American-born parishioners. Also, in 1927, the Soto sect of Japanese Zen opened its own mission with Zenshuji temple in Los Angeles, although it did not make attempts at the time to attract non-Japanese members.

One American who made his own attempt to establish an American Buddhist movement was Dwight Goddard (1861 – 1939). Goddard had been a Christian missionary to China, when he first came in contact with Buddhism. In 1928, he spent a year living at a Zen monastery in Japan. In 1934, he founded "The Followers of Buddha, an American Brotherhood", with the goal of applying the traditional monastic structure of Buddhism more strictly than Senzaki and Sokei-an. The group was largely unsuccessful: no Americans were recruited to join as monks and attempts failed to attract a Chinese Chan

(Zen) master to come to the United States. However, Goddard's efforts as an author and publisher bore considerable fruit. In 1930, he began publishing *ZEN: A Buddhist Magazine*. In 1932, he collaborated with D. T. Suzuki, on a translation of the Lankavatara Sutra. That same year, he published the first edition of *A Buddhist Bible*, an anthology of Buddhist scriptures focusing on those used in Chinese and Japanese Zen, which was enormously influential.

However, another Japanese person, also an associate of Soyen Shaku's, had an even greater literary impact. This was D. T. Suzuki. At the World Parliament of Religions in 1893, Paul Carus befriended Soyen Shaku and requested his help in translating and preparing Oriental spiritual literature for publication in the West. Shaku instead recommended Suzuki, then a young scholar and former disciple of his. Starting in 1897, Suzuki worked from Dr. Carus's home in Illinois; his first projects were translations of the *Tao Te Ching* and Asvaghosa's *Awakening of Faith in the Mahayana*. At the same time, Suzuki began writing his first major book, *Outlines of Mahayana Buddhism*, which was published in 1907. Suzuki returned to Japan in 1909 and married an American Theosophist and Radcliffe graduate in 1911. Through English language essays and books, such as *Essays in Zen Buddhism* (1927), he established himself as the most visible literary expositor of Zen Buddhism, its unofficial goodwill ambassador to Western readers, until his death in 1966. His 1949 book, *An Introduction to Zen Buddhism*, featured a 30-page introduction by Carl Jung, an emblem of the deepening relationship between Buddhism and major Western thinkers.

MODERN AMERICAN BUDDHISM

Some scholars, such as Charles Prebish, have suggested that the social phenomenon of Buddhism in America can be seen to be comprised of three broad types. The oldest and largest of these is "immigrant" or "ethnic Buddhism", those Buddhist traditions that arrived in America along with immigrants who were already believers and that largely remained with those immigrants and their descendants. The next oldest and arguably the most visible and best-heralded type is referred to as "import Buddhism", because it came to America largely in response to the demand of interested American converts who sought it out, either by going abroad or by supporting foreign teachers; this is sometimes also called "elite Buddhism" because its practitioners, especially early in the process, tended to come from social elites. The newest trend in Buddhism is "export" or "evangelical Buddhism", groups which are based in another country and who are actively recruiting members in America from various backgrounds; by far the most successful of these has been Soka Gakkai.

IMMIGRANT BUDDHISTS

Immigrant Buddhist congregations in North America come in an extremely wide variety, exactly as wide a variety as exists in the different peoples of Asian Buddhist extraction who have settled there. The New World is home to Chinese Buddhists, Japanese

Buddhists, Korean Buddhists, Sri Lankan Buddhists, Vietnamese Buddhists, Thai Buddhists, and Buddhists with family backgrounds in nearly every Buddhist country and region in the world. The passage of the 1965 Immigration Act in the United States greatly increased the number of immigrants arriving from China, Vietnam, and the Theravada-practicing countries of southeast Asia.

It is common for Buddhist temples and societies to serve as foci for the social life of an immigrant community, helping to maintain a connection to Old World traditions in a foreign environment. However, as the passing of time produces congregations increasingly dominated by persons born in America, which is especially common among Japanese Buddhists, questions arise about how their religious customs should adapt.

JAPANESE BUDDHISM

The largest and most influential national immigrant Buddhist organization in the United States is the Buddhist Churches of America and the Honpa Hongwanji Mission of Hawaii. The BCA is an affiliate of Japan's Nishi Hongwanji, a sect of Jôdo Shinshû, which is in turn a form of Pure Land Buddhism. Tracing its roots to the Young Men's Buddhist Association founded in San Francisco at the end of the 19th century and the Buddhist Mission of North America founded in 1914, it took its current form in 1944. All of the Buddhist Mission's leadership, along with almost the entire Japanese American population, had been interned during World War II.

The name Buddhist Churches of America was adopted at Topaz War Relocation Center in Utah; the use of the word "church", which normally implies a Christian house of worship, was significant. After internment ended, some members returned to the West Coast and revitalized churches there, while a number of others moved to the Midwest and built new churches. During the 1960s and 1970s, the BCA was in a growth phase and was very successful at fund-raising. It also began to publish two periodicals, one in Japanese and one in English. However, since 1980, BCA membership has declined markedly. The Honpa Hongwanji Mission of Hawaii has 36 temples throughout the state of Hawaii. The history and organization of the Mission is quite similar to the BCA.

It is interesting to note that, while a very large majority of the Buddhist Churches of America's membership are ethnically Japanese, it does have some members from non-Asian backgrounds. Thus, it can be seen as having some, currently very limited, aspects of an export Buddhist institution. As declining involvement by its ethnic community creates questions about its future, there has been internal discussion as to whether it should devote more attention to attracting the broader public.

TAIWANESE BUDDHISM

Another institution with some appeal both to a specific ethnic group as well as to Americans generally is Hsi Lai Temple in Hacienda Heights, California. Hsi Lai is the American headquarters of Fo Guang Shan, an enormously successful modern Buddhist group in Taiwan. Hsi Lai was built in 1988 at a cost of $10 million and is often described as the largest Buddhist temple in the Western hemisphere. Although it continues to cater primarily to Chinese Americans, it also has regular services and outreach programs in English. Hsi Lai was at the center of a bizarre incident in the history of American Buddhism when a 1996 fund-raising event by Vice President Al Gore provoked a controversy; at the time Hsi Lai was often referred to in the media as simply "the Buddhist temple".

IMPORT BUDDHIST

Since Henry Steele Olcott travelled to Sri Lanka in 1880, interested Americans have sought out Buddhist teachers from a variety of countries in Asia, many of which have now established their teachings in America. The three most notable trends of this type are Zen, Tibetan Buddhism, and Vipassana, which is an outgrowth of Theravada Buddhism. Because its membership tends strongly to be among educated, white, native English speakers, import Buddhism has come to enjoy a higher level of prominence and prestige than other types of Buddhism in America.

ZEN

Beginning with Soyen Shaku's invitation to San Francisco and then the ministries of Nyogen Senzaki and Sokei-an, Zen Buddhism was the first import Buddhist trend to put down roots in North America. In the late 1940s and 1950s, writers associated with the Beat Movement, including Gary Snyder, Jack Kerouac, Allen Ginsberg, and Kenneth Rexroth, took a serious interest in Zen, which helped increase its visibility. In 1951, an octagenarian Daisetz Teitaro Suzuki returned to the United States to take a visiting professorship at Columbia University,

Sanbo Kyodan Zen is a contemporary Japanese Zen lineage which had an impact in the West disproportionate to its size Japan. It is rooted in the reformist teachings of Harada Daiun Sogaku (1871-1961) and his disciple Yasutani Hakuun (1885-1971), who argued that the existing Zen institutions of Japan, the Soto and Rinzai sects, had become complacent and, with few exceptions, were unable to teach real Dharma. Harada had studied with both Soto and Rinzai teachers and Yasutani founded Sanbo Kyodan in 1954 to preserve what he saw as the vital core of teachings from both schools. Sanbo Kyodan's first American member was Philip Kapleau, who first travelled to Japan in 1945 as a court reporter for the war crimes trials. In 1947, Kapleau visited D. T. Suzuki at Engaku-ji in Japan and in the early 1950s, he was a frequent attendee of Suzuki's Columbia lectures. In 1953, he returned to Japan, where he met with Nakagawa Soen, a protégé of Nyogen Senzaki. At Nakagawa's recommendation, he began to study with Harada and later with Yasutani, whose disciple he became. In 1965, he published a book, *The Three Pillars of Zen*, which recorded a set of talks by Yasutani outlining his approach to practice, along with transcripts of dokusan interviews and some additional texts.

The book quickly became popular in America and Europe, contributing to the prominence of the Sanbo Kyodan approach to Zen. Later in 1965, Kapleau returned to

America and, in 1966, established the Rochester Zen Center in Rochester, New York , making him the first American-born Zen priest to found a training temple. In 1967, Kapleau had a falling out with Yasutani over some of Kapleau's moves to Americanize the style of his temple, after which it became independent of Sanbo Kyodan. The Rochester Zen Center is now part of a network of related centers in the United States, Canada, Europe, Mexico, and New Zealand, referred to collectively as the Cloud Water Sangha. One of Kapleau's most notable early disciples was Toni Packer, who herself left Rochester in 1981 to found a nonsectarian meditation center, not specifically Buddhist or Zen.

Robert Aitken is another important American member of Sanbo Kyodan. He was first introduced to Zen as a prisoner in Japan during the Second World War. After returning to the United States, he began studying with Nyogen Senzaki in Los Angeles in the early 1950s. In 1959, while still a Zen student himself, he founded the Diamond Sangha, a zendo in Honolulu, Hawaii. Three years later, the Diamond Sangha hosted the first U.S. visit by Yasutani Hakuun, who would visit various locations in the U.S. six more times before 1969. Aitken travelled frequently to Japan and became a disciple of Yamada Koun, Yasutani's successor as head of the Sanbo Kyodan. Aitken became a dharma heir of Yamada's, authored more than ten books, and developed the Diamond Sangha into an international network with temples in the United States, Argentina, Germany, and Australia. In 1995, he and his organization split with Sanbo Kyodan in response to reorganization of the latter following Yamada's death. The Pacific Zen Institute led by John Tarrant, Aitken's first Dharma successor continues as an independent Zen line.

Another influential Japanese Zen teacher was Taizan Maezumi, who arrived as a young priest to serve at Zenshuji, the North American Sôtô sect headquarters in Los Angeles, in 1956. Like Shunryu Suzuki, he showed considerable interest in teaching Zen to Americans of various backgrounds and, by the mid-1960s, had formed a regular zazen group. In 1967, he and his supporters founded the Zen Center of Los Angeles. He was later instrumental in establishing the Kuroda Institute and the Soto Zen Buddhist Association, the latter an organization of American teachers with ties to the Soto tradition. In addition to his membership in Soto, Maezumi was also recognized as an heir by a Rinzai teacher and by Yasutani Hakuun of the Sanbo Kyodan. Maezumi, in turn, had several American dharma heirs who have become prominent, such as Bernie Glassman, John Daido Loori, Charlotte Joko Beck, and Dennis Genpo Merzel. His successors and their network of centers have organized as the White Plum Sangha.

Matsuoka-Roshi was a great dynamic influence in both America and Japan, lecturing and providing true Zen training to all people. Rev. Dr. Soyu Matsuoka-roshi served as superintendent and abbot of the Long Beach Zen Buddhist Temple and Zen Center. The Temple was headquarters to Zen Centers in Atlanta, Chicago, Los Angeles, Seattle, and Everett, Washington. Matsuoka-Roshi was born in Japan into a family that has a history of Zen priests dating back six hundred years. Matsuoka attended Komazawa University in Tokyo, where he graduated with a bachelor's degree. He was sent to America to serve as a founder of temples both in Los Angeles and San Francisco. He furthered his extensive graduate work at Columbia University with Dr. D.T. Suzuki. He finally established the Temple at Long Beach in 1971 where he resided until his passing in 1998.

Not all the successful Zen teachers in the United States have been from Japanese traditions. There have also been teachers of Chinese Zen (also known as Chan), Korean Zen (or Seon), and Vietnamese Zen (or Thien).

The first Chinese Buddhist priest to teach Westerners in America was Hsuan Hua, a disciple of the preeminent 20th century Chan master, Hsu Yun. In 1962, Hsuan Hua moved to San Francisco's Chinatown, where, in addition to Zen, he taught Chinese Pure Land, Tiantai, Vinaya, and Vajrayana Buddhism. Initially, his students were mostly ethnic Chinese, but he eventually attracted a range of followers. In 1970, Hsuan Hua founded Gold Mountain Monastery in San Francisco and in 1976 he established a retreat center, the City Of Ten Thousand Buddhas, on a 237 acre (959,000 m^2) property in Talmage, California. These monasteries are noted for their close adherence to the vinaya, the austere traditional Buddhist monastic code. Hsuan Hua also founded the Buddhist Text Translation Society, which works on the translation of scriptures into English.

Another Chinese Chan teacher with a Western following is Sheng-yen, a master trained in both the Caodong and Linji schools (equivalent to the Japanese Soto and Rinzai, respectively). He first visited the United States in 1978 under the sponsorship of the Buddhist Association of the United States, an organization of Chinese American Buddhists. In 1980, he founded the Ch'an Mediation Society in Queens, New York. In 1985, he founded the Chung-hwa Institute of Buddhist Studies in Taiwan, which now sponsors a variety of Chinese Zen activities in the United States.

The most prominent Korean Zen teacher in America was Seung Sahn. Seung Sahn had been the abbot of a temple in Seoul and had also lived in Hong Kong and Japan when, in 1972, not speaking any English, he decided to move to America. On the flight to Los Angeles, a Korean American passenger offered him a job at a laundry in Providence, Rhode Island, the city which was to become the headquarters of Seung Sahn's Kwan Um School of Zen. Shortly after arriving in Providence, he attracted a group of America students and founded the Providence Zen Center. The affiliated Kwan Um School now has more than 100 Zen centers on six continents. Another notable Korean Zen teacher in America is Samu Sunim, who moved to America in 1968 and founded Toronto's Zen Buddhist Temple in 1971. He is now the head of the Buddhist Society for Compassionate Wisdom, which has temples in Ann Arbor, Chicago, and Mexico City.

Two notable Vietnamese Zen teachers have been influential in America: Thich Thien-An and Thich Nhat Hanh. Thich Thien-An came to America in 1966 as a visiting professor at UCLA and taught traditional Thien meditation. Thich Nhat Hanh was a monk in Vietnam during the Vietnam War, during which he was a peace activist. In response to these activities, he was nominated for the Nobel Peace Prize in 1967 by Martin Luther

King, Jr. In 1966, he left Vietnam in exile and now resides at Plum Village, a monastery in France. He has written more than one hundred books about Buddhism, which have made him one of the very few most prominent Buddhist authors among the general readership in the West. In his books and talks, Thich Nhat Hanh emphasizes mindfulness (*sati*) as the most important practice in daily life. His monastic students live and practice at two centers in the United States: Deer Park Monastery in Escondido, CA, and Blue Cliff Monastery in Pine Bush, NY.

TIBETAN BUDDHISM

Perhaps the most widely visible Buddhist teacher in the world is Tenzin Gyatso, the current Dalai Lama, who first visited the United States in 1979. As the exiled political leader of Tibet, he has become a popular cause célèbre. His early life was depicted in glowing terms in Hollywood films such as *Kundun* and *Seven Years in Tibet*. He has attracted celebrity religious followers such as Richard Gere and Adam Yauch. The first Western-born Tibetan Buddhist monk was Robert A. F. Thurman, now a noted academic supporter of the Dalai Lama. The Dalai Lama maintains a North American headquarters at Namgyal Monastery in Ithaca, New York.

The best-known Tibetan Buddhist lama to live in the United States was Chögyam Trungpa. Trungpa, part of the Kagyu school of Tibetan Buddhism, moved to England in 1963, founded a temple in Scotland, and then relocated to Barnet, Vermont, and Boulder, Colorado in 1970. He established a series of what he named Dharmadhatu meditation centers, which were eventually organized under a national umbrella group called Vajradhatu (later to become Shambhala International). The methods and techniques he developed for teaching Westerners he termed Shambhala Training. Following Trungpa's death, his followers built the Great Stupa of Dharmakaya, a traditional reliquary monument, near Red Feather Lakes, Colorado. Consecrated in 2001, it is the largest stupa in the United States.

The first Tibetan Buddhist lama to come to the United States was Geshe Ngawang Wangyal, a Kalmyk-Mongolian of the Gelug lineage, who came to the United States in 1955 and founded the "Lamaist Buddhist Monastery of America" in New Jersey in 1958. Among his students were the future western scholars Robert Thurman, Jeffrey Hopkins and Alexander Berzin. Other early arrivals included Deshung Rinpoche, a Sakya lama who settled in Seattle, WA, in 1960, and Tarthang Tulku Rinpoche, the first Nyingma teacher in America, who arrived in the U.S. in 1968 and established the "Tibetan Nyingma Meditation Center" in Berkeley, California in 1969.

There are four major schools of Tibetan Buddhism: the Gelug, the Kagyu, the Nyingma, and the Sakya. Of these, the greatest impact in the West was made by the Gelug, which is led by the Dalai Lama, and the Kagyu, specifically its Karma Kagyu branch, which is led by the Karmapa. As of the early 1990s, there were four significant strands of Kagyu practice in the United States: Chögyam Trungpa's Shambhala movement; Karma Triyana Dharmachakra, a network of centers affiliated directly with the Karmapa's North American seat in Woodstock, New York; a network of centers founded by Kalu Rinpoche; and an organization established by Ole Nydahl, a Danish-born lama with many supporters in Europe.

In the 21st century, the Nyingma lineage is increasingly represented in the West, by both Western and Tibetan teachers. Lama Surya Das is a Western-born teacher carrying on the great rimé, or non-sectarian, branch of Tibetan Buddhism. H.E. Chagdud Tulku Rinpoche, before his death in 2002, founded centers in Seattle and Brazil. Khandro Rinpoche is a modern female Tibetan teacher who has a strong presence in America. Jetsunma Ahkon Lhamo, in 1988, was the first Western woman to be recognized and enthroned as a Tulku, has also established Nyingma Kunzang Palyul Choling centers in Sedona, AZ and Poolesville, MD.

The Gelug tradition is most strongly represented in America by the Foundation for the Preservation of the Mahayana Tradition (FPMT), founded by Lama Thubten Yeshe and Lama Zopa. Another prominent Gelugpa teacher is Geshe Michael Roach, the first American to be awarded a Geshe degree, who has established centers in New York, NY, and at Diamond Mountain University in Arizona.

Also quite active in the United States is the self-described New Kadampa Tradition (NKT) established by Geshe Kelsang Gyatso. A schismatic offshoot of the Gelug school founded in the 1990s in the UK, the NKT has over 50 Kadampa (NKT) Buddhist Centers and branches in the United States. Geshe Kelsang Gyatso is the only Tibetan associated with the movement—most of its followers are Westerners or in the far east, principally in Hong Kong and Singapore.

VIPASSANA

Vipassana, also referred to by the rough translation "insight meditation" is an ancient meditative practice described in the Pali Canon of the Theravada school of Buddhism, and in similar scriptures of other schools. Vipassana also refers to a distinct movement which was begun in the 20th century by reformers such as Mahâsi Sayâdaw, a Burmese monk. Mahâsi Sayâdaw was a Theravada bhikkhu and Vipassana is rooted in the Theravada teachings, but its goal is to simplify ritual and other peripheral activities in order to make meditative practice more effective and available both to monks and to laypeople. This openness to lay involvement is an important development in Theravada, which has sometimes appeared to focus exclusively on monasticism.

In 1965, monks from Sri Lanka established the Washington Buddhist Vihara in Washington, D.C., the first Theravada monastic community in the United States. The Vihara was fairly accessible to English-speakers, and naturally vipassana meditation was part of its activities. However, the direct influence of the Vipassana movement would not reach the U.S. until a group of Americans returned there in the early 1970s after studying with Vipassana master in Asia. Joseph Goldstein, after journeying to Southeast Asia with the Peace Corps, had lived in Bodhgaya, where he was a student of Anagarika

Munindra, the head monk of Mahabodhi Temple and himself a student of Mâhâsai Sayâdaw's. Jack Kornfield had also been in the Peace Corps in Southeast Asia, after which he studied and ordained in the Thai Forest Tradition under Ajahn Chah, who was perhaps the most influential figure in 20th century Thai Buddhism. Sharon Salzberg went to India in 1971 as a spiritual seeker and studied with Dipa Ma, a former Calcutta housewife trained in vipassana by Mâhâsai Sayâdaw.

Goldstein and Kornfield met in 1974 while teaching at the Naropa Institute in Colorado. The next year, Goldstein, Kornfield, and Salzberg, who had very recently returned from Calcutta, along with Jacqueline Schwarz, founded the Insight Meditation Society on an 80 acre (324,000 m^2) property near Barre, Massachusetts. IMS became the central Vipassana institution in America, hosting visits by Mâhâsi Sayâdaw, Munindra, Ajahn Chah, and Dipa Ma. In 1981, Kornfield moved to California, where he founded another Vipassana center, Spirit Rock Meditation Center, in Marin County. In 1985, Larry Rosenberg founded the Cambridge Insight Meditation Center in Cambridge, Massachusetts. Another important Vipassana center is the Vipassana Metta Foundation, located on Maui.

In 1989, the Insight Meditation Center established the Barre Center for Buddhist Studies near the IMS headquarters, with the goal of promoting scholarly investigation of Buddhism from various perspectives. It director is Mu Seong, a former Korean Zen monk.

S. N. Goenka is a Burmese-born meditation teacher who can also be considered part of the Vipassana movement. His teacher, Sayagyi U Ba Khin of Burma, was a contemporary of Mâhâsi Sayâdaw's, and taught a style of Buddhism with similar emphases on simplicity and accessibility to laypeople. Goenka has established a method of instruction which has proven very popular in Asia and throughout the world. In 1981, he established the Vipassana Research Institute based in Igatpuri, India. He and his students have built several active centers in North America.

EXPORT BUDDHISTS

Although ethnic-based institutions, such as Hsi Lai Temple and the Buddhist Churches of America, show some evangelical tendencies, there is only one Buddhist group in North America which has focused on recruiting converts from among the general public and been successful: Soka Gakkai, a Japan-based society which promotes Nichiren Buddhism.

Soka Gakkai, which literally means "Establishing Value Education Society", was founded in Japan in 1930 as a fraternal auxiliary to Nichiren Shoshu, the largest sect of Nichiren Buddhism. It was perhaps the most successful of Japan's new religious movements, which enjoyed tremendous growth after the end of the Second World War. During the occupation of Japan, some American soldiers became aware of it, and it was the Japanese wives of veterans who became the first active Soka Gakkai members in the

West. A U.S. branch was formally organized on October 13, 1960. Its Korean-Japanese leader took the name George M. Williams to emphasize his commitment to reaching the English-speaking public. Soka Gakkai expanded rapidly in the U.S. through an aggressive recruitment technique called shakubuku. One of the results of this outreach is that Soka Gakkai has been much more effective than any other group at attracting non-Asian minority converts, chiefly African American and Latino, to Buddhism. It has also been successful in attracting the support of celebrities, such as Tina Turner, Herbie Hancock, and Orlando Bloom.

Soka Gakkai has no priests of its own and was originally part of Nichiren Shoshu, a formal religious sect in Japan. In fact, its United States branch was originally named Nichiren Shoshu America (NSA). However, in 1991 Soka Gakkai split from Nichiren Shoshu and became a separate organization; at that time, the U.S. branch changed its name to Soka Gakkai International - United States of America (SGI-USA). Nichiren Shoshu proper maintains six temples of its own in the U.S. and another Nichiren group exists which is primarily the domain of ethnic Japanese.

The main religious practice of Soka Gakkai members, like other Nichiren Buddhists, is chanting the mantra *Nam Myôhô Renge Kyô* and sections of the Lotus Sutra. Unlike import Buddhist trends such as Zen, Vipassana, and Tibetan Buddhism, Soka Gakkai does not teach meditative techniques other than chanting.

DEMOGRAPHICS OF BUDDHISM IN THE UNITED STATES

It is not easy to arrive at an accurate idea of the number of Buddhists in the United States. The simplest reason is that it is not at all clear how to define who is and who is not a Buddhist. The easiest and most intuitive definition is one based on self-description, but this has its pitfalls. Because Buddhism exists as a cultural concept in American society, there may be individuals who self-describe as Buddhists but have essentially no knowledge of or commitment to Buddhism as a religion or practice; on the other hand, others may be deeply involved in meditation and committed to the Buddhadharma, but may refuse the label "Buddhist". Despite these difficulties, several scholars have investigated this question. Most studies have indicated a Buddhist population in the United States of between 1 and 4 million. The U.S. State Department's International Religious Freedom Report for 2004 indicates that 2% of the U.S. population is Buddhist, which would mean a total of 5,973,446 Buddhists. Other estimates, perhaps relying on a greater degree of intuition, are larger: in the 1990s, Robert A. F. Thurman stated his opinion that there were 5 to 6 million Buddhists in America, and others might speculate there are more. Whatever the total number, it appears that roughly 75 to 80 percent of Buddhists in the U.S. are of Asian descent and inherited Buddhism as a family tradition; the remaining 20 to 25 percent are non-Asians.

ETHNIC DIVIDE

Discussion about Buddhism in America has sometimes focused on the issue of the visible ethnic divide separating ethnic Buddhist congregations from import Buddhist groups. Although many Zen and Tibetan Buddhist temples were founded by Asians, they now tend to attract very few Asian-American members. With the exception of Soka Gakkai, almost all active Buddhist groups in America can be readily classed as either ethnic or import Buddhism based on the demographics of their membership.

There is often very limited contact between these Buddhists of different ethnic groups. This divide can be disturbing in view of the historical necessity of relying on Asian peoples to transmit Buddhism, and in light of ongoing and complex tensions surrounding ethnicity and immigration in America. Some Asian-American Buddhists feel that their non-Asian counterparts ignore the many contributions of their ethnic communities toward the development of American Buddhism.

However, the cultural divide should not necessarily be seen as pernicious. It is often argued that the differences between Buddhist groups arise benignly from the differing needs and interests of those involved.

Convert Buddhists tend to be interested in meditation and philosophy, in some cases eschewing the trappings of religiosity altogether. On the other hand, for immigrants and their descendants, preserving tradition and maintaining a social framework assume a much greater relative importance, making their approach to religion naturally more conservative.

Further, Kenneth K. Tanaka suggests, based on a survey of Asian-American Buddhists in San Francisco, that "many Asian-American Buddhists view non-Asian Buddhism as still in a formative, experimental stage" and yet they believe that it "could eventually mature into a religious expression of exceptional quality".

Additional questions come from the demographics within import Buddhism. Researchers and casual observers alike report that the vast majority of American converts practicing at Buddhist centers are white, often from Christian or Jewish backgrounds. Only Soka Gakkai has attracted significant numbers of African-American or Latino members. A variety of ideas have been broached regarding the nature, causes, and significance of this racial uniformity. Journalist Clark Strand noted that

> ...that it has tried to recruit [African-Americans] at all makes Soka Gakkai International utterly unique in American Buddhism.

Strand, writing for Tricycle (an American Buddhist journal) in 2004, notes that SGI has specifically targeted African-Americans, Latinos and Asians, and other writers have noted that this approach has begun to spread, with Vipassana and Theravada retreats aimed at non-white practitioners led by a handful of specific teachers.

A key question is the degree of importance ascribed to discrimination, which is suggested to be mostly unconscious, on the part of white converts toward potential minority converts. To some extent, the racial divide is indicative of a class divide, because convert Buddhists tend strongly to be drawn from the more educated segments of society. Among the African American Buddhists who have commented on the dynamics of the racial divide in convert Buddhism are Jan Willis and Charles R. Johnson.

ENGAGED BUDDHISM

An important trend that has developed in Buddhism in the West is socially engaged Buddhism. While some critics have asserted that the term is redundant, as it is mistaken to believe that Buddhism in the past has not affected and been affected by the surrounding society, others have suggested that Buddhism is sometimes seen as too quietistic and passive toward public life. This is particularly true in the West, where almost all converts to Buddhism come to it outside of an existing family or community tradition. Engaged Buddhism is an attempt to apply Buddhist values to larger social problems, including war and environmental concerns. The term *engaged Buddhism* was coined by Thich Nhat Hanh, who developed the idea during his years as a peace activist in Vietnam. The most notable engaged Buddhist organization is the Buddhist Peace Fellowship, which was founded in 1978 by Robert Aitken, Anne Aitken, Nelson Foster, and others and received early assistance from Gary Snyder, Jack Kornfield, and Joanna Macy. Another engaged Buddhist group is the Zen Peacemaker Order, which was founded in 1996 by Bernie Glassman and Sandra Jishu Holmes.

Buddhist Education in the United States

A variety of Buddhist groups have established institutions of higher learning in America. The first four-year Buddhist college in the U.S. was the Naropa Institute (now Naropa University), which was founded in 1974 by Chögyam Trungpa. It has enjoyed consistent involvement both from convert Buddhists and counterculture personalities, such as Allen Ginsberg, who christened the Institute's poetry department the "Jack Kerouac School of Disembodied Poetics". Naropa is currently fully accredited and offers degrees in some subjects not directly related to Buddhism. Another Buddhist university is the University of the West, which is affiliated with Hsi Lai Temple and was, until recently called Hsi Lai University. Soka University of America, in Aliso Viejò California, was founded by the Soka Gakkai as a secular school closely committed to philosophic Buddhism. The City of Ten Thousand Buddhas is the site of Dharma Realm Buddhist University, a four-year college teaching courses primarily related to Buddhism but including some general-interest subjects. The Institute of Buddhist Studies in Berkeley, California, in addition to offering a Masters Degree in Buddhist Studies acts as the ministerial training arm of the Buddhist Churches of America and is affiliated with the Graduate Theological Union. The school recently moved into its new headquarters within the Jodo Shinshu Center in Berkeley.

The first Buddhist high school in the United States, Developing Virtue Secondary School, was founded in 1981 by the Dharma Realm Buddhist Association at their branch monastery in the City of Ten Thousand Buddhas in Ukiah, California. A second Buddhist high school, Tinicum Art and Science, which combines Zen practice and traditional liberal arts, opened in Ottsville, Pennsylvania in 1998. It is associated informally with the World Shim Gum Do Association in Boston. The Pacific Buddhist Academy, opened in Honolulu, Hawai'i in 2003. It shares a campus with the Hongwanji Mission School; an elementary and middle school. Both schools are affiliated with the Honpa Hongwanji Jodo Shinshu mission.

PROMOTING BUDDHISM IN EUROPE

We can divide the history of the Western engagement with Buddhism into three major phases. These phases are not totally discrete, for they intersect and overlap, but the threefold division provides a useful way of determining general trends.

PHASE I: THE DISCOVERY OF BUDDHISM

Phase I consisted in the academic study of Buddhist texts, aimed at discerning the broad contours of Buddhist history and doctrine. This project took place during the peak of the colonial period, when European countries were busy subjugating Asian peoples and incorporating their nations into their hungry empires. In many cases European interest in Buddhism was bound up with the Christian missionary enterprise of converting the native populations to Christianity.

Although reports about Asian Buddhist beliefs and practices had been drifting back to Europe since the thirteenth century, a clear picture of Buddhism as a unitary whole did not take shape in Europe until the middle of the nineteenth century, just a little more than 150 years ago. Before then, the sundry reports that had reached scholars in Europe were generally haphazard, inaccurate, and conjectural, if not utterly fantastic. The first person to comprehend Buddhism as a unitary tradition and establish its historical origins was the brilliant French philologist Eugene Burnouf. Burnouf had studied Pali, Sanskrit, and Tibetan manuscripts that had been sent to him in Paris from the East. Based on these texts, with barely no other clues, he wrote his 600-page tome, *Introduction to the History of Indian Buddhism* (1844), in which he traced in detail Indian Buddhist history and surveyed its doctrines and texts. Though later generations of scholars have greatly expanded upon Burnouf's work and filled in many missing pieces, they regard as essentially accurate the outline of Indian Buddhism he proposed in his groundbreaking study.

In the decades following Burnouf, there appeared throughout Europe a galaxy of brilliant scholars who opened up the treasures locked away in all the different branches of Buddhism. These scholars fall into three main schools. The scholars of the "Anglo-Germanic School" focused on the Pali tradition. Their work emanated from the Pali Text Society, founded by T.W. Rhys Davids, and their ranks included Caroline Rhys Davids, Oldenberg, Woodward, Hare, and Horner; the Danish scholars Trenckner, Fausboll, and Anderson; and the Swede Helmer Smith. The "Franco-Belgian School" investigated Indian Buddhism both Hinayana and Mahayana in Sanskrit, Tibetan, and Chinese texts; its luminaries were de la Valle Poussin, Sylvain Levy, and Lamotte. The "Russian School" — represented by Stcherbatsky, Rosenberg, and Obermiller — concentrated on scholastic Indian Buddhism as preserved especially in Tibetan texts. Although these scholars usually remained reticent about their own religious beliefs, by collecting Asian manuscripts, publishing modern editions of these texts, and providing translations and scholarly studies of Buddhist thought, they laid the indispensable foundation stone for the spread of the Dhamma in the West, namely, access to the original Buddhist sources.

The academic study of Buddhism initiated by these pioneers has continued through to the present time, despite the setback of two world wars and frequent shortages in funding. In Western universities and institutes, scholars map in ever finer details and with broader sweep the entire Buddhist heritage — from Sri Lanka to Mongolia, from Gandhara to Japan. Thus what I call "Phase I" in the history of Western Buddhism is not so much a temporary stage superceded by its successors as a preparation for the further evolution of Buddhism in its Western setting.

PHASE II: ELITE APPROPRIATION

Phase II in the European encounter with Buddhism I shall call "elite appropriation." By this, I mean the adoption of Buddhism as a living creed by an increasing number of intellectuals, writers, artists, and professionals. In the German-speaking world the catalyst for the transition from the mere academic investigation of Buddhism to its active appropriation was the philosopher Arthur Schopenhauer. Schopenhauer published the first edition of his philosophical masterpiece, *The World as Will and Representation*, in 1819, before he had come across reliable accounts of Buddhist thought. However, his philosophical intuitions showed such striking parallels to the Dhamma that several decades later, when Schopenhauer did gain access to accurate material on Buddhism, he at once recognized the affinity of his own thought to the Buddha's doctrine. Thus, in the second edition of his book, he hailed Buddhism as "the most perfect" of all the world's religions. Such was his admiration for the Buddha that he kept a small statue of the Master on his mantle alongside a bust of his philosophical hero, Immanuel Kant.

Schopenhauer did not become a Buddhist himself, which would have been almost unthinkable in the Europe of his day, but his writings had a profound impact on later European thinkers and guided many to the Dhamma. At least three major figures owed their discovery of Buddhism to Schopenhauer's influence: the Austrian Indologist K.E. Neumann, who translated the Digha and Majjhima Nikayas and other Pali texts into German; the Bavarian judge George Grimm; and the Berlin homeopath Paul Dahlke. The last named pair, through their writings and promotional work, became the two leading proponents of Buddhism in Germany during the early part of the twentieth century. Their writings did not simply analyse Buddhism in terms of objective, impersonal categories, but tried to explain it from the inside, as experienced by one who had made the personal leap of faith.

Arnold and the Theosophists

In the English-speaking world, the primary impetus for the adoption of Buddhism by educated Westerners came from Sir Edwin Arnold's inspirational poem on the Buddha's life, *The Light of Asia*. Arnold depicted the Buddha as a figure of heroic stature whose personality combined deep compassion for all humanity with a masterly capacity for rational thought. These two characteristics dovetailed perfectly with the intellectual milieu of the period and aroused in Arnold's readers a new respect for the Buddha and interest in his teachings. Though conservative Christians were indignant at the poem's success, the British intelligentsia of the period were liberal enough not to feel constrained by Christianity's claims to sole possession of the truth. The Theosophical movement, founded by Madame Blavatsky and Henry Steele Olcott, also gave Buddhism a profile in the Anglo-American world. While their interpretation of Buddhism as a popular expression of esoteric wisdom bordered on the chimerical, the Theosophists helped to make Buddhism fashionable among those attracted to alternative ways of thought.

The First Flowering

Inspired by the Dhamma, a few adventurous spirits, not content with mere book knowledge, left their homelands to travel to the East to learn Buddhism at its sources. Others like Childers and Rhys Davids, working in colonial administrations in Asia, already had access to native authorities on the Dhamma. By the turn of the century several Westerners took the decisive step of coming to the East to enter the Sangha. The pioneers in this development were the Englishman Allen Bennett, who became Ven. Ananda Metteyya in Burma (1901), and Anton Gueth, who became Ven. Nyanatiloka (1903). Though Ven. Ananda Metteyya later disrobed after a tentative mission to Britain, Ven. Nyanatiloka settled permanently in Sri Lanka, where in 1911 he founded Island Hermitage as a monastery especially for Western monks.

Within Europe, starting early in the twentieth century, Buddhist societies began to sprout, Buddhist journals commenced publication, and numerous books on Buddhism, of varying degrees of authenticity, attempted to bridge the gap between classical Buddhism and the Western intellectual heritage. During this phase of "elite appropriation" most proponents of Buddhism favoured the Pali tradition, as being far closer to the Buddha's original teachings than the baffling and ornate Mahayana sutras. What these thinkers emphasized in Buddhism was its rationality and realism, its ethical purity, its tolerance, its non-dogmatic approach to truth, and its compatibility with modern science. In this phase, with a few exceptions, the meditative, communal, and devotional aspects of Buddhism were left quietly on the sidelines. In other words, theory prevailed over practice.

PHASE III: THE POPULARIZATION OF BUDDHISM

Phase III in the spread of Buddhism in the West began roughly in the 1960s and continues through to the present. This third phase might be described as the popularization of Buddhism. During this phase, Buddhism comes to exert its appeal on an increasing number of people of different lifestyles and its following proliferates rapidly. At the beginning of this phase Buddhism was largely a counter-cultural phenomenon, adopted by those in rebellion against the crass materialism and technocratic obsessions of modern society: hippies, acid heads, disaffected university students, artists, writers, and anarchists. But as these youthful rebels gradually became integrated into the mainstream, they brought their Buddhism with them.

Today Buddhism is espoused not only by those in the alternative culture, but by businessmen, physicists, computer programmers, housewives, real-estate agents, even by sports stars, movie actors, and rock musicians. Perhaps several hundred thousand Europeans have adopted Buddhism in one or another of its different forms, while many more quietly incorporate Buddhist practices into their daily lives. The presence of large Asian Buddhist communities in the West also enhances the visibility of the Dhamma. Thousands of books on Buddhism are now available, dealing with the teachings at both scholarly and popular levels, while Buddhist magazines and journals expand their circulation each year. Buddhist influences subtly permeate various disciplines: philosophy and ecology, psychology and health care, the arts and literature, even Christian theology. Indeed, already three years ago *Time* magazine devoted a full-length cover story to the spread of Buddhism in America, and at least five books on the subject are in print.

Facilitating Factors

The transition in Western Buddhism from Phase II to Phase III was facilitated by two main factors. One was the increasing number of Asian Buddhist teachers who travelled to the West — Theravada bhikkhus, Japanese Zen masters, Tibetan lamas — either to give lectures and conduct retreats, or to settle there permanently and establish Buddhist centres. The second factor was the return to the West of the young Westerners who had trained in Asia in the late 1960s and early 1970s, and now came back to their home countries to spread the Dhamma.

From the mid-1980s on we see even a new sub-phase of Phase III, or perhaps an incipient Phase IV: the emergence of a generation of Western Buddhist teachers who have never been to Asia but have received their full training in the West.

What is characteristic of Western Buddhism in Phase III, in distinction from the earlier phases, is the focus on Buddhist practice, especially the practice of meditation. In this phase it is not the academic study of Buddhist texts and doctrines that dominates (as in Phase I), or the attempt to interpret the Dhamma through the prism of Western thought (as in Phase II), but the appropriation of Buddhism as a practice that can bring deep transformations in one's innermost being as well as in the conduct of everyday life. This does not necessarily mean that Buddhist practice is being taken up in accordance with canonical or traditional Asian models, nor that it is pursued to attain Nibbana in the sense upheld by classical Buddhist doctrine. Often Western Buddhists give their own twist to Buddhist concepts, sometimes in ways that depart drastically from canonical standards and from an Asian standpoint might border on "heresy." But in Phase III, Buddhism is viewed as in some sense a path to awakening, a way that brings deep understanding of the mind and makes accessible new dimensions of being. Hence at this stage Buddhism becomes a means of spiritual transformation through direct experience, through insights not arrived at by mere conceptual reflection.

A Variety of Schools

In Phase III, we also find the arrival of various schools of Asian Buddhism, which peacefully coexist, pursuing their own growth and cooperating with each other to secure common aims. With the passage from Phase II to Phase III a noticeable shift takes place in the type of Buddhism generally adopted by Western Buddhists. In Phase II, Pali Buddhism was dominant, though I must stress that this adherence to the Pali heritage did *not* entail a commitment to any form of Theravada Buddhism as practised in Asian lands. In fact, the elite Buddhists often looked upon Asian Theravada as a degeneration from the pristine canonical doctrine, which they believed was a unique possession of their own. But with the rise of Phase III the focus of attraction shifts away from the Pali tradition: first to Zen Buddhism in the 1960s and 1970s; and then to Tibetan Vajrayana Buddhism in the 1980s and 1990s. Further, new types of Buddhism come onto the scene, schools peculiar to the West, such as Thich Nhat Hanh's Order of Interbeing, the Arya Maitreya Mandala (centred in Germany), and the Friends of the Western Buddhist Order. These are partly syncretistic, partly innovative attempts to create new styles of Buddhist practice conformable to the Western temperament. Also the age range of Buddhist followers varies between the schools. Today in Germany most followers of the Pali tradition are in their 50s and 60s, while the followers of Zen and Tibetan Buddhism are in their 30s and 40s. This development is critically important for us, as followers of the Theravada, to understand, and I will therefore return to it later.

THE WESTERN RECEPTIVITY TO BUDDHISM

At this point, I want to raise the question: How are we to understand the surge of interest in Buddhism among Westerners in recent years? How do we account for the eagerness with which so many today are ready to explore the Dhamma and often to deeply embrace it? It is necessary to address this question in order to begin to see the needs that we must fulfil as we try to make our own contribution to the spread of the Dhamma in Europe.

NATURE ABHORS A VACUUM

I think the answer to this question unfolds in roughly two distinct stages, corresponding to the last two phases in the Western adoption of Buddhism that I spoke of just before. During Phase II, "the phase of elite appropriation," intellectuals were drawn to Buddhism because it filled a vacuum that had been growing ever wider in Europe since the seventeenth century. This vacuum was the absence of any comprehensive body of wisdom teachings that could offer a key to the deeper meaning of human existence. The responsibility for shedding light on the meaning of existence had traditionally been assigned to philosophy, but from the seventeenth century onwards philosophy came to renounce this task in favour of other concerns. Besides, such guidance that philosophy did offer, as in Spinoza's *Ethics*, was usually embedded in systems of thought so subtle and complex that few people could understand them.

Of course, Christianity too staked out for itself a claim to hold the key to the riddle of existence, but the main thrust of orthodox Christianity has not been to show the way to wisdom. Its purpose is to offer the prospect of an eternal afterlife in heaven through faith in God and Christ the Saviour, and it was just such faith that was coming into question. Further, Christianity's own record as a defender of human values was far from impressive. Its legacy of crusades, inquisitions, forced conversions, and intolerance repelled rather than attracted ethically sensitive minds, while its alliance with the colonial regimes confirmed suspicions about its imperialistic designs. Moreover, as science strode boldly into one arena of knowledge after another, often in the face of staunch resistance from the Church, it discredited Christian claims to the infallibility of revelation. Thus for a growing number of independent thinkers the Christian religion had become irrelevant.

When translations of Buddhist texts and expositions of Buddhist thought began to appear in the late nineteenth century, they seemed to offer the West exactly what it was lacking: a system of spiritual wisdom that could give illumination and moral guidance yet did not demand unquestioning faith in theological dogmas. Instead, it rested its claims upon human reason and personal insight into fundamental truths and universal laws. The way Buddhism impinged on the Western mind during this period reveals both the strength and weakness in the Western perception of Buddhism. The strength lay in a deep and clear grasp of the doctrinal principles of the Dhamma, expressed in works that were utterly compelling in their insights, logic, and literary eloquence. The weakness was the understanding of Buddhism as primarily a rational, ideational system, to replace the tottering belief system of the Christian churches. Another limitation was that Buddhism in this phase still appealed mainly to the educated elite and thus could attract only those astute enough to break away from the cultural and religious mainstream, which was still predominantly Christian.

THE CONDITIONS FOR POPULARIZATION

For the transition to Phase III to take place, that is, for Buddhism to spread more widely through the general population, certain additional conditions were necessary, and these only became sufficiently widespread in the second half of the twentieth century. One was the triumph of liberal democracy over autocratic political systems. Under the heading of democracy we must include not only political democracy, but also the democracy of the mind, an openness to new ways of thought and tolerance for viewpoints that differ radically from those of one's own intellectual heritage. This openness was encouraged by a partial change in the attitude of the Christian churches towards other faiths, which in the West after the Second Vatican Council (1963–65) swung towards greater respect and tolerance for non-Christian religions.

A second preparatory factor was a fair degree of economic affluence, which freed Europeans from excessive concern with material security and gave them the leisure to explore new avenues of thought. The rise of the consumerist society also helped them see the limitations to material development as a final solution to our quest for happiness.

A third factor was the relatively high standard of liberal education established in the 1960s, enabling a large proportion of young people to attend the university. Higher education exposed them to multiple viewpoints in all the domains of human knowledge, and also trained them to think critically and deeply about new ideas.

A fourth preparatory factor was improved means of transportation and communication, which facilitated contacts between East and West. Now curious Westerners could easily travel to the East to experience Buddhism first hand in its own native setting, while Buddhist teachers from Asia could move West to propagate the Dhamma.

The fifth factor, following naturally from the fourth, was the actual arrival in the West of Buddhist teachers, both Asians and Westerners trained in Asia. These teachers brought Buddhism as a dynamic faith that they embodied in their lives through years of serious training.

THE GREAT TRANSITION

While the five factors constituted the necessary conditions for Buddhism to become accessible to a sizable number of Europeans, they are not a sufficient explanation for the rapid escalation of Western interest in Buddhism. To pinpoint the decisive cause for this phenomenon, I must refer back to the vacuum or void that had opened up right beneath the feet of European civilization, that is, the absence of a solid, authoritative spiritual tradition that could give guidance in the mastery of life. In the late nineteenth and early twentieth centuries this void was acutely felt only by the more discerning Western minds, disenchanted with both doctrinaire Christianity and economic materialism. Ordinary people were somehow able to balance their ancestral Christian faith with a bright optimism about the coming Golden Age, to be achieved through science and technology.

By the late 1950s, however, the picture had drastically changed. After two world wars and a prolonged cold war that threatened the whole world with thermonuclear destruction, countless people found their trust in the intrinsic goodness of human nature crumble into dust. Such horrors as the Nazi Holocaust and the Hiroshima atom bomb not only undermined faith in a benevolent God guiding the whole creation, but also brought to light the dangers in mere rationality not illuminated by a higher wisdom and staunch commitment to ethics.

The most brilliant minds of the West, relying on the rational intellect, had twice plunged the whole world into barbaric irrationality, with death tolls numbering in the tens of millions. Now, with even more lethal weapons of destruction at hand, they threatened to do so again. Thus the void that sensitive nineteenth century thinkers had seen on the horizon had expanded until it had swallowed up almost everyone. And not only had it expanded, but for many it had acquired a sharp and compelling urgency that could not be quenched by any system of ideas, however noble. What they needed was a programme of action, which in many cases meant a deep personal engagement in the spiritual quest.

At the same time that the fear of nuclear war cast long shadows over the entire globe, unprecedented material affluence in the West brought into easy reach the comforts, conveniences, and sensory delights that earlier generations had only dreamt about. Yet while this consumerist paradise mesmerized many (and still continues to do so), at least a few people "with little dust in their eyes" realized that such mundane pleasures could bring no lasting peace to the heart. At this point, for such spiritually sensitive Westerners, the message embedded in the Four Noble Truths was no longer a splendid system of ideas, to be admired in the comfort of an armchair. The message had become, rather, a medicine for curing a terrible disease, the disease of suffering, and the one sensible thing to be done with it, as with any medicine, was to take it. Hence for the Buddhists in Phase III of Western Buddhism, the Dhamma presented itself as a path of practice pivoting on the training and mastery of the mind. As teachers and centres became available, growing numbers of Westerners took up the practice eagerly, ready to follow it wherever it might lead.

THE NEED FOR A SOCIAL ETHIC

But Buddhism offered not only a method of mind training that could bring inner peace and deeper self-knowledge, it also fulfilled another profound need of the Western soul. As part of its deep intellectual heritage, Western civilization was committed to the idea that human happiness largely depends on the reformation of the social order in ways that eliminate political tyranny, economic oppression, and social injustice. The commitment to this premise was responsible for the rise of democracy in the West, as well as for less successful experiments with various forms of socialism. However, the experience of the nineteenth and twentieth centuries had shown that without some code of ethical guidance, mere aspirations for freedom and democracy could easily give birth to their opposites. Thus the French Revolution, launched under the motto of "liberty, equality, and fraternity," ended up with the guillotine. The Bolshevik Revolution, with its promise of a "dictatorship of the proletariat," culminated in the Soviet police state. Western idealists saw in Buddhism the foundations for a lofty social ethic devoted to world peace, social justice, and ecological sanity, yet internally protected by its moral code against the deformities to which secular political utopianism was prone.

THE SEARCH FOR COMMUNITY

To understand the appeal of Buddhism to many present-day Westerners, another factor we must consider is the general breakdown of community in modern Western culture. With increasing industrialization and urbanization, the older human-scale social structures that allowed each person to find a meaningful place in the whole gave way to huge, monstrous institutions that reduced individuals to mere cogs in an impersonal social order. People have come to feel isolated, alienated, cut off from the bonds of social solidarity, trapped in a system that fuels ruthless individualism. These destructive values have provoked a widespread psychological crisis marked by chronic stress, anxiety, and depression. The escape routes people seek are promiscuous sex, violent entertainment, alcoholism, and drugs; but these, of course, do not offer a real solution.

When Buddhism arrived on the scene it seemed to offer a counterweight to the loneliness and isolation so many people felt even in their overcrowded cities. For one thing, it stressed such values as universal love, compassion, cooperation, and altruism, half-forgotten ideals of the Christian legacy. But just as importantly, it ushered in a new sense of community. As Buddhist groups sought their own organizational forms, they gradually evolved towards the model of the Buddhist centre, where fellow practitioners meet regularly in a spirit of friendship to practise and study the Dhamma together, usually under the guidance of a teacher. Many Buddhist societies now have residential facilities where the more dedicated members live either temporarily or permanently. Some have urban centres accessible to people during the working week, and country centres some distance away to which members can resort for longer meditation retreats.

THE SHIFT AMONG TRADITIONS

When Buddhism in the West enters Phase III, a shift occurs away from the Pali tradition towards Zen and Tibetan Vajrayana. One explanation for this might be the more attractive, more exotic surfaces of these schools of Buddhism; another factor might be the charismatic personalities of their teachers, the Zen masters and Tibetan lamas. But such an explanation is not complete. The main reason these traditions have gained in popularity over the Theravada is, I believe, because within their fold the lineage of meditation practice has been kept more alive than in mainstream Theravada.

Certainly in the Pali Canon the Buddha repeatedly emphasizes the urgency of meditation above all else, and this message does live on in small pockets of earnest Theravadin practitioners throughout southern Asia. However, the European Buddhists of the older generations had set the pace by viewing Pali Buddhism largely in rationalistic terms, as a lofty ethic and impressive system of thought. Almost as if to confirm this, the few representatives of Asian Theravada to settle in the West have tended to present Buddhism largely in doctrinal and ethical terms. Rarely do they exhibit the same degree of spiritual vitality as the Mahayana and Vajrayana masters. Since present-day Western seekers are looking for a practice they can incorporate into their lives, not just a system of ideas they can admire and discuss, they naturally feel the appeal of the alternative forms of Buddhism — Zen, Vajrayana, and new Western Buddhist schools — over the Theravada.

This, however, is not to say that a meditation tradition rooted in the Theravada is lacking in the West. A number of Westerners who had come to Asian countries years ago to practise under qualified teachers later returned to the West to teach and establish Buddhist centres. But what we find, as an interesting development, is that often such Western teachers of Theravada-based meditation do not consider themselves adherents of Theravada Buddhism in its doctrinal sense. Instead, explicitly or implicitly, they distance themselves from Asian Theravada and call their style of Buddhism "the Vipassana tradition" or "the practice of mindful awareness." While they have evolved a rigorous system of training, they often lift Vipassana meditation out from its setting in Buddhist faith and doctrine, presenting it almost as an autonomous discipline of psychological insight and self-awareness.

This is certainly a weak spot in the Western approach to the Dhamma, for the religious and philosophical dimensions of classical Buddhism are necessary for insight meditation to lead to its real goal, "the taintless liberation of the mind." Neglect of the textual and doctrinal side of Buddhism can result in a diluted, shoddy understanding of the Dhamma. But the stripped-down style of practice — non-religious, non-doctrinal, non-monastic insight meditation — is the dominant mode in which Westerners are taking up Theravada Buddhism. This development might induce us to examine our own tradition more closely to ask ourselves why the Dhamma is being approached in such a partial fashion, through such a pick-and-choose policy, instead of being embraced as an organic whole.

THE CHALLENGE OF BRINGING THERAVADA TO THE WEST

This brings me to the third major division of my talk, the special challenges we face in transmitting Theravada Buddhism to the West. When I ponder this issue, the question that immediately lodges itself in my mind is this: "What exactly is the type of Theravada Buddhism that we wish to spread?" For one thing, it is not merely texts and ideas that Westerners are looking for, not merely the Buddhism of the books. Books are certainly needed to introduce people to the Dhamma, to give them material for study and reflection. The point I wish to make is not that literature on Buddhism is dispensable, but that it is insufficient. For the Dhamma to take deep root in people's hearts, it must come to them, not between the covers of a book, but in living, breathing persons who display the truth of the teaching in their lives.

THE IDEAL FORM

Thus when I raise the question, "What type of Buddhism do we wish to spread?" I am not thinking of the pure canonical Dhamma, which exists as such only in the books. In actuality, Buddhism has always been expressed in concrete practices, embedded in social structures, and embodied by real human beings. Thus we have to consider this aspect of Theravada Buddhism and not merely the doctrinal formulas of the Pali Canon. So when we ponder how to bring Buddhism to the West, we have to decide which of the many faces of Theravada we want to bring. To some extent, this is premature, since if Buddhism does eventually take root in the West, it will assume forms particular to Western social and cultural conditions. But to begin we need something to serve as a seed or nucleus.

The ideal form of Theravada to present would be one that fuses all healthy aspects of the tradition into an organic whole. The transmission would have to focus on the practice of meditation, yet it should include a strong emphasis on Buddhist ethics (including Buddhist perspectives on contemporary ethical issues), textual and doctrinal study, devotional practices, and a fair share of ritual, too; but ritual would have to be integrated into the spiritual path, not pursued in compliance with mere cultural norms. The meditation practice should be the heart of the transmission. Once students experience the beneficial effects of meditation on their lives, in time they will develop keener interest in the study of texts, in devotional practices, in the precepts, and in ritual. Ritual will then serve to cement these varied aspects of Dhamma into a coherent whole, animated from within by the meditative experience.

A MONASTIC TRANSMISSION

But now we come to the heart of the issue. Theravada Buddhism, in its orthodox mould, has always looked upon the monastic order, the Sangha, as the bearer of the Buddhist heritage. Thus, if Theravada is to take hold in the West, it seems it should be through a monastic transmission guarded and upheld by lay support. Without this, we would probably wind up with a watered-down or secularized version of the Theravada, as we find today in the Vipassana sanghas. A monastic transmission is needed to keep alive the stress on renunciation and restraint so characteristic of the true Dhamma.

The need for a monastic transmission, however, immediately runs up against a practical problem. In Sri Lanka today it is extraordinarily difficult to find monks who possess the personal qualities needed by a Buddhist "messenger of Dhamma" (*dhammaduta*), including the ability to communicate the Dhamma effectively to people from a very different cultural background. This has adverse repercussions for the whole project of propagating Theravada Buddhism abroad, making the Theravada something of a still backwater on the otherwise lively Western Buddhist frontier.

Of all the Asian Theravada communities, I feel the Sri Lankans have the strongest potential for transmitting the Dhamma to the West. From what I have observed, the Thai, Cambodian, and Burmese monks cater almost exclusively to their own communities and seldom even imagine that the Dhamma can have any pull on Westerners. It is the Sri Lankans who have been most inspired by the ideal of passing the Dhamma to the West, and again it is the Sri Lankan Sangha that includes monks ready to learn Western languages and translate the teachings into a message meaningful to Westerners.

Yet, despite this, when we survey the Western Buddhist scene, the results are disappointing. We see a tremendous surge of interest in Zen and Tibetan Buddhism, in new Buddhist movements like the Order of Interbeing and the Friends of the Western Buddhist Order, and in Vipassana as a secular practice. But apart from Ajahn Sumedho's Amaravati network, which consists of Western monks and nuns, the orthodox Theravada Sangha has had relatively little impact in the West. Of course, one might just interpret this as evidence that Westerners are too decadent to appreciate the true Dhamma. However, that interpretation would not only be uncharitable, but it would also be wrong. A sizeable number of Western Buddhists feel themselves powerfully drawn towards the Theravada tradition and are on the lookout for monks to offer teachings. Thus the desire is there; it is just the resources to satisfy it that are in short supply.

THE STATE OF MONASTIC EDUCATION

Although I do not have an easy solution to this problem, it would be useful to make a preliminary diagnosis of its origins. I believe part of the explanation lies in the system of monastic education that prevails here in Sri Lanka. This system is extremely inadequate and needs drastic revision from the ground up: revision with respect to the aim, depth, and breadth of monastic training. When monks trained in this system go overseas to expound the Dhamma, they find themselves facing severe handicaps. Not only must they learn to adapt to a society where social relationships are not governed by clearly defined roles and expectations, but they must really strike at the existential concerns of Western students. Routine preaching and ceremonies simply won't do.

The only way for the Sri Lankan Sangha to help meet the challenge of promoting Theravada Buddhism in the West is by making exponential improvements in monastic education right here in Sri Lanka. If a monk is to go abroad to spread the Dhamma, he must have not only a thorough knowledge of his own Theravada tradition, but acquaintance with other subjects too. He will need some knowledge of the history and schools of Buddhism, comparative religion, and English. He should also know, or be ready to learn, the language of the country in which he will work.

Beyond these specific areas of competence, he will require the intellectual openness and acuity to comprehend the dispositions, attitudes, and worldviews of people from a different culture and relate to them in meaningful ways. He must also have some grounding in the real practice of the Dhamma, for knowledge of books and doctrines, however wide, will be fruitless if not coupled with dedication to the practice. Unfortunately, it is almost impossible to find a monastic institute that can impart the necessary training, and the Buddhist prelates, due to their conservatism, resist proposed reforms. In this respect Buddhist educational institutions compare poorly with Christian seminaries, which equip their own missionaries with a thorough and wide-ranging education that often excels the Buddhist institutes even in the field of Buddhist studies.

THE REVIVAL OF MEDITATION

The problem of deficient education is compounded by the decline of the practical training in meditation throughout the Sri Lankan monastic system. Thus the training of the monks focuses not so much on guiding them along the Buddha's path to awakening as on teaching them how to serve as custodians of a distinct social and cultural heritage. I do not want to dismiss the value of this service, for within this country it is quite necessary to preserve the cultural and social pillars of Sri Lankan Buddhism, especially against the incursions of evangelical Christianity and materialistic consumerism. But this function should be subordinated to the more important one of teaching the young monks the path to wisdom and peace; it should not become so domineering that the original path gets covered with mist and weeds.

The decline of a living meditation tradition in the bhikkhu training centres seems to stem from the sharp distinction that the Theravada tradition makes between village monks and forest monks. In this division, the village-and-town monks devote their time to preaching and community service, while the forest monks engage in full-time meditation. This division creates a situation where a monk not intent on winning the path to Nibbana in this present life postpones the practice of meditation to some future existence, justifying his life in robes as a service to society. Such social service, however, takes on a largely secularized hue and easily veers off into political activism. Seldom is it integrated into a true path of spiritual development.

On the other side of the divide, those monks who are keen on winning the goal in this life withdraw into the forest for full-time meditation and rarely show any inclination to share their insights with the wider community. Also, given their method of training, they will generally lack the linguistic and social skills needed to propagate the Dhamma in foreign countries. Thus we have this sharp dichotomy: educated town monks without deep personal insight into the Dhamma or experience in meditation, and meditation monks without much inclination to propagate the teaching.

Since it would be inappropriate to force monks devoted to full-time meditation to take up a more active vocation, the remedy needed to redress this imbalance seems to require a revitalization of meditation practice within the bhikkhu training institutes. This cannot be done, however, merely by imposing meditation on the monks from the outside as a mandatory discipline. Meditation practice does not occur in a vacuum. It must spring up from an inner need, under the impetus given by a clear understanding of the foundations and objectives of Buddhist spirituality. So what is really needed is a rejuvenation of the spiritual challenge at the heart of the Buddhist monastic life.

THE TRAINING OF DHAMMADUTAS

It is not prudent to try to create institutions expressly for the purpose of training monks as "Buddhist missionaries" or *dhammadutas*. Such institutions could easily attract monks who want to go abroad for the wrong reasons: to gain prestige, to become popular, perhaps to find employment and disrobe. I feel it is wiser to strengthen programmes in the existing bhikkhu training centres. At the same time, we should keep an eye open for capable bhikkhus enrolled in these programmes who display the qualities needed to propagate the Dhamma in the West. We must also remember that the purpose in training monks is not to make them *dhammadutas*, but to lead them along the way to enlightenment. Thus the training should focus on the inner development of the monk, both in those qualities conducive to personal growth and in those that allow for a compassionate outflow of his spiritual development to others. Monks who have the special skills, and the inclination to work for the spread of the Dhamma, can then be chosen for overseas assignments, providing they also display the inner maturity required by such a task.

AN INCONCLUSIVE CONCLUSION

At the present stage in its evolution, Buddhism in the West is taking on a form that focuses on the Dhamma as a path of inner transformation through meditation and contemplation, with other aspects of Buddhist practice subordinated to this concern. We should not immediately conclude that Western Buddhism is therefore an ideal model for Asians to emulate. Western Buddhists often lack a solid knowledge of the texts, and thus are prone to bend the teachings to fit their own agendas and expectations. It is here, I think, that Asian monks with a sound scholarly knowledge of the Dhamma can make a valuable contribution. But while corrective measures are needed in Western Buddhism to ensure right understanding, it is clear that the central focus of Western Buddhists will be on personal meditative experience as the way to inner peace and wisdom.

If Sri Lankan Buddhists are to make a significant contribution to the healthy growth of Buddhism in the West, we will need representatives of the Dhamma who are also living embodiments of the Dhamma. That is, we need monks — and nuns as well — who express in their lives and characters the potentials of the Dhamma as a way of life that brings real wisdom, purity, and peace within, and overflows in expressions of kindness and compassion for others. This is a difficult challenge, but it is an indispensable requirement if Sri Lanka is to contribute to the development of Buddhism in the West. Since the main responsibility for transmitting the Dhamma rests with the monastic order, the Sangha in this country must set its own house in order if it is to be qualified to perform this task. This will require some intense internal criticism and attempts at genuine reform, especially in the system of monastic training. If such changes do not take place, it is unlikely that Sri Lanka will be able to contribute much more to the growth of Buddhism in Europe than to maintain viharas that serve Sri Lankan expatriates.

BIBLIOGRAPHY

Adikaram, E.W. (1953) *Early History of Buddhism in Ceylon,* (2nd ed.) Colombo: Gunasena.

Anisaki Masaharu (1916) *Nichiren: The Buddhist Prophet,* reprint Gloucester, Massachussets (1966).

Aris, Michael (1978) *Bhutan, the Early History of a Himalayan Kingdom,* Warminster, UK: Aris & Phillips.

———————— (1994) Raven *Crown: The Origins of Buddhist Monarchy in Bhutan,* London: Serindia.

Banerjee, A.C. (1957) *Sarvastivada Literature,* Calcutta.

Basham, A. L. (1954) *The Wonder That Was India,* London.

Beyer, Stephan V. (1973) *The Cult of Tara: Magic and Ritual in Tibet,* Berkeley: University of California Press.

Chakravarti, Uma (1987) *The Social Dimensions of Early Buddhism,* New Delhi: Oxford University Press.

Ch'en Kenneth (1964) *Buddhism in China: A Historical Survey,* Princeton.

Cozort, Daniel (1986) *Highest Yoga Tantra: An Introduction to Esoteric Buddhism of Tibet,* Ithaca, NY: Snow Lion.

Dasgupta, Shashi Bhusan (1974) *An Introduction to Tantric Buddhism.* 3rd ed. Calcutta: University of Calcutta.

Dutt, Nalinaksha (1970) *Buddhist Sects in India,* Calcutta.

Dutt, Sukumar (1957) *The Buddha and Five After-Centuries,* London.

——————— (1962) *Buddhist Monks and Monasteries of India,* London: G. Allen & Unwin.

Gombrich, Richard F. (1996) *How Buddhism Began: The Conditioned Genesis of the Early Teachings,* London: Athlone.

———————————— (1988) *Theravada Buddhism: A Social History from Ancient Benares to Modern Colombo,* London: Routledge & Kegan Paul.

Grousset, Rene (1931) *The Civilizations of the East, vol. 2,* India, London.

Hanayama Shinsho (1960) *A History of Japanese Buddhism,* Tokyo.

Hazra, Kanai Lal (1982) *History of Theravada Buddhism in South-East Asia: With Special Reference to India and Ceylon,* New Delhi: Munshiram Manoharlal.

Hirakawa, Akira (1974-1979) Indo bukkyoshi, 2 vols., Tokyo.

Hirakawa, Akira (1990) A *History of Indian Buddhism: From Sakyamuni to Early Mahayana,* Honolulu: University of Hawaii Press.

Holt, John Clifford (1996) *The Religious World of Kirti Sri: Buddhism, Art, and Politics in Late Medieval Sri Lanka,* New York: Oxford University Press.

Hopkins, Jeffrey (1985) *The Kalacakara Tantra,* trans. London.

Horner, I.B. (1936) *Early Buddhist Theory of Man Perfected,* London.

Jayatilleke, K.N. (1963) *Early Buddhist Theory of Knowledge,* London.

Joshi, Lal Mani (1967) *Studies in the Buddhistic Culture of India, During the 7th and 8th Centuries A.D.* Delhi: Motilal Banarsidass.

———————— (1967) *Studies in the Buddhistic Culture of India,* Delhi.

King, Winston Lee (1980) *Theravada Meditation: The Buddhist Transformation of Yoga,* University Park: Pennsylvania State University Press.

Kitagawa, Joseph M. (1966) *Religion in Japanese History,* New York.

Law, B.C. (ed.) (1931) *Buddhistic Studies,* Calcutta.

Legge, James (1886) *A Record of Buddhist Kingdoms,* Oxford.

Lester Robert C (1973) *Theravada Buddhism in Southeast Asia,* Ann Arbor.

Malalgoda, K. (1976) *Buddhism in Sinhalese Society, 1750-1900.* Berkeley: University of California Press.

Masuda Jiryo, (1925) 'Origins and Doctrines of Early Indian Buddhist Schools', *Asia Major, vol. 2, pp.1-78.*

Matsunaga, Alicia (1969) *The Buddhist Philosophy of Assimilation,* Tokyo.

McGovern W.M. (1922) *An Introduction to Mahayana Buddhism,* New York.

Miler, Robert J (1959) *Monasteries and Culture Change in Mongolia,* Wiesbaden.

Mitra, Rajendaralala (1971) *The Sanskrit Buddhist Literature of Nepal,* Calcutta.

Mullin, Glenn H. (1986) *Death and Dying: The Tibetan Tradition,* East Grinstead, W. Sussex: New Knowledge Books.

Nakamura Hajime (1980) *Indian Buddhism: A Survey with Bibliographical Notes,* Tokyo.

Narain, A.K. (1980) *Studies in History of Buddhism,* Delhi: B.R. Pub. Corp.

Radhakrishnan, Sarvepalli (1927) Indian Philosophy, vol.1 (2nd ed.), London.

Rahula, Walpola (1956) *History of Buddhism in Ceylon,* Colombo: Gunasena.

—————————— (1974) *What the Buddha Taught* (Rev. ed.) New York: Grove.

Rao, S. K. Ramachandra (1979) *Tibetan Meditation: Theory and Practice,* New Delhi: Arnold-Heinemann.

Ray, Reginald A. (1994) *Buddhist Saints in India: A Study in Buddhist Values and Orientations,* New York: Oxford University Press.

Reynolds, Frank E (1981) *Guide to Buddhist Religion,* Boston.

Rhys Davids, T.W. (1903) *Buddhist India,* London.

Robinson, Richard H., and Willard Johnson (1982) *The Buddhist Religion: A Historical Introduction* (3rd ed.) Belmont, CA: Wadsworth.

Ruegg, David S. (1967) *The Study of Indian and Tibetan Thought,* Leiden.

———————————— (1981) *The Literature of the Madhyamaka School of Philosophy in India,* Wiesbaden.

Sarao, K.T.S., (ed.) (1995) *A Textbook of the History of Theravada Buddhism,* Delhi: University of Delhi.

Saunders, E. Dale (1964) *Buddhism in Japan,* Philadelphia.

Seneviratne, H. L. (1978) *Rituals of the Kandyan State,* Cambridge: Cambridge University Press.

Skilton, Andrew (1994) *A Concise History of Buddhism.* Birmingham: Windhorse.

Snellgrove, David L. (ed.) (1957) *Buddhist Himalaya,* Oxford.

————————————— (1984) *Indo-Tibetan Buddhism: Indian Buddhists and their Tibetan Successors,* Boston: Shambhala.

Snellgrove, David, and Hugh Richardson (1968) *A Cultural History of Tibet,* New York: F.A. Praeger.

Streng, Frederick J. (1967) *Emptiness: A Study in Religious Meaning,* Nashville.

Suzuki, B.L. (1938) *Mahayana Buddhism* (3rd ed.), NewYork.

Thomsen Harry (1963) *The New Religions of Japan: Rutland,* Vt.

Tucci, Giuseppe (1949) *Tibetan Painted Scrolls, 2 vols.* translated by Virginia Vacca, Rome.

Varma, V.P. (1973) *Early Buddhism and Its Origins,* New Delhi.

Warder, Anthony Kennedy (1980) *Indian Buddhism* (2nd ed.) Delhi: Motilal Banarsidass.

Watters, Thomas (1904-1905) *On Yuan Chwang's Travel in India, 2 vols.* London.

Wayman, Alex (1973) *The Buddhist Tantras: Light on Indo- Tibetan Esotericism,* New York.

INDEX